Constructing Democracy in Southern Europe

Why are some regimes democratic while others are not? Specifically, how have Spain and Italy managed to become democratic while Turkey, which shares many similar characteristics, has not?

Spain, Italy, and Turkey have shared common historical features which would have been disruptive to any new democracy; however, they represent a wide array of democratization experiences. Providing a comparative case-study analysis, this book offers some clues as to the reasons for successful transitions to democracy. This is done through a range of variables which include:

- the degree of 'stateness' problems
- learning from previous experiences with democracy and authoritarianism
- economic development
- the procedures used for designing the new rules of the regime
- the existence or absence of 'civil society' and the connection between society and political institutions
- the democratic rules themselves
- the professionalization of the military
- the influence of external factors on democratic consolidation.

By examining these variables across the three countries, Lauren McLaren narrows the range of possible explanations for differences in democratic consolidation. The book will be of particular interest to students and researchers of European Politics and Democratization Studies.

Lauren M. McLaren is Associate Professor of Politics at the University of Nottingham, UK.

Democratization studies
(formerly Democratization studies, Frank Cass)

Series editors: Peter Burnell and Peter Calvert

Democratization Studies combines theoretical and comparative studies with detailed analyses of issues central to democratic progress and its performance, all over the world.

The books in this series aim to encourage debate on the many aspects of democratization that are of interest to policy-makers, administrators and journalists, aid and development personnel, as well as to all those involved in education.

Constructing Democracy in Southern Europe

A comparative analysis of Italy, Spain, and Turkey

Lauren M. McLaren

Routledge
Taylor & Francis Group

LONDON AND NEW YORK

Transferred to digital printing 2010

First published 2008
by Routledge
2 Park Square, Milton Park, Abingdon, Oxon OX14 4RN

Simultaneously published in the USA and Canada
by Routledge
270 Madison Ave, New York, NY 10016

Routledge is an imprint of the Taylor & Francis Group, an informa business

© 2008 Lauren M. McLaren

Typeset in Garamond by Wearset Ltd, Boldon, Tyne and Wear

British Library Cataloguing in Publication Data
A catalogue record for this book is available from the British Library

Library of Congress Cataloging in Publication Data
A catalog record for this book has been requested

ISBN10: 0-415-43819-5 (hbk)
ISBN10: 0-415-59161-9 (pbk)
ISBN10: 0-203-92805-9 (ebk)

ISBN13: 978-0-415-43819-3 (hbk)
ISBN13: 978-0-415-59161-4 (pbk)
ISBN13: 978-0-203-92805-9 (ebk)

Contents

Illustrations

Maps

Tables

Preface

My interest in writing this book developed while I was employed at Bilkent University in Ankara, Turkey between 1998 and 2002. Although I was new to the study of Turkish politics and society, these quickly became topics of keen interest. As a scholar and teacher of comparative politics, my interest naturally moved toward comparative themes. Most perplexing to me was a question that had also perplexed me during many of my years of graduate study: why is it that some countries are able to establish stable regimes that protect and respect the rights of citizens while others struggle with this, sometimes for years. Turkey turned out to be one of those in the latter position, and as I read and learned more about its modern-day history, the parallels between it and other countries in Southern Europe led the comparativist in me to wonder how those other regimes, which faced extremely difficult, potentially destabilizing times, managed to succeed in their attempts to create stable democracy while Turkey had not.

Particularly surprising to me was the fact that Turkey did not appear to be an extremely poor country. This came as a surprise because of the long-proven empirical connection between a country's wealth and its regime type. Such analyses might point to the conclusion that Turkey has been unable to achieve democratic consolidation because it is poor. The comparative statistics provided in this book indicate that Turkey was indeed poorer than Spain and Italy during their early transitional periods and thus provide some support for this contention. On the other hand, my own experience of travelling around the country, including the less developed eastern regions indicated that the country was not poor, at least in the sense that a westerner might view poverty: there were very few homeless people or beggars, and very few individuals who appeared to have been malnourished. This is in stark contrast to verbal accounts of poverty in countries like India or Nigeria by people who have visited Turkey and these other countries and travelled extensively in both. One can imagine that in a place where people are barely able to survive, democracy may be difficult to create and nurture. Turkey did not appear to be one of those places. Again, the hard-core statistics provided in part of the text of the book contradicts this general perception and so the book itself will draw contradictory conclusions to those mentioned here, but it seemed worth mentioning as a casual observation.

My appreciation of Italian and Spanish politics and history developed from less of a participant observer perspective and more from teaching students about these two countries. Although I have taught about the politics of many other European democracies, these two seemed to be most ideal for comparison with Turkey. Italy provided a case that, much like Turkey, had experienced worker and student unrest and political violence in the 1960s. In Turkey, this unrest provoked military interventions and thus transitions away from democracy whereas in Italy it did not. The obvious question then became one of why the outcomes were so different in the two countries. Spain also seemed like a promising comparative case for Turkey because like Turkey, there is a long history of military involvement in politics in Spain. Given that the regression toward authoritarianism in Turkey is often a result of military interventions in politics, it is important to consider why interventionism in other cases did not undermine democracy. Another component of Turkish politics and history that seemed to require comparative analysis is the issue of regional separatism. Italy provides a couple of very mild examples of this, but nothing on the scale that Turkey has experienced. Again, Spain represented a promising case for comparison because it has also experienced violent nationalist separatism.

Thus, though far from perfect, the research design sought to use as much information as possible about the three countries on the dimensions thought to be important for explaining democratic consolidation to determine what has gone wrong with the Turkish experience with democracy thus far. Many will criticize the design, particularly the fact that a country that some consider to be in the region of the Middle East rather than in Europe is compared to European countries. The Appendix attempts to explain the reasoning for case selection further, and it is hoped that readers will find that the book has been able to reveal useful insights into the problems of democratic consolidation in Turkey, and into democratic consolidation more generally.

Lauren McLaren

Acknowledgements

There are many people who deserve acknowledgement for their part in helping to create this book.

First and foremost is Steven Thrower, who has listened patiently to my ideas and arguments, and helped me learn how to explain these ideas to a non-specialist and non-political-scientist.

I also owe a great deal of gratitude to the staff at Bilkent University. Hootan Shambayati was an excellent teacher of Turkish politics, and I learned a great deal about my new country of residence while sharing kebabs at Haci Arif Bey or mezes and fish at Agora Restaurant with him. I also wish to thank Professor Metin Heper at Bilkent for giving me the opportunity to teach in Turkey in the first place. Many others at Bilkent were also helpful during my stay there including Bilkent University Political Science department secretary Güvenay Kazancy, colleagues Evren Esen, Meltem Müftüler-Baç, Dilek Cindoğlu, Süheyla Pynar, Zerrin Tandoğan, Fuat Keyman, Ahmet Içduygu, and PhD student (now university professor) Murat Çemrek. Hootan Shambayati and former colleague Ömer Faruk Gençkaya were also instrumental in helping me obtain some difficult-to-find materials on Turkish politics.

Thanks to Clese Erikson for encouraging me to take the risk and migrate to Turkey. Also thanks to my colleagues at Nottingham University who supported my application to win an extra semester of sabbatical to complete this book, and to the university itself for granting the extra semester off. Special thanks to Nottingham colleague Paul Heywood for providing extensive feedback on the book proposal, and to Fülya Memisoğlu for gathering some of the information used in the book and for invaluable assistance in manuscript preparation.

And, of course, very special thanks to Ouida and Eusevio and their spouses, Michael and Connie, for their long-term support for my academic endeavours.

Finally I would like to thank http:flagspot.net for granting me permission to reproduce Maps 2.1 and 2.2 for this book, as well as the staff at Routledge, particularly Heidi Bagtazo and Amelia McLaurin, and three anonymous reviewers for their invaluable comments and suggestions.

Abbreviations

AKP	*Adalet ve Kalkınma Partisi* (Justice and Development Party)
AP	*Alianza Popular*
DC	Christian Democrats
DLP	Democratic Left Party
DP	Democrat Party
CEDA	*Confederación Española de Derechas Autónomas* (Confederation of Autonomous Rightist Groups)
CHP	*Cumhurriyet Halk Partisi* (Republican People's Party)
CNL	Committees of National Liberation
CNT	*Confederación Nacional del Trabajo* (National Confederation of Labour)
DISK	*Devrimci İşçi Sendikaları Konfederasyon* (Confederation of Revolutionary Trade Unions)
ECSC	European Coal and Steel Community
EEC	European Economic Community
ETA-M	ETA-Military
ETA-PM	ETA-Political Military
EU	European Union
FAI	*Federación Anarquista Ibérica* (Iberian Anarchist Federation)
GRAPO	*Grupos de Resistencia Antifascista Primero de Octubre* (armed left-wing branch of PCE)
IO	international organization
JP	Justice Party
MHP	*Milliyetçi Hareket Partisi* (Nationalist Action Party)
NATO	North Atlantic Treaty Organization
NSC	National Security Council
NUC	National Unity Committee
OECD	Organization for Economic Co-operation and Development
PCE	Communist Party of Spain
PCI	Communist Party of Italy
PSOE	Socialist Party of Spain
RPP	Republican People's Party
TPP	True Path Party

TURK-IS	*Türkiye İşçi Sendikaları Konfederasyonu* (Confederation of Trade Unions of Turkey)
UDC	Union of the Democratic Centre
UGT	*Unión General de Trabajadores* (General Union of Workers)
UMD	*Unión Militar Democrática*

1 Introduction

Why are some regimes democratic while others are not? What explains differences in regime types across countries? These questions have perplexed philosophers and political scientists for centuries. Although this book does not pretend to answer such grand questions definitively, it does attempt to provide some clues as to the reasons for successful transitions to democracy by examining three case studies: Italy, Spain and Turkey.

The general topic of democratic transition and consolidation is one that was of particular interest to academics in the 1980s and 1990s in the midst of the 'Third Wave' (Huntington 1991) of transitions to democracy but seems to be somewhat less of a major focus of study at the start of the twenty-first century. Interest in the topic of democratic consolidation in Southern Europe appears to have waned even more. Presumably this is because so many landmark books were written in these decades[1] that for many researchers perhaps the 'book' on democratic transition and consolidation is closed, particularly in this region. This is unfortunate for at least two reasons. First, one of the Southern European regimes of interest to these scholars – Turkey – has continued to struggle somewhere between full democracy and authoritarianism. This is despite the fact that in the early post-World War II era it was clearly counted as being amongst the South European transitional regimes and had begun to make its regime transition long before many of the other Southern European countries (e.g., Spain and Portugal). As will be shown throughout this book, the Turkish Republic faced many similar circumstances to other South European transitional regimes but unlike these has thus far failed to achieve full democracy. Thus, this creates a perplexing puzzle that still needs to be resolved. The declining interest in this topic is also unfortunate because there are still many other regimes that have attempted to become democratic but have thus far failed to do so as well. A comparative analysis such as the one provided in this book may, therefore, lead to clues about the reasons for failed democratization in other regions of the world.

In fact, many may contend that Turkey really ought to not be compared to other Southern European countries like Spain and Italy, and that instead it should be compared to (other) Middle Eastern, predominantly Muslim countries. Given that no other country in the Middle East, other than perhaps Israel (which is not predominantly Muslim), would be counted as a fully functioning democracy, it is unclear as to what such comparisons might tell us about why Turkey's transition has thus far failed. To answer this question, it seems that we need to compare with regimes that have *succeeded* in consolidating democracy. Moreover, the chapters that follow will show that Turkey has had many similar experiences to other Southern European countries and that comparisons with these regimes provide useful insights about the differences that might have produced different regime type outcomes. (For further discussion of the case-study selection in this book, see the Appendix.)

It is a basic premise of this book that in order to determine why the transitional outcomes have been different in Italy, Spain, and Turkey, we must examine the historical development of each, focussing upon key variables that prior theory and academic research indicate are likely to be important in explaining regime type. The book assumes that readers may have very limited knowledge of the history and politics in the three countries and thus is designed primarily for those who may be new to the topic. At the same time, it is expected that the analysis and insights provided here will also be of interest to the general scholarly community.

Before discussing the importance of these three cases for our general research puzzle, we must begin with a few definitions. In the next section, I thus explain how I define and measure democracy. Following this, I provide a brief overview of the academic literature on democratic transitions and consolidation. The chapter then provides a summary of the transitions and consolidations in the three countries, as well as a summary of where each country lies in terms of the definition of democracy. In the final section of the chapter, each of the potential explanatory variables is described briefly. The chapters that follow this introduction will then be devoted to analysing each potential predictor of successful democratic transitions in Italy, Spain, and Turkey, using an historical case-study approach.

Defining and measuring democracy

Gerardo Munck (2001) indicates that there are considerable lapses in analytical writings between definitions of transition to democracy, definitions of democratic consolidation, and definitions of quality of democracy (see also Collier and Levitsky 1997 on the conceptual difficulties in defining 'democracy'). I attempt to avoid such lapses here by first indicating what I mean by 'democracy' and then outlining the ways in which we might know that a regime has moved from transition to consolidation. It is assumed here that if there are issues related to the quality of a democracy that render a regime non-democratic, that regime is still potentially in transition.[2] This will be discussed further below.

The definition of democracy used in this book draws heavily upon that outlined by Robert Dahl in *On Democracy* (1971). For Dahl, the concept of democracy centres upon the notion of political equality, which means that everyone has the same right or opportunity to have her preferences translated into government policy. Specifically, this implies that all members of the polity have equal and effective opportunities for making their views known. It also means that all votes count equally; no one's vote or perspective should carry more weight than anyone else's. Political equality further means that all have equal and effective opportunities for learning about alternative policies and their likely consequences; that is, information is available to those participating in the polity so that they are able to choose what they view as the most appropriate policies. Political equality also means that members have the right to decide what matters are to be placed on the agenda. Agenda-setting power is one of the most significant of those available to political actors. Indeed, some have defined power specifically in terms of the ability to set agendas (Schattschneider 1960; Bachrach and Baratz 1970). Based on Dahl's definition, then, democracy cannot consist of only a small group of elites that present a limited menu of choices to participants in the polity; others must also be allowed to insert items onto the political agenda. Finally, Dahl argues that all adults must be included in the political process if there is to be political equality. People cannot be restricted from participation because of property restrictions, race, gender, etc. (see Held 1996 for a comprehensive overview of theories and models of democracy).

While conceptually appealing, this specification may leave us rather confused as to how to then go about identifying which regimes to count as democracies. Fortunately, Dahl proposes several criteria that together help to meet these requirements of political equality: that officials are elected, that elections are free, fair, and frequent, that there is freedom of expression, that there are alternative sources of information, that there is associational autonomy, and that there is inclusive citizenship.

Although many scholars have focussed on the electoral component of this definition, such a focus is generally seen as problematic because elections only occur intermittently and only allow citizens to choose between highly aggregated alternatives offered by political parties (Schmitter and Karl 1996). Thus, it is important to also consider the other aspects mentioned by Dahl such as freedom of expression, alternative sources of information, and associational autonomy. Additionally, Diamond (1999) provides further specification of what must be present if a regime is to be counted as democratic. First, elected officials must control the state and key decisions. Key decisions cannot be made by democratically unaccountable actors or foreign powers. Second, executive power should be constrained constitutionally by the power of other government institutions; thus an elected government cannot have the institutional mechanisms to become tyrannical after winning elections. Third, no group that adheres to constitutional principles can be denied the right to form a party and contest elections. Fourth, cultural, ethnic, religious, and other minority groups should not be prohibited from expressing their interests in the political process or from speaking their language or practising their culture. Fifth, there must be an impartial institution – presumably a judiciary – to protect the individual and group liberties of citizens without interference from other institutions. Finally, citizens in a democratic regime are protected from unjustified detention, exile, terror, and torture. In the absence of any one of these characteristics, the democratic credentials of a regime are called into question.

Explaining transitions to democracy

Academic research on transitions to democracy tends to be divided between those taking a 'functional' approach and those taking a 'genetic' approach. It is argued that the former have tended to mistakenly assume that the factors that help preserve democracy are the ones that will bring it about in the first place (Rustow 1970). Most of these theories focus on the role of the economy and particularly economic development, or modernization. The contention is that economic development produces a large middle class, which then begins to press for greater inclusion in political decision-making via democratization (e.g. Lipset 1959). This idea makes some logical sense, in that the vast majority of stable democracies are indeed economically developed – perhaps leading the analyst to conclude that there is something about economic development that produces the pressures for change. One only need look at the key counter-example of the US, however, a country that began life in economic backwardness but for which there were very early pressures for democratization (see Rustow 1970).[3] Also, case-study resesarch has shown fairly convincingly that the supposedly democratic middle classes often press for repressive measures rather than democratization (Rueschmeyer *et al.* 1992). This is a topic that will be discussed far more extensively in Chapter 4.

Thus, the contention of those taking a 'genetic approach' to democratic transitions is that the factors that make democracy likely to survive are not necessarily the ones that bring it about in the first place, and there are a whole range of variables that can potentially bring regime change from authoritarianism to democracy. These include the death or defeat of a dictator, along with the inability of any single individual or group to gain a solid foothold of power following this death or defeat; the installation of democratic institutions by foreign powers; restoration of democratic regimes after external conquest; alternatively, authoritarian regimes may perceive that they are losing legitimacy and attempt to bow gracefully out of power by initiating a transition to democracy; or it is possible for oppositional forces to come together to initiate a transition (see Stepan 1986). The key point to note about the transition process is that it is an uncertain period, during which it is far from clear that a democratic regime will be installed because there is generally conflict between key actors over control of the political arena. In addition, it is not clear that any particular economic or other circumstances must prevail for a transition to occur.[4]

Democratic consolidation

As discussed above, consolidation and transition are two different matters, and a transition to democracy in no way guarantees democratic consolidation. How do we define consolidation, though? This section will specify what we mean by consolidation; later sections of the chapter discuss the factors believed to be associated with democratic consolidation (i.e. the predictors of democratic consolidation).

Andreas Schedler (1998) points out that the term 'consolidation' has become a moving target in the academic literature (see also Munck 2001). In the 1980s literature on democratic transition and consolidation, the meaning was clearer: the sudden death of democracy by way of a coup or some other dramatic event was taken to signify the breakdown of democracy, while the absence of such events was taken as a sign of consolidation. In the 1990s and beyond, though, scholars have pointed to more gradual transgressions that slowly move a regime away from democracy, and so the meaning of consolidation has become less clear. To quote Schedler, consolidation

> has come to include such divergent items as popular legitimation, the diffusion of democratic values, the neutralization of antisystem actors, civilian supremacy over the military, the elimination of authoritarian enclaves, party building, the organization of functional interests, the stabilization of electoral rules, the routinization of politics, the decentralization of state power, the introduction of mechanisms of direct democracy, judicial reform, the alleviation of poverty, and economic stabilization.
>
> (Schedler 1998: 90–1)

Differing definitions then create problems for case classification – a regime that might be highly consolidated under one definition may also be unconsolidated in another. Schedler's proposed solution is to use consolidation to refer to avoidance of democratic breakdown or democratic erosion and nothing else.

The most commonly accepted definition of consolidation, however, is that offered by Linz and Stepan (1996: 5): consolidation is a political situation in which democracy has become 'the only game in town'. This means that:

- 'No significant political groups seriously attempt to overthrow the democratic regime or secede from the state.'
- 'Even in the face of severe political and economic crises, the overwhelming majority of the people believe that any further political change must emerge from within the parameters of democratic formulas.'

- All actors 'become habituated to the fact that political conflict will be resolved according to the established norms' (Linz and Stepan 1996: 5).

Similarly, O'Donnell (1994) refers to consolidation as the effective functioning of a democratic regime after the creation (or re-establishment) of democratic rule (see also Whitehead 1989).

Some have also argued that a key indicator of whether consolidation has occurred is whether government peacefully changes hands from one party or block to another after elections. Huntington, for instance, argues that a regime must pass the 'two-turnover test', whereby a democracy can be viewed as consolidated if the party or group that takes power after the initial election at the time of the transition loses a subsequent election and hands over power to the new election winners, *and* if those election winners then peacefully hand over power to the winner of a later election (Huntington 1991: 266–7). This definition is thought by many to be problematic, however – would we count Japan as a non-democratic country until the early 1990s because one party maintained control of the government for an overwhelming 38 years after the end of World War II, for instance? Similarly, scholars of politics in Southern Europe object to its applicability to most cases in the region (see Morlino 1998).

How will we define consolidation in this book then? Conceptually, we adopt Linz and Stepan's notion of democracy being the only game in town. Empirically, we will adopt Schedler's suggestion: that consolidation refers to (a) avoidance of dramatic democratic breakdown, for instance via a coup and (b) avoidance of democratic erosion (i.e. the slow progression away from democracy being the only game in town). Because the definition of consolidation fundamentally depends on the attitudes and behaviours of actors within the political system, we can adopt the following indicators of consolidation: the absence of any significant anti-system party or movement and the absence of any serious conflict among politically significant groups over the basic framework for political contestation. That is, there is no disagreement over the basic rules of the political game (Gunther *et al*. 1995: 13–15). The next section discusses the transitions to democracy in Italy, Spain, and Turkey, and the following section addresses democratic consolidation in the three countries.

Overview of the transitions in Italy, Spain, and Turkey

In the case of Italy and Spain, the most recent democratic transitions came shortly after the defeat and/or death of a dictator. As discussed above, this particular circumstance does not necessarily guarantee a transition to democracy, as other dictators or groups of dictators (including the military) could presumably take over and keep the country in authoritarian rule. However, in the case of Italy, the period of dictatorship was short enough that many of the pre-fascist political groups were still in existence and were prepared to join forces to press for re-democratization shortly after the end of World War II. In the case of Spain, the death of a dictator initially was expected to produce another seemingly dictatorial regime – a monarchy. However, the monarch himself, along with other members of the former fascist regime, orchestrated a transition from authoritarianism and to democracy (Gilmour 1985; Maravall and Santamaria 1986; Linz and Stepan 1996: Chapter 6; on the uncertainty of the transition period in Spain see Colomer 1991).

In Turkey, the transition process was initiated by elites as well. Prior to the start of this transition toward democracy, the regime in many ways bordered on the totalitarian. Very much unlike the sultans who had ruled before him, the founder and first president of the Turkish Republic, Mustafa Kemal 'Ataturk', advocated the development of a regime that would connect the citizenry to government. Some basis for such a connection was required, however, and that ideology came in the form of Kemalism. Nowadays we would most likely refer to the tenets of Kemalism as policy goals rather than ideology (an ideology generally being understood as a logical, coherent set of propositions that usually have some linkage to philosophers, academic writings, etc.), but many scholars of Kemalism do at times refer to it as an ideology (see Aksoy and Robins 1997; Müftüler-Baç 1999; Kogacioğlu 2003).

Mustafa Kemal's key ideologies included modernization, westernization, and secularization of the Turkish public. Specifically, they were built upon six 'isms' (referred to by Kemal as Six Arrows): Republicanism, Populism, Secularism, Revolutionalism, Nationalism, Statism. The essence of all of these when combined was that the state would be actively used to modernize Turkish society, and that the new state would be built upon the principles of nationalism (i.e. the creation of a Turkish nation-state), secularism, and republicanism. The latter of these took some time to develop, as Kemal attempted to address other elements of his goals by building a powerful state. The fledgling state struggled to carry out its developmental goals in the face of widespread traditionalism and economic backwardness, and several years after Kemal's death in 1938, the elites who had taken over from him (and ran his one-party state via the Republican People's Party) decided to open politics up to multi-party elections, marking the start of the transition to democracy in Turkey in 1946. In terms of the general explanations for transitions discussed above, in the case of Turkey, the explanation for the transition appears to lie in the combination of loss of legitimacy, as many of the modernization goals were nowhere near to being met, along with calls from the more traditional-leaning elites for democratic representation for the masses.

The post-war transitions to democracy across our three cases thus occurred under varying circumstances. In Spain, the transition began shortly after the death of a long-term dictator (Franco ruled Spain from 1939 until his death in 1975). In Italy, it began shortly after Italy's defeat in World War II and Mussolini's execution. In neither of these cases, however, was it 'guaranteed' that democracy would be the route taken. In Spain, Franco had re-established a monarchy which was to succeed him at his death; in Italy, at the time of Mussolini's death, there was still a monarchy in place, and the monarch in question (Victor Emmanuel III) was immediately recognized as the head of state by the Allied powers at the end of World War II. Prior to this, and after Mussolini had initially been captured, King Victor Emmanuel began to form a government in Italy with a military marshal as his prime minister, despite the existence of a cross-party Committee of National Liberation which had played a pivotal role in Italy's resistance to German occupation. In fact, there was a seven-month stand-off between the king and the Committee, which only ended when all of the parties in the CNL (and most crucially, the Communist Party) agreed to collaborate in the creation of a democratic post-war Italy whether the king stayed on the throne or not. Thus, it was entirely possible at the end of the war that Italy was going to return to its pre-fascist situation of quasi-democracy/quasi-monarchy. Indeed, this appears to be the direction that King Victor Emmanuel was taking (Pasquino 1986; Hine 1993). The start of the post-war transition to democracy actually thus came in a very close referendum in 1946 in which 54.3 per cent of the Italian public voted to abolish the monarchy. In contrast to the two cases of Spain and Italy, in Turkey, there was no specific pivotal defining moment which caused the start of the transition. The initial opening up of elections to opposition parties in 1946 came suddenly and unexpectedly, to the point that the opposition had little time to organize itself to contest the election.

All three of the cases studied here have thus begun processes that aim to transform the country away from authoritarianism and toward democracy. I am not, however, attempting to provide an analysis of why these transition processes began, as these reasons have already been outlined briefly above. The three cases have also experienced widely varying *consolidations*, and it is to this topic that we now turn.

Democratic consolidation in Italy, Spain, and Turkey

Our three cases differ considerably both in terms of their length and degree of consolidation. Since the beginning of the transition in 1946, Turkey has experienced both erosion and dramatic breakdown in the form of military coups, and this book contends that it is still in transition toward democracy. Italy also had a very slow transition phase, and scholars differ as to when exactly Italy's democracy became consolidated. Although there was no clear breakdown or erosion of democratic principles, there was a long period during which major political players – in particular, the very popular Communist Party – were perceived as not being completely committed to the rules of democracy, and so while these players were in existence and perceived to be committed to overthrowing the 'bourgeois' democratic government, it was not possible to speak of consolidation in Italy. In stark contrast, after one brief period during which a few military officials attempted an overthrow of democracy in Spain (see Chapter 9), the consolidation was rapid. Consolidation in each of these three countries is now discussed in turn.

Although the initial transition began immediately prior to the 1946 elections in Turkey, many scholars would put the clear start-date at the 1950 general elections, which are argued to be the first to have been contested freely and fairly (whereas the 1946 elections are believed to have been heavily influenced by the governing Republican People's Party). Ironically, however, after the ruling authoritarian party was defeated by the opposition in 1950, this opposition – once in government – began to adopt fairly non-democratic means itself, including spying on *its* opposition (the former ruling party), confiscating the key opposition party's property, attempting to place restrictions on the opposition party leader's ability to travel to party rallies (which were being used to criticize the governing party), and subjecting the opposition party to a parliamentary investigatory committee which was armed with the right to deny permission for the party to hold meetings. Also, the non-democratic practices included the jailing of journalists. In this particular era, there was no constitutional way to hold a government majority in check (e.g. no Constitutional Court) (see Ahmad 1993; Özbüdün 2000; Zurcher 2004; also see Chapter 5 of this book).

By 1960, the Turkish military had intervened by staging a coup, during which the governing party was closed down and the prime minister and two other ministers were executed (see Chapters 3 and 9). The military and other officials proceeded to develop a democratic constitution which would include the sorts of checks and balances that were thought to be missing in the pre-coup period (a topic that will be discussed further in Chapter 5 on constitution building). However, it is not clear that all of the key actors were committed to democratic principles in the post-1960 period: powerful, popular extremist groups on both the left and right were becoming increasingly radicalized and their commitment to the rules of the regime was questionable. The ideological differences in the country and resulting political violence prompted the military to intervene again in 1971 with a 'soft' coup: tanks did not roll, but the government was forced to resign and parties were generally warned to tone down the extremist dialogue, amongst other things (see Chapter 9; also see Ahmad 1993; Zurcher 2004).

The warning was not heeded, and in 1980, there was another real coup. Military officials decided that the constitution needed to be re-written, and it is difficult to argue that the resulting document created entirely democratic institutions and practices. Specifically, it guaranteed strong, formal oversight powers for the military via the National Security Council,[5] restricted the political activities of labour unions and other professional associations, and allowed for government to confiscate newspapers and periodicals prior to their publication (i.e. engage in censorship), amongst other things.[6] Thus, the constitution in itself points to the lack of possibility for consolidation of democracy and perhaps even a clear transition toward authoritarianism. Moreover, the actual practice of the regime confirms this: the military continued to exercise influence on civilian decision-making in all aspects of policy-making, including economic policy. One of the most significant military interventions in recent years has been the forced collapse of the civilian government in 1997, and there has been a clear threat of intervention over the 2007 presidential election results (see Chapter 9). In addition, given that the most recent coup was not brutal and that it is credited with bringing a great deal of order to Turkish politics and society, it is not clear that major actors are all that committed to preventing a return to military rule. Indeed, actors that are not opposed to military intervention in the future generally take this perspective because they worry that other actors in the system (particularly, Islamists) are not committed to democracy themselves.

In the past few years, Turkey has in many ways inched toward democracy again. However, there are still significant factors that keep Turkey from being considered as consolidated. These include continued limitations on individual freedom of expression and association, limitations on press freedom, continued political involvement by the military, as well as some reported incidents of torture (see Freedom House or Amnesty International on the latter). One of the most egregious violations of the norms of democracy can be found in the 2005 revised Turkish penal code, which makes it illegal (and punishable by imprisonment) for a person to publicly denigrate Turkishness, the Turkish Republic, the Grand National Assembly of Turkey, the Turkish government, the judicial institutions, or the military or security organizations.

The Italian consolidation was also relatively slow and it is difficult to determine a clear point at which the country became firmly democratic. Some might put this at the time of the holding of the 1946 referendum to decide whether the country would be a monarchy or a republic; others might put it at the first post-war parliamentary elections in 1948. Still others might contend that the transition was not complete until the 1990s because it was not until then that there was a clear alternation of government power between one block and another (see Leonardi 1991).

As mentioned above, for some time after the start of the transition to democracy, many in the political system questioned the commitment of one large group – the Communists – to the maintenance of the democratic system, and thus significant actors may not have been convinced yet that democracy was 'the only game in town'. The Communist Party's origins were in radical communist ideology, advocating overthrow of the existing system and establishment of dictatorship of the proletariat. Even after it began moving away from these roots and participated in democratic government immediately after the end of World War II, its true leanings were often in question (Cotta 1992; Hine 1993; Partridge 1998; Koff and Koff 1999; Foot 2003; Bull and Newell 2005; Parker and Natale 2006). Specifically, although the party had clearly rejected the option of revolutionary insurrection by the end of 1948, its continued links with the totalitarian Soviet Union and its claims about the superiority of the Soviet-style regime over bourgeois democracy helped to fuel suspicion about the party's 'real' intentions (Cotta 1992: 167). (This will be discussed further in Chapter 6.) While it is still difficult to pinpoint when the party became a less feared element, there are a few key moments in this regard: one is 1968 when the party condemned the Soviet invasion of Czechoslovakia; another is 1976, when the party openly supported a centre-right ('bourgeois') party in order to avoid a government collapse and what many perceived as potential system collapse in the face of extreme political mobilization and terrorism (see Chapter 6); still another is the early 1980s when the Italian Communists condemned the imposition of martial law in Poland (and thus openly opposed Soviet Union policy) (Hine 1993). Again, identifying any particular moment in which democracy in Italy was consolidated is difficult, but certainly by the late 1970s and early 1980s, there could not have been much fear of a transition away from democracy (see Absalom 1995: Chapters 9 and 10); moreover, there had been little attempt to move Italy clearly toward authoritarianism since the public rejection of the monarchy in 1946, although it must be noted that in 1953 the government veered dangerously close to authoritarianism by changing the electoral law such that any alliance of parties which received one vote more than 50 per cent of the votes cast at a national election would receive two-thirds of the seats in the lower house of the Italian parliament (see Chapter 6). However, no party won such a majority in the 1953 elections, and the electoral law was returned to a pro-portional formula shortly after this.

Spain's democratic consolidation, on the other hand, is far clearer. The transition process began very shortly after Franco's death in 1975, and within three years, Spain had ratified a democratic constitution and had held democratic elections. This is not to say that there was no underlying threat to the new democratic regime. First, there were influential political actors in the Basque region who fundamentally rejected the rules of the Spanish democratic regime. However, many of the more extreme of these, including Euskadiko Ezkerra and the Basque Nationalist Party, moved away from being anti-system and only the group Herri Batasuna and its allies in ETA remained persistently hostile to the Spanish state (Gunther *et al.* 1995: 21–2). In addition, Franco had had extremely powerful supporters within his own political party and in the military, and so during the transition process, there was a continued danger that a coalition of these forces would undermine the process and push Spain back into authoritarian rule. Indeed, after the constitution had been ratified, and prior to the second set of parliamentary elections to be held in 1982 in which one of Franco's and the military's most hated groups, the Socialists, was expected to win, a Lieutenant-Colonel marched his men into the Spanish parliament and held it hostage for more than 18 hours. The coup attempt was quickly stopped, and a potential regime crisis was averted (see Chapter 9). Many would thus put the consolidation date at this point. Although another coup was apparently planned in 1985 (Heywood 1995: Chapter 3) – this one extremely brutal, in that it involved assassinating the king and government ministers – it was averted as well. As Linz and Stepan contend, 'There is broad scholarly consensus that Spanish democracy was consolidated no later than the peaceful transfer of power to the socialist opposition after the October 1982 general elections' (1996: 108).

Current levels of democracy in Italy, Spain, and Turkey

Although citizens and observers may complain about the *quality* of democracy in countries like Italy and Spain (see Morlino 1998), as implied by the above discussion, there are no serious questions as to whether either country is a democracy, as defined in the early sections of this chapter. In terms of the specific indicators discussed above, both countries regularly hold elections which are thought to be fairly contested. That is, political opponents are not bullied, jailed, or murdered by state elites. In addition, there is associational autonomy in both countries – citizens can belong (or not belong) to any association they like – and freedom of expression is generally widely accepted (see Preston 1986; Heywood 1995, 1998a; Arango 1996; Partridge 1998; Gibbons 1999; Koff 1999; Foot 2003; Balfour 2004; Gunther *et al.* 2004; Magone 2004; Bull and Newell 2005; Parker and Natale 2006). The only one of Dahl's indicators that might be seen as not being met fully is that of alternative sources of information. Specifically, in the last decade many observers noted the control of a vast media empire by the former Italian prime minister, Silvio Berlusconi. The accusations indicate that Berlusconi was able to use his control of the media to keep himself in power and to prevent views of opponents from getting televised exposure (see Ginsborg 2005). While this may indeed be the case, the defeat of Berlusconi's party, *Forza Italia*, in the 2006 general elections would indicate that his control over television broadcast did not prevent alternation in government. It is also important to note that there are many other media sources as well in Italy (particularly radio and newspapers).

If we consider Italy and Spain in terms of Larry Diamond's additional indicators of democracy, first, it does not appear to be the case that democratically unaccountable officials are responsible for key political decisions in either country. Moreover, institutions in both countries are designed to provide some constraint on majority governments. In both countries, for instance, there are regional institutions which are growing in power and these presumably keep a check on what the national government is doing. Both countries also have independent judiciaries, and they both have Constitutional Courts which are responsible for ensuring that governments act within the guidelines set out in their respective constitutions. In fact, Italy's Constitutional Court was responsible for making sure that Berlusconi's self-granted immunity from prosecution for corruption was removed in 2004 and that he would face trial, as would any ordinary citizen. In both countries, there are also few limitations placed on the forming of parties and both political systems have even allowed former extremists – fascists and communists – to contest elections, including during times when these groups were thought to be potential dangers to the democratic regime. And while the Italian constitution makes the re-formation of a fascist party illegal (according to Article XII of the Transitory and Final Provisions of the 1948 Constitution), such a party was indeed allowed to contest elections and win seats in parliament in the post-war period.

Furthermore, while Spanish elites were traditionally divided over whether to allow minority languages and cultures to operate freely in the country, nowadays this right is recognized and protected. This has been less problematic in Italy, where the vast majority in almost all regions now speak Italian as their first language (see Chapter 2 of this book). Finally, there are no major reported incidents of torture or unjustified detention in either country in the modern day, although there are some reports of excessive use of force by police in Italy.[7]

While Turkey is not at the opposite end of the spectrum – i.e. completely undemocratic – it is thought thus far to fail in meeting a few of the basic requirements of democracy outlined in previous sections. On the one hand, elections themselves are free, fair, and frequent, and there is considerable opportunity for agenda setting and critique of government on the part of ordinary citizens, with a media that can at times be scathing of government policy.[8]

On the other hand, there are limitations on freedom and equality that must be taken into account. First, although elections themselves are conducted freely and there are very few examples of parties being restricted from participating in elections, there are many examples of parties being closed by the Constitutional Court after an election for violating one of the basic constitutional principles, such as secularism or the indivisibility of the Turkish state and people.[9] Thus, for instance, parties designed to represent the interests of Kurds and parties with a clear religious bent have been closed after elections. Since 2003, the laws on party closures have attempted to circumscribe the reasons for closure of a political party. However, a party can still be shut down if its programme is not in agreement with the constitution, and the word 'agreement' can be widely interpreted.[10]

It must be recognized that some countries that are argued to have firm democratic credentials in the modern day also allow for the possibility of party closures and thus this deficiency in Turkish democracy may be less problematic than stated above. Scholars like Larry Diamond recognize that a democracy must protect itself from groups that threaten to undermine completely the basis on which the regime is built. Thus, it should come as no surprise that extremist parties in Germany may be legally banned, for instance, and as mentioned above, neo-fascist parties are technically illegal in Italy.[11] However, in practice, the only party that has been declared to be unconstitutional by the German Federal Constitutional Council is the Communist Party (17 August 1956); efforts to close the nationalist party, the National Democratic Party of Germany, on grounds that it had direct links with the National Socialist Party (Nazi) failed and the party still exists today, as does the Italian fascist party (formerly the National Social Movement, now renamed the National Alliance). Thus, it appears that party closures in Germany are not taken lightly in that they do not occur very often. In contrast, there have been multiple party closures since the adoption of the democratic constitution in 1960 in Turkey, and these parties have at times represented a fairly large portion of voters.[12] Such closures, in turn, raise the potential problem of government using state institutions to keep the opposition out of parliament.

There are other elements of democracy on which Turkey still experiences difficulty as well, however. One of these is freedom of expression. The trials of novelists like Orhan Pamuk and Elif Shafak for violating the above-mentioned penal code by 'insulting Turkishness' in their novels and essays is indicative of this particular shortcoming.[13] Moreover, insulting the founder of the Turkish Republic, Mustafa Kemal Ataturk, is still considered to be a major offence, along the lines of insulting Turkishness.[14] In addition, the government agency, Supreme Council of Radio and Television (RTUK), regularly sanctions broadcast media for violating a very broad range of regulations. Thus, freedom of expression is not completely respected in Turkey. Until very recently, freedom of expression in languages other than Turkish – particularly expression in Kurdish – was also curbed but, importantly, restrictions have been lifted and broadcasting in Kurdish is now possible (see Chapter 8).[15]

Similarly, questions continue to be raised about freedom of association in Turkey. A new law on associations came into force at the end of 2004, but the regulation implementing the law still allows restrictions on associations that are deemed to be contrary to the Turkish Constitution. In practice, this means that associations whose objectives include promoting a certain cultural identity (e.g. Kurdish identity) or a particular religion, will not be able to register as an association. At the same time, some associations based on race, ethnicity, sect or other minority status have been allowed to form, leading the European Commission to conclude that the legislation on associations has not been consistently implemented, with, for instance, a Gay and Lesbian Cultural Research and Solidarity Organisation being temporarily blocked by Ankara's Deputy Governor, who noted that the law restricts the establishment of an association that is 'contrary to law and morality'. Also significant is that human-rights groups continue to be harassed and at times shut down.[16]

The final key factor that prevents Turkey from being considered as a fully functioning democracy is related to the role of the Turkish military in politics. Recall that one of Diamond's suggested requirements for democracy is that elected officials control the state and key decisions rather than such decisions being made by unaccountable officials. If decisions *are* being made by the latter, this calls into question the concept of political equality by allowing the views of some (the unaccountable officials and their supporters) to take priority over the views of everyone else. As will be discussed below, the Turkish military has played a fairly active part in what it perceives as holding the regime together. While early military interference was made with the stipulation that the civilians would be returned to power as quickly as possible, in the periods after 1971 and 1980, military presence in day-to-day decision-making was stepped up, with the military gaining a constitutionally protected advisory capacity on any issue related to national security via the institution known and the National Security Council (see Cizre 2004, 1997). While the latter has always included elected civilian representatives as well as military officials, it has also clearly been a place for military officials to have a legitimate say in policy-making. Importantly, 'national security' has tended to be broadly defined, and so economic crises as well as domestic political issues have often been on the agenda of the National Security Council.

Although the NSC's constitutional role has been downgraded to 'advisory' in recent times and the number of military personnel on the council reduced (see Chapter 9), military generals are still in the habit of making public proclamations on domestic and foreign policy. As stated in the most recent Freedom House report on Turkey: 'the opinions of the top generals continue to generate press attention, and the possibility of military intervention in controversial policy making remains'.[17] Given the military's history of active intervention via military coups, it can only be expected that such public statements undermine the authority and accountability of elected officials. That is, if policies are being made because a military general proclaims that he supports such policies, it is difficult for the citizenry to hold anyone (particularly the generals) accountable for policy-making which results from these proclamations. The response of the military to this accusation would likely be that elected politicians have come very close to allowing Turkey to fall to extremists on the left and right and that perhaps rather than going the way of pre-fascist Italy or Spain (see the next two chapters), they would prefer to rescue the regime from such a fate and attempt to put it back on track toward democracy (as they see democracy, at least). Still, this – along with deficiencies in the realm of freedom of expression – prevents Turkey from being considered as fully democratic.

The puzzle: explaining variation in democratic consolidation

The chapters that follow will show that there were considerable similarities across the cases chosen for analysis in this book. All were relatively backward economically when their transitions began, and all have had multiple experimentations with democracy, as well as experiences with repressive authoritarianism. Two of the cases (Italy and Turkey) contained groups with strong or growing elite–mass linkages that were believed to be subversive to the democratic nature of the regime. All three countries are also relatively large, both in terms of population size and land mass, raising potential difficulties of governance and consolidation that may be less likely to exist in smaller Southern European countries (such as Greece and Portugal). All of the cases (but particularly Spain and Turkey) also faced threats of regional separatism that in turn threatened to undermine democracy, if only through the gradual erosion of democratic principles as the regimes were forced to tighten security against separatist movements. They all also faced potential threats from their own armed forces, although the threat has been more substantial in the cases of Spain and Turkey, both of which had militaries that were firmly committed to the principles of the previous authoritarian regimes. The key question to be answered, therefore, is: given these similarities, why did Spain and Italy manage to consolidate their democracies by the start of the twenty-first century while Turkey continues to fail in its attempt to consolidate? In addition to illustrating the similarities in variables such as economic backwardness, subversive political groups, regional separatism and the threat of a powerful military, the following chapters will point to a few key variables that help explain differences in the outcome (or dependent variable) under investigation here. These include factors connected to the writing of the democratic rules and the rules themselves (i.e. writing the constitution and other key rules) and the degree of rapid professionalization of the military by civilians (which is, in turn, connected to degree of political will on the part of civilians to bring the military under civilian control). The role of external factors in consolidating democracy in the three countries will also be examined.

The factors thought to be potentially causally related to differences in levels of democratic consolidation are briefly outlined here and each will be explored further as they relate to our three case studies in the chapters that follow. These factors include: the degree of 'stateness' problems in the early phase of the transition and the regime's handling of such problems; learning from previous (failed) experiences with democracy and authoritarianism on the part of elites and masses; economic development and economic crisis at the time of the transition; the procedures used for designing the new rules of the regime; the existence or absence of 'civil society' and the connection between such society and parties; the democratic rules themselves, particularly the clarity of rules regarding powers of various institutions and the degree of consensualism incorporated in those rules as well as the solution to stateness problems incorporated within the institutions; the professionalization of the military; and the influence of external factors on democratic consolidation.

Stateness

A basic fact of the modern international system is that it consists of states. Most of the world is now carved into territorial units which are expected to represent and govern the individuals contained within them. Some states exist in territories where most of the citizenry are willing to accept the authority and legitimacy of the state, while other states have been created despite an unwillingness on the part of a significant portion of the population to be governed by the institutions of the state. The latter situation is thought to create severe problems for democratic consolidation (see Rustow 1970; Linz and Stepan 1996). In these circumstances, there is usually little hope of finding institutional arrangements that will satisfy all major contenders and prevent them from undermining the institutions themselves.

It is unclear, however, what proportion of the public failing to support the state institutions would be required for a breakdown of democracy: 5 per cent, 10 per cent, 20 per cent, 50 per cent? Research does indicate, however, that the larger the size of ethnolinguistic minorities in a territory, the higher the likelihood of failure of democracy (see Almond 1956; Dahl 1971; Rabushka and Shepsle 1972; Lijphart 1977; Powell 1982; also see John Stuart Mill 1861 for an early discussion of these ideas).[18] Although some might point to a stateness problem as the key to explaining Turkey's failed democracy, Chapter 2 of this book will argue that Turkey's stateness problem has been no more severe than that experienced in Spain, and so this argument does not reasonably explain differences in democratic consolidation between these two particular cases.

Learning and previous experience with the breakdown of democracy

Elites and masses in a country making a transition to democracy do not make the transition in a vacuum of the present conditions and circumstances. It is highly likely that past experience becomes part of political and cultural memory and that elites prefer to avoid mistakes that may have produced dramatic regime collapse in the past. Thus, it is possible that a country currently making a transition is more likely to move to consolidation if that country had some previous experience with democracy (see Huntington 1991; Valenzuela 1992; Plattner 1998; Beliaev 2003).[19]

Bermeo defines political learning as

> the process through which people modify their political beliefs and tactics as a result of severe crises, frustrations, and dramatic changes in environment.... Crises often force people to reevaluate the ideas that they have used as guides to action in the past. The changed ideas may relate to tactics, parties, allies, enemies, or institutions.
>
> (1992: 274)

For instance, the failures of democracy in both Spain and Italy prior to the fascist dictatorships established in those countries may imply that the same mistakes would not be repeated in subsequent transitions. However, again, the evidence for the importance of this variable is unclear: in our case of failed consolidation – Turkey – there were also democratic periods followed by dramatic breakdown of democracy, and these periods were followed by significant learning in the development of new democratic institutions. However, this learning process has not yet led to consolidation. Thus, this book contends that prior experience with (failed) democracy does not necessarily improve the likelihood of later achieving democratic consolidation. Prior experience with lengthy authoritarian rule after the dramatic breakdown of democracy may, however, be important.

Economic development and economic crisis

One of the general findings that has been replicated across a wide range of research is that economic development is strongly associated with democratic development: countries that have the highest levels of GDP per capita (and Purchasing Power Parity per capita) tend to also be stable democracies and vice versa (Lipset 1959; Cutright 1963; Bollen 1979; Huntington 1991; Diamond 1992; Londregan and Poole 1996; Przeworski *et al.* 1996; Przeworski and Limongi 1997; Gasiorowski and Power 1998; Geddes 1999; Bunce 2000; Boix and Stokes 2003). There are, of course, exceptions to this trend, but these are few, and so this book considers this to be one of the key potential explanations for differences in democratic consolidation in Spain, Italy, and Turkey.

Perhaps more important for the transition period and whether this transition moves toward democratic consolidation is whether a country is experiencing economic *crisis*, with rapid inflation, rapidly rising unemployment and/or negative growth. When the economy is in freefall, there may be more actors with incentives to disrupt the transition process in the name of gaining firm control over the economic tools of the state. The assumption is that democratic institutions have more difficulty addressing economic crisis quickly because of the need to (a) satisfy constituents and (b) negotiate. Thus, actors operating under democratic rules may not be capable of forcing potentially difficult economic medicine on the population as a whole, leading non-democratic contenders to stage a takeover. Therefore, periods of economic crisis during a transition period may result in the breakdown of democracy (Przeworski and Limongi 1993, 1997; Gasiorowski 1995; Haggard and Kaufman 1995).[20]

Chapter 4 will be devoted to exploring the levels of economic development at the time of the transitions to democracy in Spain, Italy, and Turkey but will also examine economic crisis during the transition periods to determine whether either of these variables were likely to be key to explaining differences in democratic consolidation across the three countries. The findings indicate that while economic development may have been an important indirect factor affecting democratic consolidation in the three countries, economic crisis does not provide a major explanation for such differences.

Constitution building

Constitutions lay the foundation for the functioning of a polity. This is particularly the case in democracies, where elites occupying different roles within the polity can point to the foundational document when there are disputes regarding the distribution of power. The rules themselves dictate how power will be distributed, and so the rules have a major influence on how the political system functions. There are widely varying methods of creating the basic rules, and one chapter of this book will investigate the development of rule-making procedures in the three countries under examination. It is here that we find a clear potential explanatory variable for differential outcomes across the three regimes: the constitutional design process in Spain and Italy was vastly different than that in Turkey, and we will argue that this difference is likely to have played a key role in subsequent levels of consolidation in the three countries.

Civil society, social and political cleavages, and political parties

Another argument that has been put forth in academic literature relates to the attitudes, values, and behaviours of the ordinary citizens in a transitional regime. Namely, the contention is that without an organized civil society in place to hold government accountable, the likelihood of survival of democracy is very low (Almond and Verba 1963; Inglehart 1989; Uslaner 2002; see also Putnam 1993, 2001 on civil society in 'making democracy work'). This is an argument that has been highly contested, and Chapter 6 outlines the reasons for this contestation. One of the counter-arguments that is potentially very important to the analyses here is that a highly organized, active civil society can actually produce instability and breakdown of democracy if it cannot be channelled directly to the state institutions via organized groups like political parties (Berman 1997). Early research on political stability also pointed to the importance of a developed political party system in maintaining stability (see Barnes 1966; Huntington 1968). However, the evidence will indicate that this variable is unlikely to be crucial in the cases of Spain, Italy, and Turkey: Spain managed to consolidate democracy quickly despite having a relatively weak party system at the time of its transition to democracy, Italy also managed to consolidate democracy (albeit more slowly) with a highly developed party system, and Turkey failed to consolidate despite having a party system that appeared to be consolidating and a society which was becoming active and connected to political parties in the 1960s and 1970s.

The rules: executives, parliaments, and executive–parliamentary relations

Not only is it important *how* the rules are designed, but the rules themselves may also be crucial in explaining democratic consolidation. At the very least it appears that the locus of executive power must be clear and that executive power divided across multiple institutions with differing sources of authority may be extremely problematical for consolidation. For instance, Linz (1990) argues against adopting presidential systems in new democracies because these systems create problems of dual legitimacy. Essentially, since both the president and the legislature are popularly elected, but in different elections and using different means to conduct the elections, they both have legitimate claims to ultimate power. Although none of the cases studied in this book have (yet) adopted presidential systems of governance,[21] it must be noted that there are other potential sources of dual legitimacy. One of these is heredity and the other is the power given to a political role via the constitution.

As this book will show, disputes over executive power in Italy may have contributed to weakness and ultimately collapse of democracy in the 1920s, and the clarification of the locus of executive power after the end of World War II may have similarly contributed to stability and consolidation. In contrast, we will see that the most recent Turkish constitution introduces ambiguity regarding the exercise of executive power, and we will also see how this has contributed to instability and ultimately the failure to consolidate (Heper and Çinar 1996).

Also important to consider is the distribution of power between the executive and parliament. Do strong parliaments help to consolidate democracy, or is a strong executive more promising for consolidation? The evidence presented in Chapter 7 indicates that the relationship varies, depending on the nature and strength of political cleavages, and that the weakness of the Turkish parliament vis-à-vis that of the Italian parliament may be one of the key factors explaining the differences in consolidation across these two countries. Also investigated is the degree of consensualism adopted in the rules governing parliamentary decision-making and parliamentary–executive relations.

The rules: stateness problems and regional autonomy

As discussed above, internal divisions over ethnicity, nationality, and religion often spell the death knell for democracy. If a state has not resolved these divisions prior to the transition to democracy (e.g. via repression, propaganda, etc.), there is a reduced likelihood of making the transition successfully. However, some scholars (e.g. Lijphart 1968, 1977, 1985, 1999; Lijphart and Waisman 1996) believe that it is possible to design institutions that address these divisions and placate national, ethnic, and religious minorities, allowing the democratic institutions to take root and flourish. Chapter 8 will be devoted to explaining how the three countries under investigation have addressed their stateness problems. The findings indicate that the handling of such conflicts may indeed be highly relevant to the consolidation of democracy.

The army

One of the components of democracy discussed at the start of this chapter was that elected officials must have control of all major policy-making power; unaccountable officials cannot exercise political power if the country is to fit within the concept of 'consolidated democracy'. If there are officials exercising political power without accountability in a polity, these are often within the military (see the O'Donnell *et al.* 1986, *Transitions from Authoritarian Rule* volumes). We thus explore differences in the professionalization of the military, including the reasons for such differences across our three cases. The findings point to the conclusion that one of the key reasons for the failure to consolidate Turkish democracy lies in the failure to professionalize the military, but that this failure has its roots in the failure on the part of civilians consensually to agree to have sole control of political power in their own hands. Chapter 9 explores military interventionism in our three cases, and the professionalization techniques thought to be available to transitional regimes, as well as the reasons the Turkish government has been unable to adopt such techniques, using Spain and Italy as cases for comparison.

External influences on democratic consolidation

No democratic transition, especially in the modern day, takes place in a vacuum apart from the rest of the world, and while many of the earlier studies of democratic transition and consolidation tended to emphasize domestic factors in the transitional countries, it is now widely recognized that external factors may be equally crucial in pushing regimes toward consolidation (or preventing them from transitioning to authoritarianism). Thus, Chapter 10 discusses which of these external actors are thought to be relevant, as well as the role of such factors in consolidating democracy in Italy, Spain, and Turkey.

Plan of the book

As indicated above, the chapters that follow are devoted to exploring each of these variables in turn. Each chapter will begin with a discussion of the theory and logic behind the hypothesis under investigation, and then the hypothesis will be tested on the three cases. This book is not based on quantitative analyses, and it is assumed here that the answers to the questions posed in the book lie as much in the historical development of the three countries as in basic statistics regarding economic development, party membership, etc. All of the chapters therefore provide information about all three cases and include historical information that is deemed to be relevant to the questions posed in the book.

Although the book is based on the qualitative analysis of factors that potentially influence democratic consolidation in the three countries, it uses the logic of comparative case study methods, particularly John Stuart Mill's 'Method of Difference' (or Przeworski and Teune's 1970 'Most Similar Systems'). Namely it will be assumed that where the dependent variable – democratic consolidation – differs across the three cases but the values of an independent variable are similar across the cases, that potential explanatory factor can be ruled out as a main cause of the phenomenon under study. The logic of this system and the selection of cases are explained further in the Appendix to this book.

As with any historical, qualitative analysis, a potential critique against this approach is that it may be unclear as to which historical details are important and which ones may be omitted. It is for this reason that the chapters are structured as variables to be discussed and measured where possible. Historical and political circumstances surrounding each variable are also discussed, and so the reader is free to draw alternative conclusions to those drawn here. Readers may also, of course, consult the histories of the three cases analysed here for the development of alternative explanations.

2 Problems in state building

Modern states can be distinguished from other territorial entities by the fact that they demand at least a minimal degree of commitment and loyalty from their citizenry. In contrast to prior governing units such as the Ottoman Empire or Hapsburg Empire in which local languages, cultures, and religions could exist with little government interference and in which the only demand was obedience to the sovereign and its laws, the modern state, in its quest for ultimate commitment and loyalty, has undertaken numerous activities to alter factors like language spoken and perceptions of community. Specifically, most modern states have adopted a single language which serves as the official language of the state and which is taught in schools, used in official government proceedings, including legislative debates, official addresses, and court cases.[1] States have also participated in the development of common myths to try to further the impression of community amongst the citizenry (Hobsbawm 1990; Anderson 1991; see also the collection of essays in Hutchinson and Smith 2000).

Gaining and maintaining control over the population contained within the territory of a state is one of the main difficulties faced by all modern states, but it is particularly problematic for democracies. In stark contrast to authoritarian regimes, the methods of control available to democracies are – at least in theory – far more limited, as brutal coercion may be seen to violate some of the underlying tenets of democracy discussed in Chapter 1. While democracies may attempt validly to use authoritarian methods to maintain control over territory by placing separatist movement organizers in a specific legal category (e.g. terrorists) that allows for coercive measures, the fact of the matter is that when a large sector of the population feels that the state's institutions do not represent people like them and that laws are being made for them by foreigners, this creates inherent tensions within a democracy. Indeed, it is argued by some that if a country cannot resolve its stateness problems, there is little hope for achieving stable democracy (see Rustow 1970; Linz and Stepan 1996), and some empirical research points to the conclusion that large ethnolinguistic minorities in a state create an increased likelihood of a breakdown of democracy (Almond 1956; Dahl 1971; Rabushka and Shepsle 1972; Lijphart 1977; Powell 1982).

One of the most basic defining features of a state is that it has clear boundaries that are generally recognized and acknowledged by the rest of the international community; the state's leaders then – in theory – have the absolute right to make policy that applies to the population residing in that territory with the expectation of non-interference by other states (although Chapter 10 will provide examples of some external interference). The process of setting these boundaries is rarely easy or natural – for instance, driven exclusively by natural boundaries like waterways or mountains – and indeed boundaries are often settled by war. The potential problem for state building and ultimately for democratic consolidation is that even once a territory is conquered, there may be groups of elites and masses who are adamantly opposed to having been conquered in the first place. Thus even after boundaries are apparently set and recognized by the international community, dissatisfied groups within the state may still contest these and contest the new state's authority. Therefore, the chapter briefly describes how the boundaries were established in each of the three cases and whether there were any domestic groups which contested these boundaries. Also of importance for the modern state is the creation of national myths and a common language and the sections below outline these processes for our three case studies. The chapter will conclude with a discussion of whether state-building is likely to have had a direct impact on democratic consolidation in the three countries. It is important to note that the topics covered in this chapter mostly relate to the unification of territory and development of shared language and myths and that Chapter 8 addresses the issue of ethno-linguistic minorities in our three case studies, as well as these states' attempts to address potential problems caused by ethno-linguistic or nationalist minority identities.

Italy: the speedy transition from feudalism to modern state?

European state-building processes in the eighteenth and nineteenth centuries tended to emphasize centralization of government power in the state capital and standardization of local administrative procedures.[2] The three cases examined in this book are no exceptions – although as will be shown below, the Spanish state did briefly experiment with alternative methods of state-building that were centred on the assumption that autonomous communities existed within the state territory.

In comparison to our other two cases, the creation of the modern Italian state was arguably relatively smooth and rapid. There were important setbacks in the process, and these will be outlined below. However, it is argued here that these were relatively minor when viewed in terms of stateness; that is, the rebellions that did occur against the newly forming state did not significantly threaten to undermine the creation and maintenance of the state itself.[3] On the other hand, the state was arguably of questionable legitimacy until the 1920s because of its openly hostile treatment of the Catholic

Church and the Church's supporters; furthermore, problems of illiteracy may have reduced the state's ability to spread a common language and myths until the 1940s and 1950s. Additionally, at the end of World War II, the state faced some separatist movements in its peripheral regions. These issues will be discussed below, and the case of the post-war uprisings will be discussed further in Chapter 8.

Until the mid-1800s, Italy did not exist as a unified entity. The territory now known as Italy had, in fact, been partitioned into city states and papal states after the decline of the Roman Empire. Between the fifteenth and eighteenth centuries, the territory was under foreign control by the great European powers of the day – France, Spain, Germany, and Austria – as well as the Catholic Church. The territory was then unified for a brief period

Map 2.1 The regions of Italy, original image provided by Flags of the World, flagspot.net.

while it was under Napoleon I's control (1797–1815), but after Napoleon's defeat, the old configuration of foreign rule was restored in the Vienna Settlement of 1814–15, in which European powers struck agreements as to how to re-establish the balance of power in Europe following the defeat of Napoleon's France.[4]

In the years leading up to the Vienna Settlement and afterward, intellectuals had begun to romanticize about creating an Italian state. Secret societies began to form with a view to overthrowing the settlement, and various groups (lawyers, doctors, shopkeepers, and students) began staging uprisings. The uprising (the *Risorgimento*) was generally the pursuit of intellectuals, students, and the growing bourgeoisie which had begun to see potential economic benefits from throwing off foreign rule (see Riall 1994, 1998; Ziblatt 2006: Chapter 4). Thus, this uprising was not a mass-based nationalist movement, although organizations like 'Young Italy' and the Italian National Society helped to draw public attention to the nationalist cause.

It was ultimately through diplomacy that unification became possible. With the help of France the rulers in the northern region of Piedmont (see Map 2.1) managed to gain control of the central part of what is now the Italian state. With the help of Britain, the South was also annexed. Along the way, most papal territory was also claimed, a point to which we return below. In 1861, it was declared that a new kingdom existed, and only Venice and Rome still remained outside the kingdom. These were then captured in 1866 and 1870, respectively (see Absalom 1995, Chapters 1 and 2).

Besides dealing with the integration of several different administrative and legal systems, and the delicacy of maintaining regional balances in government posts, the new state faced a potentially devastating counter-revolution in the Southern part of Italy between 1860 and 1865. There were already rumblings of discontent because the nationalist revolutionaries had betrayed the Southern peasants by at first playing for their support by promising land re-distribution and cheaper food in exchange for their support for the *Risorgimento*, and then supporting the landlords instead and executing many of the peasants along the way.

It also became immediately apparent that the intention of the *Risorgimento* leaders was to impose Piedmontese laws and administrative systems on the entirety of Italy. Thus, the process of 'piedmontization' provoked a revival of local sentiment. The ex-king of Naples (which had been an independent kingdom prior to the *Risorgimento*) led efforts at counter-revolution, relying on support from both the aristocracy and the peasants in the former kingdom of Naples. However, the counter-revolution used banditry against the rich as its key weapon. Rather than being a movement inspired by loyalty to the king of Naples or any form of nationalism, it seems to mostly have been inspired by poverty and the tradition of highway robbery.

Amongst the leaders of the new government, however, there were many who believed that the Southern rebels were actually fighting for an alternative dynasty and for the Church (which had been ousted from most of its territory during the *Risorgimento*). The response of the new government was therefore fairly brutal. Martial law was declared in areas that were deemed to be overrun with bandits, and brigands and their accomplices were punished in military courts. Soldiers were instructed to shoot any peasant carrying arms, men were shot on suspicion of being brigands, and villages were sacked and burned for sheltering bandits. Over 120,000 soldiers – almost half of the new national army – were concentrated in Sicily and the South of Italy (Mack Smith 1959: 69–75).

By 1865, although bandits still roamed the South, the region appeared to be pacified. At the very least, the organized rebellion had ended. Furthermore, even though the interests of the South appear to have been generally neglected with new government policies – particularly related to taxation and tariffs – and Catholic interests were a potentially incendiary force, there was no major organized effort to undermine the existence of the new state after 1865 until the rise of Northern nationalism and the Northern Leagues in the 1990s. At the end of World War II, the regime did face uprisings in Sicily and some of the smaller Northern regions, but separatist activity in these regions was halted fairly quickly, as will be discussed in Chapter 8. In short, the brigands of the South simply did not manage to wage any sort-of coordinated guerrilla war against the new state, and the post-war separatist activity was short-lived.[5] Thus, in comparison to Spain and Turkey which will be discussed below, Italy had mostly managed to resolve stateness problems prior to the start of early democratic experimentation in the late 1800s (see the next chapter).

As discussed at the start of this chapter, the modern state entails far more than the conquering of territory. Specifically, modern states demand loyalty and commitment on the part of their citizenry. Without such a commitment, the state is likely to encounter severe legitimacy problems which in turn create problems of control. As discussed above, non-democratic states are able to use coercion to maintain some degree of control, whereas democratic states must generally rely on other means. At the very least, these states must teach a common language and develop some way of connecting citizens to one another and to the state via unifying myths (Hobsbawm 1990; Anderson 1991). While the above historical overview of the creation of the Italian state illustrates the way in which the state came into existence, it says very little about the *citizens* of that state. Thus, we now turn to the question of loyalty and commitment to the Italian state on the part of ordinary Italians.

In terms of developing a common language by which people could communicate with each other and with the state leaders, it is estimated that only 2–3 per cent of people living in Italy actually spoke Italian at the time of unification, with most people speaking local dialects (Mack Smith 1959; de Mauro 1976; Hobsbawm 1990: 38; Moss 2000). Much of the intellectual and political leadership behind the *Risorgimento* were not even fluent in Italian (Mack Smith 1959). Moreover, the process of teaching Italian,

particularly in the countryside was slowed by the illiteracy of the vast majority of the population and resistance by poor parents to the implementation
of compulsory education, which was established in 1877.[6] Indeed, Antonio
Gramsci contended that governments of the late nineteenth century had
failed to recognize that they needed to impose cultural hegemony at a much
faster pace, and that the slow progress of the development of a national language was an indicator of the slowness of the promotion of national identity
among the citizenry. Gramsci further argues that Italy fell 'prey to Fascism
precisely because its post-unification governments had been backward in
creating a solid "national-popular" identity between the classes', and this
was in large part connected to the failure of greater widespread mastery of
the country's national language (quoted in Moss 2000: 104–5). In addition,
despite Mussolini's attempt to alter this situation, by the time his regime
collapsed after more than 20 years, Italian was still the regular language of
only a minority of Italians, at most 37 per cent (Moss 2000: 105–6, 110).

However, it is clear that Italian has indeed been learned, as almost 100
per cent of Italians now claim that the language they primarily speak at
home is Italian and approximately 99 per cent speak no other language at
home (see, for instance, the 1995 International Social Survey Project). Scholars contend that the factors that contributed to this dramatic change are:
internal migration and urbanization, industrialization, state education,
national bureaucracy, military service, the press, and mass entertainment
(see Moss 2000: 110). In addition, there are no large regional pockets of
Italy in which citizens systematically speak any language other than Italian
(but see Chapter 8 on languages spoken by very small minorities). Thus, the
project of teaching Italians Italian would appear to have generally been a
success.[7] As Moss (2000: 110) contends, 'the sharing by most Italians of
a language they did not share before has been a contributory factor in
the shaping of a feeling of Italianness among people of diverse cultural
origins'. What this overview of linguistic diversity also indicates, however,
is that at the time of the start of the post-World War II experiment with
democracy in Italy, the country was still not nationally unified in terms of
language and so the new state was faced with both a democratic transition
and a nation-building process simultaneously. Moreover, democratizers were
facing rebellions in some of the peripheral territories, including Sicily (see
Chapter 8).

With regard to unifying myths, the key myths of the Italian nation-state
centre around the *Risorgimento* and national unification. Events such as the
charismatic *Risorgimento* soldier Giuseppe Garibaldi's 'defence of the Roman
Republic' in an attempt to defend Venice against Austria in 1866 have been
recorded as 'episodes of extraordinary popular heroism' (Riall 1994: 68; see
also Ginsborg 1991). Despite the fact that the *Risorgimento* was waged
without much of a mass following, it still became a defining part of Italy's
common past and provided a basis for cultural identity which was more
important than ethnic or linguistic identity (Lanaro 1988; Tobia 1991).

Moreover, journalists and publishers had already begun to 'discover' Italy's common past in the late 1700s. Italians also appear to have been further unified by the myth of Italy being cheated of her due by other victorious nations after World War I, a myth that was eventually used by Nationalists to rally support (see Mack Smith 1959: 321). During the fascist period in Italy, the regime drew upon the ancient Roman imperial past and began excavating Roman ruins and erecting marble reliefs showing the extent of the Roman Empire in order to further build Italian national identity. The *Risorgimento* heroes and Italian writers and thinkers were used to build nationalism as well. Propaganda was used in children's textbooks for the same purpose, and given that illiteracy was reduced considerably, it is expected that these texts had at least some impact on the building of Italian nationalism (Mack Smith 1959: 414–23).[8]

A key issue to note with regard to the creation of the Italian nation-state, however, is the potentially undermining effect that the Catholic Church had on the process of state-building. The conquest of papal territory and seizure of papal possessions in the unification of Italy virtually guaranteed the Church's opposition to the new state. Given the religious nature of Italian society at the time, the notion of the creation of a secular nationalism as promoted by the thinkers of the *Risorgimento* was likely to have rung hollow with most people residing in the new state. Moreover, Pope Pius IX (1846–78) required Italians to choose between loyalty to the Church and support of the new state, thereby dealing 'a devastating blow to the legitimacy of Liberal Italy' (Riall 1994: 79). Thus, it is possible that this disconnect between the state and society that resulted from the Church's insistence that its followers exclude themselves from participation in the new state institutions was not fully resolved until the time of Mussolini's fascist dictatorship, during which the state entered into a Concordat with the Church. Although the Church lifted its ban on participation in elections for certain constituencies prior to the rise of Mussolini (for instance, in the 1904 election), this was because of fear of a leftist victory (Clark 1984: 146). It was primarily the 1929 Concordat between the Fascist state and the Church, which comprised restoration of some of the Church's funds and land, including the creation of the Vatican City State with sovereign immunity, as well as the restoration of the Church's moral policy-making role, that ended the Church's hostility to the Italian state. Therefore, there is likely to have been considerable delay in the creation of loyalty on the part of ordinary Italians, as Catholics were being instructed to be loyal to the Church rather than the state.

Also of importance is that because of the elite nature of the creation of the new state, the ruling class failed to create a uniform sense of national identity. However, it can be argued that in addition to the effects of post-war modernization, *partitocrazia* (party control over the state) in the post-World War II era provided a means by which Italian citizens could finally be connected to their state, and that this served to help create relatively stable institutions – a point which will be further developed in Chapter 6.[9] Further, the new anti-fascist, democratic institutions may have provided Italians with a revitalized sense of common identity, particularly given the lack of participation on the part of most of these citizens in the discredited fascist regime (Ragionieri 1976; Barbagallo 1994).

The fact that national identity was indeed created in Italy is confirmed by modern national survey data. It is clear from these data that Italians *do* very much identify with their nation-state: 87 per cent claim to feel close to their country, with minimal regional deviation from this average, and when asked whether it is essential that the country remains as one or whether parts of the country should be allowed to become fully separate countries, 84 per cent insist that the state should remain as one (International Social Survey Project 1995). There are regional differences to note, however, and these are displayed in Table 2.1. What is reflected in these figures is the movement in the North for separation that developed in the mid-1990s, but it is interesting to note that the vast majority in the South – the part of Italy that had been conquered or 'piedmontized' – prefers unity rather than dissolution. Moreover, it is an overwhelming majority in *both* regions that prefer unity, indicating that somewhere along the way, the nation-state building process in Italy was quite successful.

What conclusions can we thus draw about the relationship between state-building processes and democratic consolidation in Italy? On the positive side, the Italian state appears to have faced relatively small-scale organized challenges to its authority in the form of armed resistance movements. Thus by the time of the start of the post-World War II transition to democracy the issue of stateness had been resolved to a great extent, and so the new democracy was not forced to simultaneously address the problems of large-scale armed resistance and consolidating new democratic institutions, although it was faced with threats of break-away regions at the end of World War II.[10] At the same time, if 'stateness' also refers to factors like the building of loyalty and common language, it is clear that the state had some way to go in consolidating its authority and this appears to have occurred simultaneously with democratic consolidation. Thus, this case seems to illustrate that the state-building process does not need to be entirely complete prior to the transition in order for consolidation to succeed but that

Table 2.1 Allow parts of Italy to separate from the Italian state?

	Remain one state (%)	*Become Separate (%)*	*Number of cases*
North West	75	25	280
North East	74	26	197
Centre	93	7	203
South + Islands	92	8	385

Source: Adapted from International Social Survey Project, 1995.

the lack of large groups of organized armed challengers to the state may be a necessary condition for democratic consolidation. We now turn to the next two case studies in order to determine whether this argument is likely to hold in the face of further empirical evidence.

Spain: a troubled state-building process

In contrast to the development of the state in Italy, the actual boundaries (and very existence) of the Spanish state have been set for much longer, having been established in 1512.[11] Also in contrast to Italy, though, is that there have been significant periods in which the degree of stateness has clearly been called into question. For instance, one of these significant periods was the Portuguese war of independence from Spain in the seventeenth century.

Although Spain's boundaries have been more or less clear far longer than those of the Italian state, this does not necessarily mean that the Spanish territory began developing as a modern state at this early date of 1512. In fact, the founding of a Spanish kingdom was only possible because of the *Reconquista*, or re-conquering of Iberian territory from the Muslim Moors, but this *Reconquista* was carried out by warriors who proceeded to establish themselves as political rulers (counts or princes) in the territory that had been re-conquered (Oliveira 1946). With this divided territory facing

Map 2.2 The regions of Spain, original image provided by Flags of the World, flagspot.net.

powerful neighbouring competitors like France and Britain, King Philip II decided to formally unite Spanish territories in 1580. However, leaders of the re-conquered territories continued to be protective of their power, and the newly unified state did not pursue heavy centralization policies. According to one historian, the Spanish state was, in fact, founded on the basis of religious homogeneity and all other differences – political and cultural – were met with tolerance (Oliveira 1946: 356). In the 1620s, there was some movement toward creating national solidarity by the ending of all regional autonomies, but this is mostly counted as a failure; the minister who proposed and attempted to enact the reforms (Philip IV's chief advisor, the Count-Duke of Olivares) was hugely unpopular, and Spain's failures at foreign policy and its economic bankruptcy made the creation of national unity all the more difficult. The centralization policies resulted in a Catalonian rebellion in 1640 and King Philip IV's subsequent backing down on most of these (even though the Catalans were defeated). It was not until the early 1700s (under Philip V) that centralization was begun in earnest (Oliveira 1946: 371–4).

In terms of identity and loyalty, through the mid-1700s, Spain was merely a kingdom that had been created by marriage between various rulers (including the Bourbons, who ruled Southern Italy as well) and as in other kingdoms and empires there was little interest in building the sorts of connection between the masses and the state that have been evident in more modern times (Heywood 1995: 13). Indeed, as with other kingdoms, monarchs of Spain often did not even speak any of the languages of the country, as they were brought up in other parts of Europe. (There was a similar situation in the early days of the new Italian state – the thinkers behind the *Risorgimento* could barely write in Italian and tended to prefer French.)

Countless scholars of Spanish politics and history point to the relative dearth of studies about the creation of Spanish national identity (see Flynn 2001; Muro and Quiroga 2005; but see Holguin 2002 and Ortiz 2000 on the creation of Spanish national myths and identity). As will be discussed further in Chapter 8, however, the concerted effort at centralization and standardization that was witnessed in Italy from the founding of the new Italian state until the early 1970s was not in evidence in Spain. Because of ongoing wars of succession in Spain, the process of nation-state creation was rather slow. Also, fundamental disagreements between liberals and nationalists over the construction of the Spanish state meant that state-building policies often changed radically between administrations.

Although the process of standardization began to progress in the 1800s, with local administrative reform in 1833 and the establishment of a national system of secondary education in 1857, these reforms also coincided with civil war in Spain (the First Carlist War of 1833–9 and the Second Carlist War of 1872–6), a military *pronunciamiento* (coup) in 1868, and the establishment of a Republic that survived a mere 11 months in 1873. It is difficult to imagine that much real movement toward the creation of a common Spanish nation-state occurred under these circumstances.

Additionally, as mentioned above, there was fundamental disagreement about the form that the Spanish state should take. The 1st Republic, for instance, established a *federal* republic of 17 states, thereby recognizing the autonomy of Spanish regions. Again, this experiment was short-lived, and what followed was a more consistent campaign of nation-state building, including regaining of centralized control over local administration (del Mar del Pozo and Braster 1999), the requirement that the *Spanish* national flag be raised everyday in all public schools in 1893, and the reinstatement in 1921 of a government decree from the late 1800s that required a portrait of the king, as the 'head of the power that represents the unity of the father-land' be placed in a visible location in all public schools (del Mar del Pozo Andres and Braster 1999). In addition, it was ordered in 1902 that the catechism be given in Castilian only rather than in any regional languages or dialects; following protests in Catalonia, the order was rescinded. However, in 1923 and 1924, primary-school teachers were reminded that they were obliged to teach in Castilian only (as required by a 1902 law), and that to speak Catalan or Basque in the classroom would be severely punished. A royal decree in 1923 stipulated that symbols like regional flags could not be displayed in public buildings, and that primary school teaching – as a state activity – must be in Castilian (see Vincent 2007). It is important to note that one of the key factors leading to increased activities in the realm of identity creation was the loss of the last few colonies in the Americas (Cuba, Puerto Rico, and the Philippines) in 1898. Without the grandness of empire to form the basis of unity, scholars and intellectuals began to contemplate other factors that might contribute to national consciousness (Heywood 1995: 14).

However, these stepped up efforts at developing a common nationality were followed by the creation of the Second Republic (1931–6), which included liberal governments (from 1931–3 and from 1936 until the out-break of the Spanish Civil War) that allowed for regional autonomy, even giving Catalonia its own parliament and president. The Spanish Civil War (1936–9) resulted in the defeat of the liberals and the creation of the Franco dictatorship, which had amongst its goals the creation of a unitary Spanish nation-state. Thus, the use of languages other than Castilian was severely repressed and government decision-making and administration was re-centralized. As will be discussed in later chapters, these efforts at forced assimilation have been a failure and in the case of the Basque Country, they appear to have produced support for extremist separatist groups (see Chapter 8).

The Spanish state-building process has thus clearly been problematical. Regional languages and identities still persist in regions like Catalonia, the Basque country, Galicia, and Valencia. As argued above, a key component of the failure has been the existence of civil wars and the resulting lack of con-certed effort at establishing a common national identity.

Some also point out that in contrast to the Italian case, the regions in

Spain which have been the fiercest in resisting government attempts at control have also been amongst the most economically developed, industrialized regions. That is, the regions of Italy that were prime candidates for rebellion against the centre – and in which there was indeed a brief rebellion – were also amongst the least industrialized. What this is likely to have meant is that the prime places in which resistance could be fomented – factories and other urban centres – simply did not exist to the same degree that they existed in regions like Catalonia and the Basque country in Spain.[12]

Thus, the failure of the Spanish state-building process appears to lie in the rather delayed attempt to build a nation-state long after the process of industrialization in the north began. Based on the Italian example, it seems that repression of peasants who would very likely have more difficulty organizing themselves is far easier than repressing groups that reside and work in the most industrialized portion of the country. This particular failure in the Spanish case, in turn, may in great part be a result of the very long period of succession wars and military pronouncements that hindered any consistent state-building process. The post-Franco Spanish state leaders have, however, recognized that methods of nation-state building that might have been appropriate in previous centuries are not at their disposal in the current period and have begun another experiment at Spanish state building which will be discussed further in Chapter 8.

It should be noted that in contrast to the potentially severe problems created by disassociation with the Catholic Church in Italy, for the most part, this was less of a problem for the Spanish state. There were periods throughout the 1800s in which liberalizing regimes began passing legislation to remove the Church's wealth and role in providing education, but in 1851, a Concordat was signed between the Church and the Spanish state guaranteeing priests an income and recognizing Catholicism as the religion of Spain. The Church remained fairly neutral toward the state, but during the periods in which liberal parties formed the government in the 1930s, the church became more hostile toward the regime as the liberal leaders themselves became more openly anti-clerical.[13] This was relatively short-lived, however, as Franco restored much of the power of the Catholic Church, instituted moral policies in line with the Church's teaching, and allowed the Church considerable autonomy in the realm of social policy. The close relationship between the Church and state ended in the late 1950s when the Church began to distance itself from the regime. For the most part, though, it can be argued that during the creation of the Spanish state, the Church was not hostile to the state itself and thus was not an undermining force as had been the case in Italy.

As in our previous section on Italy, it is worth investigating the degree of stateness problems in modern-day Spain. While the terrorist activities of groups like ETA can be taken as one possible indication of a serious stateness problem, without additional information, it is difficult to know whether the problem is limited to a few radical groups or is more widespread. Thus, we turn to data on language usage and national identity to gain a more thorough picture of the level of commitment and loyalty to the Spanish state in the modern day.

Recall that the efforts at state building, particularly from the 1930s onward, have included a process of trying to Castilianize the language spoken in Spain. This process has been somewhat successful outside a few key regions, as roughly only 16 per cent of the Spanish population still does not speak Castilian at home (according to the 1995 and 1999–2000 waves of the World Values Survey). Those who do not speak Castilian at home tend to be concentrated in particular regions, though. For instance, approximately 51 per cent of respondents in Catalonia speak Catalan at home, about 58 per cent of survey respondents in the Galician region speak Galician (which is similar to Portuguese); approximately 37 and 35 per cent in Valencia and the Balearics, respectively, speak native languages at home rather than Castilian (see World Values Survey, 1995; see also Graham and Labanyi 1996). Recall that in stark contrast, there are no regional patterns in languages spoken in Italy, indicating that the vast majority of the Italian population has been assimilated to the new state, at least in this regard.

Despite not speaking the same language at home, it is still possible for citizens of Spain to feel that they share a common destiny and to feel themselves to be part of the Spanish state. When asked the question about how close they feel to their country, 89 per cent of survey respondents in Spain claim to feel close; moreover, the only region where the vast majority do *not* express such sentiments is the Basque Country, where approximately 52 per cent claim to not feel close to their state (see the 1995 International Social Survey Project). Moreover, approximately 84 per cent of Spanish survey respondents feel that it is essential for their country to remain as one country rather than allow certain regions to separate. Not surprisingly, however, 50 per cent of the Basque sample believe that regions wanting separation should be allowed to leave the country, and about 40 per cent in Catalonia also felt this way. On the other hand, the region which contains the smallest number of Spanish speakers – Galicia – is very much in favour of the Spanish state staying together (88.5 per cent are in favour of this option).

Overall, then, it would appear that despite an earlier start date as a unified state, Spain's 'stateness' problems are potentially more severe than Italy's. The majority in some Spanish regions have not adopted the state's traditionally preferred language, Castilian, and large minorities across Spain have failed to do so as well. Further, in contrast to Italy, there are significant regional pockets of citizens who do not identify with the Spanish state and believe that regions wishing to leave should be allowed to do so. As will be discussed further in Chapter 8, the most potentially problematic regions in terms of separatist sentiment and/or activity have been the Basque Country and Catalonia, with the former currently representing roughly 5 per cent of the total population of Spain, and the latter representing approximately 16 per cent (according to the *Instituto Nacional de Estadística*, Madrid).

The evidence presented in this chapter, along with the evidence of ETA violence, indicate that it is not clear that modern Spain has completely solved its stateness problems. As discussed in the book's introduction, however, Spanish democracy is clearly consolidated. It thus appears that democratic consolidation can indeed occur despite severe stateness problems. Chapter 8 will discuss the issues of regional identity at greater length and will explain how the new Spanish democracy confronted this potentially disruptive issue.

Turkey: the latecomer state

As mentioned above, all of the case studies included in this book began their processes of state-building relatively late in comparison to other European countries like France and Britain. However, amongst our three case studies, Turkey is the most recent to start such a process. This section outlines the events leading up to the establishment of the Turkish state, the government policies that have been adopted in the state-building process, and the difficulties in state-building that elites have faced.

The intense concentration on building a nation-state is at times tied to the decline of empire. This certainly seems to be the case in Spain, where nation-building policies were stepped up after the final loss of its American empire in 1898 (see Heywood 1995: Chapter 1). This is also true in Turkey.

Map 2.3 The regions of Turkey, original image provided by the University of Texas Perry-Castañeda Library, www.lib.utexas.edu/maps.

Although the Ottoman Empire began to decline toward the end of the seventeenth century and reforms were adopted in the 1800s to try to maintain what was left of the Empire, it was not until the establishment of the Turkish Republic in 1923 through a war of independence conducted against foreign powers – who were in the process of carving the Empire up – that anything resembling a modern state began to develop. Prior to this point, the Empire was in many ways run in a similar manner to other empires – that is, with feudal lords assisting in the process of tax collecting, but with no concerted attempt to create a loyal citizenry (or nation).[14]

At the end of the nineteenth century, three key movements related to identity-creation developed: Ottomanism, Pan-Islamism, and Turkism. Ottomanism, which was promoted by the group known as the Young Ottomans and later the Young Turks, did not see the religious differences (e.g. Muslim, Greek Orthodox, Armenian Orthodox and other forms of orthodoxy) among ethnic groups within the Empire as an obstacle to unity under the Ottoman banner. Pan-Islamism was developed partly in reaction to the activities of the Young Ottomans/Young Turks; its aim was to establish contacts with oppressed Muslims and to promote a return to the values and traditions of Islam. Finally, Turkism came into being as a result of a search for a new foundation for the Empire's political existence, and for those ascribing to Turkism, the new foundation was to be located in Turkish culture (Çağlar 1990: 81–2).

The founder of the new Turkish Republic, Mustafa Kemal, was very much influenced by several of these strands of thought. He and his colleagues were particularly keen to look to the pre-Islamic past for inspiration regarding identity building. To this end, the Turkish Historical Society was founded in 1932 to explore Turkish history, and this institution eventually put forward the notion that Turks belonged to a proto-race called Touro-Aryene, which was argued to be the original race of the European nations. In addition, the Turkish Linguistic Society was founded to simplify and re-establish the language of the pre-Islamic Turkish past (Çağlar 1990: 83).

First and foremost, however, the founder of the Republic took as his primary goal the creation of a modern state. The process of making the country modern included banishing the formal place of the Muslim religion in Turkey by abolishing the Caliphate,[15] closing religious schools, abolishing the Ministry of the Holy Law, banning dervish orders, closing Muslim shrines, banning the wearing of headgear associated with religious affiliation, adopting the Swiss Civil Code in place of sharia law, and removing any reference to Islam as the state religion of Turkey. Other modernization policies included the banning of the Arabic alphabet and replacing it with the alphabet that Kemal associated with modernization – the Latin alphabet (adapted slightly for the Turkish language) – and allowing for participation of women in elections (see box, 'Chronology of Kemalist Reforms'). Thus, the new leadership was attempting to make a solid break from the past. Moreover, unlike Spain and Italy in which there was very little concerted attempt to convince the new state citizens to give up their religious beliefs and traditions, the Turkish leadership was attempting to do this while simultaneously creating new state symbols and a common state language with a new alphabet. Moreover, by the time of the start of the transition to democracy in the 1940s, the relationship between the state and religion was still one characterized by hostility.

In addition, the state was trying to create new Turkish citizens with relatively limited resources. As discussed above, one of the ways in which intellectuals and state leaders have generally managed to create nation-states is by perpetuating myths about the territory, its people, etc. In turn, one of the key ways to accomplish this is through the written word – particularly literature and school books. This process requires literacy on the part of the masses. While there is no shortage of myths about the impressive nature of the Turkish tribes, the accomplishments of the Ottoman Empire, and the rescue of that Empire from foreign rule by Mustafa Kemal, teaching these

---

Chronology of Kemalist Reforms

1922	Abolition of Sultanate (1 November).
1923	Treaty of Lausanne signed (24 July).
	Republic of Turkey with capital at Ankara announced (29 October).
1924	Abolition of Caliphate (3 March).
	Closure of traditional religious schools, abolition of sharia law, adoption of Constitution (20 April).
1925	Abolition of Dervish groups.
	Abolition of the fez (November 25) and veiling of women discouraged;
	Western attire for men and women encouraged.
	Adoption of Western (Gregorian) calendar.
1926	Adoption of new civil, commercial, and penal codes based on European legal systems.
	Ending of Islamic polygamy by new civil code; introduction of civil marriage.
1928	Adoption of new Turkish alphabet (a modified version of the Latin alphabet). Turkish State declared to be secular (10 April); removal of constitutional provision establishing Islam as official religion.
1933	Islamic call to worship and public readings of the Kuran (Quran) to be held in Turkish rather than Arabic.
1934	Granting of right to vote and right to hold office for women.
	Law of Surnames adopted; Grand National Assembly gives Mustafa Kemal the name Kemal Atatürk (Father Turk); Ismet Pasha takes the surname of Inönü.
1935	Sunday made the legal weekly holiday.

Source: adapted from US Library of Congress, Chronology of Major Kemalist Reforms: countrystudies.us/turkey/14.htm (consulted 13 July 2007).

myths through literature and textbooks would have been enormously difficult because of the limitation on resources, which had implications for the
basic literacy of Turkish citizens. Even by 1970 – over 45 years after the
foundation of the new Republic – it is estimated that approximately 43.5
per cent of the population was still illiterate.[16] This can be compared to Italy
and Spain, where illiteracy in 1970 is estimated to have been 5.5 and 8.5 per
cent, respectively. Furthermore, although a great portion of the illiteracy
figure in Turkey is a result of overwhelming female illiteracy (in 1970, 60.5
per cent of women were illiterate), even amongst the male population in
1970, illiteracy was at 27 per cent; in contrast, approximately 4 per cent of
males in both Italy and Spain were illiterate by 1970. Thus, high levels of
illiteracy and the fact that more than half of the population were not likely
to be attending school at all would have made the spread of foundational
myths difficult.[17]

The final key difficulty to note in the Turkish state-building process is
that a significant portion of the population does not claim to have links to
the Turkic tribes that arrived from the east. Immediately prior to the creation of the Turkish Republic, this would have mostly included Christians
of Greek and Armenian descent. However, other than a relatively small
portion of the population, the latter are believed to have died during or fled
after an attempted uprising during World War I; most of the former (other
than a small community of Greeks living in Istanbul) were transferred to
Greece, as agreed in the Lausanne Treaty of 1923. (Most of the Turkish
Muslims living in Greece were also transferred to Turkey as part of this
agreement.) Thus, measures had been taken to ensure that the new state
would have little difficulty in becoming a nation-state. It became clear
shortly after the foundation of the new Republic, however, that another
group – Kurds – also did not appear to be historically or ethnically part of
the Turkish nation. Although only 10–20 per cent of the entire population,[18] this group is concentrated in specific regions of the country and has
managed to wage a powerful resistance against assimilating to the new
Turkish nation-state. As in Spain during the Franco years, the traditional
policy pursued by the Turkish government – until very recently, that is –
has been forced assimilation via repression of the public use of languages
other than Turkish.

Obtaining estimates of linguistic assimilation in Turkey is far more difficult than is the case with Spain and Italy. Amongst the most recent estimates of the numbers of native Kurdish speakers in Turkey is the 1959
census, in which the estimate was put at about 10–20 per cent. Current estimates are that 'as many as one in five inhabitants of Turkey' maintain
Kurdish as their mother tongue (Ergil 2000). While linguistic assimilation
figures are still sketchy and so determining the extent of stateness problems
in Turkey is difficult, we may turn to statistics on levels of national pride
similar to those presented for our other two cases in order to ascertain
whether such problems appear to be significant. Based on the 1999–2000

wave of the World Values Survey conducted in Turkey, roughly 87 per cent of the Turkish population expresses pride in being Turkish. While this figure varies by region, with 'only' about 72 per cent expressing national pride in Istanbul versus well over 90 per cent expressing pride in places like Isparta (western Turkey), Manisa (also in western Turkey), Konya (central Turkey), and Antalya (southern Turkey), in the region believed to contain the highest level of Kurdish population – Van (in eastern Turkey) – only 49 per cent express pride in being Turkish. Moreover, 51 per cent claim to not be at all proud of being Turkish. This evidence is consistent with what would be expected based on anecdotal evidence from the area. That is, it is not just the small minority who have carried out acts of terrorism who do not identify with the Turkish state.

Thus, at the start of the transition to democracy in 1946 in Turkey, the state still faced severe legitimacy problems. Despite the removal of several potentially key minority groups (e.g. Greeks and Armenians), the new democracy had two main potentially difficult stateness problems with which to contend: the lack of loyalty to the state on the part of ethnic Kurds and the lack of loyalty because of the potentially alienating secularization policies which were likely to still be anathema to the beliefs of the majority of the population of the state. Future chapters will continue to explore how these issues have played out and whether they have been instrumental in the failure to consolidate democracy in Turkey. For now, we draw some tentative conclusions about the stateness variable using a comparative analysis of these cases.

Conclusions

Where do our three case studies fall on the stateness variable at the time of their post-World War II transitions to democracy? Italy appears to have had the least amount of stateness problems, in that there was very little organized opposition to the existence of the state itself even in the early days of unification – although some small peripheral instances of separatism were witnessed at the end of World War II, which will be discussed further in Chapter 8. As will be seen in Chapter 6, the most organized of the groups in Italy by the late 1800s (e.g. the Communists) were not opposed to the existence of the Italian state per se, but their ideas as to how that state should be governed were initially in opposition to the regime. By the end of World War II there were still doubts about the democratic loyalty of this group which will be discussed further in Chapter 6, but they were not fundamentally opposed to the Italian state itself. Moreover, the signing of the Lateran Pacts in 1929 very likely went a long way toward gaining the loyalty of devout Catholics to the state and so this particular problem had begun to be resolved by the start of the post-World War II transition, although it must also be noted that it was initially unclear as to whether the World War II resistance leaders would not reverse Mussolini's policies regarding the

Church (see Chapter 5). At the same time, the new post-war democracy still faced problems of spreading the common language of the state, a process which appears to have been greatly assisted by industrialization and internal migration.

It seemed that Turkey was on the road to resolving stateness problems via the population exchanges provided in the Lausanne Treaty of 1923, but then spent much of its subsequent history (and funds) fighting separatism in the East and Southeastern parts of the country. At the time the country began a transition to multi-party politics in the mid-1940s, the 'Kurdish problem', or 'problem in the Southeast', as it was referred to in Turkish politics, was still unresolved. Thus, in contrast to Italy, Turkey did face a potentially severe stateness problem at the start of the democratization process.

Like Turkey, Spain similarly faced stateness problems in the post-Franco era of democratization, with ethnolinguistic minority groups comprising a similar percent of the overall population as was the case in Turkey. Also similar to the Turkish experience, Franco's policies of forced assimilation failed miserably in Spain, and instead, they seem to have ignited even stronger opposition to the Spanish state within the Basque region (see Chapters 3 and 8). The newly democratizing Spanish state was thus left with a situation that threatened to undermine the democratization process. However, given that Spain *is* now counted amongst the world's stable democracies (as discussed in Chapter 1) it is difficult to argue that stateness problems related to ethnic or regional identity are necessarily a cause of breakdown of democratic institutions. Since Turkey and Spain share the characteristic of stateness problems, and the size of this problem seems to be roughly similar (based on population sizes and reported levels of national pride), but the two countries differ on our dependent variable, democratic consolidation, it is unlikely that stateness problems are a cause in and of themselves of failed consolidation.

On the other hand, the failure of a new state to reconcile religious identity with secularization in a manner that is acceptable to the population may be important. Italian and Spanish dictators managed to go a very long way in this regard, whereas the Turkish state had failed to strike balance on the issue of religion that would be acceptable to its fairly devout population at the time of the post-World War II transition. The next chapter will show that in the most recent pre-World War II experiment with democracy in Spain, the failure to reconcile religious and secular interests in a manner acceptable to the vast majority may have directly contributed to the breakdown of democracy, although in the Italian case, the relationship between religion and the breakdown of democracy is less direct. In the case of Turkey, at times the tension between religious and secular interests has been a direct cause of the breakdown of democracy (e.g. the military intervention in 1997 and threat of intervention in 2007), while at other times it appears to have served as an indirect factor contributing to breakdown. Chapters 3 and 6 provide further exploration of these issues.

3 Experiencing the breakdown of democracy

For many countries trying to establish democracy, the process of creating institutions that produce stability and ultimately democratic consolidation may be an iterative one. That is, institutions may be tried but if those institutions fail to help create circumstances that will favour consolidation, new institutions may be tried in the next democratic transition (or even during an uninterrupted transition period). In extreme cases, the democratic experiment may end in civil war or military dictatorship, as has been the case in our three case studies. This chapter examines prior experience with democracy in each of the three countries, and contends that while these experiences may have something to do with (a) the types of institutions that are developed later and (b) the behaviour of political elites within those institutions, the evidence from the three cases indicates that prior experience with democracy alone may not be a crucial factor guaranteeing democratic consolidation.

Does theory provide any guidance regarding the role that previous experience with democracy might play in consolidating a democracy? One form of social-science theory – historical institutionalism (Steinmo *et al.* 1992; Thelen 1999; Pierson 2000) – might lead us to the conclusion that prior failed experiments do not bode well for current attempts at democracy. This is because the institutions developed in previous rounds of experimentation are unlikely to be completely abandoned, and so it is possible that the institutions chosen at the first attempt to establish democracy will persist in later rounds: the path initially chosen by a country in many ways predetermines the options available later.

However, such approaches generally have considerable difficulty explaining *change* in institutions (see Thelen 1999), and it seems logical that if enough key participants desire change and are able to develop new institutions that are acceptable to all relevant players, institutions can be changed. In the case of democratization, failed democratic experiences that led to negative consequences for all major players may thus be expected to produce a situation whereby these players alter institutions in order to attempt to prevent an experience similar to the previous collapse of democracy (Bermeo 1992). Note that in this context, 'institutions' may be interpreted in its broadest sense, referring not only to the specific bodies like parliaments, prime ministerships, etc. or rules, but also to the culture and norms that further serve to bind those who participate (see March and Olsen 1989). The three cases presented below demonstrate that institutional learning did occur in all three countries to some extent, but it is contended that the alteration of institutions appears to have little or no effect on whether a country becomes a consolidated democracy or not.

In addition, it is argued that the experience with authoritarian rule may have an impact on the survival of democracy. Memories of human-rights violations and the terror of an authoritarian regime may make individuals in the post-authoritarian era inclined to press on with democracy even during difficult times. Moreover, the previous experience with authoritarian rule may have shown that the authoritarian rulers are no better at governance, particularly managing the economy, than democrats – despite the claim in most cases when there is a takeover that it has been partly to alleviate economic difficulties (Bermeo 1992; Valenzuela 1992; Pridham 2000; but see Linz and Stepan 1996).

This chapter briefly outlines the nature and functioning of the three regimes under investigation in this book prior to their most recent transitions to democracy. While the emphasis is on the issue of learning from failed experiences with democracy, some aspects of the non-democratic regimes will also be summarized. Although we are mostly concerned with the time period closest to these most recent transitions, relevant historical context is provided where there have been multiple prior experiments with democracy.

Italy's liberal regime: from *Risorgimento* to fascism

In the first four to five decades following the establishment of the new Italian state, the regime was a mix of monarchy with some parliamentary control over the monarch.[1] The constitution was simply the old Sardinian Constitution of 1848, and under the rules outlined in that document considerable executive powers were constitutionally reserved to the king (see Clark 1984: 45). The king had the power to nominate and dismiss his ministers, but he was under no obligation to follow ministerial advice.[2] It was constitutionally unclear as to who had the chief initiative in legislation, and the king could issue proclamations having the force of law (Mack Smith 1959: 27). The monarchy also had clear constitutional domination over foreign affairs, declaring war, making peace treaties, commerce treaties, and commanding the armed forces. Although ministers were constitutionally responsible to the king, the Italian parliament developed some control by interrogating them in 'interpellations', by using votes of no confidence (Mack Smith 1959: 30), and by limiting the king's budget (Clark 1984: 45). However, even as late as 1915, the king was able to decide to enter World War I without asking parliament and unilaterally instituted military rule during Italy's participation in that war (Mack Smith 1959: 329). More-over, during times of social and political unrest, prime ministers, in con-junction with the king, tended to rule by decree rather than via legislating in parliament. Thus, the political system was far from being clearly democratic.

Also indicative of the non-democratic nature of the regime was the fact that it was not unusual for the government to persecute political opponents or those they deemed to be potentially hostile to the new state. In the very early days (under the first Italian Prime Minister, Cavour), the targets were, in fact, republicans (Mack Smith 1959: 33); in later years, the targets became Socialists and Catholics. Moreover, elections were rigged at times to ensure the defeat of groups – particularly the extreme left – and government officials regularly used bribery and intimidation of the press to ensure very little in the way of open or organized opposition (Mack Smith 1959: 34). In addition, the electorate in these early days was highly restricted. Prior to the adoption of universal male suffrage in 1912 (Clark 1984: 156–7), there were literacy and age restrictions on voting rights, along with the requirement of paying a special tax for the privilege of voting. Thus, the vast majority of the population – and particularly the poorer elements of the population – were legally excluded from participation in politics.

Although the pre-1912 regime could hardly be called 'democratic', the way that it functioned was highly indicative both of the manner in which the brief period of Italian democracy of 1912–22 operated and the way that post-World War II democracy functioned in Italy. As in the decades follow-ing the creation of the Italian Republic in the 1940s, the 1860–1922 period was marked by constant government 'collapse', with almost 40 different governments in this 42-year period (see Mack Smith 1959: Appendix). As in later years as well, however, 'collapse' was often simply a matter of the king or prime minister wanting to reshuffle the cabinet or remove one or two cabinet ministers. Heads of government (prime ministers) often lost their posts only to return a few months later to once again take charge of the government. Thus, most 'new' governments consisted of the same indi-viduals, perhaps rotated to different posts (Clark 1984: 45). Governments and parliamentary coalitions were built around fairly temporary sets of inter-ests and thus could (and did) easily fall apart (Mack Smith 1959: 202); members of parliament and government ministers were generally interested in clientelism, not ideology (Mack Smith 1959: 203–4). There was also no notion of collective cabinet responsibility and no real sense on the part of the government that members were part of a group; instead, it was like working free-lance (Mack Smith 1959: 30). Indeed, parliamentary life in the very early days (under Cavour) consisted of an alliance across the Centre Right and Centre Left; there was very little in the way of unifying ideology across these groups and indeed the differences were fairly large (e.g. centralizers versus decentralizers, state control over church versus free church in a free state). The priority at this time, however, was to put national over sectional interests and so groups that raised oppositions were often treated as traitors and/or were suppressed. The system inhibited the growth of a clear-cut party system and a clear-cut organized opposition and tended to leave governments dangerously free from opposition and criticism (Mack Smith 1959: 31). Additionally, parliament itself in the late 1800s was not conducted in a very dignified way. The speaker was on occasion showered with paper missiles, and more than once there was a brawl on the floor of the house (Mack Smith 1959: 201).

Thus, much of the pre-1912 period was marked by a lack of organized interests via political parties. Political groupings were, however, beginning to form in the late 1800s. When suffrage was extended at local level elections to all literate males over 21 in 1889 and councils with municipalities larger than 10,000 were then allowed to elect their own mayors (and then shortly thereafter – in 1896 – all municipalities could elect mayors), this gave Catholics and Socialists a greater voice at the local level (Clark 1984: 93). The introduction of universal suffrage in 1912 provided these groups with clearer opportunities to participate in national institutions, although the Catholic Church still only reluctantly supported participation in the new regime to counter the threat from the left.

After this transformation to mass democracy, the leaders of the 'Liberal' traditional governing groups used the same techniques that had been used with other political groupings – they attempted to buy off as many different factions as possible in order to maintain peace and stability in the parliament and in government. It was a system that had worked to co-opt other potential subversives such as Southern landowners, and so it seemed like a useful way forward for mass Italian democracy. In the case of Socialist and Catholic interests, this meant going much further than offering bribes or engaging in clientelism, however; it meant adopting policies that would placate these groups. In particular, social welfare and other public works spending increased: by 1907, the government was spending 50 per cent more on these than in 1900. The working day was also limited and a maternity fund set up; one rest-day per week was made compulsory; accident insurance had to be provided by employers. Government subsidized public goods like trams, water, electricity, which were run at the local level. The government also began to use arbitrators to resolve disputes between workers and owners rather than using repression, as had been the case in previous years (Clark 1984: 137–8). The intention was to buy these groups off and absorb them into the system. Some were indeed absorbed into government fairly easily; union leaders, for instance, were 'absorbed', as were many Socialist members of parliament (Clark 1984: 141).

Not all were absorbed, however, and in fact, many socialists were becoming more and more radicalized as party members began to believe that a socialist revolution was eminent. In the late 1800s, the party had agreed to adopt an approach of cooperation with other parties to make parliamentary democracy work; they would not, however, be able to openly support any *bourgeois* party. By the early 1900s, some in the party were becoming more radicalized, and when multiple prime ministers (Giolitti, Nitti, Bonomi) made further attempts at absorption by asking the Socialists to join the government (around 1910), even though the most hard-core realized that this was a reasonable move, they refused to join the government because they thought that acceptance of government posts would be misunderstood by the rank and file. Namely, one of the party's attractions was that it was *different* from the bourgeois parties, was uninterested in government posts, and was strongly opposed to patronage and corruption; joining a bourgeois government was likely to give the impression that the Socialists were really no different from the other parties. Moreover, it would very likely mean having to compromise over economic and social policy, which is not something the party was prepared to do at the time (Mack Smith 1959: 218–19, 327).

In the process of trying to absorb the Socialists by gaining their indirect support, government leaders came to be seen by many industrialists and landowners as being in cahoots with the Socialists, which became problematic. In addition, the response of the government to workers' strikes was simply to allow the groups to go on strike; that is, unlike previous governments, Prime Minister Giolitti and other like-minded liberals felt that repression was counter-productive and that a better policy was to simply allow the strikes to die out on their own. Naturally, these were not policies that were supported by all industrialists, and the country was generally starting to appear to be out of control politically and socially. As argued by Allen and Stevenson, 'Certainly during the late summer of 1920 a left-wing revolution seemed distinctly possible and, in the context of the period, such an event would not have been remarkable' (Allen and Stevenson 1974: 5).

It was eventually the policy of absorption that produced the end of Italy's first experience with democracy. Besides the Socialists, the other key group that was growing in power appeared to be the Nationalists. Although the latter had not been very successful in elections, they had been successful in creating paramilitary fascist groups that were being used – sometimes under payment from industrialists – to beat the strikers and other 'subversives' into submission. After failed attempts at harnessing Socialist groups and co-opting them into the system of absorption, government leaders – Prime Minister Giolitti in particular – began to try to harness the rising Nationalist forces. This was done initially by inviting Benito Mussolini's newly created party to participate on the governing party list during the first elections held under proportional representation in 1919 (previous elections had been held under single-member-district-plurality rules). Although Mussolini's party did not win many seats (35 of 535), after many failed attempts by government party leaders to form stable coalitions with the left, Mussolini was invited by the king to try to form a government himself. Mussolini then very easily used powers that had also been used by previous governments – such as declaring a state of emergency and getting parlia-

ment to agree to allow him to govern by decree law for a year – to undermine the democratic institutions and establish an authoritarian regime that
lasted for 20 years (Lyttelton 1973: Chapter 1; see Forsyth 2002 on politics
in the early 1900s in Italy).

Linz and Stepan (1996) contend that the nature and functioning of the
authoritarian regime is likely to have an impact on the prospects for democratic consolidation. Thus, we briefly review the nature and functioning of
the fascist regime under Mussolini. Compared to the other fascist regimes
which took on this same description at the time (i.e. Germany and Spain),
Mussolini's brand of fascism was relatively mild. In Italy, although a Special
Tribunal for the Defence of State was set up in November 1926 to try terrorists and those accused of political crimes using military judges and military law, and the Tribunal had the power to impose the death penalty, there
were only 26 executions up to the time of the collapse of the fascist regime
(Clark 1984: 233). On the other hand, alternative viewpoints such as those
espoused by Socialists and Communists were repressed and leaders of these
groups were imprisoned or exiled to the southern islands of Italy; many fled
to other countries, with opposition parties being officially banned from
1926 onward (Clark 1984: 231–2). Mussolini himself took over the running
of much of the press and was able to use it, along with new media such as
radio and cinema, to promote the regime's propaganda.

Fascism in Italy contained many different strands of thought. There were
syndicalists who wanted to create a 'producers" state; there were provincial
radicals who wanted to do away with the Church, the king, and the parliament; and there were those promoting national pride; still others wanted a
strong state and planned economy. They were, however, united against what
was perceived as a common enemy – anyone who had conspired against the
Italian nation. This included Bolsheviks, Freemasons, and even international
bankers. The group was held together by nationalism, promotion of empire,
and promotion of Italian greatness via reference to ancient Rome (Clark
1984: 242–3). The regime seemed to manage to socialize at least one generation of youngsters to its version of nationalism and provided other benefits
that older generations enjoyed, including recreation schemes and poverty
relief (Clark 1984: 242–5). Thus while the youth were being mobilized and
socialized into fascist thinking, their elders were being entertained by recreation, sporting events, radio, and cinema. Mussolini was fairly popular, at
least until the late 1930s, and the regime was stable; however, most
observers contend that there was never much enthusiasm for fascism (Clark
1984: 247).

Part of the reason that the country was so stable after years of workers'
strikes was in great part due to the existence of the syndicalist strand of the
fascists. Although one component of the fascists – the squads – had been
tamed, Mussolini allowed the syndicalists to establish a state bureaucracy
that would manage worker–producer relations using syndicalist ideology.
Specifically, the idea was that workers and business elite would collaborate

in running the country's economy. Generally, it seemed highly innovative and a reasonable alternative to socialism and communism. In fact, the business elite were strongly opposed to allowing worker participation in major economic decisions and Mussolini realized the scheme could not be carried out precisely as planned by the syndicalists. Initially the latter had formed fascist unions and had led workers in strikes and protests; Mussolini and his advisers decided that while syndicates should continue to be used to allow workers to express grievances and negotiate with owners and managers, the regime could not be seen to be participating in organizing strike activity. (Indeed, many of the fascist squads had been paid by industrialists to halt the strikes.) Thus, in 1926 a law was passed that confirmed the monopoly of the syndicates over negotiations and provided for compulsory arbitration of collective disputes via special labour tribunals, but also made strikes, go-slows, and lockouts illegal. Strike leaders were threatened with prison sentences. Thus, there would be negotiation between major groups, but there was not to be any corporatist planning of the economy. However, the system is still argued to have worked fairly well to maintain stability over the course of the regime (Clark 1984: 248–9).

One final point to note about the functioning of the Italian fascist regime is that while organized opposition was banned, there was still some criticism of the regime and some important alternative sources of power. First and foremost was that the parliament still existed. Although the Chamber of Deputies consisted mostly of Mussolini supporters (a result of the electoral system adopted by Mussolini, the rigging of some elections, and the fact that the few remaining members of the opposition left the parliament in protest against Mussolini's policies), the upper chamber – the Senate – contained many individuals who had been appointed by the king during the liberal period. Several of these individuals were critical of the regime's policies. Moreover, the monarchy still existed and while it was weak throughout much of Mussolini's reign it was still an alternative source of power and authority; indeed, as will be discussed in Chapter 9, the monarch continued to command control over one of the main instruments of force, the military. More importantly, though, was that the Catholic Church was a major alternative source of power and authority. Particularly problematical was that many Catholics had started to become politically active via the organization Catholic Action. Fascists squads had attempted to halt much of this activism, but the fact of the matter was that Catholicism was still a major force in Italian society and the populist approach being taken by Mussolini could not be successful with the regime still in opposition to the Church. Thus, instead of repressing Church interests as in much of the liberal era, Mussolini co-opted it. Although he was an atheist himself, he converted to Catholicism and began to provide government support for the Church: he increased clerical salaries, granted funds for the repair of damaged churches, restored the Crucifix in schools and courts of law, and ultimately signed the Lateran Pacts in 1929. There were still disputes between the Church and

Mussolini, predominantly over organized Catholicism; an ambiguous agreement was eventually struck which had the effect of allowing Catholic youth movements to flourish. These became a clear rival to the fascist movement (Clark 1984: 254–5).

The fascist regime under Mussolini remained fairly popular, though, and until the late 1930s the opposition was still disorganized and the groups on the left continued to squabble amongst themselves. The problems for the regime seemed to lie in (a) its imperialistic activities and the fact that it was getting Italy involved in seemingly unnecessary wars and (b) the anti-Jewish policies adopted around the same time as *Kristallnacht* in November 1938.[3] It seems to be this period – and the period when Italian Communists, Socialists, and Republicans went to Spain to fight on the Republican side of the Spanish Civil War between 1933–6 – that finally produced a change in the perspective of the opposition parties.

Did early experiences with democracy ultimately have any impact on the success of Italian democracy after World War II? (Note that 'success' is still defined here as the continued existence of parliamentary democracy, or the lack of reversion to authoritarian rule.) Most commentators on Italian history and politics would argue that they did for two reasons. One is that leaders and society as a whole learned to be wary of the extremes; to this end, both the Nationalists and the Communists were actively kept out of government in the post-World War II period of democracy, as discussed in later chapters of this book. At the same time, these groups were still allowed participation and representation through parliamentary and other (e.g. local-level) institutions – a policy that seemed to flow from former Prime Minister Giolitti's philosophy on allowing official outlets for organized opposition. Second, it became clear that – given the percentages of seats that were won by Italian parties – government would have to rely on Socialist and/or Communist support at times in order to prevent the deadlock that occurred prior to inviting Mussolini to form a government in the 1920s. While supporting a bourgeois government or even a Catholic government (as became common in the post-war era) was previously unthinkable for Socialists, the potential consequences of *not* doing so were perceived to be fairly severe, and so both Socialists and Communists became far more accommodating and cooperative – and openly so – in the next attempt at democracy in Italy (see Hine 1993; Foot 2003; Bull and Newell 2005; Parker and Natale 2006), a point to be discussed again in Chapters 5, 6, and 7.

The degree of continuity of the functioning of Italian politics despite the 20-year authoritarian interlude is also surprising, however. *Trasformismo*, absorption, etc. continued to be the name of the game. As in the pre-Mussolini days, there simply was not a clearly organized government party or coalition and a clear opposition. It might have been expected that the post-Mussolini leadership would have made efforts to alter this situation, for instance, by changing the electoral system back to single-member-district elections. However, as will be discussed in Chapters 5 and 6, there were multiple political groupings at the negotiating table, and many of these would have worried about the effect of this type of electoral system on their parties' chances of winning seats in parliament. Moreover, the single member district system had been in place prior to 1919 and did not seem to produce clearer electoral majorities or stable governments then. Thus, it may not have been clear as to what lesson could be learned with regard to the electoral system in any case.

As will be shown in subsequent chapters, in many ways neo-institutional path dependency may help to explain several aspects of the functioning of democracy in Italy in the post-World War II era, but at the same time there was clearly learning on the part of political elites and this had impacts both on their general behaviour in the political system and on the institutions they designed – e.g. with regard to the monarchy and the creation of constitutional checks and balances (see Chapter 5). The Italian case points us in the direction of concluding that previous (failed) experience with democracy may actually be helpful for subsequent attempts at democratic transition in that elites learn methods and design rules so as to prevent failure in the future. We now turn to examine Spain's early experience with democracy to determine whether this is likely to have had any impact on the functioning and stability of Spanish democracy in the post-1975 (post-Franco) period.

Spain: liberalism, the monarchy, and dictatorship

As indicated by the above discussion, Italian progression toward political liberalism was relatively gradual and major political upheavals occurred mostly as a result of the consequences of these gradual changes. For instance, the widening of the electorate made it possible for mass-based parties with fairly rigid ideologies (socialist or anti-socialist) to win enough seats to produce political instability. In contrast, Spain's movements toward a liberal regime appear to have been part of a cycle in which movement toward liberalism was followed by military *pronunciamientos* (coups) re-establishing the monarchy or the supremacy of the monarchy over parliament, and this followed by military *pronunciamiento* establishing a liberal regime. This was the general cycle up to the period of the Franco dictatorship. Thus, if there was a learning process in successive experiences with democracy, it appears to have been a slow one. This section discusses Spain's experience with political liberalism and democracy, with the aim of discerning whether there are aspects of this experience that are likely to have been key in explaining the country's later success with democracy after Franco's death.

Spain's liberal tradition began in earnest with a constitution developed in 1812 by a temporary parliamentary body that was set up at Cadiz outside French-occupied Spain. The parliamentary body was dominated by liberals who took their ideas from the French Revolution: equality before the law, a centralized government and administrative system, an efficient, modern civil service, the replacement of feudal privileges with freedom of contract and property rights. This new constitution included a limited monarchy that governed with ministers who would be subject to parliamentary control, suffrage for those who meet minimum property requirements, and a central administrative system based on newly created provinces and municipalities rather than on historic provinces. After Napoleon's defeat in 1815, the monarch who was returned to the throne (Ferdinand VII) rejected the Constitution, claiming that it was invalid because he had played no role in drafting it, and thus returned Spain to a system of absolutism (Pierson 1999; Barton 2003: Chapter 4; Ross 2004: Chapter 1).

Around this time, Spain's American colonies began proclaiming independence and by 1825, only Cuba and Puerto Rico remained as Spanish American colonies. Thus, Ferdinand's foreign and military policies were hugely unpopular with the Spanish military, and a military *pronunciamiento* in 1820 successfully toppled the government and forced Ferdinand to accept the liberal constitution. With the help of French intervention, Ferdinand restored absolutism after only three years of liberal government (known as the Constitutional Triennium) (Pierson 1999; Barton 2003: Chapter 4; Ross 2004: Chapter 1).

When Ferdinand died in 1833, his only heirs were daughters. While Ferdinand had persuaded parliament to set aside the principle of male lineage so that one of his daughters could become head of state, some felt that Ferdinand's successor should instead be his brother, Don Carlos. What ensued was a war of succession which the supporters of Ferdinand's daughter, Isabella II, won. Liberals managed to dominate the regime at this time – Isabella was only three years old when she was declared queen and her mother served as her regent, supported by Progressives and Liberals. Thus, the liberal constitution was restored, and revised such that the power of the parliament was increased further. Also important is that the new constitution provided for state responsibility of upkeep of the Church. The latter provision was a compromise to the Church's many supporters (more on this below), but was also very unpopular with many anti-clerical liberals. At the same time, however, the new constitution abolished all monasteries and small convents and abolished tithes and so still remained somewhat unpopular with devout Catholics. What followed until 1873 was a series of coups and counter-coups on the part of various military officers who would then establish themselves as regents to the queen; the policies preferred by each of these continued to vary between dictatorship and rule by royal decree, along with protection of the church and church property, on the one hand, and more liberal-leaning government that simultaneously attempted to strip the church of its power and wealth, on the other (Pierson 1999; Carr 2001a; Carr 2001b: Chapter 1; Barton 2003: Chapter 5; Ross 2004: Chapters 1 and 2).

Rather than being a result of revolution or citizen demands, the declaration of Spain's First Republic in 1873 came about because of these problems with succession of both monarchs and regents. Queen Isabella was forced by military coup to abdicate in 1868 and the coup leader's choice of successor, Amadeo of Savoy (son of Italian king Victor Emmanuel II) abdicated the post shortly thereafter (in 1873), claiming that Spain was simply ungovernable. Parliament took this opportunity to proclaim Spain to be a federal republic. In the 11-month period of this republic, there were four presidents, none of whom could find a prime minister to form a stable government. Also, while the constitution that established the republic provided for self-governing provinces that would be bound to the federal government by voluntary agreement, the government could not decentralize quickly enough and cities and provinces began to make unilateral declarations of autonomy. It appeared that Madrid was losing control over the country and so once again the army stepped in to rescue the 'national honour', and an interim military dictatorship was established (Carr 2001a; Barton 2003: Chapter 5; Pierson 1999; Ross 2004: Chapter 2; Carr 2001b: Chapter 1).

For a brief period, during 1875–85 (with Isabella's son Alfonso XII as the new monarch), Spanish politics began to stabilize. Alfonso XII and his chosen government adopted the British model to politics. The electoral system was designed in such a way to produce a two-party system, as in Britain, and was successful to some degree in this regard, but also relied on manipulation of votes to ensure that two parties dominated the *Cortes*. However, very much unlike the British example in which the political parties were formed around shared ideologies, values, and beliefs, the two parties that gained representation during this decade of Spanish politics differed very little from one another. As was the case in Italy, the two dominant party groupings represented the bourgeois classes, and other interests were generally excluded via electoral manipulation. Also similar to Italy is that in the absence of an ideologically-based party system, patronage and bribery were used to deliver votes to parties. Further paralleling the Italian experience, this system did work to stabilize the country for some time, but as interests that did not fit within those of the governing parties (e.g., workers unions and Catalan and Basque groups) began to organize, the system was unable to maintain stability.

Although the late 1800s and early 1900s saw the continuation of parliamentary methods – as in Italy – political instability was on the increase as a result of the newly forming socialist parties and labour unions, as well as popular anarchist unions (see Chapter 6). Like Prime Minister Giolitti in Italy, a reforming prime minister (Antonio Maura) came to power in Spain in the early 1900s and attempted to accommodate the growing diversity of interests by legalizing strikes, reforming the judiciary, regulating rural rents and making elections fairer. At the same time, this particular leader was intolerant of the anarchists and used repression to try to quell the growing movement. This policy was hugely unpopular with other leftists and also with one of the main governing parties (the Liberals). Also problematic was that Spain's colonial ventures in Morocco were to be carried out partly by conscripted Barcelonan workers, a policy which incited riots in Barcelona. Thus, Spanish politics was dominated by labour unrest, strikes, and nationalist agitation, along with organized calls for the creation of a republic (Pierson 1999; Carr 2001a; Carr 2001b: Chapter 7; Barton 2003: Chapter 5; Ross 2004: Chapter 4).

Governments generally managed to avoid military coups during this period, which was a marked change vis-à-vis the 1800s. However, when the government attempted to reform the military budget and reduce the size of the officer corps in particular, officers began organizing juntas and refused to obey orders of state officials. The government backed down, but the rumblings from the military continued, particularly as the military was increasingly being used to repress the anarchist protests and terrorism. In the face of growing strikes and terrorism, as well as colonial failings – Spain had lost Cuba, Puerto Rico, and the Philippines in 1898 and was losing its battle against Moroccan independence – the military stepped in again and a coup was staged by General Miguel Primo de Rivera in 1923. Spain was then run by military dictatorship for almost two years and then by a combined military–civilian government (Primo de Rivera remained prime minister and had a civilian cabinet). Some progress was made in terms of public-works projects and improving schools and universities during Primo de Rivera's reign, but the civil strife continued, as did regionalist uprisings in Catalonia and military discontent.

The monarchy was also becoming increasingly unpopular, and in the 1931 municipal elections, republican candidates won majorities in most of the country's provincial capitals. The king (Alfonso XIII) went into exile, and a new provisional government declared the start of Spain's Second Republic. Parliamentary elections were held shortly thereafter and a new republican constitution was approved in the Cortes by the end of 1931.

The functioning of this new regime was far from smooth, however. The newly elected Cortes was dominated by a coalition of republican parties and the socialists. The government passed considerable progressive reforms, including removing any remaining restrictions on voting (including gender restrictions) and granting autonomy to Catalonia and the Basque country. Social reforms were enacted as well, such as increased provisions protecting workers, changing the taxation system, and redistributing large estates to peasants. Education was secularized, church and state separated, and divorce legalized. These policies alienated large landowners and the Church, however, and peasants also became dissatisfied with the slow pace of land reform. Opposition amongst Catholics began to increase, and the government began to collapse in the face of opposition to secularization of education and closure of Catholic schools (Esenwein and Shubert 1995; Pierson 1999; Carr 2001b: Chapter 8; Barton 2003: Chapter 6; Ross 2004: Chapter 5).

New elections were called, and conservative parties won enough seats to form a government. The new government then proceeded to repeal the reforms that had been made by the socialist–republican coalition, particularly those related to the Catholic Church. Thus, the battle between the anti-clericals and supporters of the Church that had begun a century prior simply continued under the new republic. In addition, provisions regarding regional autonomy were repealed and social reforms were halted. Worker discontent began to increase again, and government was having difficulty controlling strikes. Socialists led an insurrection in Asturias (in northern Spain) that lasted for two weeks; the government eventually repressed the uprising and imprisoned hundreds of leftist supporters, with the effect of radicalizing these groups even further. The governing coalition collapsed in 1935 and called for new elections, which were won by an even more radical republican–socialist coalition of parties, including the then Communist Party of Spain. The government began reinstating the policies it had passed between 1931–3 – reestablishing regional autonomy, secularizing education, etc. Right-wing parties began to fear the increasing radicalization of the government, particularly as the country was experiencing further strike action. In the last few months of the Republic, as violence was escalating, with Falangists attacking and sometimes killing left-wing strikers, the latter attacking and sometimes killing the former, the police killing both, the response in parliament was for the left-leaning parties to blame the right and for the right to blame the left-wing strikers and revolutionaries. Many in the right-wing parties in parliament moved further toward the right, arguing that a fascist state might be necessary, or at the very least that authoritarian measures needed to be taken (Payne 1993: 347). Moreover, the left-wing government was in a sense being a belligerent on one side (Payne 1993: 349). To quote historian Stanley Payne:

> The final long, conflictive Cortes debate began at 7:00 P.M. on 1 July and lasted twelve hours, marred by frequent shouts and incidents. Deputies were involved in pushing and punching each other on at least two occasions.... This was also the session in which the Socialist Angel Galarza replied to [prominent right-wing politician] Calvo Sotelo with the remark that against the latter 'anything was justified, even personal assassination'.
>
> (Payne 1993: 351)

After multiple killings and assassinations of leftist workers and of Falangists, the leftist government arrested hundreds of Falangists but no Socialists (Payne 1993: 354). When a leftist Assault Guard was assassinated, Socialist and Communist activists and militia went to the Ministry of the Interior to demand action, and the Assault Guard and civilian leftists arrested dozens of rightists in Madrid that night (Payne 1993: 354–6). These Guards (Civilian Guard and Assault Guard) somehow managed to get leading politicians onto their list of suspects to arrest (even though they had immunity and there were no charges pending against them). One of these –

the leader of the parliamentary opposition, Calvo Sotelo – was killed after he was picked up (apparently not the intention of those who led the arrest, but done by an excitable Socialist militant). The government's only apparent response was to begin a process of abolishing right-wing political activity (Payne 1993: 356–7; see also Preston 1978).

In the circumstances, it is thus not surprising that – almost in keeping with tradition – plots for a military coup began to develop. The street fighting between leftists and right-wing groups and amongst the left-wing groups, along with the newly forming fascists, descended into warfare and so began the Spanish Civil War (Pierson 1999; Barton 2003: Chapter 6; Ross 2004: Chapter 5). The details of the war are far too lengthy to outline here (but see Schubert and Esenwein 1995; Browne 1996; Preston 1996, 2006; Carr 2000; Carr 2001b: Chapter 8; Ross 2004: Chapter 6; Romero Salvado 2005; Payne 2006), but the war was eventually won by Francisco Franco and his supporters who then proceeded to establish a dictatorship that lasted from 1939 until his death in 1975.

As argued by Stanley Payne, the problems for the Spanish Second Republic began with the founders of the Republic themselves who failed to try to overcome and transcend the divisions of the past, instead representing the zeal of a new group imposing its own values on the regime and taking revenge on ousted predecessors (Payne 1993: 375). The Constitution of 1931 was clearly the creation of one significant sector of society, to be imposed on that portion which did not share its values. In fact, these groups were not committed to the rules either and demanded annulment of an election outcome that was not favourable to themselves in 1933 (Payne 1993: 375–6). Social antagonisms may have been so intense that no liberal democratic regime could have survived, but no moderating strategy was even attempted during the Second Republic (Payne 1993: 378).

As discussed above, Linz and Stepan (1996) contend that the nature and functioning of the authoritarian regime is likely to have an impact on the prospects for democratic consolidation. Here we therefore outline very briefly how the Francoist brand of authoritarianism functioned.

The regime brought together multiple groups with an interest in putting a halt to the republican regime and included: conservatives who were interested in preserving the system of large landowners commanding a large but weak peasantry; monarchists who included previous opponents (Carlists and Alfonsists); and the increasingly popular fascists who wanted to preserve Spanish traditions and ultimately to carry out a national-syndicalist revolution (see Carr 1985: Chapter 1). It was the latter of these that gave the regime its general ideological stance which led to the initial impression that the regime was set to become fascist. In fact, the main aspects of syndicalism remained a key part of the regime's ideology throughout its forty years, despite the fact that Franco and most of the elites around him did not really believe in it.

The philosophy behind syndicalism *was* one that Franco bought into, which was that Spain needed to be an 'organic democracy' rather than an 'inorganic' one as during the previous periods of liberalism. It was argued that everyone fitted naturally into certain groups – their families, their workplace, their municipalities, etc. – and that it was these groups that ought to be represented in government, not political parties. The belief was that all Spaniards were just that – Spaniards – and were working together for national causes; political parties damaged this organic structure and approach by dividing Spaniards from one another into unnatural groups. In theory, the main groups mentioned above would instead join forces to make policies that benefit all. In practice, this is not how the regime functioned. As in Italy, the fascists were used to establish and administer a system of syndicalism and were used to maintain the propaganda of the regime, but in fact, Franco had a low opinion of the working classes, and business elites and large landowners appeared to have direct access to Franco and his government ministers rather than operating through the parliament and the other institutions designed for the purpose of syndicalism (Carr 1980: Chapter 10; Gilmour 1985: Chapters 1 and 2). The regime was not totalitarian in this sense especially after 1945 (when fascism in Germany and Italy had clearly collapsed), as it was clear that it was not being run by a single, coherent party that had a clear structure and apparatus apart from the regime itself, and there was no real attempt at mass mobilization (see Linz 2000 on totalitarianism). To the contrary, beginning in the 1950s the goal was to keep people demobilized and to have them divert their energies into the new consumer culture (see Chapter 4), sport, entertainment, etc. – in other words, anything except politics (Carr 1980, Chapter 10; Gilmour 1985: Chapters 1 and 2).

On the other hand, the regime was extremely repressive, particularly at the start. Estimates vary, but clearly hundreds of thousands were executed, again mostly during and after the Civil War, near the beginning of the regime. According to David Gilmour, anyone who had been a member of a trade union, a Masonic lodge, any of the republican parties or a left-wing political party, a supporter of Basque or Catalan nationalism, or in anyway had 'helped to undermine political order or... impeded the *Movimiento Nacional...*' was likely to be imprisoned or executed (quoted in Gilmour 1985: 28). Military tribunals were often used for trials for political crimes, and in 1963 the Public Order Court was established to deal with those suspected of 'undermining the foundations of the state, altering political order, or creating anxiety for the national conscience (quoted in Gilmour 1985: 29). Although some of the repression was relaxed and some liberals and Christian democrats were able to publish mild criticism of the regime, the repression of communists and Basque separatists continued (Gilmour 1985: 28). In general, then, the regime appears to have been far more repressive than was Mussolini's brand of fascism.

Ultimately the regime appears to have been held together by (a) the belief on the part of those in the governing coalition that Spaniards were not suited to liberty because if given too much freedom, the country descended into anarchy, (b) maintaining a balance of forces within the regime and making sure that none of them became too powerful and (c) Franco making all important decisions, including the hiring and firing of ministers, himself. Toward the end of the regime and particularly as Franco became less able and interested in the daily affairs of running the country, these old factions began to rise again, along with a new group that had become powerful in the 1950s and 1960s, the Opus Dei technocrats (see Chapter 4).

As will be discussed in Chapter 5, it is clear that post-Franco leaders bore the scars of the pre-Civil War period and Franco's dictatorship. As should also be clear from this very brief summary of Spain's political history, though, the learning process appears to have been extremely slow. The nineteenth century witnessed vast policy differences across the key government parties and groupings and adoption of policies that would only a few years later be radically altered when different groups took control of government. These periods were interspersed by military intervention aimed at supporting one or the other of the coalitions of interests. Radically different perceptions of how Spain should function as a modern state meant that compromise was apparently impossible, even for the sake of providing some semblance of governance. Given that this process repeated itself during the Spanish Second Republic after 100 years of similar difficulties and a seven-year military leadership, it is difficult to argue that prior experience with democracy has much influence on whether subsequent experiments with democracy are relatively successful or not. Indeed, these events would appear to support a path dependency/inertia model. On the other hand, given that this seemingly iterative process in Spain was halted by fascist dictatorship, perhaps subsequent democratizers were able to learn from mistakes of the nineteenth century up to the Civil War and develop a system that would make peace, stability and governance possible.

Turkey: Ottoman liberalism, fascism, democracy, and military coups

As discussed in the previous chapter, the predecessor to the modern Turkish Republic was the Ottoman Empire which ruled the territory currently known as Turkey until the Turkish Republic was formally established in 1923. The Ottoman system was in many ways similar to other empires of the time: it was built upon the assumption that all conquered land belonged to the monarch – the sultan – who granted use of it to feudal lords in exchange for military service. Taxation was centralized and in order to keep the landlords under control, a force of men was established to serve the sultan. The unusual component of Ottoman rule was that not only were military and political power concentrated in the hands of the sultan, but after the assumption of the Caliphate in 1517, the sultan was also considered to be the religious, spiritual leader. This is in contrast to European monarchs who might claim to have God on their side but did not simultaneously take on the role of spiritual leader (see Shaw and Shaw 1977; Ahmad 1993; or Zürcher 2004 for overviews of Turkish history).

The previous chapter noted that the de-linking of these roles was part of the legitimacy problem for the early Turkish Republic. However, it must be noted that the Ottoman Empire began to witness reforms in the 1800s that attempted to limit the absolute power of the sultan. These included the so-called *Tanzimat*, or 'reorganization', which was a new system guaranteeing equality to all Ottoman subjects and promising them the right to life and property, regardless of religion. These reforms culminated in the creation of a Constitution in 1876. According to this constitution, the rights of individuals were to be inviolable, no matter what their religious background, press freedom was guaranteed 'within the limits of the law', individuals were given the right to establish independent companies and the right to private property, the inviolability of private dwellings was outlined, and torture was forbidden. As in the case of Italy's early experience with democracy, the Ottoman Empire at this stage was ambiguously democratic, but clearly vested more power in the hands of the sultan than would be the case in a popularly elected parliament. For instance, under the 1876 constitution, ministerial government was to be established, with ministers being appointed by the sultan, and the sultan making the final decision if there was a dispute between a minister and the chamber of deputies. A bicameral General Assembly was also established: Senators would be appointed for life terms by the sultan and the Chamber of Deputies would be elected by popular vote but with limitations based on property ownership. Again, while not very democratic by modern standards, compared to other quasi-democratic constitutions of the time, this one was not all that unusual (Lybyer 1913; Shaw and Shaw 1977; Ahmad 1993; Zürcher 2004).

It must be noted that these changes were made mostly in response to the pressure being placed on sultans by a rising influential group, the Young Ottomans mentioned in the previous chapter. The Empire had been haemor-rhaging territory for many years, and this group believed that to become powerful again, the Empire would need to modernize and develop along the lines of the powerful European countries. Given the lukewarm response of sultans to attempts at curbing their power, it is not surprising that the constitution was revoked very quickly – in 1876, the same year it was created; the constitution then remained suspended until 1908. The Young Ottomans, eventually the Young Turks, continued to grow in power, however, and by 1908, they had formed military cells strong enough to force the sultan to reinstate the constitution and summon another parliament (see Chapter 9; also Tanör 1990).

This essentially sparked a regime crisis, as the Young Turks then proceeded to depose the sultan in 1909 and take control of running the empire themselves. By 1920, it was unclear as to whether the sultan or Young Turks were in charge, and the Allies at the end of World War I recognized the sultan as head of state (giving him the power to sign peace treaties, for instance). As outlined in the previous chapter, the outcome of these disputes over power and regime type was that the sultanate was finally abolished shortly before the Turkish Republic was founded in 1923, and the Caliphate – the religious title that had previously been held by sultans – was also formally abolished in 1924 (Shaw and Shaw 1977; Ahmad 1993; Zürcher 2004).

Given that the new regime was named the Turkish *Republic*, it might be assumed that this regime was indeed republican in the modern sense. Far from it, however: the regime functioned more like Italy under Mussolini or Spain under Franco. During the adoption of the reforms discussed in the previous chapter, those opposed to the reforms did create an opposition party, the Progressive Party. The party was accused of complicity in a revolt in eastern Turkey in 1925, however, and several of its members were put before 'Independence Tribunals' (which had originally been established to try Greeks in Anatolia who were subverting the Turkish War of Independence). Many of the opposition politicians were jailed or sent into exile, and repression continued for two years, partly in response to the alleged discovery of a plot on founder Mustafa Kemal's life. After this, there was no real organized opposition left: Young Turk leaders who were believed to have participated in the plot were hanged or exiled. Although Mustafa Kemal periodically attempted to 'create' opposition parties, these tended to be short-lived when it became apparent that they would be able to attract a large popular following. It was not until after his death in 1938 that a real opening came in the political system. As discussed in the book's introduction, the 1946 elections were the first in which an opposition party was allowed to participate and it did manage to win a few seats. Given the relatively small number of seats won by the opposition, however, it is unclear as to how free these elections were, but by the next round of parliamentary elections in 1950, elections were conducted freely and fairly, and the key opposition party managed to win a vast majority (more than 80 per cent) of the seats in the Turkish parliament.[4] Thus, the Turkish 'Republic' did not get into full swing until more than 25 years after it was established.

This first experiment with democracy was to be short-lived, however. The constitution under which this experiment took place included very few checks and balances (see Chapter 5), which meant there were no means by which to hold a majority government in check. Thus, the new government (led by the Democratic Party) became the repressors and increasingly adopted measures to crush any opposition to it. The government became increasingly intolerant of criticism and began jailing journalists on charges of publishing false reports or reports that were likely to breach the peace. It also began to conduct intrusive enquiries into the functioning of the opposition party (the Republican People's Party), arguably with the ultimate intent of closing it down and establishing a one-party state of its own (Robinson 1963; Shaw and Shaw 1977; Ahmad 1993; Zürcher 2004).

The result was a military coup in 1960 and the execution of three government leaders, including the prime minister, in 1961. A new constitution was designed which clearly drew upon the past ten years of experience by trying to guarantee limitations on majorities: the electoral system was changed to proportional representation (which would presumably limit the possibility of majority government in the first place); a second chamber (Senate) was created, which would consist of university graduates only; a Constitutional Court was created; and a bill of rights was adopted. In addition, Universities and the Turkish Radio and Television Corporation were made autonomous. All of these new rules were designed specifically to guarantee that there would be multiple sources that could hold government in check (see Chapter 5).

Despite these reforms, this experiment with democracy was also to be short-lived. The new electoral laws had the effect of fragmenting the party system and parties on the extreme left and extreme right began to appear (including an Islamic fundamentalist party and a neo-fascist party) (see Chapter 6). Neither of these parties won large percentages of the vote, but they did manage to radicalize dialogue. The main centre-right party (the Justice Party) began to appear extremist by participating in coalition governments with the extreme right parties and by radicalizing its own language in order to win votes. The left accused this party of collaborating with 'fascist political forces', and both sides contended that the other was anti-system. Terrorism on the part of left-leaning and right-leaning groups was on the increase and it seemed that ideological polarization was seeping down to the masses. In 1971, the military issued a warning which is nowadays referred to as a 'polite coup' or 'soft' coup that forced the resignation of the centre-right government and warned the parties to tone things down. The warning did not appear to have been taken seriously, and in 1980, there was another coup (and not a polite one) (see Chapter 9).

Again, it was clear that previous experience with democracy had a strong bearing on the democratic institutions that were created after the 1980 coup. The new constitution attempted to centralize power more and to allow strong, formal oversight powers for the military and presidential powers were also increased. There were other key aspects to the new constitution that also call into question the new regime's democratic credentials, aspects which were included in response to the problems of previous decades. For instance, universities were to be returned to state control; political parties were restricted from forming auxiliary branches, labour unions and other professional associations were restricted from participating in politics, other than by voting, that is, and the government was given strong censorship powers. Also in reaction to the previous two decades, a restricted form of proportional representation was introduced, with a 10 per cent nation-wide threshold.

Thus, it is clear that the structure created by the 1982 constitution necessarily restricted Turkey to quasi-democracy. Rather than attempting to learn from previous failures and apply this learning to new democratic rules, leaders reacted by moving the regime in an even more authoritarian direction.

Chapter 5 outlines the reasons for this, but generally, the evidence indicates that learning does not always lead to an improvement on *democratic* institutions and may indeed push the regime (back) towards authoritarianism.

In addition, the periods of military rule in Turkey have not generally been seen by civilians as highly repressive nor as political or economic failures. Indeed,

> the positive evaluation of military rule was one reason why the political actors have found it difficult to regard a democratic regime as 'the only game in town'... the Turkish experience has given rise to a conviction that the costs of abandoning democracy are not so high' and 'weakened the civilian resolve to seek remedies within the democratic system'.
>
> (Demirel 2005: 246)

Even the 1980–3 military regime, during which 171 individuals died as a result of torture in prison and 43 people were sentenced to death in military courts for political crimes, the regime was not widely discredited or disliked (Demirel 2005: 251). In contrast to much of the Italian opposition which was exiled or jailed, Turkish elites from the 1961–80 era were generally sent to military holiday camps for a short period. Thus, the consequences of the coup for them were fairly minimal. Moreover, it is contended that the period of one-party rule by the Republican People's Party was not overly repressive either (Demirel 2005: 248). Thus, the consequences of a breakdown of democracy appear to have been less severe in Turkey than for Spain or Italy, thus giving political elites less incentive to change their behaviour in the former to prevent such regression in the future.

Conclusions

Does prior democratic experience have any bearing on the successful consolidation of democracy? Perhaps not, as indicated by our three case studies. All three spent decades operating democratic systems or quasi-democratic systems that eventually collapsed – either by military coup or civil war. The case in which there appears to have been clear learning from failed experiences with democracy is Turkey, where constitutional design following the breakdown of democracy consisted of attempts to alter institutions in such a way as to guarantee stable democracy, or stable quasi-democracy. At the same time, however, more than two decades after the adoption of the most recent Turkish constitution, the country's democratic credentials are still in question. Thus, notions of institutional redesign provoked by crises and learning appears not to work as might be predicted in this case. Moreover, in the cases of Spain and Italy, the failure of democratic institutions and practices were generally not followed by successful institutional reforms. It was only after extremely serious crises of democracy leading to a

20-year dictatorship in Italy and a 40-year dictatorship in Spain that leaders appeared to contemplate the failings of previous institutions. In Spain, this appears to have led to a very careful consideration of institutional design issues. In Italy, it is unclear that post-World War II institutions were completely altered to take into account the problems that had allowed for the rise of Mussolini (including the system of proportional representation). The clearest institutional reform was actually one so divisive that it was put to the Italian people – the abolition of the monarchy. Politicians themselves were apparently unwilling to make this decision, despite the authority problems that had been created by a quasi-parliamentary system with a monarch who had ambiguous powers. Many would argue that there was indeed a learning process in Italy, in that politicians themselves found ways to prevent the extremes from becoming too powerful by adopting a far more consensual approach. Our final case study – Turkey – would indicate that such learning is not guaranteed: even after a relatively bloody military coup in which the former prime minister and two other government officials were executed, politicians failed to alter their behaviour to prevent another such coup. Thus, previous experience with democratic or quasi-democratic institutions does not appear to necessarily create promising conditions for democratic consolidation. That is, on the basis of the comparative analysis, what we have seen is that all three cases have had multiple experiences with democracy and opportunities to redesign political institutions, and they all show some signs of institutional learning eventually – as will be further outlined in Chapter 5 – but in one of these cases, institutional learning has not produced democratic consolidation.

On the other hand, it may be that previous failed experiences followed by lengthy dictatorships *does* create conditions in which politicians are more willing to regulate their own behaviour for the sake of the maintenance of the democratic regime. Specifically, the two consolidated democracies in this book experienced fairly lengthy periods of repressive dictatorship following a breakdown of democracy and so the logic of comparative analysis dictates that this may be a cause of differences in democratic consolidation. Later chapters of the book will continue to explore the behaviour of political elites within their political institutions. The next chapter considers an alternative explanation, however, which is that democracy may only work well when government is wealthy enough to placate important socioeconomic groups, in turn preventing them from rebelling and creating the sort of public instability that served as backdrops to general political instability in all three of our cases.

4 Pre-transition economic structures and economic development

One of the few established near-facts in comparative politics research is that democracies tend to be relatively economically developed. There are exceptions to this tendency – the most significant being India – but in general, the relationship between economic development and democracy is very strong (Lipset 1959; Cutright 1963; Huntington 1991; Diamond 1992; Londregan and Poole 1996; Przeworski et al. 1996; Gasiorowski and Power 1998; Geddes 1999; Boix and Stokes 2003). Although exceptions like India may lead us to the conclusion that high levels of economic development are not necessary for consolidating democracy, given the cross-national strength of this relationship, we must ask the question of whether varying levels of economic development have played an important role in the differing democratic outcomes across our three case studies. This chapter begins with an overview of the theoretical propositions thought to explain this particular relationship – that is, *why* are democracy and economic development so consistently related to one another? – and then turns to an analysis of economic development in Italy, Spain, and Turkey.

Modernization theory, economic development, and democracy

As argued in the introduction to this book, it is not clear that high levels of economic development are necessary to begin a transition to democracy, and such transitions occur in widely varying circumstances.[1] Thus, it is difficult to claim that any particular level of economic development is required for a transition to begin. However, it may be possible to argue that what happens after the transition *is* fundamentally dependent upon economics, given the very strong relationship between consolidated democracy and level of economic development. As argued by Przeworski and Limongi (1997), when a country that is developed happens to choose democracy, the likelihood of it surviving is considerably higher than when a poor country chooses democracy.

What is the nature of this relationship, though? Why is there such a strong connection between these variables? There are at least two possible explanations. The first stems from early modernization theory (e.g. Lipset 1959), and revolves around the growth of the middle class and the demands of that class. The assumption of this approach is that upper classes tend to try to use government to protect their interests, and this protection often involves repression of lower classes so that labour and wage demands are kept low. Lower classes, for their part, tend to be short-sighted, intolerant, not all that interested in democracy, and easily swayed by charismatic authoritarian leaders, according to the theory. Thus, in a political system where there is a small upper class and a large lower class, it is relatively easy for the former to use authoritarian techniques to maintain control over the latter. The implication is that any attempt to push the system toward democracy would be met with repression by a group that has considerable state power on its side and that the impetus for democracy is probably lacking in the first place. As a country becomes more economically developed, however, this often implies a burgeoning middle class, and this class is far more difficult to control via repressive means. It must be noted that modernization theory also assumes that development is associated with *industrialization*, and it could be industrialization that creates the key conditions for the growth of a middle class. Namely, industrialization requires a new class of workers in the form of middle management, which are necessary to run industries efficiently. The economic position of this class, along with their increased time available for things like newspaper reading means that they have the knowledge and strong economic base to make demands for an increased say in government decision-making. According to this approach, any attempt to move away from democracy once a transition is under way would be met with protest from this group. However, Rueschmeyer *et al.* (1992) make a convincing case against the democratic tendencies of the middle classes, with empirical findings indicating that the latter often press governments to use authoritarian measures against the poorer classes when these classes become disruptive (e.g. engage in strikes). Beyond the class-based arguments mentioned above, modernization theory also emphasises that economic growth generally leads to increased literacy and improved channels of communication, both of which are prerequisites for exercising effective control over the state (see Maravall 1997 for a summary of these arguments).

The second possible explanation for the connection between development and democratic consolidation lies in government capacity for redistribution. Democracy is a fragile way of running a government. It requires that interests be balanced against one another in such a way that key groups and individuals do not have strong incentives to overthrow the democratic rules, opting for authoritarian ones instead. That is, it is a system in which those who are political or economic losers must be unwilling (or unable) to resort to extra-democratic means. Politically, this simply means that losing groups have some hope of eventually becoming winners (i.e. via elections).

Economically, though, the cost of losing can be rather severe. The cost to lower classes when upper class or bourgeois parties take power after democratic elections can include unfavourable taxation systems, lack of wage protection, as well as inadequate social and heath-care systems. Essentially, a takeover by parties representing upper classes may imply a decline in personal economic circumstances for the lower classes, and this – rather than intolerance – may mean that such classes are willing to resort to non-democratic means. Similarly, when lower class or socialist-leaning parties win elections, the threat to those in the upper classes can also be severe, particularly in terms of taxation and land reform designed to strip the upper classes of their wealth and transfer it to the poor.

Both of the above scenarios imply that if government is going to maintain a balance across these interests, there must be a high level of national wealth and development. Particularly when a democracy adopts universal (or universal male) suffrage, there can be no doubt that the lower classes will have the power to make redistribution demands via government institutions. How can a regime adequately meet these demands, however, if resources are scarce? Similarly, how will the regime prevent the upper classes from combining forces amongst themselves and with authoritarian-leaning elites to overthrow the system (as appeared to be the case in Italy in the 1920s when the bourgeoisie collaborated with fascist thugs to repress strike activity)? It seems that there must be an economic situation whereby extracting some of the wealth of the upper classes is not so painful that they prefer some other system of government, and such a circumstance would need to be one in which these groups have enough wealth to provide for themselves and further growth of their wealth even if government expropriates a significant portion of that wealth to provide social welfare and other benefits to the lower classes. That is, the economic pinch cannot be too hard. Indeed, recall that one of the many causes of the outbreak of the Spanish Civil War was likely to have been economic: strike activity was on the increase (and note that this was organized through the CNT and UGT), with better wages being demanded, but the main reason business owners did not negotiate was because economic circumstances were such that they could not meet the demands being made by workers (Payne 1993: 338).

These two main explanations for the relationship between democracy and development in turn imply that we need to examine two key factors of development in our three case studies: industrialization and overall levels of wealth. Thus, we will examine levels of industrial development in the three countries, attempting to draw inferences about the growth of middle classes and working classes across the three. At the same time, overall levels of wealth must be examined in order to attempt to make inferences about the distributional capacity of the three states during the early part of their democratic transitions.

It is also important to consider whether the regimes were in the midst of an *economic crisis* during the early days of their transitions. Economic crisis consists of a combination of slow growth and high inflation (Haggard and Kaufman 1995). These economic circumstances present any regime –

authoritarian or democratic – with difficult decisions, the result of which may prompt regime collapse. In the modern day, the economic remedies suggested for solving economic crises, including wage restraint and the reduction of government budgets, with extremely negative implications for public services, are particularly difficult for democracies to undertake precisely because of the need to balance interests, as outlined above. If the economic medicine is not taken, however, the economic situation is likely to worsen, creating circumstances in which those willing to use more authoritarian measures take control of government. In the words of Diamond and Linz, 'Economic crisis represents one of the most common threats to democratic stability' (1989: 17). Thus, economic crisis increases the likelihood of a breakdown of democracy (O'Donnell 1973; Remmer 1990; Huntington 1991; but see Gasiorowski 1995 and Gasiorowski and Power 1998), and new, transitional democracies seem more vulnerable to this possibility, as attachment to and institutionalization of the new democratic rules is still generally weak.

What do the theories outlined above lead us to predict for the three cases? The expectation is that if these theories are correct, our empirical findings will point to the conclusion that Turkey has failed to carry out a successful consolidation of democracy because of its lack of industrialization and subsequent small (and weak) middle class and because the overall level of wealth was too low to provide the Turkish state with any real distributive powers. On the other hand, if these theories are incorrect, we would expect to find that levels of industrial development and overall wealth were very similar in each of the three countries during the early stages of their transitions to democracy. Additionally, it may be the case that Turkey's transitions occurred during economic crises whereas the economic situations in Spain and Italy were more stable during their post-war transitions to democracy.

Before discussing each case individually, it is important to stress the fact that these countries experienced relatively similar economic development patterns, patterns which set them apart from countries like Britain, France, and Germany. First and foremost is that they were all late industrializers, and in the cases of Spain and Turkey, even once industrialization got under way, it was slow and very much incomplete (again, in comparison to Northern Europe). Because of the lag behind the industrialized European economies, all three of the cases investigated here tended to rely on government impetus for industrialization. That is, rather than industry and market economies being a result of entrepreneurship in society, they were led from the centre, using government direction, subsidies, and tariff and non-tariff barriers to protect newly established indigenous industry. All three economies have tended to be heavily agrarian and have had difficulty switching from traditional to modern agricultural production techniques, although this is far less the case in Italy than in the other two countries. The domination of agriculture by small land-holders who lacked the financing to purchase equipment for mechanization has meant that a very large portion of the workforce continued to be employed in agriculture; this also means that fewer workers are available for non-agricultural production, and so labour in industrial enterprises remained fairly expensive. Finally, in the cases of Spain and Turkey, the shift in the nature of employment was rather different than that experienced in Northern Europe. In the latter, as agriculture became mechanized and workers moved to cities to work in industry, the percentage employed in agriculture dropped while the percentage employed in industry rose. It was only when the Northern economies reached a 'post-industrial' phase that the number of industry workers declined and the tertiary, or service, sector increased in size. In Spain and Turkey, by contrast, the eventual decline in the number of agricultural workers almost immediately coincided with an increase in service workers, with only marginal increases in industrial labour. Thus, these two never really experienced the sort of industrial revolution that was experienced in Northern Europe (see Sapelli 1995). We now turn to an overview of the development of the economies in each of these three countries, and at the end of the chapter will provide some comparative statistics in order to try to determine whether differences in economic development or economic crisis might explain the differences in levels of democratic consolidation across the three.

Pre-transition economic structures and conditions in Italy

Amongst the three countries analysed in this book, Italy was the clear leader when it comes to economic development and industrialization. Although a latecomer to industrialization by Northern European standards, Italy was fairly far ahead of Spain and Turkey in this regard. This section begins with a brief summary of development and industrialization in Italy in the decades prior to the country's transition to quasi-democracy in the late 1800s and early 1900s. It then focuses on economic development during the fascist era; this is because it is entirely possible that growth during this period created conditions which put the country in ideal circumstances for creating a consolidated democracy. We then turn to a discussion of the economic situation during and immediately after World War II in Italy, as these were the circumstances in which the country was making the most recent transition to democracy. We finally address Italy's economic conditions during the period of initial political instability – the 1950s and on through the 1970s – in order to determine whether a high level of economic development helped the country to withstand the political instability of those decades by providing governments with the resources needed for redistribution, thereby placating the demands that provoked the instability (demands related to wages and working conditions).

The empirical evidence on factors like urbanization and railroad construction indicate that Italy's levels of industrialization and general development were on the increase, starting in the late 1800s. For instance, Denis Mack

Smith (1959) provides statistics on population growth in the three largest Italian cities (see Table 4.1). These statistics indicate fairly large-scale migration to these cities during this period. Other evidence indicating a significant rise in industrialization is the level of coal imports; these apparently doubled between 1879 and 1885 (Mack Smith 1959: 154). Evidence also indicates that by the 1890s, the transportation system and rail network in Italy was virtually complete, and that protectionist policies that had been adopted in the 1880s had encouraged a number of basic industries (Allen and Stevenson 1974: 2). Moreover, the adoption of German banking techniques, along with guidance from banks regarding channelling funds to expanding industries is thought to have helped with Italy's industrialization at this time (Allen and Stevenson 1974: 3; Gerschenkron 1955: 374–5). However, it also appears that there was fairly slow growth between the mid-1890s and 1913, along with a low rate of investment and stagnant international trade (Allen and Stevenson 1974: 1), and growth was 'disappointing' by international standards – far below the levels of Germany, Russia, and Sweden, for instance (Allen and Stevenson 1974: 4). Such information would indicate that the industrialization process was off to a relatively slow start during this period.

By late 1913, there was an economic downturn in Italy (and many other countries) and with the onset of the world depression in the 1920s, many Italian businesses failed (Clough 1964: 171, 205). World War I actually created the circumstances in which further industrialization and growth could have occurred, though. Urbanization increased during the war years as a result of the demands of war-making industries for labour. Industry clearly benefited for the first two years of the war: there was rapid growth in demand and high profits, all of which encouraged technical innovation and the development of new products. However, many firms had difficulty adapting to peacetime conditions, as increased profits had not gone far enough toward preparing for the post-war economic conditions and the need to produce non-war-related goods (Allen and Stevenson 1974: 4–5). According to Clough (1964), the lengthy war meant that Italian economic development was seriously distorted toward the war industry and away from industries designed for civilian demand. In addition, foreign trade was interrupted because former trading partners became enemies; the costs of the war itself were also extremely high (Clough 1964: 178). On the other hand, a

Table 4.1 Population size of major Italian cities

	1871	*1921*
Milan	200,000	700,000
Turin	250,000	500,000
Rome	220,000	700,000

Source: Mack Smith (1959: 189–90).

few industries, like steel and automobiles (particularly Fiat) developed well during the war (Clough 1964: 178).

Allen and Stevenson contend that in general the 1914–45 period was an economic (and political) disaster for Italy (Allen and Stevenson 1974: 4). It must be noted, though, that the fascist period (1922–43) did produce some key economic achievements. For instance, the government pursued a policy of agricultural self-sufficiency by developing selected seeds and increasing the use of tractors and other machinery (Allen and Stevenson 1974: 6–7).[2] In addition electricity production was subsidized and increased fivefold between 1917 and 1943 (Mack Smith 1959: 403). Mainline tourist trains ran on time and by 1939, 5000 kilometres of track had been electrified; major roads were built to connect Turin to Milan, Milan to the Lakes, and Florence and Rome to the sea (Mack Smith 1959: 408; Allen and Stevenson 1974: 7). Before and during World War II, attention was given to industry related to goods that Italy was dependent upon; refineries were developed and there was a search for coal, oil, and alternative energy sources (Clough 1964: 258). The banking system was also reformed under fascism: the Bank of Italy was turned into a public institution and the three main banks were declared 'banks of national interest' and were to avoid the investment banking that had caused many other Italian banks trouble previously (eventually producing bank failure). A better system of bank inspection was also established (Clough 1964: 258).

The fascist regime attempted to develop social services, but these were still far lower than in most other European countries at the time (Mack Smith 1959: 405). Similarly, wages and labour conditions did not improve; the previously adopted eight-hour working day was abandoned in 1926, and wages were estimated to be lower than in Spain in 1930 (Mack Smith 1959: 405–6). Average consumption of basics like wheat decreased between the 1920s and 1930s (Mack Smith 1959: 407). In addition, Mussolini attempted to stop migration to the cities, using populist rhetoric about Italians being close to the land to do so, along with requiring migrants to obtain permits to move to the cities (Mack Smith 1959: 405–6). Although there was some economic recovery in the 1922–5 period, world depression put an end to this. The Italian economy suffered from serious deficit and a drop in gold reserves by 74 per cent between 1927–39. In 1937, the government began adopting desperate measures, including selling arms to other countries (friendly or otherwise) in order to obtain hard currency. Estimates are that per capita growth in national income was only 1.5 per cent per year during the fascist period, and most of this was absorbed by attempts at colonization and the war effort (Allen and Stevenson 1974: 6–7).

Thus, the economy might have improved somewhat under fascism, except that World War II was extremely costly. The country did not have adequate funds to prepare for the war and it did not have the necessary materials, like coal, to do so. Industrial output was extremely low compared to the enemies. For instance, in 1938, Italy produced only 70,000 automobiles, tanks, and buses compared to 444,877 for the UK; Italy mined only 1.48 million tons of coal to the UK's 230.64 million tons (and France's 46.5); and had 6214 railway locomotives to the UK's 21,629 (Clough 1964: 261).

Toward the end of World War II, Italians were reduced to near-starvation levels. At the end of the war, agricultural livestock had been reduced to 75 per cent of pre-war levels, much agricultural equipment was destroyed, and agricultural capacity was cut by 40 per cent. Damage to industry was less severe, but the estimates are that much of what survived was suffering from heavy wear and tear or was obsolete. Not surprisingly then, industrial output in 1945 was at about 25 per cent what it was in 1941 and roughly equal to its 1884 level. The transportation system was also damaged by the war, with one-quarter of railway tracks having been destroyed, along with one-third of bridges and about 60 per cent of wagons and trucks. Merchant shipping was reduced to one-sixth of its wartime peak, and port facilities were almost decimated. Real income per person was equal to about half of the 1938 level and below the income level at the time of Italian unification. There was large-scale unemployment, and, as mentioned above, the country was close to starvation. Moreover, inflation was a major problem (Clough 1964: 289, 308; Allen and Stevenson 1974: 7–8).[3]

Thus, taking into account the hypotheses of modernization theory, given these circumstances, the prospect of a successful transition and consolidation of democracy would seem unlikely. Namely, a country at such a reduced level of industrial capacity of Italy at the end of World War II and in such extreme poverty and also suffering from high inflation would not appear to have the economic circumstances necessary to sustain democracy.

However, despite the dire conditions, the economy regained strength. GDP per capita was almost back to 1938 levels by 1950, as was the agricultural sector; manufacturing had exceeded 1938 levels by 1950 (Clough 1964: 308). A great deal of this recovery was a result of grants and food aid provided by the Allies: between 1948–51, Italy received about 1310 million dollars, mostly in grants (Allen and Stevenson 1974: 8–10).

By 1950, the country was still relatively poor and backward with regard to industrialization. For instance, 44 per cent of the workforce was employed in agriculture, agricultural techniques were still far from modern and productivity was low; agricultural production accounted for only 23 per cent of GNP despite holding 44 per cent of the labour force. Much of industry was also backward and on a small scale. In 1951, the average manufacturing establishment employed less than six people; over 90 per cent of the manufacturing establishment had a workforce of less than five. Income per head in 1950 was $290, which was not much above the $200 by which according to UN convention, a country was deemed to be underdeveloped (Allen and Stevenson 1974: 11). Even by 1958, Italy had a per capita income that was $\frac{3}{7}$ that of France, and $\frac{3}{14}$ that of the US (Clough 1964; statistics from *Annuario Statistico 1960* Rome: Instituto Poligrafico dello Stato,

1961: 418). Once again, these circumstances would not appear to bode well for the prospect of sustaining Italian democracy.

The period 1951–71 marks a significant turnaround for the Italian economy, however. During these years, there was rapid economic growth, a high rate of investment, high growth in exports, reduced unemployment, and change in the employment structure (Zamagni 2000: 49–50). Unions were weak until the mid-1960s and so wages could be kept below productivity; this meant industry could reinvest in itself and also that export prices were highly competitive. The dismantling of tariff barriers with the EEC helped Italian industry to flourish; the country was able to achieve a surplus on balance of payments and build up gold and foreign currency reserves, and thus able to weather temporary fluctuations in the balance of payments (Allen and Stevenson 1974: 14).

The structure of employment also changed markedly. In 1951, agriculture accounted for 44 per cent of the total labour force; by 1970, this had declined to 19 per cent, representing an absolute exodus of five million people from the countryside into industry (Allen and Stevenson 1974: 14). This shift provided a reservoir of labour, which in turn, helped to keep wages down and kept trade unions weak, thereby increasing profits and allowing high levels of self-financed investment (Allen and Stevenson 1974: 15). The state holding sector was able to purchase the most advanced technologies and was thus able to produce high economic activity in iron, steel, cement, oil, chemicals, and energy (Allen and Stevenson 1974: 16). Agricultural mechanization also increased, as did the number of large firms. Much of the change has been aided by government grants and other policies, including the expropriation of large, poorly managed farms for redistribution to peasant owners (Allen and Stevenson 1974: 16–17). In earlier periods, one of the key problems hampering industrial development in Italy was the lack of natural resources that were necessary for industrial production – resources like oil and gasoline (Mack Smith 1959: 403; Clough 1964: 170); in the 1951–71 period, the country discovered oil and natural gas deposits, and the latter have been quite large, providing a source of energy self-sufficiency (Allen and Stevenson 1974: 18).

It is important to note the role and importance of the Italian state in producing economic growth after World War II; the state managed to developed railways, the metallurgical industry, and shipbuilding. It also controlled banking in such a way as to favour industrial development, and established welfare policies that were 'extensive', accounting for 11 per cent of Italy's national income in 1959 (Clough 1964: 10). Also, as noted above, there was considerable reliance on the Italian state and state finance to catch industry up to the standards of those ahead in economic development. In addition, both public- and private-sector firms were able to meet demands for wage and social benefit increases in the 1960s because government was able to borrow more money to pay for the former or to bail out the latter (Clark 1984: 352; Zamagni 2000: 50).

Any discussion of the Italian economy would not be complete without mention of the North–South gap in economic development. The gap – both in terms of wealth and industrial output – existed at the time of political unification in 1861, but it widened over the next 100 years (Clough and Livi 1956; Lutz 1962; Clough 1964; Allen and Stevenson 1974: 12; King 1992). It must be noted, though, that as the north of the country improved economically, government policies of redistribution were adopted, and so the lot of the South has also improved considerably (Clough 1964: 345–52; King 1992).

What are the implications of the above discussions for the role of modernization in Italy's successful democratic consolidation? First, the increased industrialization in the late 1800s and then in the 1950s–1970s clearly produced a much larger middle and working class. Chapter 6 will address the degree of organization of these classes, particularly the working class, but for now, it can be assumed that they increased considerably, as did their concentration in the major cities of Italy. Different strands of modernization theory would argue that one or the other of these two classes would be likely to pursue further democratization, and it is particularly to the advantage of the working class to gain power through democratization in order to produce governments that develop policies that benefit them. It would not be surprising if these groups were indeed pressing for continuation of democracy once it had been established. Initially, large segments of them pressed for communist revolution, but this goal was dropped shortly after Italy's post-war transition to democracy, and the working classes – or at least their representatives – generally became more committed to democracy.

However, it is unlikely that this would have been the case if the overall level of development had not been improved in Italy. Namely, the sorts of demands being made by the working classes in the 1960s require funds, and a government that lacks the funds to provide these (old-age pensions, unemployment insurance, and the like) risks considerable instability and potential collapse in the face of too many demands. Thus, it may be contended that the rapid improvement in economic conditions in Italy in the early transition period, particularly the 1950s, created circumstances in which democracy could take root. These improvements are, in turn, at least to some degree connected to emergency aid provided by the Allies at the end of World War II, a point to be discussed again at the end of this chapter.

Pre-transition economic structures and conditions in Spain

The above discussion illustrates that while Italy was extremely poor at the time of the start of the post-war democratization, the economy improved considerably during the first few years after the transition and this may have provided governments the economic tools with which to placate key economic interests in Italy. At the same time, unions were still fairly weak, and so extreme policies to benefit the working class were not necessary until the 1960s, and this may have also contributed positively to creating a period during which democratic institutions could take root because there was little risk of the bourgeois class attempting to overthrow this system in the face of large-scale working-class demands. We now turn to a discussion of our next case study, Spain. As in the previous section, this one will begin by providing an overview of the state of the economy prior to the transition to democracy in Spain in the mid-1970s, focussing upon industrialization and economic development. This section also explores the state of the economy under the Franco dictatorship to determine whether economic conditions were created under that regime that then made democracy more likely to survive by the mid-1970s. Finally, the section discusses the Spanish economy during the early years of the transition to determine whether the prevailing conditions in those years were also promising for the creation of stable democratic institutions.

In general, industrial expansion was far slower and less developed in Spain than in Italy. The Spanish government did take some action, like the development of the railway system, most of the main arteries for which were completed by around 1865 due to a fairly generous government system that attracted foreign railway companies. Lieberman argues that the development of the railway system had very little impact on inducing other industries to develop, however (Lieberman 1995: 107). Many other industries, such as mining, were also under foreign control – by the beginning of World War I, for instance, most railroads, streetcars, utilities, mining, and the chemical industries were controlled by foreign interests – and it is thought that the foreign investment failed to stimulate economic development in Spain because profits were not re-invested there but instead were invested in the home countries of those establishing the industries (Lieberman 1995: 107).

In addition, even with the industrial activity that was taking place, as late as 1914 almost 62 per cent of the Spanish labour force was employed on the land, with only 18.5 per cent in mining and manufacturing, and almost 20 per cent in the service sector (Alcaide 1976, vol. 1: 1136). Agricultural production was relatively backward, with cultivated land being divided into small plots and larger plots, many of which were not being cultivated (Harrison 1985: 16–18; see also Harrison and Corkhill 2004: Chapter 3).

Industrial development was concentrated mostly in Asturias, the Basque region, and Catalonia (Harrison 1985: 15; see also Harrison and Corkhill 2004: Chapter 4). The Catalonian cotton textile industry was the most advanced of the industrial development in Spain, but much of its development in the 1890s was dependent on sales in the remaining Spanish colonies; when Spain lost the Spanish-American war in 1898, this meant a loss of crucial markets in Cuba, Puerto Rico, and the Philippines; this produced a lengthy depression from which the textile sector was never to recover (Harrison 1985: 19–20). One of the failings of this industry was that it was characterized by very small enterprises, frequently family firms

(Harrison 1985: 21). The Basque region did much better in the longer term, particularly in the Vizcaya province, and was involved in steel production (note that the region has iron ore deposits); the big economic take-off for the province was the late 1870s (Harrison 1985: 22). According to Harrison, however, 'Outside of Catalonia and Vizcaya, Spain remained a backwater in terms of industrial development' (Harrison 1985: 26; see also Harrison and Corkhill 2004: Chapter 4).

During World War I, unlike Italy, Spain remained neutral and some Spanish industries did well out of the war, selling food products, war materials and clothing. Very similarly to the situation in Italy, however, the industry that developed failed to find ways to readjust to civilian needs. Entrepreneurs who did well apparently failed to reinvest their profits in things like agricultural efficiency or civilian industry (Harrison 1985: 35; see also Harrison and Corkhill 2004: Chapter 4).

With the economy still struggling, dictator Primo de Rivera came to power and ruled Spain during 1923–30. In terms of improving Spain's economic situation, Primo de Rivera had lofty ideals about making agriculture more efficient, but he tended to come up against powerful landowners (and was one himself) (Harrison 1985: Chapter 3). He also emphasized modernizing the railways in his rhetoric but in fact, the length of the standard track was only extended very marginally. On the positive side, however, the number of locomotives and new carriages and wagons that came into service was indeed increased (Ceballos Teresí no date: 374–5). Furthermore, the length of roads doubled (Velarde Fuertes 1973: 95) and the number of cars and lorries rose sharply. For instance, official records indicate that the number of vehicles registered in 1923 was 37,169 compared to 201,249 in 1929 (Calvo Sotelo 1974: 308). Electricity supply was also improved and increased, but was still low compared to France and Italy at the time (Harrison 1985: 62–3; see also Harrison and Corkhill 2004: Chapter 4). One of the biggest problems that the government had was with tax reform (in great part trying to get landowners to stop evading paying taxes) and with monetary policy (the value of the peseta was in perpetual decline) (Harrison 1985: Chapter 3). Also, heavy industry had to be propped up with government contracts for products (Harrison 1985: 72). Thus, the economy and government reserves were only marginally improved under Primo de Rivera. Still, official statistics indicate that the degree of industrialization had increased: in 1930 47 per cent of the Spanish workforce were employed in agriculture; 31 per cent in industry; 22 per cent in the service sector (Alcaide, vol. 1: 1136), compared with 63 per cent, 18 per cent, and 20 per cent in 1914.

The Spanish Second Republic (1930–6) appears to have been an economic disaster for Spain. The new Republic began at the start of the most profound depression ever experienced in capitalist Spain (Harrison 1985: 77). There were radical revolutionary movements, peasant land occupations, strikes, military plots, and political polarization on both the Left and the Right. Economic reform was simply impossible (Harrison 1985: 78–9). It is argued that Spain was not as hard hit by the Great Depression as other parts of the world in great part because the country was so economically backward and isolated from the mainstream international economy (Harrison 1985: 80–5). Still, unemployment amongst agricultural workers was very high and in some places, anarchist-led peasants staged revolts, despite the fact that the left-leaning government initially in power was adopting agricultural reform policies to try to improve the lot (and rights) of peasants (Harrison 1985: 92–3).

When the centre-right government came to power in 1933, it did not immediately give up on land reform but switched to emphasizing small tenant farmers rather than landless peasants; eventually land reform was abandoned and 'the Law for the Reform of Agrarian Reform' was passed (Harrison 1985: 95). When a left-leaning government returned to power in 1936, there is a further increase in unemployment in the countryside and the government once again began to push through agrarian reform measures. There was an escalation of wages and landlords were obliged (not for the first time) to take on local labour before accepting migrant workers: 'Such developments almost certainly reinforced the overwhelming support of Spanish landowners for the military rising which took place on 18 July 1936' (Harrison 1985: 95).

The economic emphasis of the Second Republic was clearly on agricultural and land reform. There was very little in the way of industrial policy during this period and industrialists appeared to fail to get the government to consider industrial concerns (Harrison 1985: 99).

Amongst the other economic problems of the Second Republic, the currency depreciated considerably (Harrison 1985: 99). In addition, although Republican governments were committed to balancing the budget, in the face of increasing levels of social pressure, government spending increased and so did the budget deficit (Harrison 1985: 101–3). That is, governments simply did not have the economic resources to finance the meeting of the demands of the poor and unemployed.

In 1936, the Spanish Civil War began, and the war was costly for all sides. The republicans drew on state funds and reserves to purchase weapons. The military rebels raised funds domestically but also received help from the Italian and German governments (Harrison 1985: 110–13).[4] Many of the large land owners (*latifundistas*) took flight or were assassinated by Republicans or leftists, leaving large plots of land uncultivated. The Republican government's minister of agriculture issued a decree in October 1936 calling for the expropriation without indemnity of all rural estates belonging to everyone who had participated in the insurrection against the Republic (although this was opposed by most other Socialist and Republican ministers). The confiscated lands were to be given to peasants living within the municipal boundary. In Nationalist controlled areas, land reform policies were reversed (Harrison 1985: 113).

Thus, by the time the rebels won the Civil War, the Spanish economy was a shambles. Very much like that of Italy's dictatorship, Franco's initial economic policy was one driven by the quest for economic self-sufficiency (Harrison 1985; Rees and Grugel 1997: 106–12). On the positive side, this encouraged the development of domestic industry, which was protected by tariffs and quotas, allowing it to survive despite high operating costs. However, it also meant industry had little inducement to become cost-efficient. High production costs and low quality adversely affected Spanish exports (Lieberman 1995: 108; see also Lawlor and Rigby 1998, part II: 100). Until the 1950s, then, Spain's economy was stagnant and many of Franco's key policies, like establishing corporatist style interest groups (or *sindicatos*) and breaking up the *latifundios* were completely ineffective.[5]

The 1950s marked the beginnings of a profound transformation of Spain's economic structure. Approximately one million workers left the land for towns and the government accepted the need for international exchange and began adopting a liberal economic ideology (Harrison 1985: 122; see also Harrison and Corkhill 2004: Chapter 4). Not until 1950 did the index of industrial production rise above the peak year of 1929, while agricultural production remained below that level until 1958 (Schwartz 1976: 85). The 1935 level of national income measured at constant 1964 prices was not attained until 1951 (Alcaide, vol. 1: 1142). National income rose during 1950–59 by 54 per cent (Harrison 1985: 131).

Moreover, although Spain was not a recipient of Marshall Plan Aid, in 1953, Spain began receiving economic aid from the US in exchange for permission to construct US military bases in Spain (Harrison 1985: 123; also Lawlor and Rigby 1998: 100; Lieberman 1995: 2). During 1951–7, the US paid $625 million of aid; $260 or 41.6 per cent of this came through the Defence Support Program (see Table 6.3 of Harrison 1985: 133). The high levels of aid from the USA during 1951–7 allowed Spain to import products that were deficient, like raw cotton, olive oil, and capital goods. The foreign currency also meant that goods like fertilisers and machinery could be purchased. Famine in the countryside began to recede (Harrison 1985: 133–4). In addition, there were investment programmes for electricity and railways; the government also encouraged licensing arrangements with foreign companies to acquire skills and technology. This is how the motor-vehicle sector (e.g. SEAT) made progress (Harrison 1985: 136).

However, the early liberal reforms were half-hearted and almost completely uncoordinated. By the mid-1950s, Spain's economic situation was deteriorating sharply; inflation was on the rise and foreign reserves were being depleted (Harrison 1985: 123).[6] There were divisions within the regime about how to deal with the economic difficulties and eventually the neoliberals – the Opus Dei technocrats[7] – won out. In 1959, the Franco regime sent a memorandum to the International Monetary Fund and Organization for European Economic Cooperation, which became known as the Stabilization Plan (Harrison 1985: 124, 140; also Lawlor and Rigby 1998: 101; see also Harrison and Corkhill 2004: Chapter 4).

Between 1959 and 1973, Spanish national income rose by 156 per cent (*Servicio de Estudios del Banco de Bilbao* 1983: 232). The proportion of the active labour force employed on the land fell from 41.9 per cent to 25.3 per cent by 1973; approximately two million Spaniards left the countryside in the 1960s (Harrison 1985: 145). The contribution of agriculture to Spain's GDP almost halved during the 'miracle' years, dropping from 20 per cent in 1959 to 11 per cent in 1973. The contribution of industry rose from 30 per cent to 41 per cent over the same period (*Servicio de Estudios del Banco de Bilbao, Informe economico, 1982* (Bilbao, 1983: 228). Foreign trade also increased; imports rose 13-fold and exports 14-fold during 1959–73; the import–GDP ratio more than doubled from 6.9 per cent to 15.9 per cent; the export–GDP ratio rose from 6.1 per cent to 14.1 per cent (*Servicio de Estudios del Banco de Bilbao* 1983: 234, 250).[8]

Thus between 1959 and the mid-1970s, there were unprecedented rates of economic growth (Rees and Grugel 1997: 112–22; Gilmour 1985: Chapter 3). Among members of the OECD, only Japan enjoyed faster and more sustained growth in this period (Harrison 1985: 144; also Lawlor and Rigby 1998: 101). Growth was due not only to government plans but to growth in exports, particularly textiles, footwear, and oranges, along with tourism, foreign investment, and emigrant remittances; all of this was made possible by the increasing growth and prosperity of the main European economies and the US (Lawlor and Rigby 1998: 101). Roads, railways, airports, water, health, and public works were improved for the sake of tourism; people started moving into the service sector and the building industry, transport, and commerce (Harrison 1985: 155–6; see also Harrison and Corkhill 2004: Chapter 4). In agriculture, the mass exodus of rural labourers had the indirect effect of modernizing agricultural production. This is because the reduction in large numbers of cheap labourers available for agricultural work produced a sharp increase in labour costs; for instance agricultural wages rose by 269 per cent during 1957–67. Thus, where possible, farmers began to try to use machinery (Harrison 1985: 158). Small farms could not really afford mechanization and in the face of problems with making ends meet, many sold their lands. According to the Agrarian Census, half a million farms disappeared during 1962–72 (Naredo 1974: 135).

At the time of Franco's death in 1975, Spain's economy was faltering, however, as a result of the early 1970s oil crisis. Although Spain had been exempted from the oil boycott of 1973 because of friendly relations with the Arab states, the country did not escape the massive price increases that followed. The country was particularly hard-hit by this. Heavy industries were dependent on the cheap oil and many goods were being transported by lorry because of the inadequate railway structure (Harrison 1985: 171). By 1974, it is argued that the oil crisis had put an end to 15 years' economic progress (Harrison 1985; see also Harrison and Corkhill 2004: Chapter 4; Rees and Grugel 1997: 117–22).

After Franco's death, the government was extremely slow to respond to the economic difficulties, though, and it was clear that the economic crisis took a secondary role to the democratic transition (Harrison 1985: 168–9). Because of the extreme delicacy of the political situation no government was initially willing to introduce severe measures which were needed to put the economy back on track. Thus, labour costs rose by 30 per cent during 1974–8, contributing to the rise in inflation of 26.4 per cent in 1977. The trade deficit also rose (Lawlor and Rigby 1998: 102) but so did consumption (Lieberman 1995: 173–4). Moreover, growth rates fell to 1–2 per cent, with a low of 0.9 per cent for the 1972–82 period (Harrison 1985). Unemployment rose to 20 per cent in the mid-1980s, whereas it had been around 3 per cent in the early 1970s under Franco, and growth rates dropped from over 7 per cent per year to 1.7 per cent between 1975 and 1985 (Linz and Stepan 1996: 113). That is, the country was facing economic crisis.

By 1978, things appeared to have turned around with regard to the trade deficit. The reasons include a 20 per cent devaluation of the peseta in 1977; in addition, political stability meant that foreign investment nearly doubled during 1977–8; tourism also increased (Harrison 1985: 175; Lieberman 1995: 185–6). Lieberman additionally puts the turnaround down to good weather and abundant rain, which produced bumper crops, which in turn limited the rise in food prices and strengthened agricultural exports (Lieberman 1995: 185–6). Unemployment increased considerably, though (Lieberman 1995: 185–6). Also, budget deficits were very large, as was inflation. In 1965–72, inflation was about 6.4 per cent per year; in 1975–9 it was 17.4 per cent per year. By the summer of 1977, it stood at 37 per cent. The reasons seemed to be that the Bank of Spain continued to finance the large public-sector deficit; also, 'unstable governments chose to buy short-term social peace by sanctioning large rises in monetary wages in advance of increases in productivity' (Harrison 1985: 176). Unemployment increased from around 3 per cent to around 17 per cent during 1974–82 (Harrison 1985: 176).

The economic situation continued to deteriorate in the early 1980s. The budget deficit doubled between 1981 and 1982; foreign debt rose by US$1.5 billion; there was a loss of US$3.8 billion in international reserves (Lieberman 1995: 245). The second oil crisis in 1979 and its aftermath coincided with a period of political instability culminating in the resignation of Prime Minister[9] Adolfo Suárez in January 1981 and an attempted coup in February 1981 (see Chapter 9). Because of the delicate political situation during which leaders were trying to establish stable democratic institutions, the government was again hesitant to introduce radical economic policies (Lawlor and Rigby 1998: 102–3).

However, the socialist government under Felipe González pursued economic liberalism with considerable vigour from 1982 onward (Lieberman 1995: 9; see Chapter 6 on the conversion of the Spanish Socialist party into a supporter of neoliberal policies); it was not until the mid-1980s that the economy experienced a spectacular recovery, though. Rapid economic growth in the mid- to late 1980s allowed the Spanish standard of living to approach West European levels (Lieberman 1995: 248). The budget deficit was still very high, though, and unemployment continued to rise (Lieberman 1995: 250; see also Harrison and Corkhill 2004).

During 1983–5 the González government managed to reduce the rate of inflation by maintaining a restrictive monetary policy and by restraining the rate of growth of salaries and wages. However, this meant raising interest rates, which restricted the pace of economic recovery. Fortunately, improvement in the world economy helped increase productive investment (Lieberman 1995: 257). The government managed to negotiate labour reform, limit salary growth and wages, along with other reforms, but it still included concessions on increased retirement benefits and unemployment pay, which contributed to an increasing budget deficit (Lieberman 1995: 258–9).

Still, by 1990, Spain's GDP per person was only 76.7 per cent of the entire European Community (EC) average ratio and was 70.7 per cent of that of France (Lieberman 1995: 331). Generally, though, the last half of the 1980s experienced high levels of growth in GDP and Spanish employment increased by 15.7 per cent; however, with an unemployment rate of 16.3 per cent in 1990, Spain's unemployment rate was nearly twice as large as the average rate for the entire EC (Lieberman 1995: 332; see also Harrison and Corkhill 2004: Chapter 7).

In the early days of the transition, the Spanish economy needed foreign capital in order to finance the growing trade deficit that was resulting from a rise in imports of consumer goods. During 1980–5, the EC supplied Spain with 52 per cent of its foreign-financed investment; during 1986–90, this increased to 75 per cent. Foreign capital mostly went into energy production, construction, banking, and insurance (Lieberman 1995: 337; see also Harrison and Corkhill 2004: Chapter 6). In the mid-1980s, the Spanish government extended generous financial assistance to the private industrial sector to allow the latter to import needed foreign technology and expand its own research and development efforts. Public aid particularly benefited domestic industries seriously affected by rapid technological development. The government channelled its financial support to the chemical, electronics, precision instruments and telecommunications industries. Despite all of this, the share of domestic industry in Spain's GDP continued to diminish in the early 1990s (Lieberman 1995: 356–7).

What are the implications of these developments for Spain's prospects for democratic consolidation? On the one hand, the considerable amount of development that occurred in the Franco years until the first oil crisis in 1973 may have placed the country in an economic situation whereby new democratic governments could afford to buy off potentially destabilizing elements, particularly the working classes. In addition, as the economy became more industrialized, working classes began to organize themselves; strike activity increased, and by the late 1960s these strikes included

political as well as economic demands (Maravall and Santamaria 1986: 77).
Also of considerable importance is that the economic policies carried out in
the late 1950s and 1960s began to divide the regime, with Opus Dei technocrats favouring increasing openness and the hard-line right preferring to
keep Spain inward looking (Maravall and Santamaria 1986: 76; Gilmour
1985: Chapter 4). It was these fundamental cracks in the regime that made
it very difficult for the regime to survive after its leader had passed away.

At the same time, the economic crisis facing Spain at the time of Franco's
death could have served to create precisely the destabilizing conditions that
would have brought about the end of Spanish democracy. The government
managed to continue to buy off the working classes by increasing budget
deficits and was financed in great part by foreign investment. It is unclear as
to how long this economic policy could have continued before the Spanish
economy was in severe difficulty. According to Tovias (1984), however,
Spain's high level of reserves and general credit-worthiness, and the general
attitude of the international finance community as a whole toward the
country allowed it to overcome circumstances similar to those which had
contributed to the collapse of the Second Republic in the 1930s. As discussed above, though, there was a clear turn-around in the mid-1980s, and
despite the austere measures adopted by the Socialist government, the
economy as a whole grew. Thus, Spain rapidly advanced toward being
amongst the more developed world economies. As with Italy, then, we may
conclude that despite initial economic difficulties in the transitional
economy, it is possible that the rapid recovery did indeed create positive
conditions for the creation of stable Spanish democracy.[10]

Pre-transition economic structures and conditions in Turkey

The Ottoman Empire first began to promote industry by granting the right
of private property in 1808: the Treasury gave up its purchasing monopoly
and allowed landlords to sell their produce directly to foreign buyers and
their agents at this time. This accelerated the commercialization of agriculture and landlords prospered. By 1876, they emerged as an interest group
capable of furthering their interests in the new parliament discussed in the
previous chapter. However, the shelving of the constitution by Abdulhamid
in 1878 froze these developments for the next 30 years until the constitution
was restored in 1908. Wherever possible, liberal economic practices were
abandoned, although protectionism was not pursued because of legal concessions (known as 'capitulations') granted to the foreign bourgeois class
(Ahmad 1993).

In the late 1800s, the regime began creating the sort of infrastructure
thought to be necessary for the creation of a developed, industrial economy
by investing in postal and telegraph systems, railroads, and roads. A mainline train service connected most of the major trading centres of the

Ottoman Empire, roads were connected to these to provide access to the regions that lacked rail service. However, very much like the development of Spanish railways, in Ottoman Turkey, railroad building fell mostly to foreign financiers who had the capital and technical expertise that the Ottoman government and capitalists lacked. Thus, the government offered concessions to foreign investors who were granted monopolies to operate the lines they built (for a certain number of years, that is); the government also guaranteed profits and paid minimum agreed sums to builders for every kilometre of railroad built. As Shaw and Shaw point out, this project took its toll on the treasury budget, but it did also mean the development of a transportation system that would have otherwise been impossible (1987: 120–2).

The trade agreements that were made with England and other industrial powers at the time meant an influx of foreign merchants starting in the mid-1800s, and these merchants helped to develop industries like silk, carpet-weaving, flour production, olive oil production, glass, canning, paper, and cotton-gin. Minerals were also exploited by foreign industrialists, but as had been the case in Spain, most of the product was shipped back to the home country of the industrialist to help further feed industry in those countries rather than using the materials for developing the Ottoman economy (Shaw and Shaw 1987: 123; see also Issawi 1980: Chapter 5; Pamuk 1987: Chapter 2; Hansen 1991: 294, 301).

Even in the face of foreign competition, the Ottoman Empire did manage to develop some factories themselves. Given that the Empire was almost constantly at war, it is not surprising that these domestic enterprises tended to create materials for this purpose. Thus, government sponsored factories to manufacture uniforms and headgear for the army; later factories also began to produce artillery and rifles, as well as shoes, boots, cartridge belts, etc. However, these were inefficient and poorly run and failed to meet even the domestic needs of the army and state (Shaw and Shaw 1987: 122–3).

The Empire also attempted to modernize agriculture in the late 1800s by helping to finance imported machinery and establishing schools that showed farmers how to use the equipment and taught them other modern farming techniques. Although output did increase, the schemes favoured large landowners and the smaller landowners, who still represented the majority of farmers, continued to use traditional labour-intensive methods. Thus, the Empire appears to have made little headway in shifting workers off of farms, which would have been required for an industrial revolution (Shaw and Shaw 1987: 230–4).

By the start of World War I, there had been no significant increase in urbanization, and Turkey was far less urbanized than other European countries. The exception within Turkey was Istanbul, with 1.3 million people by 1913. However, it was four times the size of the next largest city, Izmir (Hansen 1991: 295).

During the late Ottoman period, much of the Ottoman bourgeoisie consisted of Greeks and Armenians and their expulsion during the 1914–24 period left only a fledgling Muslim bourgeoisie; at the same time, the state was controlled by the party associated with the Ottoman bureaucracy and attempted to direct a state-centred socioeconomic transformation (Keyder 1987: 2). The population exchanges also had a profound effect on the urban population, and urbanization actually decreased (Hansen 1991: 295).

As discussed in previous chapters, when the new Turkish Republic was founded in 1923, one of its primary goals was the accelerated modernization of the Turkish economy and ultimately Turkish society. Initially, policies focussed on providing incentives in the form of capital, which in turn was provided by banks established by government directives. In 1927, the Turkish parliament passed the Law for the Encouragement of Industry, which provided for an extensive range of measures to encourage native industrial development. The provisions included the granting of free land for factories and mines, exempting factories from property, land, and profit taxes and from telephone and telegraph charges; government departments were required to purchase native-made products even if the price was higher and quality lower, and government was authorized to subsidize up to 10 per cent of factory output. In addition, those who built factories under this law were allowed to have monopolies in their fields for 25 years without any government intervention, except to enforce the law itself. Prior to the passage of this law, government had also been actively buying up all of the major foreign-owned industries, particularly public works and natural resource industries (Hershlag 1959: 62–7; Shaw and Shaw 1987: 390).

At the same time that government was promoting industrialization, it also continued with attempts to expand agricultural output. At the time of the founding of the Turkish Republic, there was still a vast expanse of uncultivated land, and the government adopted a policy of distribution to smallholders. The main agriculture-investing bank was also directed to provide loans to these smallholders rather than concentrating only on the large landowners (Hershlag 1959; Hansen 1991: 257).

Government became dissatisfied that these incentives were not producing the rapid growth it expected and began to turn to far more heavy-handed measures, referred to as *etatism*. The system relied on five-year plans, very similar to those in use in the Soviet Union (see Hansen 1991: 323). Although the system was still a mixed economy, government did use its position to try to create major industry. The government did, in fact, make considerable progress toward industrialization. For instance, coal production increased by almost 100 per cent in only a decade (1930–40); chrome production increased by 600 per cent over the same period, and iron and mineral production also increased. The textile industry developed to the point of being able to meet 80 per cent of the country's textile needs. The numbers of kilometres of roads and railroads nearly doubled between 1927 and 1940. National income was on the increase and foreign trade was at surplus levels for the first time since the late 1800s (Hershlag 1959: 127–8,

134; Shaw and Shaw 1987: 395). At the same time, while the growth rate of the manufacturing industry was high in terms of its share of GDP, the impact on employment was modest, as the percentage of the population employed in industry changed only marginally. Industries also continued to be small-scale and family-run (Hansen 1991: 330–1).[11] Moreover, comparative statistics indicate that Turkish coal output (per worker) was still far lower than in countries like the USA and Great Britain (Hershlag 1959: 129), and income in 1938 was far lower than developed countries, as well as Italy, and the standard of living during the inter-war period remained low for most of the population.[12]

As in the other countries studied here, progress virtually came to a halt during World War II. Turkey remained neutral during most of the war, but because the country was under threat of invasion from both the Soviet Union and from Germany it had to remain fully mobilized during the war (Shaw and Shaw 1977: 398; Altuğ and Filiztekin 2006: 19). This meant that much of the male working age population was drafted into military service and that military expenditures took a much higher proportion of the government budget; these were funds that would have previously been directed toward industrial development for civilian purposes. As a result of the lost labour, wheat production fell by 50 per cent and national income declined by an average of 5 per cent per year during the war years (Altuğ and Filiztekin 2006: 19). As in Italy, there were severe shortages of food and other goods, and extreme inflation. For instance, the overall price index in Istanbul increased from 101.4 in 1939 to 354.4 by 1945 (Shaw and Shaw 1977: 398).

Eventually, the Allied powers began to provide Turkey with funds and equipment in exchange for Turkey declaring war on Germany. In addition, US funds in the form of Marshall Plan aid further helped to restore the postwar economy (Hershlag 1959: 203; Shaw and Shaw 1977: 399).[13] Thus, at the end of the war, like Italy, it looked as if the Turkish economy was on the road to recovery, although the economy was not without difficulties. It was in these circumstances that – under pressure from the opposition within the governing party – the country made its first transition to democratic rule.

In 1950, a new democratically elected government came to power promising to relax statist policies and to encourage private enterprise. This approach was successful for the first few years: investment increased, the economy grew rapidly, production increased, including in agriculture, which was increasingly being mechanized. Agricultural output almost doubled, and industrial production more than doubled; coal output doubled, roads were extended, and the number of commercial vehicles and cars on the roads increased tremendously. Factories were being built at unprecedented numbers (Shaw and Shaw 1977: 408). To quote Shaw and Shaw, 'The statistics are impressive, and the mass of Turks certainly benefited. But the tremendous economic expansion was achieved at a price that eventually undermined the regime and seriously threatened democracy itself' (1977: 408).

The problem was that much of the progress was financed with the government budget,[14] which was in chronic debt. The balance of foreign trade was also massively in deficit, and inflation was extremely high (Shaw and Shaw 1977: 409). Thus, despite the apparent progress, the economic situation worsened, and this culminated in 1958 with the government agreeing to a major devaluation and other measures under the auspices of an IMF-sponsored programme (Altuğ and Filiztekin 2006: 19). Recall that the political and economic stability ultimately resulted in a military coup in 1960 and the re-establishment of democracy in 1961.

One important social breakthrough, however, was the introduction of a social-security system in 1950 that consisted of a retirement programme for government employees and other public-sector employees, as well as a partial social-insurance system. Statistics from the 1960–80 period indicate that the system did redistribute substantial amounts of money (Hansen 1991: 350–1; see ILO *Statistical Yearbook of Turkey*, 1979 and 1985; OECD *Economic Survey of Turkey*, 1987). Note that there was no unemployment insurance, though.

In the period immediately following the reestablishment of democracy (the 1960s), there was rapid growth from around 1963. Government pursued import substituting industrialization in a more comprehensive manner than before. For much of the 1960s, Turkey was mentioned as being amongst the more rapidly growing developing economies (Altuğ and Filiztekin 2006: 19). Production in agriculture, manufacturing, construction, etc. increased by more than 35 per cent during 1962–70. By the early 1970s, a favourable foreign-exchange situation based on large foreign workers' remittances allowed the Turkish economy to grow at a rate of about 8–9 per cent until 1975–6 (Altuğ and Filiztekin 2006: 20). The main problem was inflation: the influx of capital from other governments and from organizations like the EEC, World Bank, etc., along with remittances from Turks who had migrated to Europe, produced massive inflation (Shaw and Shaw 1977: 427). By the early 1970s, import substitution policies were taking their toll on the Turkish economy; in 1970, there was a balance of payments crisis (Altuğ and Filiztekin 2006: 19). In addition, in 1975–6, the effects of the first oil shock were apparent. Growth halted. Turkish industry had failed to change its orientation toward exports and to more capital-intensive sectors. The import substitution system had to be stopped as well (Altug and Filiztekin 2006: 20).

In general terms, it appears that the *etatist* policies and import substitution were actually fairly successful, insofar as growth rates remained high and distribution appears to have improved. This was true up until the second half of the 1970s when domestic inflation and foreign borrowing had already increased beyond sustainable levels and foreign lending to Turkey began to dry up. As Hansen argues, one factor that made growth and government-led policy unsustainable was the excessive increase in real wages, a consequence of both the liberalization of the labour market and the legalization of labor unions, which had been guaranteed in the 1961 constitution (1991: 353–4).

Unemployment increased and in the absence of unemployment insurance, the lot of many Turks appears to have worsened. Moreover, despite attempts to alter the taxation system, the bulk of the tax burden fell on wage and salary earners, who suffered increases in real taxation as inflation accelerated and their nominal incomes rose, pushing them into higher tax brackets. It is thus highly likely that economic distribution of after-tax income tended to worsen during the 1970s (Hansen 1991: 382).

In the 1980s, with the liberalization policies being pursued under Özal, first as part of the military's technocratic administration and later as Prime Minister, restrictions on imports were almost totally abolished; measures to liberalize foreign markets were also put in place (Altuğ and Filiztekin 2006: 20; Hansen 1991: Chapter 12). The government invested in infrastructure and the share of government expenditures in current GDP increased from 18 per cent in 1982 to 24 per cent by 1990. However, this was financed by domestic and external borrowing, which had the effect of increasing Turkey's deficit (Altuğ and Filiztekin 2006: 21).

By 1994, the country was again in financial crisis. International capital flows had turned out to be short-term, volatile, 'hot money'. The lira was overvalued and deficits were increasing. A speculative attack on the lira was followed by a devaluation of 150 per cent, skyrocketing overnight interest rates, and inflation reaching 107 per cent. Average inflation in the 1980s had been in the range of 50.4 per cent whereas it increased to 73.2 per cent in the 1990s. GDP was very volatile during the 1990s, declining by 6 per cent in 1994 and by 5 per cent in 1999. It declined by a further 7.5 per cent during the banking and financial crisis of 2000–1 (Altuğ and Filiztekin 2006: 21–2). According to the OECD, the 1990s represent a 'lost decade' in Turkey (Altuğ and Filiztekin 2006: 22). On the positive side, in 1996 the customs union agreement with the EU came into effect and inflation had subsequently declined to single digits by 2004. There was strong output growth in 2003 and 2004 as well as expansion of trade (Altuğ and Filiztekin 2006: 22).

The above discussion points to the possibility that Turkey's economy may have played a role in its failure to consolidate democracy. Although government was clearly making some headway in promoting industrialization, the first transition to democracy came after prolonged failed attempts at state-led economic development. Moreover, this was also the immediate post-World War II era and the overall level of wealth was low. In addition, while there have been some periods of considerable growth since the first transition to democracy, these have been followed by crisis conditions and a subsequent reduced willingness on the part of the international community to continue lending to Turkey. These conditions may have thus made consolidation difficult as wage demands could not be met. The next section provides comparative statistics for our three cases before drawing more definitive conclusions about the effect of economic development and economic crisis on democratic consolidation in the three.

Comparative analysis of macroeconomic statistics

The overviews of economic development in these three countries indicates considerable similarities across the three during their transitions to democracy. Both Turkey and Italy were in a state of extreme poverty, with reduced agricultural production and very limited industrial capacity after World War II, at least in terms of equipment, roads, etc. Also similar to Turkey, Spain experienced extreme inflation and budget deficits during the early days of its transition (between 1975 and 1982 in the latter and the 1950s in the former). All three countries thus faced economic circumstances that did not bode well for establishing stable democracies.

What do the comparative statistics for the three countries indicate, though? First, Table 4.2 indicates that in terms of GDP per capita in the early days of their democratic transitions, Spain was economically in much better shape than Italy or Turkey, with the latter lagging fairly far behind (the key years are highlighted in bold). Table 4.3 provides statistics representing the per cent of GDP earned by agriculture, industry, and services (again with the most relevant periods highlighted in bold). These indicate that both Italy and Spain were considerably more industrialized than Turkey at the time of their democratic transitions. They also indicate that Turkey may have finally begun to catch up with Italy and Spain by the 1990s. On the other hand, Table 4.4 indicates that the problem of inflation was no more difficult in Turkey during its early transition years than was the case in Spain – although the 1970–80 period experienced very high inflation, which may have, in turn, played a role in prompting the 1980 military intervention.

Recall that all three sections above pointed to the importance of Marshall Plan aid or other US-based aid in financing post-war economic development in these three countries. While there is some disagreement as to how much this aid actually helped recipient countries (see, for instance, Wexler 1983), given the near-starvation levels in countries like Italy, it seems that such aid was likely to have been instrumental in paving the way for a more rapid economic recovery than would have otherwise been possible. Moreover, without the aid the new democracies in Italy and Turkey would have very likely been even more destabilized than was the case in these countries.

Table 4.2 Real GDP per capita in international prices (constant prices; US$ at 1985 exchange rate)

	1950	1955	1960	1965	1970	1975	1980	1985	1988
Italy	2548	3377	4375	5315	6937	7775	9986	10,584	11,741
Spain	1823	2497	2701	4161	5208	6413	6514	6433	7406
Turkey	1097	1462	1669	1875	2293	3035	3003	3204	3598

Source: Adapted from Political Data Handbook (Lane *et al.* 1996, Table 4.2).

Table 4.3 Origin of GDP by sector (percentage)

	1950	1960	1970	1980	1990
Agriculture					
Italy	22	12.2	8.1	6.4	3.1
Spain	NA	NA	10.5	7.1	5.3
Turkey	49	40.8	26.7	21.4	16.6
Industry					
Italy	40	41.3	42.9	42.7	33
Spain	NA	NA	37.1	37.9	35
Turkey	15	20.5	24.5	28.6	35.4
Services					
Italy	38	46.5	49	50.9	63.8
Spain	NA	NA	52.4	55	59.7
Turkey	36	38.7	48.8	50	48

Source: Adapted from Political Data Handbook (Lane *et al.* 1996, Table 4.4).

Table 4.4 Inflation: average growth rates (consumer price index)

	1950–60	1960–70	1970–80
Italy	3.0	4.0	14.9
Spain	4.2	6.8	15.9
Turkey	9.5	6.1	32.9

Source: Adapted from Political Data Handbook (Lane *et al.* 1996, Table 4.7).

Given that Turkey was included as one of the recipients of post-war aid, it is worth considering why its economy did not improve in the same way Italy's or Spain's did. First of all, the statistics in Table 4.2 indicate that the level of industrialization may have been far lower in Turkey than in Italy at the end of World War II. Italy already had a very large industrial workforce capable of making the transition to a post-war industrial economy, given a bit of investment. At the same time, Table 4.5 indicates that the overall amount of funds given to Italy and Spain after World War II far exceeded that given to Turkey. Thus, it seems possible that foreign investment in the economies of these countries may have been key in determining their economic development, and in turn, their further development and eventual redistributive capacities.

Moreover, recall that Spain's transitional economy was financed with extreme budget deficits which were partly financed by foreign governments. On the other hand, during key periods of economic difficulty in Turkey, foreign investors refused to continue financing the government's wage increases for workers and other measures designed to keep the economic

Table 4.5 Post-war aid

Country	1948–9	1949–50	1950–1	Cumulative	1950 Population size (in millions)	Cumulative aid per capita (US$)
Italy	594	405	205	1204	47	25
Spain	–	–	–	625	28	22
Turkey	28	59	50	137	21	6.5

Note
The figures provided for Italy and Turkey are the levels of Marshall fund aid given to these countries; Spain did not receive Marshall Plan aid, and the figure in the table represents the amount given to Spain in the 1951–7 period. The former are adapted from en.wikipedia.org/wiki/Marshall_Plan (consulted 26 April 2007); the latter is adapted from Harrison 1985, pp. 133–4).

situation stable while the democratic transition was under way. In essence, policy-makers in Turkey simply did not have the foreign investment tools that were available to Spain. At the same time, it may also be worth considering why foreign governments were hesitant about continuing to invest in the Turkish economy, which may have been connected to political instability.

Conclusions

Based on the above analyses, it appears that differences in economic development may have had some impact on differences in democratic consolidation in Italy, Spain, and Turkey. Recall that it was argued that there were two main aspects of development to consider, industrialization and overall wealth. In terms of the former, despite government attempts to promote industrialization, Turkey's industrialization lagged behind that of Italy and Spain's during much of its transitional period. What are the implications of this? First, weak industrialization implies the lack of development of a strong middle class or business class that might have been able to press government leaders, including the military, to avoid constant breakdowns of democracy; part of the reason they were unable to do so was precisely because they did not represent a large enough sector to allow them to become a large party with largely similar economic interests that required the maintenance of democratic institutions. Second, weak industrialization implies a small working class as well, and according to some researchers (such as Rueschemeyer *et al.* 1992), this class is often the one that presses for improvements in democratic norms and institutions. On the other hand, this class was clearly growing in Turkey, particularly in the 1960s and 1970s and was becoming more active and organized (see Chapter 6). Some might contend that this was, in fact, partly what led to subsequent moves away from democracy.

Turkey has also lagged behind Italy and Spain in terms of overall wealth. The implication of this is that when the working classes began to make demands involving better social-welfare provisions, the government and economic elites were unable to oblige, prompting further strikes and radical behaviour. This, in turn, could have contributed to the collapse of democracy and continued failure to fully consolidate.

However, it is also important to consider the fact that Spain managed to create a stable democratic system despite facing economic (and political) crisis in the late 1970s and early 1980s. This would seem to indicate that democratic consolidation *can*, in fact, occur despite the existence of very problematic economic circumstances.

Was economic development then the key factor in the differential outcomes across the three countries? Clearly it may have been important, but it is also clear that countries in the midst of economic crisis can adopt stable democratic institutions. The remaining chapters consider how this might be possible.

5 Constitution building

Arend Lijphart has put forth the notion of consensualism to describe the functioning of some types of democratic institutions. This idea will be discussed further in Chapters 6 and 7, but the general notion behind Lijphart's argument is that some democratic institutions are designed to promote consensual decision-making whereas others are designed to promote a more conflictual style of decision-making. The idea of consensualism can also be applied to the initial design of those institutions via the process of creating a constitution. For scholars like Lijphart, deep divisions in society (which are often reflected in elite issue positions) have the potential to disrupt democracy if significant portions of that society are permanently excluded from the decision-making process by the institutions of democracy. Thus, the need to build consensus in such systems is an ongoing problem, but one that may guarantee the very existence of the institutions themselves. It can also be argued that the development of a constitution and institutions that are acceptable to the key (elite) players in a country at the time of that country's transition to democracy is equally important. This is because these are the participants that are likely to have the power to undermine the newly developing system, either indirectly by withholding support or directly by co-opting those with control over mechanisms of force into bringing about a collapse of democracy.

Similarly, Giuseppe di Palma (1990) contends that the key to launching a successful democracy is a 'negotiated transition', whereby all major players participate in the discussions, even those who may have also participated in undermining democracy previously or were leaders in the previous non-democratic regime. For di Palma, the important point is that the old elite from the non-democratic regime must be given an opportunity to compete in the new political system because otherwise they will not cooperate with the new order. Moreover, the rules themselves must be designed such that these old elite believe themselves to have a realistic opportunity of continuing to govern. This chapter extends this general idea and argues that no matter what the role of elites in the previous regime, they must be allowed to negotiate the rules of the new regime; otherwise, as di Palma points out, they have strong incentives to attempt to undermine the system at every opportunity, or to withhold support at crucial times.

This chapter examines the constitution-building process in Italy, Spain, and Turkey. The findings from this chapter and the next point to the conclusion that while the institutions that are adopted at the outset of the new regime may not actually be all that consensual (e.g. Spain), obtaining agreement amongst the major contenders for power on the nature of these institutions (as in Spain and Italy) is likely to be important in ensuring later cooperation and cooptation. The contrasting case examined in this chapter is Turkey, where constitutional design has proceeded with most of the impetus for change coming from military leaders, in consultation with a limited range of other elites. Ultimately, those who participated in the actual functioning of the democracy as elected officials have generally had little input into the initial rules and institutional design, thereby potentially undermining support for the new system (see Özbudun 1998). Therefore, it is argued in this chapter that one of the main explanations for the failings of Turkish democracy is the unwillingness to put such major decision-making into the hands of elected elites, and forcing them to come to some form of lasting compromise regarding the functioning of the democratic institutions.[1]

The creation of the 1948 Italian constitution

The development of acceptable rules of the new Italian regime after the end of World War II was fundamentally dependent on the particular configuration of key players at the time. Not surprisingly, during the last couple of years of the war there were multiple players jockeying for different sorts of agreements that they believed would influence the running of the regime. The first of the institutions that had to be considered was the monarchy. Although the monarchy continued to exist during Mussolini's dictatorship, it was clearly subordinated to the dictator. In many ways, once it became clear that fascism was on its way out, the monarch was perceived by many (including himself) as being the only real player in Italy who had the authority to act on behalf of Italians.[2] Nonetheless, this idea was highly contested.

Toward the end of the war, in 1943, Italy was essentially divided into two zones – the North which was occupied by Germany and the South which was still under the control of the monarch. There was considerable resistance to German occupation in the North, however, and this resistance was highly organized and worked in collaboration with the Allied powers who had begun their invasion of Italy. The organized resistance comprised three different components. The first consisted of organized groups that had always been opposed to Mussolini and fascism; by the end of the war, many of the leaders of these groups were in exile or in prison, but many of those in exile returned to Italy to help fight off the encroaching German troops. The most important player in this group was perhaps the Communists. The group had suffered under fascism, but it had remained fairly organized nevertheless. There were other players in this category as well, particularly the Socialists and the newly formed 'Justice and Liberty' Brigades of the Action Party. The latter were firmly committed to establishing democracy in Italy, as well as a capitalist economic framework, but were not economic liberals in the sense that they also wanted the regime to also pursue policies that would correct the distortions of a market system. The desires of the former two groups would have initially been highly ambiguous. Were they planning to replace fascism with communism, for instance? As it turns out, the Communists in particular made it clear that they wanted to persuade the other resistance groups to join the royal government (see Chapter 6). Note that the communists were strongly opposed to the monarchy, but they were clearly willing to sacrifice this position to rid Italy of fascism.

The other two major anti-fascist parties were the Liberals and the Christian Democrats. Recall that the Liberals had participated in bringing Mussolini into government in the first place. By this time, they realized this had been a fatal error, but their desire was simply to return Italy to its pre-fascist state. At the start of the Nazi occupation of Italy, the third group, the Christian Democrats were still organizing themselves and so were not yet a major force.

None of the groups mentioned above were numerically strong enough individually to serve as a clear resistance to Nazi occupation, and so in 1944, they came together to form the National Committee of Liberation. There is no doubt that the CNL played a key role in helping the Allies win control over Italy from Germany. In at least one case – the freeing of Genoa – the Committee appeared to play *the* key role. Thus, in terms of military power, many in the CNL felt that they should have been the natural group to take over governing toward the end of the war (see Ginsborg 1990 for a more thorough overview of Italy during and immediately after the war).

Given that there were fundamentally different views on who or what should exercise ultimate sovereignty in Italy after the war, one of the main decisions that had to be made was whether Italy was to continue to be a monarchy or if it was to convert itself into a republic. This was a contentious issue within the CNL itself and one which had the potential to fundamentally divide one of the parties, the Christian Democrats. It was therefore decided to allow Italians to make the decision by voting in a referendum. The result of the 1946 referendum was 54.2 per cent against the monarchy and 45.8 per cent in favour. Immediately following the vote, the king stalled for time and tried to argue that the Republicans had only won a majority of valid votes rather than all votes cast (i.e. including those who spoiled their ballots). There were rumours of a possible military coup in support of the king, but 11 days after the ballot, the king went into exile (Ginsborg 1990: 98–9). Therefore, an issue that had the potential to split the leaders of the CNL was resolved relatively peacefully; once the public had made their views clear, it would have been difficult for those supporting the king and the monarchy to contest these wishes.[3]

The popular vote on abolishing the monarchy helped pave the way for the creation of full democracy in Italy, but what kind of democracy would it be? A presidential system, a parliamentary system? And what specific rules would regulate the relations between different governing bodies? It was argued in the introduction to this chapter that this phase of the democratic transition is terribly important, not only because the institutions that are chosen may themselves have an impact on the likelihood of survival of the democracy (see Chapter 7) but because the agreements made at this stage must be acceptable to the key actors in the regime. If any major groups or their representatives are excluded from the process itself, those groups are likely to believe that the rules have been designed in such a way that they fail to benefit them and therefore will have every incentive to undermine the new institutions, thereby destabilizing the democracy. So what was the Italian approach to constitutional design, then?

The Italian case is one in which constitutional design proceeded in a fairly consensual manner. At the same time as the referendum on the monarchy, voters were asked to choose representatives to a Constitutional Assembly. It is the groups that were elected to this assembly that were the major powers in Italy at the time, and so it is these group leaders who had to come to an agreement about the nature of the constitution. So who were these groups?

Table 5.1 provides a summary of the percentage of votes and seats each party received in the 1946 election. Recall that the Christian Democrats (DC) had still been trying to organize themselves in 1944. Clearly they managed to do so. By 1946, they had converted themselves to a mass-based party with a wide appeal. They became one of the primary outlets for the capitalist bourgeois class, as the other natural outlets (e.g. the Liberals) proved to be a weak, elitist party; they also appealed to family values and aimed their ideas at 'believers of all social classes' (Ginsborg 1990: 75). The key turning point for the party seems to have been the Vatican's support, granted in the summer of 1944. Along with the Church's verbal support came the support of the Church's main civil society organization, Catholic Action. Thus, the largest single group within the Constituent Assembly represented a conglomeration of interests, and at times was internally divided itself, particularly over social-welfare issues (see Chapter 6). The

Table 5.1 The 1946 Italian Constituent Assembly

Party	Votes	Seats (%)
Christian Democrats	35.2	38.1
Socialists	20.7	21.2
Communists	19.0	19.2
Others	25.1	21.5

Source: Adapted from en.wikipedia.org/wiki/Italian_general_election,_1946 (consulted 15 July 2007).

party was not the natural ally of the bourgeoisie, but the leadership wanted to ensure continued support of this group in the design of the constitution.

Amongst the left-leaning groups, it had been expected that the Communists would be the largest force. The fact that they came in third was a blow to the leadership and very likely dictated a higher level of compliance and negotiation than might have been required if the party had won the plurality of seats in the Constituent Assembly. It is not clear as to why the party performed relatively poorly, other than the fact that – as mentioned above – the Catholic-based party managed to do very well. Also, many Italians are likely to have still recalled the leftist strikes that were associated with bringing the previous democratic regime down and making fascism possible. Even with the disappointing results for the Communist Party, when combined with the socialist share of the seats, it is clear that the leftist parties were equal in strength to the Christian Democrats. Either of these camps (the left of the right) could have attempted to negotiate a new constitution with other parties and ignored one another, and indeed the Christian Democrats probably could have succeeded in creating a constitution that would be acceptable to these other small groups. However, the main parties did indeed negotiate amongst themselves and with the smaller parties on the specific provisions of the constitution. Ultimately, the constitution was approved in the Assembly by a vote of 453 to 62, with only the extreme right voting against (see Hine 1993; Sassoon 1997: Chapter 12; Foot 2003: 62–70). This in itself is a testament to the consensual nature of the document. But what were some of the key negotiated provisions?[4]

A key area of compromise was in the realm of devolution. One of the themes being emphasized by DC leaders was the need to create a constitution that had as many layers as possible between the state and the individual in order to try to provide a wide array of institutional counter-balances to the national government. It was believed this would help prevent the rise of fascism in the future. Thus, the Christian Democrats promoted strong local and regional governments and pushed for a fairly federalist system, in which the regions would have legislative powers that were outlined in the constitution. At the time, Italian Communists were opposed to the idea of decentralization, but were won over by the argument that decentralization could promote the development of unions and parties at the local level, which the Communists favoured. The compromise was that the principle of devolution was included in the Constitution but much of the devolution process would require enabling legislation for its implementation (see Chapter 8; Sassoon 1997: Chapter 12).[5]

Another issue that was to prove difficult was the role of the Church. The PCI would have preferred to make Italy a constitutionally secular state but was faced with the reality of a very religious society and with the reality that the arrangements made by Mussolini via the Lateran Pacts had helped to legitimize the Italian state. Thus, the PCI recognized that there would need to be some constitutional provision recognizing the Church. Their preferred

text was: 'The State recognizes the sovereignty of the Catholic Church within the juridical order of the Church itself. The relations between the State and Church are determined by both' (quoted in Sassoon 1997: 214). The DC proposed the following: 'The State and the Catholic Church are, each in its own order, independent and sovereign. Their relationships are regulated by the Lateran Pacts. Modifications of the pacts, which have been accepted by the two sides do not require constitutional amendment' (quoted in Sassoon 1997: 214). The article did not satisfy the Socialists, but the PCI voted for it, and this was the adopted provision.

Striking a balance between protecting the bourgeoisie and providing social rights for the working classes was also difficult. After compromises amongst the leftist parties, liberal parties, and the Christian Democrats, Article 1 of the Constitution stated that 'Italy is a democratic republic founded on labour' and Article 4 enshrines the 'right to work' (Sassoon 1997: 209). Article 40 enshrines the right to strike but also specifies that the right must be exercised 'within the spheres of laws which regulated it'. This article had been a point of controversy, with the DC arguing that civil servants should not have the right to strike while the PCI trade-union leader insisted there should be no legal restriction. The text of the article is a compromise which establishes a right to strike but not an absolute one (see Sassoon 1997).

One of the most controversial parts of the constitution was Article 3, containing two sections. In the first paragraph, there was a declaration of formal equality for all: 'All citizens have equal social dignity and are equal before the law, without distinction of sex, of race, of language, or religion, of political opinion, of personal and social condition.' According to the second paragraph:

> It is the task of the Republic to remove the obstacles of an economic and social nature which, limiting in fact the liberty and equality of citizens, prevent the full development of the human personality and the effective participation by all workers in the political, economic and social organization of the country'. The combination of these two is ambiguous, but there is strong evidence that the intentions of the legislators were radical.
>
> (Sassoon 1997: 210–11)[6]

Just as the Christian Democrats and other parties with bourgeois leanings were willing to negotiate on these provisions that were put forth by the left, the left was also willing to negotiate on the issue of private property, even though this concept is anathema to communist ideology. Thus, the protection of private property is endorsed in Articles 41 and 42. Article 41 represents a clear trade-off between bourgeois capitalist interests and those of the socialists and communists. It states that 'private economic initiative is free', with a limiting clause that it should not develop 'in conflict with social utility or in such a manner as to damage security, liberty and human dignity'. The article goes on to specify that legislation could try to coordinate the public and private sectors of the economy towards social ends, thus giving constitutional legitimacy to economic planning (Sassoon 1997: 211–12). Similarly Article 42 on private property is a clear compromise. It recognized private property *and* state property or other forms of collective property such as cooperatives. It also gave nationalization of industry a degree of constitutional validity by asserting that 'private property may be expropriated with compensation for reasons of general interest' (Sassoon 1997: 212).

One key issue that was not all that difficult to address had to do with the power of the executive versus the parliament. Faced with the dissolution of the monarchy, the Constituent Assembly had to decide whether to adopt a presidential system similar to that of the US or a parliamentary system. They decided on a weak presidency and a parliamentary system in which the parliament would be relatively powerful vis-à-vis the prime minister. This represented a relatively easy convergence on the part of the DC and PCI. Recall that the DC at this point was still suspicious of state power and was trying to keep executive powers to a minimum. The PCI, for its part, wanted a strong parliament and weak executive because they realized that their electoral weight would ensure them a major role in parliament, while the onset of the Cold War could (and would) preclude them from government (Hine 1993).

Overall then, the process of writing the 1948 democratic constitution in Italy appears to have been a fairly consensual one. Concessions were made by both major blocs – the left-leaning Communists and Socialists as well as the centre-right Christian Democrats. Although the consensual behaviour broke down to some extent as soon as the constitution was adopted (see Chapter 7), the fact that all major parties had agreed to the ground rules is likely to have helped ensure compliance with those basic rules of governance. Thus, even when the country was once again faced with turbulent times in the 1960s that were similar to those of the early 1920s, political elites continued to operate through the parliament to effect change. This could partly be a result of the dire consequences that resulted from failing to cooperate in the 1920s, but it also seems very unlikely that cooperation would have necessarily been guaranteed after 1948 if the key groups had not agreed initially to the rules of the democratic game.

The Italian case points to the potential importance of constitutional settlements in helping to create stable consolidated democracy. Previous Italian constitutions had not been written in a consensual manner and were simply various iterations of the old Piedmontese constitution. Of course, given the existence of the extreme left in Italian politics from the start of the twentieth century, it is entirely possible that the creation of a consensus on a new constitution would have been impossible in any case. The post-war settlement was built upon new-found common ground across all major parties that institutions must be designed to prevent the rise of fascism again. Those institutions then in turn were used by the parties to create a consensual political system whereby major interests could gain representation and have a say in policy-making. This is an issue that will be discussed further in Chapters 6 and 7. For now we turn to the question of constitution-making in Spain. What techniques were used in the design of the Spanish constitution, and what is thought to be the impact of these techniques on consolidation?

Spain's 1978 constitution[7]

One of the failings of the Spanish Second Republic had been the failure to design basic rules and agreements in the consensual manner described above. In particular, the Constituent Assembly that designed the 1931 constitution included mostly democrats and republicans and excluded the more conservative right-wing elements. As a result, many of the provisions included in that constitution, such as the provisions regarding the church – including the banning of Jesuit orders and the possibility of banning other teaching by religious orders, along with removal of state support for religious orders, and the eventual confiscation of Church property – provoked a walkout of the right-wing minority and the resignation of two prominent Catholic Republican ministers in the Constituent Assembly (Payne 1993: 62). Another point of contention was the issue of devolution and regional powers, which were incorporated in the institutional design in 1931 despite clear hostility to this idea on the part of the right. Not surprisingly, once the right had managed to reorganize itself, it halted and even reversed many of these policies. Ultimately, the legitimacy of the political regime, which had been founded on the basis of secularism and regional autonomy, was in question right from the start. By the time of Franco's death in 1975, these were still highly contentious issues in Spain and it was perceived that the manner in which they were addressed could produce yet another civil war. What was the strategy of post-Franco elites for constitutional design?

The situation faced by constitution writers who were trying to design Spain's new democratic institutions was fairly different from that faced by Italy's Constituent Assembly. In Italy, the fascist regime had been discredited by its poor performance during the Second World War, and so a rupture from that fascist past was possible. When Franco died, on the other hand, his form of fascism was not discredited, and there were elites within the regime who believed Francoist values and ideas should continued to be pursued. Thus, democratic reformers were faced with a far more ambiguous situation than was the case in Italy, in that they needed to develop a constitution that would be acceptable to Falangist Francoists. This section briefly reviews the process by which the initiation for reform came about in the first place, and then explains how the Constitutional designers addressed seemingly disparate desires for both democracy and continuation with Francoist ideas.

Prior to Franco's death, there were already many in the regime who were in favour of significant reform; at the same time, there were many others who preferred to continue with the regime Franco established, but with the new monarchy – re-established by Franco himself in the Law of Succession of 1947 – as the head of state. The monarch, Juan Carlos, however, was in favour of reform, and a few months after Franco's death managed to appoint a new prime minister (Adolfo Suárez) to lead the reform process. Many would argue that his choice of prime minister was brilliant; Heywood refers to it as 'inspired' (Heywood 1995: 41). Although initially Suárez seemed an unlikely candidate to push through any sort of major reform because he was seen as a loyal Francoist, it soon became clear that he would indeed do just that. The reason the choice is thought to be 'inspired' is that it ensured that the democratic transition would be led by an individual who was more or less trusted by the hard-line Francoists. If King Juan Carlos had selected someone who was clearly in the reform-minded camp, any attempted reforms would have likely sparked conflict and the reforms themselves would have been halted.

Thus, Prime Minister Suárez managed to convince the Francoist assembly that reform of some sort was necessary and inevitable, but that they could be part of this reform process. He managed to convince them to potentially vote the Franco regime out of existence and vote themselves out of a job by getting them to pass the Law for Political Reform in 1976. According to this law, the assembly would be abolished and a new parliament would be established, with a popularly elected lower chamber (see Chapter 7). Also of importance was that the law guaranteed continued strong executive powers for both the prime minister – referred to as the 'president of the government' in Spain – and the king, and also guaranteed that Suárez would have strong powers to manage the period leading up to the first elections. He was also instrumental in creating an electoral system that would favour large parties and rural areas, thereby creating the potential for a conservative party to win a majority or plurality of seats in the newly established parliament.

The potential gamble paid off and Suárez's newly established party, the Union of the Democratic Centre (UDC; see Chapter 6), which contained many of the key Franquist elites, won the most seats in the lower house of the Cortes. This meant that the UDC was able to lead the way in setting the agenda of the Cortes, and the main item on Suárez's agenda was the writing of a new constitution. Again, it is of tremendous importance that he and his party were able to lead this process. If, for instance, a left-leaning party had won the most seats in parliament and had been in charge of reforms, the Francoist hardliners would have very likely resisted the reforms.

Given the difficulties that had plagued attempts at creating democratic institutions in Spain previously, it is not surprising that there were a few key issues that would prove to be fairly contentious, and the stability of the post-Franco settlement was likely to hinge upon how these issues were addressed constitutionally. Some of these were quite similar to the questions facing Italian constitutional designers after World War II. For instance, in Spain, the role of the Catholic Church was still contentious. Also potentially contentious was whether Spain was to remain a monarchy or not, as was the case in Italy.

For both Italy and Spain, whether the country was to be unitary or federal was also a point of contention, but for different reasons. In Italy, the centre-right favoured decentralization as a check on executive power, while the left was opposed because of the ideological inconsistency of this with communist ideology. In Spain, the issues raised did not revolve around checks on the executive but instead had to do with the fact that some regions in the country claim a unique, non-Spanish territorial identity, as discussed in Chapters 2 and 8. Even though Franco had tried to obliterate these sentiments, he had failed and probably only increased separatist identity as a result of the use of repressive tactics (see Chapter 8). Therefore, in contrast to Italy where there was not a strong sense of territorial nationalism pushing the country toward federalism (other than in a few peripheral regions, to be discussed in Chapter 8), in Spain, there *is* a strong sense of nationalism, particularly amongst the Basques and Catalans. Moreover, traditionally, the left in Spain had been strongly in favour of a federal Spain which would give the regions far greater powers of governance, essentially sharing power with the central government in Madrid. This was, in fact, one of the policies that sparked the Spanish Civil War. Recall that prior to the outbreak of war, government changed hands between left-wing and right-wing parties and that the left-wing parties would adopt decentralizing policies, which the right-wing government rescinded. It was shortly after the left-wing government returned to power and once again pursued decentralization that war broke out in 1936. Even by 1975, both sides still maintained the same positions on this issue that they had held in the 1930s (and long before). Thus, the handling of territorial issues in the new constitution was clearly going to be a major source of conflict.

How were each of these contentious issues resolved then? We begin with the monarchy. It is argued that King Juan Carlos's actions themselves helped to ensure that the monarchy would be retained. By pursuing a democratic transition, he helped to guarantee that the aims of the left to establish a republic would not be fulfilled. The left also wanted to avoid a potential backlash against the creation of a republic (as had been the case in 1936), and thus accepted the monarch as the head of state.

Territorial issues were addressed by several constitutional provisions and will be discussed at greater length in Chapter 8. It is important to note that the way potential conflict over this question was resolved appears to be simply by including ambiguous and contradictory constitutional provisions in which each camp could recognize their own positions. For instance, Article 2 of the Constitution states that

> The Constitution is based on the indissoluble unity of the Spanish Nation, common and indivisible country of all Spaniards, and recognizes and

guarantees the right to autonomy of the nationalities and regions of which it is comprised and solidarity amongst them.

As Heywood (1995) argues, this is a fairly extraordinary provision because it seems to both prevent the possibility of regional autonomy (in the first part of the provision) but also create the possibility for it to occur. Moreover, the meaning of 'autonomy' was left unspecified, and was apparently used in different ways by those writing the constitution. Provisions like these have created subsequent problems in governing, but they may have been key to guaranteeing initial cooperation with the new regime.

The role of the Catholic Church was not nearly as contentious as it had been in Italy after the World War II. The Church itself had changed dramatically by 1975 and had already begun to distance itself from the Franco regime. Thus, many in the Church hierarchy were clear about their desire to see a separation of church and state. Still, there were others in the hierarchy who were concerned about the loss of influence of the Church over policies like divorce and education. Also, the hardliners within the Franco regime would have still been very committed to maintaining a strong role for Catholicism in the new democracy, particularly with their growing concerns about moral degradation (see Chapter 9). In an attempt to address these differing perspectives, Article 16 disestablishes Roman Catholicism as the official religion of the state and provides that religious liberty for non-Catholics is a state-protected legal right, but it also states that 'The public authorities shall take the religious beliefs of Spanish society into account and shall maintain the consequent relations of cooperation with the Catholic Church and the other confessions'. In addition, Article 27 provoked controversy by appearing to pledge continuing government subsidies for private, church-affiliated schools, something that the left adamantly opposed. The Constitution, however, includes no mention of the fact that the majority of Spaniards are Catholics or that the state should take into account the teachings of Catholicism. Thus, as was the case with devolution and decentralization, the constitution was relatively vague in order to try to accommodate the main interests on this issue.

For the sake of accommodating major interests, even Franco's army was granted pride of place in the constitution. Section 8 of the preamble states that

> The mission of the Armed Forces, comprising the Army, the Navy and the Air Force, is to guarantee the sovereignty and independence of Spain and to defend its territorial integrity and the constitutional order.

This provision was clearly incorporated very much like the others mentioned above – it was somewhat ambiguous and designed to keep military officers happy and thus prevent them from interfering with the transition. As will be shown in Chapter 9, however, this strategy was not entirely successful.

The design of the constitution in Spain was clearly helped by the fact that the major party leaders were willing to compromise. The leaders of the Communist Party, Santiago Carrillo, and the Socialist Party, Felipe González, had already previously come to the conclusion that the only way to prevent the country from continuing on the path of authoritarianism was to compromise with the Suárez government. This was the approach that was used after the initial elections as well. Thus, as in Italy, it was tremendous sacrifice and compromise particularly on the part of the left that helped to create a smooth transition.

Turkish constitutional design and failed democratic consolidation

We now turn to a discussion of constitution writing in Turkey. Because three different constitutions have governed the Turkish Republic during its post-war transition period, I outline the process of writing each of these constitutions, as well as highlight some of the main features of the three Turkish constitutions.

As discussed in previous chapters, the Turkish transition to democracy did not come as a result of a sudden and dramatic event like defeat in war or the death of a dictator. At the time of the opening up to multiparty politics in the mid-1940s in Turkey, there was already a constitution in place. This was the 1924 Constitution. In fact, one scholar wrote about that constitution: 'The Constitution of 1924, if it is faithfully carried out, will provide Turkey with a representative and democratic government' (Earle 1925: 86). This same academic went on to write that 'Fear has been expressed that the great personal prestige of Mustapha Kemal Pasha, combined with his leadership of the Popular Party and his constitutional prerogatives, might lead to the gradual transformation of the republic into a virtual dictatorship' (Earle 1925: 87). These fears were not unfounded, as the Turkish 'Republic' was rapidly transformed into a one-party state, with severe restrictions on party formation and organization of the opposition. Still, as Earle (1925) argues, the constitution itself appears to create democratic institutions, particularly a parliament in which all sovereign powers were to reside and which has the power to dismiss the executive. This consists of a president selected from within the Parliament, a prime minister selected by the president, and a cabinet selected by the prime minister, all approved by the parliament.[8] Freedom of conscience, thought, press, assembly, and association are all mentioned as 'natural rights of Turks' (Article 70 of the 1924 Constitution), 'personal liberty shall not be restricted or interfered with except as provided by law' (Article 72 of the 1924 Constitution), and 'torture, corporal punishment, confiscation and extortion are prohibited' (Article 73 of the 1924 Constitution).

It was this same constitution that was in force when elections were opened up to competition in the 1940s. When a new government came to power in 1950, this government saw no need to initiate constitutional change and so the same constitution remained in effect. Thus, it was the 1924 constitution that governed the first ten years of Turkey's democratic transition.

So how was this 1924 constitution designed? Was it the result of consensual decision-making amongst the key Turkish elites at the time? It is difficult to argue that it was. Prior to the creation of the constitution, crucial decisions on maintenance of the monarchy (the sultanate) and the role of religion (the Caliphate) were made by an Assembly dominated by those supporting Mustafa Kemal. Moreover, the Assembly that designed the 1924 Constitution was also dominated by Kemalists. Those with more traditional leanings and those who might have preferred to try to incorporate traditionalism and religious values into the Constitution were generally absent. Therefore, the Constitution would have been seen as a text created by a fairly minor section of elite interests rather than being designed by all major 'groups'. It must also be noted that at the time of the drafting of the constitution, however, unlike the cases of Italy and Spain, there were no coherent or semi-coherent groups or party-like organizations to speak of. Thus, representing differing sectors of Turkish society via groups like parties or unions would have been extraordinarily difficult. Even so, the writing of the constitution could have been postponed until groups had had a chance to form. However, the conduct of the elections themselves made it clear that the leadership did not yet trust citizens, and the final decision regarding who would be selected for parliament was restricted by Kemal and his party. It was argued that until voters had the social and political skills with which to make an informed decision, it would be best to restrict the range of possible candidates who could be elected. In short, the electors to the Grand National Assembly in Turkey in 1923 were far from representative of the mass public (Shaw and Shaw 1977; Özbudun 1998). Thus, it is not clear how far the constitution they designed was legitimate.

In 1961 a new constitution was designed. The impetus for the creation of a completely new constitution came from the 1960 military coup that overthrew a government that was perceived as using increasingly repressive techniques to stifle opposition criticism and competition. Importantly, the party that had been in government prior to the 1960 coup – the Democratic Party – was banned at the time of the writing of the new constitution. The design of the new constitution was conducted by a constituent assembly, but the group of officers who had carried out the coup constituted one of the two chambers of the assembly (these officers had organized themselves into the National Unity Committee). The other chamber of the assembly was civilian, but only one-third was selected by elections, and these elections were not direct. The rest of the civilian chamber (the House of Representatives) was appointed by Mustafa Kemal's party, the Republican People's Party, as well as the head of state (a military general), the National Unity Committee, the judiciary, and trade unions. Supporters of the banned Democratic Party were not represented in the Constituent Assembly. In essence, the constitution was designed by one particular party – the Republican People's Party – under strict supervision of the military (Özbudun 1998). Given that the banned Democratic Party had won clear majorities in the Turkish parliament prior to the 1960 coup, it can be assumed that this group of elites – more so than those in the Constituent Assembly – represented the majority of Turkish public opinion. To exclude it from discussions on the development of a new constitution would thus seem to create significant legitimacy problems. Indeed, when the successor to the banned party, the newly formed Justice Party, came to power in 1965, its leaders were extremely critical of the rules established in the 1961 constitution. It seems highly likely that if they had been participants in developing the rules and rules had been developed that were acceptable to all, the legitimacy of the system would have been far less questionable and elites would have learned to work within this system rather than questioning it right from the start.

Instead, politics became far more radicalized (see the next chapter), and after a 'soft' coup in 1971, amendments were added to the constitution strengthening the executive by giving it decree powers, curtailing some civil liberties, and increasing the autonomy of the military by excluding it from being reviewed by civilian courts. Political instability and violence continued to increase, and once again, in 1980 there was another military coup. Rather than looking to examples of other constitutional design processes (such as Italy or Spain) and adopting those, the military pursued a very similar design process that was used after the 1960 coup. These officials seemed to believe that it was the rules themselves that mattered but did not appear to grasp the fact that the process of writing the rules may matter more. The rules were thus changed considerably: the 1961 Constitution had developed a system which would allow for checks and balances to try to avoid the pre-1960 situation in which a single party could dominate and use the rules to create an authoritarian system. For instance, the electoral system in 1960 was changed to proportional representation in hopes that it would encourage the need for coalition governments, as it was unlikely that a single party would win enough seats under PR to govern alone. In addition, a second chamber of parliament had been created which would consist of those with university-level education, a Constitutional Court had been created to serve as a check on government's authority, and the autonomy of universities and the media increased (Özbudun 1998; see also Dodd 1969).

Not surprisingly, the 1982 Constitution was a direct reaction to the problems that resulted from these rules. The legislature was again reduced to a single chamber, and executive powers were increased. However, these new rules were not designed in such a way as to accommodate the key interests of the time. Instead, the assembly writing the constitution once again consisted of two chambers, one of which was the National Security Council (created by the 1961 Constitution); the other chamber – the Consultative Committee – was appointed by the National Security Council. In addition, the NSC had the power to amend or reject the constitutional draft that was prepared by the Consultative Assembly. During the ratification process, a decree was issued prohibiting the expression of any views on the constitution that were intended to influence voters, and military leaders were able to conduct a pro-constitution campaign without any opposition. Importantly, no individuals who had been party members in the previous parliament were eligible for membership in the Consultative Assembly that designed the constitution (see Özbudun 1998 for a more thorough review of constitution writing in Turkey).

Thus, the document that resulted from the assembly's work can hardly be considered to have been created in a consensual way, and it is argued that this – as with the 1961 constitution – has created severe legitimacy problems for the Turkish Republic. In addition, some of the rules themselves created by the 1982 constitution push Turkey into the realm of quasi-democracy. Namely, provisions restricting freedom of expression, freedom of the press, and freedom of association were incorporated (the next chapter outlines why this was the case), and the role of the National Security Council was increased. Under these rules, it is not clear that Turkey could continue with its transition to fully consolidated democracy.

However, since 2001, the Turkish parliament has passed significant measures to change the Constitution as well as the Turkish penal code to make these more consistent with those of consolidated democracies. First, the role of the National Security Council is argued to have been down-graded: the number of civilian members was increased from five to nine while the number of military representatives was held at five. In addition, rather than being required to give the recommendations of the NSC 'priority consideration', the government is now required to 'evaluate' these recommendations.[9] Other significant changes have included a prohibition on torture, giving it constitutional status, adding the right to fair trial to the constitution, abolishing the death penalty,[10] altering the allowed detention periods of those accused of criminal activity, and lifting the ban on statements and publications in languages other than Turkish. However, while there has been some attempt to put the rights of the individual in higher standing vis-à-vis the rights of the state, there are still provisions of the constitution that could easily be used for the purpose of restricting freedom. For instance, Article 14 states that 'None of the rights and freedoms embodied in the Constitution shall be exercised with the aim of violating the indivisible integrity of the state with its territory and nation, and endangering the existence of the democratic and secular order of the Turkish Republic'. However, governments since 2001 have adopted further legislation protecting freedom of expression and assembly, as well as legislation that attempts to curb the military's power by reducing the number of meetings of the NSC and reducing the powers of the secretary-general of the NSC.[11]

It is also important to note that government officials in the present day appear to be cognizant of the potential importance of consensualism in constitutional design. For instance, the ruling party in 2005 (the Justice and

Development Party) tried to convert Turkey into a semi-presidential system similar to France. Although the party could have apparently turned to minor parties for support for this revision (which would be a major change to the constitution), the party's leadership instead was keen to make sure that the key opposition party, Mustafa Kemal's Republican People's Party, also agreed to the reform. So far the measure has failed and the ruling party has decided to allow the issue to be decided in a referendum.[12]

Conclusions

As discussed previously, democracies can be very fragile sorts of regimes, and they are unlikely to function properly without fundamental agreement on the basic rules. Rules designed exclusively by one group are unlikely to be respected by others, nor does the group that designed the rules in the first place have any incentive to remain faithful to them since the opposition is unlikely to help guarantee enforcement. In fact, it may be the case that the rules themselves, while affecting the way a democracy functions, have less of an effect on the durability of democracy than the manner in which the rules were constructed. The Spanish Civil War appears to have been a direct result of failure on the part of elites representing important groups to agree on the basics, and as will be illustrated in Chapter 6 breakdowns in Turkish democracy may have also resulted from failures to bring about consensus on the basic rules amongst key elite players representing major societal groups.

Of particular importance for constitutional design would appear to be the creation of a popularly elected constituent assembly that then negotiates the fundamental rules of the regime. In the three countries analysed here, the development of consensual rules regarding the role of religion and subnational identities in such an assembly is of particular importance. Namely, in Italy and Spain, constitutional negotiators recognized that Catholic interests and the interests of sub-national groupings could not be ignored and thus compromises were reached across elites with widely differing views on these two issues. In contrast, Turkish constitutions have been designed without the input of religiously oriented elites or sub-national groupings, with the effect that the preferences of these groups are largely ignored and eventually repressed. In the case of the sub-national groups the result has been open hostility to the state and an active attempt to destabilize the regime. This has, in turn, produced a situation of increased human-rights violations and military independence. In the case of the religiously oriented groups, it has meant a lack of willingness to support the regime in times of difficulty. Moreover, as will be shown in later chapters, even relatively mainstream centrist parties have withheld support and cooperation at crucial times partly as a result of their hostility to rules designed by the military and/or the Republican People's Party. The next few chapters of this book continue to explore the implications for democratic consolidation of the failed representation of various groups in government institutions.

6 The representation of social and political cleavages

This chapter focusses on citizens of newly democratizing countries. Although it might be expected that citizens would be key players of a democracy, the role of citizens in maintaining democratic stability and producing a consolidated democracy is still extremely unclear. Certainly, citizens in some countries have been instrumental in forcing authoritarian regimes to make the transition to democracy, as witnessed in Central Europe in the late 1980s and early 1990s. In all three of the countries analysed here, however, transitions to democracy were clearly elite- rather than mass-led. Even under these circumstances, there are countless scholars who would argue that once the transition has been made by the elites, the attitudes and behaviours of the mass citizenry are, in fact, important for ensuring the continued existence of the democracy. In this chapter, we address two aspects of the mass citizenry that are thought to be most relevant: civic culture or 'social capital' of the society and the ways in which citizen interests are mobilized via accepted democratic channels, particularly political parties. The chapter also explores the role of political parties in consolidating democracy in the three countries.

Since the 1950s (and long before as well), scholars have argued that in order for democracy to survive, a certain type of political culture should be present. Culture can be thought of as 'an historically transmitted pattern of meaning embodied in symbols, a system of inherited conceptions expressed in symbolic forms by means of which men communicate, perpetuate, and develop their knowledge about and attitudes toward life' (Geertz 1973: 89). *Political* culture refers to 'the specifically political orientations – attitudes toward the political system and its various parts, and attitudes toward the role of the self in the system (Almond and Verba 1963: 12). Findings from early survey research pointed to the conclusion that democratic political culture consisted of the certain mix of active and inactive, efficacious and inefficacious, trusting and sceptical citizens. The inference was that without this particular mix democracy had little hope of survival (Almond and Verba 1963; Inglehart 1990).

More recent versions of this approach to democracy have emphasized a related concept, social capital. This is defined by its most prominent proponent as 'features of social organization, such as trust, norms, and networks, that can improve the efficiency of a society by facilitating coordinated actions' (Putnam 1993: 167). When there is a lack of participatory culture – i.e. people do not form groups and networks for various purposes, be they political or non-political – individuals exist in a situation of distrustful 'wary isolation', and democracy cannot work very well under such conditions. By implication, there is thus the danger of breakdown of democracy in such circumstances. However, the connection between political culture and democratic stability (and consolidation) is a classic chicken-and-egg question, and it is unclear as to which of these comes first. While there is indeed an empirical connection between the two, there is also evidence to indicate that stable democratic institutions may produce a particular type of democratic culture rather than the reverse (see Muller and Seligson 1994; Rothstein 2004; McLaren and Baird 2006).

In addition, some evidence indicates that social networks can themselves be bad for democracy (Berman 1997). If such networks exist but the interests that they represent are not channelled into democratic institutions in some way, this means that *active* elements in society are – in essence – locked out of the political system and that dissatisfaction created by this situation opens up the possibility for non-democratic elites to use those already existing networks to create a movement supporting a less-than-democratic system. This is what Sheri Berman (1997) argues helped to produce the rise of Nazi Germany, for instance. Berman, and before her Samuel Huntington (1968), contend that key interests must be channelled into the democratic system, and in the modern day, this is usually done via political parties. By implication, if key groups do not gain representation via political parties, this creates a group of citizens that can be mobilized by various elites who then pursue authoritarian means with large-scale mass backing. Moreover, findings by Lai *et al.* (2005) indicate that parties play a major role both in making a transition from authoritarian rule and in producing consolidated democracy. Namely, parties serve to connect the state and society, which can be especially important in a new democracy. Note that such connections may not always be 'virtuous' and that many times in new democracies, patronage and clientelism are used to build party–society linkages (see Hopkin 2001).[1] At the same time, it is often up to party leaders to serve as sources of moderation and compromise during times when citizens become polarized and violent. Furthermore, the reaction of party elites to parties that do become radicalized is also thought to be important (Pridham 1990 on the role of political parties in consolidating democracy).

If we look to examples of fairly well-established European democracies – e.g. the UK, the Netherlands, Sweden – it becomes apparent that the party systems *have* traditionally done a fairly good job of representing the main interests in society at crucial time points in transitions to (increased) democracy. Some might argue that the opening up of representational channels at various points in history in these countries has ensured that those at the mass level – whatever their social group connections – have been able to participate in the democracy and thereby affect policy in such a way that the continued compliance of those groups with regime laws and norms is guaranteed. If, on the other hand, representational systems had permanently excluded groups from decision-making, as discussed above, such exclusion creates potentially important groups that non-democratic leaning elites can use to undermine democracy. Specifically, if democratic institutions are *not* adequately channelling interests, some may come to the conclusion that democracy is not good for them and may be persuaded by elites to collude against the democratic institutions.

It is generally widely accepted that parties and party systems in Western Europe came into existence in the way they did because of societal-level cleavages having their roots in two political/social revolutions: the National Revolution and the Industrial Revolution (Lipset and Rokkan 1967). National Revolutions refer to the process of nation-state building in Europe. As discussed in Chapter 2 of this book, prior to the development of the modern state political elites appeared to have little interest in moulding residents into citizens. Although the period of nation-building varied by country, most European countries did begin in the eighteenth and nineteenth centuries to try to reshape citizens for the purpose of developing nation-states, wherein citizens would identify with one another and their states and would pledge ultimate loyalty to the state. This process involved wresting control out of the hands of other major sources of loyalty and redirecting it to the state. Also as outlined in previous chapters, one of the main contenders for the loyalty of individuals in Europe at the time was the Catholic Church. In order to try to control the Church, state leaders adopted measures such as stripping the church of much of its property and ending of subsidies to the Church, as well as bringing legal systems entirely into the realm of the state and taking legal decision-making particularly regarding divorce and marriage out of the hands of the Church. This was not a process that was supported by all amongst elite groups or the masses, and as shown in previous chapters, it was one of the major divisions that formed as a result of state-building processes.

In addition to religious loyalty, most Europeans at the start of the national revolutions would have held local or community-level loyalties. Language and dialect was extremely localized and there would have been very little in the way of loyalty across a large territory, such as an empire. As discussed in Chapter 2, in order to develop mass-level loyalty intellectuals and state elites began to contemplate and write about the main historical connections – in many cases, mythologized connections – across the masses living in the state and to try to spread knowledge of these connections. The primary means for doing this, in turn, was the creation of a common language through which myths could be told and the creation of an education system that would teach everyone in the territory how to speak, read, and write in that common language. Again, such a process was controversial, as it involved choosing certain myths and languages over others. Naturally, there were many individuals and elites who resisted this process. This produced yet another important political cleavage between those who supported the state-building process and those who were opposed.

Thus, the National Revolutions across Europe produced two main divisions, referred to by Lipset and Rokkan (1967) as church versus state and centre versus periphery cleavages. The Industrial Revolution is also argued to have produced two divisions. First, the process of industrialization produced a new class of wealthy business owners who created factories. The interests of this class came in conflict with the traditional wealthy elites, the landed aristocracy; moreover, the interests of those living on and working the land were seen as being very different from those who were moving to the cities to work in the factories. Thus, the Industrial Revolution produced a rural–urban division in many European societies. Finally, as more and more workers moved to the cities and became concentrated in factories, the pressures created by poor working conditions, long working hours, poor health care, etc. produced considerable divisions between those doing the work and those who employed them. That is, the Industrial Revolution created a class cleavage.

While the relevance of most of these cleavages has dwindled in most European countries in the modern day (Franklin *et al.* 1992; Dalton 2001; but see Evans 1999) in that the state-building revolution has been fairly successful and economic disputes associated with the Industrial Revolution have in great part been addressed via government negotiation and social welfare policies, the important point for this book is that at the time that many European countries were adopting democratic institutions or altering institutions to make them more democratic, these main cleavages were able to gain representation through legitimate, or generally accepted, means. For instance, in countries like the UK, rather than being forced to stage a revolution, as would have been predicted by Marx and Engels, industrial workers were given the right to vote and to create a party representing their interests. This party, in turn, successfully altered the working and living conditions of the group it represented to the point that the group lost its need for militancy and accepted the legitimacy of democratic institutions.

This chapter focuses on cleavage representation in the newer democracies of Italy, Spain, and Turkey. As will be illustrated below, the political and social cleavages in all of three of these countries were largely similar to the ones described above. The chapter explores the impact of cleavage representation on the outcomes of democratic transitions in the three countries. The main questions to be answered are: To what degree were the main cleavages represented in the democratic political system? Did such representation have a positive, negative, or negligible impact on democratic consolidation? The chapter first summarizes the nature of social cleavages in our three cases and then provides an analysis of the role of this variable and political party systems in explaining the differential outcomes in consolidation across the three.

Italy: the national and industrial revolutions and cleavage representation

Italy has experienced both a National and Industrial Revolution and represents a fairly quintessential example of the general historical development of cleavage structures discussed in the introduction to this chapter. The only one of the four cleavages discussed above that has historically been relatively unimportant has been the centre-periphery cleavage. Although there was initial resistance to the elites forming the Italian state and nation in the 1800s and briefly after World War II, that resistance was extremely weak and was quickly suppressed. As indicated by the evidence presented in Chapter 2, at least in terms of language and identity, there does not appear to be a major centre–periphery cleavage. Such a cleavage did begin to develop in the 1990s with the increased popularity of the Northern Leagues, but this was long after Italian democracy had been consolidated. Thus an analysis of representation of that particular cleavage is beyond the scope of this text (but see Levy 1996: Part II; Sassoon 1997: Chapter 14; Bull and Gilbert 2001; Gold 2003).

The cleavage that did result from the nation-state building process in Italy was that of church versus state interests. The importance of the actions of Italian state builders in producing potentially damning animosity on the part of the Catholic Church in the mid-1800s cannot be overemphasized. The geographical roots of the Catholic Church lie predominantly in what is now Italian territory, and once the Italian government began to confiscate the Church's lands (the Papal Territories), the ire of the Church was clearly invoked. In addition, the Church had been facing similar displacements in other traditionally Catholic countries, and so had very little in the way of international backing to prevent Italian state leaders from carrying out its anti-Church, secularizing policies. The main weapon the Church had at its disposal, though, was the ability to ensure the illegitimacy of the new regime. Thus, devout Catholics – which would have represented the majority of ordinary Italians at the time of the creation of the Italian state – were instructed to not participate in the new regime, and it is believed that priests encouraged much of the agitation that occurred in the South shortly after the creation of the Italian state in the 1860s (see Mack Smith 1959). As discussed in Chapter 2, it was only when Mussolini entered into the Lateran Treaties with the Church in 1929 that the Church acknowledged the legitimacy of the state.[2] At this time, the Church's powers were increased and it gained considerable power to create civil society organizations (although Mussolini's government only very reluctantly allowed the Church to create such organizations), and it did so on a very large scale. Thus, by the time of the collapse of fascism in Italy, the Catholic Church, via its civil society organizations, was an extremely powerful force in Italian society and politics (Mack Smith 1959; Clark 1984).

Also strongly present in Italian society by the start of the post-World

War II democratization period were cleavages associated with Italy's Industrial Revolution. Indeed, some would argue that the existence of these cleavages brought about the end of the Italian democratic experiment of the early 1900s. The key division was between workers and employers/owners of industry, but there were also discrepancies between industrializers and those still working or managing the land (see Mack Smith 1959).

What was the nature of cleavage representation in both experiences with Italian democracy then? At the end of World War II, the main parties that existed to represent these cleavages were roughly similar to those from before Mussolini's rise to power. It must be emphasized that because of the Catholic Church's dictate against Catholic participation in the Italian state, the representation of Catholic interests in state institutions had been very weak in Italy's early experience with democracy. Thus, the main groups gaining representation primarily included the bourgeois class (e.g. the Liberals and the Radicals) and the working class (e.g. the Socialist Party of Italy). It was only in the early 1900s when Italy was faced with the realistic possibility of the Socialist Party gaining enough electoral strength to take control of the Italian government that the Catholic Church began to send signals indicating that Catholics ought to participate to keep the Socialists out of government. This began with local elections in 1904 and by 1919, a Catholic-based party, the Italian People's Party, formed and managed to win 20 per cent of the popular vote. While this is impressive given that the party was newly formed, it also seems very likely that the party's vote would have been higher if it had been formed earlier, which in turn would have required that the Catholic Church change its position regarding the Italian state. As it was, Catholics in parliament were not powerful or experienced enough after the 1919 election to help keep Mussolini out of power – and indeed, given that their primary aim was to keep the socialists out of power, Mussolini's fascist party may have seemed appealing.

In any case, it seems likely that Catholic interests were under-represented in the Italian parliament in 1919. By the end of World War II, the situation had changed dramatically. The Church was one of the few organizations that was allowed to continue operating its civil society organizations throughout Mussolini's rule, and so when World War II came to an end and Mussolini was defeated (and then executed), Catholic interests were strongly organized and immediately formed the Christian Democratic party. Furthermore, reflecting the argument made above regarding the strength of the party, after the war the party became the largest in parliament and was a leader or member of every post-war coalition government until 1992 (see Chapter 7; see Hine 1993; Sassoon 1997; on the Italian Christian Democrats, see Leonardi and Wertman 1989).

Two key parties from the pre-Mussolini days appeared again in the post-war period to represent the interests of the working classes – the Socialist Party and the Communist Party. In fact, up until 1921, there had been one working class party, the Socialists. In 1921, however, there was a major split in the party that resulted in the more radical of the group forming a separate Communist party, with the two remaining at odds with one another until the late 1930s (see Hine 1993; Sassoon 1997).

After the war, the two major forces in Italian politics and society were the religiously based Christian Democrats and the secular Communists. It is argued that the incorporation of the latter of these into the new post-war democracy was, in fact, the main feature that kept Italy on the road to democratic consolidation (e.g. Pasquino 1986; Hine 1993). One of the factors that led to Mussolini being invited to form a coalition government in 1921 was the refusal of the left to cooperate with 'bourgeois' parties. The Socialists held the most seats in the parliament that had been elected in 1919 and therefore should have been pivotal in government formation and stability. However, cooperation with bourgeois parties was fundamentally against the party's ideological approach (see Gray 1980 on the pre-war PCI; also see Lange and Vannicelli 1981). Moreover, if the Socialists had been able to form a coalition with another left-leaning party, it is entirely possible that the government would have been so radical as to spark the beginnings of a Communist revolution.[3]

Importantly, it was the radical wing of this party – which had become the Communist Party – that tended to win the second most seats in the parliament throughout much of the post-war history. Up until the early 1980s, the democratic commitment and credentials of this party were still very much in question. Under the circumstances, there are many different approaches that other parties could have taken to this one. Presumably if the party did indeed threaten the democratic institutions of the country, the other parties could have tried to ban the Communists and to repress party activity, as was the case in the United States in the 1950s, for instance. Again some claim that one of the keys to Italian democracy was in fact the approach taken to this particular party: rather than trying to rid Italian politics of it, the party was allowed to contest elections freely and, as will be seen in later chapters, was able to take part directly and indirectly in governance – although it was excluded by other parties from ever becoming part of the government itself.

It is now widely believed that the PCI leadership had no intention of waging a communist revolution in the post-World War II period. The ideology of much of the leadership had been de-radicalized by the end of the war, but still they allowed followers to believe that they were playing a double game (the so-called *doppieza*) – that is, once they managed to get into government, the communist revolution could begin – in order to continue to win large numbers of seats in the parliament (see Ginsborg 1990). Not only did the party's followers think the PCI might be playing a double game, but other party leaders also seemed to believe it. Thus, the fear of the possibility of a Red Italy cannot be overemphasized; nor can the reaction of the other parties, which was one of quiet and gradual incorporation of a party whose leaders *did*, in fact, want to participate in the new democratic regime. This will be discussed further in the next two chapters.

It should be noted that in addition to these two cleavages and parties representing them, there continued to be small bourgeois parties that had their roots in pre-Mussolini Italian politics. Moreover, the system allowed for the representation of neo-fascists, in the form of the Italian Social Movement (MSI). Given Italy's historical circumstances, it seems that this party could potentially have been banned as well. Indeed, Article XII of the 1948 constitution states that reorganization of the fascist party under any form is prohibited. However, such a party did form in 1946 and was allowed to participate in the institutions of Italian democracy by winning approximately 5 per cent of the vote in post-war national elections and thus gaining seats in the Italian parliament.

Thus, the Italian party system throughout much of the post-war era was one that allowed many parties to gain representation in the national parliament, roughly proportionate to the percentage of vote the party had received. Such a system had the effect of creating problems of governance, which will be discussed in the next chapter. Presumably, the designers of the post-war electoral system could have created electoral rules that would prevent small extremist parties from gaining a foothold. Many other countries, for instance, institute a minimum district-level and/or nationwide threshold, and if Italy had taken this approach, it would have presumably reduced the number of seats going to extremist parties like the MSI. The problem, however, would have been for the small 'bourgeois' parties. These were never mass-based parties and they simply did not have the ability to amass large numbers of votes to cross any significant threshold. Thus, it is unlikely that these parties would have gone along with any meaningful minimal threshold. Moreover, at the time of the first post-war election – that for the Constituent Assembly in 1946 – none of the parties had any idea as to how many seats they might win. Thus, they all agreed to use the Imperali system that would distribute seats on the basis of the number of votes received – a relatively pure form of proportional representation. It was this system that continued to be used in Italian national elections until 1993.

The next chapter will address the governmental implications of such an electoral system, but for this chapter, the important point to note about the effect of this electoral system is that it made representation of all major and minor cleavages possible. On the one hand, this appeared to run the risk of putting the regime in considerable danger of either a communist overthrow or a repeat of Mussolini's rise. On the other hand, both sets of extremes had toned down their extremist rhetoric, and it appears that incorporating them into the legitimate democratic institutions at the time may have been productive in terms of consolidating democracy. That is, if these extremes had *not* been incorporated in such a way, it seems entirely possible that they would have sought 'illegitimate' outlets of influence and used far more radical means than they did.

We now turn to another issue that was raised in the introductory section of this chapter: the role of civil society and social capital in guaranteeing democracy. Although finding adequate measures of these concepts for the transitional period is difficult,[4] one indication of the existence of civil society is the level of organized strike activity. Italy has a fairly lengthy history in this regard, with the first large-scale strikes occurring in 1872 in 25 different places, although these were not, in fact, organized by trade unions (Clark 1984: 71). The first nationally organized trade union (of printers) was formed later that year (Clark 1984: 73). Many of the organized interests at the time, however, joined anarchist groups. After a few dismal attempts at revolution in which very small numbers tended to show up to participate in attempted seizures of government, much of this movement was destroyed, its leaders either arrested or driven into exile. This made 'legal', 'Socialist' strategies more attractive and workers began to organize through Socialist unions (Clark 1984: 74–5). Prior to the rise of organized socialism, there were also networks of co-operatives and mutual-aid societies, providing basic social insurance such as old-age pensions, sick pay, and funeral costs (Clark 1984: 76). From the early 1900s, socialist trade unionism grew rapidly. The most important of these were the Chambers of Labour, which also grew quickly from 14 chambers in 1900 to 76 in 1902 (Clark 1984: 141). Martin Clark argues that 'they were the centres of a Socialist popular culture and a Socialist morality' (Clark 1984: 142). There was considerable rivalry between the Socialist organizations and the other main organized group – the Church – and socialism was explicitly anti-clerical (Clark 1984: 142).

It is difficult to argue that organized civil society had a positive influence on Italy's first experience with democracy – prior to the rise of Mussolini, that is. The evidence points to increased participation in organized unions in the 1918–20 period: for instance, membership in the Socialist unions in the General Confederation of labour rose from 250,000 in 1918 to two million by late 1920 (see Clough 1964: 207). The Catholic confederation consisted of approximately 1.2 million members, and the anarcho-syndicalists claimed 300,000 members. Despite concessions to organized labour, such as the creation of an eight-hour work day and the beginnings of old age, health and unemployment insurance, organized labour continued to engage in militant activities: strikes, lockouts, riots, factory occupations and gang warfare were common. In 1919, more than one million people went on strike and even more did so in 1920 (Clark 1984: 206–7).

Such activities do not necessarily result in the collapse of democracy, but in the 1920s in Italy, it can be argued that these activities – and the organized groups behind them – certainly did not contribute positively to maintaining democratic institutions. There are at least a couple of reasons for this. First is that the Russian Revolution just a few years previously contributed to the perception that a communist revolution in Italy was eminent. Thus, radical elements within the unions used strike activity to try to force the country into revolution. Second, the Socialist Party leadership refused to try to bring these organized interests under control and into the fold of legitimate political activity.

Recall from the introductory section of this chapter that many researchers believe that the existence of civil society is not enough to prevent an authoritarian takeover; organized groups must instead be channelled into democratic institutions via organized political parties. In the case of Italy, the most important of these organized groups *were* channelling behaviour into an organized party – the Socialist Party. The problem was that although the Socialist leadership participated in parliament, it refused to cooperate with most other parties in parliament, limiting its own ability to become part of government. In this way, the party could continue to remain in the opposition, criticizing government policy without actually taking responsibility for developing and implementing its own policies. In addition, despite a softening approach to the idea of violent revolution amongst the party's leadership, it continued to use inflammatory rhetoric to maintain its large number of supporters in the electorate and to win votes, and this rhetoric presumably contributed to increased militancy and also failed to instil party supporters with notions of compromise and conciliation – again, despite an actual softening of approach by these leaders. Ultimately, the behaviour of the strikers and the party resulted in deadlock, and despite multiple attempts to form governments, the apparent increase in the popularity of Benito Mussolini's *fasci* led other parties and the monarch to invite Mussolini into government, presumably as a temporary fix to the high levels of violence and economic and political chaos. Thus, partly because of uncompromising behaviour on the part of organized groups, Italy's first experience with democracy collapsed into authoritarianism. Indeed, as argued by Dylan Riley (2005), the organized groups in existence in Italy actually served the purposes of the fascist organizers because of the ease with which such groups could be used, for instance, to hold meetings for fascist speakers. As in the case of Germany during the inter-war period (see Berman 1997), Italian 'civil society' could be exploited to help create an organized system of fascism.

What about post-World War II Italian democracy, though? The period just before the end of the war, beginning in around 1944, perhaps indicates the power of organized civil society to overthrow authoritarian rule. During this period, former enemies – Catholics, Communists and Socialists – were willing to collaborate against Nazi Germany's occupation of Italy and against Italian fascism. As discussed in previous chapters, although it is unlikely that these groups would have been successful on their own (see Clark 1984: 295), their cooperation with one another and with allied forces are thought to have helped the latter in removing Nazi Germany from Italian territory (Ginsborg 1990: Chapter 2). These groups then formed the post-war government and designed the post-war constitution, once the issue of the monarchy was resolved by popular referendum.

With regard to civil society, immediately after World War II ended, the traditionally strong Italian groups – the unions – were extremely weak. By 1960, the situation had changed. Increased economic growth meant growing numbers of workers as well as their concentration in urban centres (see Chapter 4); this, in turn, meant an increase in working-class union members. Prior to the 1960s, government – operating through the main trade unions – was able to keep a lid on demands for wage increases. The argument was that industrial entrepreneurs needed the time to regenerate Italian industry; this was an idea that had been accepted by the unions and so strike activity was generally avoided. In the 1960s, on the other hand, there was a high level of labour militancy, as well as active involvement of non-unionized workers in stoking up discontent and leading strikes; this continued into the 1970s (Sassoon 1997: 132–7). Sassoon contends that the large-scale militant behaviour is in great part a result of the weakness of organized labour – stronger labour organizations tend to enforce greater restraint and control, partly to avoid jeopardizing power relations with government and other unions. Italian unions simply did not have the strength with which to control the militancy (Sassoon 1997: 137). Thus, 1960s and 1970s Italy was approaching levels of violence and strike activity not witnessed since the 1918–20 period which had eventually resulted in the invitation to Mussolini to form a government.

In the 1960s and 1970s, terrorist groups on the right and the left tended to engage in violence to publicize their ideological positions and at times simply to create chaos (Foot 2003: 83). Fascist squads revived in the early 1970s to restore order and repress the left: the former had plenty of funds and established links with the neo-Fascist party, the Italian Social Movement. Ultimately, they hoped to cause chaos that would then force the army to step in, impose martial law and overthrow parliamentary democracy. Moreover, left-wing terrorist groups were forming and by 1976 there were over 140 of these active in the country. Initially funding for these came from one wealthy individual but later Czechoslovakia, Cuba, and South Yemen became important, particularly in advance weapons training. There appears to have been considerable public sympathy for these groups. By the late 1970s there were more than 2000 terrorist acts per year, including about 40 murders (Clark 1984: 384–6).

Thus in what appeared to be a repeat of the 1910s and 1920s, one of the important differences was the approach taken by the Communist Party leadership, particularly party leader Palmiro Togliatti. It was almost thirty years since the Russian Revolution, and Italian communist leaders had begun to promote an 'Italian way' to socialism which would no longer involve any violent overthrow of existing institutions. Instead, the approach pursued during the Nazi Germany occupation of Italy toward the end of the war was one of national unity in the face of Nazis and Fascists; moreover, it was hoped that unity would be continued into the period of reconstruction. Thus, Togliatti's approach was vastly different from that of the pre-Mussolini years, and the party became willing to cooperate with previous enemies – bourgeois parties *and* the Christian Democrats (Ginsborg 1990: 42–3). Amongst the key steps in this process were the *svolta di Salerno* of

1944 when the PCI agreed to recognize the government that had been chosen by the monarch, despite being strongly anti-monarchist, as well as the compromise with other parties over including the Lateran Pacts in Article 7 of the new constitution (see Chapter 5). The party created ambiguities about its leanings, though, by continuing to receive funding from the Soviet Union, and although the PCI began to try to distance itself from the Communist Party of the Soviet Union in the 1960s, it still accepted funding from them in order to avoid opening a debate about the issue and causing severe dissent within the Italian Communist Party (Pasquino 1980: 77–80).

Early work on polarization and democratic stability contended that the Italian party system was a case of polarized pluralism, with anti-system parties at both ends of the spectrum and a fragmented and unstable centre, which implied electoral polarization and the potential collapse of the system (Sartori 1976). However, Farneti (1985) argued that by the 1960s, the system no longer fit this description, in that even if the electorate might have driven the system in a centrifugal way, the party leaders did not become radicalized and instead found compromises (although generally not very durable ones) to prevent the system from degenerating into deadlock. In fact, Hine (1990) contends that the political parties and party leaders in particular played a crucial role in consolidating Italian democracy.

Recall that prior to the rise of Mussolini, the left-wing parties refused to consider cooperating with non-left parties, particularly parties thought to represent bourgeois interests. Cooperation with the Christian Democrats, who represented bourgeois *and* religious interests in the post-war period was thus inimical to the party's general ideological predispositions. In the post-war era, there were critical junctures during which the party leaders made it clear that they were not going to allow the system to become centrifugal. The first of these, after the *Svolta di Salerno* of 1944 at the end of the war, was the 1947–8 period, during which time the party leader Giuseppe Saragat lent the support of his newly formed Social Democrat Party (a splinter party of the PCI) to the Christian Democratic-led centrist government.

Another critical juncture occurred in the 1960–4 period. During this time, the PSI was trying to establish a new identity that would be independent of the PCI in order to build up a leftist force that would serve as a viable alternative to the Christian Democrats and would banish the PCI to the radical fringe. While the party was trying to reform itself, the centrist governing coalition (consisting of the Christian Democrats and the traditional bourgeois parties) fell apart and faced two choices. One was to invite the extreme right into the coalition, thereby creating the same situation that allowed the fascist party to take control of government in the 1920s;[5] the other was an opening to the left, in which the Socialists would replace the Liberals as the main junior partner of the Christian Democrats. This posed a big problem for the Socialists: were they to capitulate their goals of reform in order to give the government a stable coalition, or were they to continue with their reforms and risk the consequences of a clear left–right polarization of the political system? The PSI decided to join the Christian Democrats in coalition, and according to Hine, this can be seen as an act of national responsibility and self-sacrifice by its leaders in that party leaders realized that they were placing the party itself in danger of electoral loss by allowing the PCI to monopolize the opposition (Hine 1990: 76).

Another critical period came in 1973–6 when a new government crisis originated with the labour unrest in 1969, which destabilized the centre-left coalition. In 1976, the centre-left coalition of Christian Democrats and Socialists collapsed and the PCI's prime concern was to restore stability. Thus Christian Democrats remained in government even after the Socialists left, with the indirect support of the PCI. This era is known as the 'historic compromise'. Again, this was a self-sacrifice on the part of the party, in that it created tremendous internal strains in the party and with the unions. In addition, in 1978–9 the PCI supported Prime Minister Giulio Andreotti during a difficult period of terrorist attacks (see Ruscoe 1982 on the 1976–81 period of the PCI). In general, it appears that in the face of political violence in the 1970s, it was the fact that the Communists were able to restrain their own militants that prevented a breakdown of parliamentary democracy (Clark 1984: 385).

Thus, at moments when parliamentary democracy has seemed close to breakdown, at least one of the left-wing parties has been willing to compromise with the parties of the centre-right, and at moments when the working class has seemed most militant, the leaders of the left have tried to establish some moderating control. That is, the party leaders have worked to bring society into the fold of the new democratic rules of the game. The parties of the left clearly suffered as a result of their compromising behaviour: the PSI's participation in the centre-left coalition reduced its level of electoral support and pushed more people into the arms of the PCI. This was partly due to the fact that once the PSI joined the government, it started using patronage resources upon which the Christian Democrats were already drawing heavily. Initially participation in government and use of patronage began as a mechanism to control policy and shore up electoral support against the extremes, but it ended up having the opposite effect by discrediting party politics as a whole and driving many voters to the extremist parties.

Hine contends that of these acts of accommodation, the historic compromise was probably the one that made the single greatest contribution to the consolidation of democracy because it enabled the PCI to imply by its actions what it was never quite able to convince others of in words: that it was committed to the democratic framework. After the Historic Compromise, it was far more difficult to maintain the view that the PCI represented a threat to democracy (Hine 1990: 78–9).

While Italian democracy appears to have stabilized, in that it is difficult to imagine a return to clear authoritarianism, it must be noted that changes were made to the electoral laws in the early 1950s which had the potential to undermine this process. Namely, Prime Minister De Gasperi, who was increasingly under pressure to form a coalition with the extreme right (monarchists and neo-fascists), eventually decided that measures must be taken to protect the new Italian democracy from the extremes. One of these was to change the electoral law such that any alliance of parties which received one vote more than 50 per cent of the votes cast at a national election would receive two-thirds of the seats in the Chamber of Deputies. Obviously, this law bore some resemblance to that passed by Mussolini in 1923, in which any party receiving more than 25 per cent of the vote would take two-thirds of the seats in the Chamber. Electoral laws in Italy can be passed as ordinary laws, and since the governing coalition had a majority of seats in the parliament, it did pass, despite attempts to obstruct its passage on the part of the Communists and Socialists (Ginsborg 1990: 142).

In a sense, the next election, 1953, could have put Italy onto a very different path, one that many would argue would be a step back toward authoritarianism. This is particularly relevant given the Turkish experience at a very similar juncture in time, which will be discussed further below. The election results were extremely close, and Christian Democratic-led alliance (which included the Social Democrats, the Liberal Party, and Republican Party) failed to cross the threshold by a mere 0.15 per cent of the vote (Hine 1993: 158).[6] Shortly after this, De Gasperi handed over power to a colleague and then died; the electoral system was subsequently changed back to pure proportionalism (Ginsborg 1990: 143; Hine 1993: 159).

Although the electoral and party systems may have helped to stabilize democracy in Italy, there have long been complaints of corruption and cronyism on the part of several main parties, along with complaints about the generally ineffective, unstable governing coalitions in the post-war period. Thus considerable changes have been made since 1993 to change the functioning of the system. Chapter 7 discusses these changes in the context of the functioning of government. For this chapter, it is relevant to note that the party system changed drastically, with the Christian Democrats reaching the point of virtual collapse. Given the vast changes in the international system, particularly the collapse of the Soviet Union and the decline of international communism, it is also not surprising that much of the traditional left has dwindled as well. Parties in modern-day Italy have been forced to coalesce into pre-election centre-left and centre-right groupings to contest elections, but whether this change has had much effect on the functioning of Italian politics is questionable. Again, the next chapter discusses this issue in greater detail.

Spain: the end of ideology and democratic consolidation

In the case of Spain, the cleavages discussed in the introduction to this chapter resulted in Civil war during 1936–39, which ended with Franco's rise to power. Not only did Spain face religious versus anti-religious and socialist versus anti-socialist forces, the country was also faced with a relatively severe centre versus periphery cleavage. Rather than simply allowing these cleavages to work their way through the democratic institutions, disputes over these issues provoked large-scale violence and destruction. Thus like Italy, Spain's history points to the possibility that cleavage representation may, in fact, be problematic for consolidating democracy. We begin with a review of the major cleavages in Spanish politics prior to the rise of the Franco dictatorship and representation of these in Spain's key experiment with democracy, the Spanish Second Republic. In addition, parties that have managed to gain representation in the modern Spanish democracy will be described, and as was the case with Italy, civil society and the degree of political activism in modern Spain will be examined.

In the mid-1800s as Socialism and Communism were becoming popular in other European countries, they were also making their way into Spanish society and politics. As in Italy, this took a radical form. In Spain, it was anarchism that initially attracted the largest of the mass followings vis-à-vis Communists and Socialists. The ideological approach of anarchists was in many ways very similar to that of other Marxists, in that they envisioned a disappearance of the state, which was viewed as a system whereby minorities repress the majority. However, unlike Marxists, anarchists were strongly opposed to the state being converted to a dictatorship of the proletariat since this would necessarily mean the continuation of repression of the majority by a minority of leaders. Anarchists pointed to measures taken by Lenin, Trotsky, and Stalin as examples of this. Ultimately, anarchists viewed small-scale violence against the state apparatus as a reasonable way to try to bring about an end to the state. Thus, at the time of the start of the Spanish Second Republic, the left was dominated by anarchism, but also contained Communist and Socialist elements as well (Carr 1980; Radcliff 2000; Heywood 2003).

The centre-right during this period had been dominated by moral and religious conservatives who tended to favour continuation of the monarchy and protection of the landed aristocracy. However, this group was discredited by its affiliation with the Primo de Rivera dictatorship (1923–30). When Primo de Rivera became unpopular and started experiencing health problems, the monarch attempted to install other military officials as heads of government. The second of these called for local elections in order to placate the demands of democrats and republicans; however, these groups won the majority in the elections and leaders of these groups and protestors began demanding the removal of the king. The military declared that it could no longer defend the king and he fled the country (Carr 1980: Chapter 7).

A constituent assembly for drafting a Republican constitution was formed, and it is at this stage that we gain some idea as to the strength of various groups in Spain prior to Franco's seizure of power. At that time, the right was in disarray and large conservative and Catholic minorities were without representation in the Cortes (Payne 1993: 59). As anarchists and communists did not participate in elections, the Socialist Party was the only dominant force of the left in parliament. As discussed in the previous chapter, the constitution and other fundamental rules created by the Cortes were thus of questionable legitimacy. Besides the Socialists, the other main groups gaining representation in the new Cortes were the centre-right Radical Republican Party and Basque and Catalan nationalist parties.

It took the right two and a half years after the creation of the new republic to fully reorganize; the lack of modern rightist political organizations and the general discrediting of the right by the preceding dictatorship and the final phase of the monarchy impeded its development, as mentioned above. The new right that did emerge consisted of four main categories: political Catholicism, monarchist forces, militant new business interests, and newly forming fascists. The most important of these was the emergence of mass Catholicism, which had never before been accomplished in the modern history of Spanish parliamentary regimes (Payne 1993: 166).[7]

The main new Catholic group that formed for the first of the republican elections was *Acción Naciónal*, which was based mostly in conservative northern central Spain. It was able to elect a handful of delegates to the Constituent Cortes, including an eloquent university professor who came to hold the reputation of being the chief parliamentary spokesman for the right.[8] This party joined with other Catholic political organizations and the Radical Republicans to form a large new umbrella party, the Spanish Confederation of Autonomous Rightist Groups (CEDA) which convened its first national congress in 1933. Although Catholicism had declined in importance in Spain by this time, there were still many Catholic identifiers, and this group soon became the largest single force in Spanish politics (Payne 1993: 167–8).

With regard to the group's ideological leanings, controversy developed over CEDA's true identity and intentions. Moderate Republicans claimed that it was a moderate centre-right group. Left Republicans and the worker left called CEDA a Trojan horse of rightist authoritarianism, 'objectively fascist' (Payne 1993: 168).

According to Stanley Payne, it seems clear that CEDA's intentions were to win political power through legal means and then to enact fundamental constitutional revisions that would protect religion and property and alter the basic political system. The platform was that of Catholic corporatism, in both economic and political structure. The aim was neither a fascist state nor restoration of the monarchy, but a corporative and conservative Catholic republic, reordered by corporative representation that would necessarily mean some limitation of direct democratic rights. Their rhetoric and behaviour (including attending a Nazi Party rally at Nurnberg) left considerable ambiguity about their intentions (Payne 1993: 168–70). What seems unambiguous was that they were not committed to democracy, except as a means to their corporatist conservative ends (Payne 1993: 171).

Also on the right, monarchists began to organize around a journal called *Acción Española*. This group was backed financially by well-organized industrial-financial elite in the Bilbao area of the Basque region. The group generally approved of Hitlerism but contended that it was no substitute for a monarchy. They pledged to revive traditional Spanish ideology, grounded in religion and in strong monarchist traditions (Payne 1993: 171). Almost all of its members had been associated with the Primo de Rivera regime and they developed much of their inspiration from this regime (Payne 1993: 171–2). CEDA was denounced for being too moderate, compromising, and ambiguous, as well as insufficiently nationalist and authoritarian. The monarchists later splintered into more conservative and radical wings and had several disputes that seemed to be based on personality clashes (Payne 1993: 172).

Monarchists eventually formed a broader coalition of radical right groups, which took shape as the *Bloque Naciónal*, organized in December 1934. This group proposed the installation of an authoritarian monarchy, which would have to be preceded by a period of dictatorship. The new state would adopt a militantly nationalist policy and foster development of the armed forces; it would reject laicism and restore the Catholic identity of Spanish government (Payne 1993: 172).[9]

Finally on the right, there was Spanish fascism. In fact, a fascist movement was slow to emerge in Spain, in great part because of the weakness of nationalism (Payne 1993: 174). There was some attempt by intellectuals to get fascism off the ground starting in 1931, but the movement did not attract many supporters. During the summer of 1933, representatives of wealthy financiers and industrialists in Bilbao searched for a possible leader of a counter-revolutionary, demagogic Spanish fascism. The figure that came to the fore was José Antonio Primo de Rivera, the oldest son of the late dictator; *Falange Española* was then founded in 1933 (Payne 1993: 175). The organization was fairly insignificant for the next two years and simply failed to gain broader support beyond student movements (Payne 1993: 175–6). The movement began to shift to the 'left' and the national syndicalism took on more radical overtones. By the end of 1934, Falangist leaders were denying that they were fascists; they admitted that they had much in common with Italian Fascists, but they insisted on the Spanishness and singularity of Falangism. According to Payne, however, neither in style, organization, nor doctrine did Falangism differ significantly from Mussolini's party (Payne 1993: 176).

In the 1933 elections, the Radicals (moderate right) and CEDA did very well, with 24 and 30 per cent of the vote, and 32 and 37 per cent of seats, respectively; Socialists received about 20 per cent of the vote and 13 per cent of seats (Payne 1993: 179–80). There was vast turnover of deputies – almost half elected in 1933 had not served in the 1931 parliament. The Socialists asked the president to rewrite the electoral law (which they had helped design) and call new elections by decree, but he refused (Payne 1993: 181–2).

The socialists temporarily moved further toward the left, and socialist groups began preparing for armed rebellion of workers. Anarchist attacks also continued during this period. The biggest of the Socialist-led rebellions was in Asturias in 1934. After this failed revolt, moderate socialists and moderate Republican leftists took as their main goal the restoration of a unified political action (Payne 1993: 223). However, groups on both the left and the right began splintering, and during much of this time there were rumours of a military coup. It was after the collapse of the centre-right coalition and the triumph of the centre-left in 1936 that Franco's insurrection began to gain momentum. As discussed in Chapter 3, what followed was a brutal civil war in which anarchists fought against other leftists, and both groups fought the Falangists and other right-wing groups. Franco eventually defeated the republicans and leftists and established a regime that incorporated CEDA's notions of conservative Catholicism, combined with corporatism. Most of the individuals affiliated with anarchism and active socialism were killed or went into exile. As mentioned in previous chapters, the regime attempted to crush most of the regional separatist movements but failed to do so and appears to have moved some of these – the Basques in particular – further toward radical separatism than had previously been the case.

Had these social and political divisions been destroyed by Franco, or were they still in existence at the time of his death? At first glance, they clearly were still in place. The major actors who were around during this period were very much tied into the old disputes that had produced the Spanish Civil War. There was the conservative, religious wing of Franco's fascist party. There was a large Socialist party and a much smaller Communist party. In addition, there were the Catalans and Basques, who had been subjected to more than 40 years of repression, particularly in the case of the Basques. It was the manoeuvring of key leaders at the time of the transition – particularly Adolfo Suárez – that ultimately made it possible for all of these groups to gain representation via parties in parliament. That is, very much like the post-war Italian experience, none of these groups was banned from participating in politics – not even the fascists – and all were incorporated into the legitimate democratic institutions via the national parliament (and regional parliaments – to be discussed in Chapter 8).

At the same time, however, there were also reformists from within the Franco regime in the new parliament in 1976. This group was pivotal in bridging the differences across the political spectrum. It is also important that anarchism appeared to have been mostly eliminated as a political force and that it was the moderate Socialist Party that attracted the majority of votes on the left, although the Communist Party was also popular in the initial parliamentary elections. Thus, despite the existence of some fairly powerful extremes and despite ongoing strike activity (see below), the regime managed to make its transition to democracy and to eventually become a stable, consolidated democracy at that (see Hanley and Loughlin

2006; Heywood 1995: Chapters 8 and 9; Newton 1997: Chapter 10; Hanley and Loughlin 2006).

Was the latter related to citizen mobilization? It is clear that the transition itself in Spain depended upon decisions of elites, and it seems unlikely that citizen mobilization contributed positively to the consolidation. First, let us consider the historical role of citizen representation and mobilization in destabilizing Spanish democracy.

As mentioned above, prior to the rise of the Falangist movement, anarchism was the largest organized force in Spanish society. This movement entered Spain in 1868, and the combination of anarchism and syndicalism, or trade unionism, later produced anarcho-syndicalism. The first major movement was established in 1910–11, the CNT (National Confederation of Labour). It had become a mass organization by the end of World War I and engaged in many acts of political violence and strikes. In 1927, a separate Iberian Anarchist Federation (FAI) was organized by hard-core anarchists (Payne 1993: 13).

The first Marxist socialist group was organized in Madrid in 1879, but it gained few members. The Socialist Party (PSOE) and trade union UGT (General Union of Workers) emerged in 1888. The Spanish Socialist party was fairly typical of the Socialist organizations of the Second International, devoted to trade union activity and contesting elections, but eschewing revolutionary militancy in exchange for tangible gains (Payne 1993: 13–14). The party did not gain a seat in parliament until 1910 (see Heywood 2003).

After 1919, the issue of Communism and the Third International divided the Socialist party; the party chose the midway between revolution and social democracy, with negative consequences in terms of its mass base of support, in that membership had plummeted by 1923 (Payne 1993: 14). By that time, anarcho-syndicalism had completely outstripped socialism in labour organization, with the CNT having nearly one million members. Many Marxists attributed this to Spanish backwardness and the small-shop structure of Spanish industry, which did not generate the dense concentrations of workers found in more advanced countries, or even in Russia (Payne 1993: 14).

Union violence began in Barcelona in 1917, and some of the CNT turned to political violence, which was countered by private vigilantism of 'employers'' police, as had been the case in Italy, this was followed in turn by state repression under martial law. The appearance of the small new Spanish Communist Party (PCE) only worsened the problem (Payne 1993: 17). In addition, there were farm strikes during 1918–20 (Payne 1993: 17). The Primo de Rivera dictatorship (1923–30) used martial law to finally get public order and little was heard from the anarchists and Communists for 7 years (Payne 1993: 20).

After the establishment of a republic, anarchist violence affiliated with the CNT resumed (Payne 1993: 52). There were anarchist attacks on churches and Catholic workers (Payne 1993: 53). Anarchists rejected social-democratic reformism and refused to work with government-backed labour arbitration committees, choosing direct action instead (Payne 1993: 53). Moderates in the CNT did support a democratic regime that would guarantee full civil rights, labour freedom, and efforts to implement greater social justice, but the radical portion of the group (FAI) became increasingly popular and rapidly won converts among the rank-and-file of the CNT. They preached a vague doctrine of 'Libertarian communism', or totally decentralized communalism to be achieved by radical strikes and armed insurrection (Payne 1993: 53). CNT called a strike in 1931 shortly after the founding of the republic, which resulted in brutal repression by the authorities. Even the Socialists were turning against them, and against the republic (Payne 1993: 54). The Communist Party contributed to the growing chaos by declaring war on the Republic in 1931, aiming to replace it with a 'Republic of Worker, Peasant and Soldier Councils' (Payne 1993: 54).

As discussed above, the more moderate socialists were not nearly as popular as their radical counterparts, and the Socialist Party's affiliated trade union, UGT, was equally unpopular until around 1932. In 1930, the union had only 277,011 members but by mid-1932, it had 1,041,539 members (Payne 1993: 57). As a group, they were actually ambivalent about participating in power and their key intellectual leader argued against it, but claimed he would do so to prevent a return of rightist forces or a major threat to reforms (Payne 1993: 58).

Thus, as with Italy, the case of pre-Franco Spain indicates that organized groups may be a problem for democracy, particularly when those groups take violent dissolution of the state itself as their main ideological stance. Post-transition observers often lament the low level of activism and organization of civil society in modern Spain, but in fact (a) in the early days of the transition, leftist groups were indeed organizing activity, particularly strike activity and (b) the more moderate approach to political activism in the modern day may have made the establishment and continued existence of democratic institutions possible.

The electoral institutions of modern Spain have also been designed to prevent the sort-of fragmentation that occurred in the elections of 1933 and 1936. The proportional system introduced by the government for the 15 June 1977 elections – the first free elections held in Spain since 1936 – was modified with corrective devices, including the allocation of seats by means of the conservative d'Hondt rule and the introduction of the 3 per cent constituency-level threshold. This electoral system, along with the cartelization of politics by the major parties, has helped to prevent most minor parties from entering the national parliament. At the same time, most of the pre-Franco groupings are able to find outlets, including those on the left, those in the centre, and those from the right. In fact, it has become the Socialist party that generally represents the interests of the centre, with the leftist Communist Party being far less popular. The latter became so unpopular, in fact, that it formed a coalition with the Greens and left-wing Socialists, known as the

United Left. On the right is the party that formed out of the right-wing Francoists, the People's Party. Regional groupings have also managed to gain representation in the national parliament.

Moreover, the sort of union activism that was apparent during the Second Republic simply did not exist any more in the early days of the new Spanish democracy. Union membership is generally very low, and many authors have commented on the general lack of participation in public life in Spain, although there was some strike activity in the early days of the democratic transition (see Chapter 4; see also Giol *et al.* 1990; they reference Tezanos, 1979, 1981; Maravall 1982; Perez Diaz 1984; Subirats 1987).

One important party to the early Spanish democracy is one that did not have such age-old roots as the Communists and Socialists. The Union of Democrats of the Centre (UCD) was the party formed by Adolfo Suárez to try to maintain unity across the reformist members of Franco's Movimiento. It was not formed on the basis of ideological unity but for the purpose of contesting elections. The key reformist groupings within the Movimiento came together under the UCD umbrella to help ensure that they would continue to gain representation in parliament and in government (see Maravall and Santamaria 1986: 94–5). The party included such disparate groups as those with social democratic leanings, those with Christian Democratic leanings, and independents. Party unity was maintained by a system of trading off government posts across the key factions – somewhat similar to the system in place with the Christian Democrats in Italy. The party was short-lived, however, and was seen as incompetent because of its inability to deal with ETA and the military (see Chapter 9), and because the secretive backstairs dealings of Suárez; he and his party came to be viewed with disenchantment, and in the 1982 elections to the Cortes the party won only 7 per cent of the popular vote and 3.4 per cent of the seats in parliament. This is in comparison to the first two elections it contested, in which it won 35 per cent of the popular vote and 47–8 per cent of the seats in parliament (see Table 6.1) (see Amodia 1983; Heywood 1995: Chapters 8 and 9; Newton 1997: Chapter 10).

The collapse of the UCD paved the way for the other parties to occupy the centre in these early years after the transition. Initially, it was the PSOE that took over this position. The leader of the party during the transition to democracy, Felipe González, thought that the party's hard-line communist approach might make it difficult for it to win enough seats to ever take over government and began trying to remove the Marxist sections of the party programme shortly after the first election in 1977. At first his attempted changes met with extreme resistance and he resigned from the leadership in May 1979; however, his party came around to his ideas and later the same year, a special party congress was held and he was reinstated as party leader. The party very soon came to adopt austerity measures and monetarist policies usually seen in parties of the centre-right. Thus, the main left-wing party in Spain had clearly moved into a centrist, catch-all position (Nash 1983; Heywood 1995: Chapter 8; Newton 1997: Chapter 10).

Table 6.1 Election results: Spain (1977–2004)

Party	1977 votes	% seats	1979 votes	% seats	1982 votes	% seats	1986 votes	% seats
UCD	34.6	47.4	35.	48.0	7.1	3.4	–	
PSOE	29.3	33.7	30.5	34.3	48.4	57.7	44.1	52.6
PCE-IU	9.4	5.7	10.7	6.9	4.1	1.1	4.6	2.0
AP-CD-CP	8.3	4.6	6.0	2.6	26.2	30.3	26.0	30.0
CDS		–		–	2.9	0.6	9.2	5.4
Regional								
PCD-CiU	3.7	2.9	2.5	2.6	3.7	3.4	5.0	5.1
ERC	0.8	0.3	0.7	0.3	0.7	0.3	0.4	0.0
PNV	1.7	2.0	1.5	2.0	1.9	2.3	1.5	1.7
EE	0.5	0.3	0.5	0.3	0.5	0.3	0.5	0.6
HB		–	1.0	0.9	1.0	0.6	1.2	1.4
PSA-PA	0.3	0.000	1.8	1.4	0.4	0.0	2.8	0.0

Party	1989 votes	% seats	1993 votes	% seats	1996 votes	% seats	2000 votes	% seats	2004 votes	% seats
PSOE	40.0	50.0	36.1	45.4	37.5	40.3	34.1	35.7	42.6	46.86
PP	25.6	30.3	34.8	40.3	38.5	44.6	46.6	52.3	37.6	42.29
IU	9.0	5.1	9.6	5.1	10.6	6.0	5.5	2.3	5	1.43
CDS	7.7	4.0	1.8	0.0		–		–		–
Regional										
CiU	9.0	5.4	5.0	4.9	4.6	4.6	4.2	4.3	3.2	2.86
ERC		0.0	0.8	0.3	0.7	0.3	0.8	0.3	2.5	2.29
PNV	1.3	1.4	1.2	1.4	1.3	1.4	1.5	2.0	1.6	2.00
EA	0.7	0.6	0.6	0.3	0.5	0.3	0.4	0.3	0.3	0.29
HB	1.1	1.1	0.9	0.6	0.7	0.6				
EE	0.5	0.6								
PA	1.1	0.6			0.5	0.0	0.9	0.3		
AIC/CC	0.3	0.3	0.9	0.9	0.9	1.1	1.1	1.1		
BNG		–	0.5	0.5	0.9	0.6	1.3	0.9	0.8	0.57
PAR	0.4	0.0	0.6	0.6						
UV	0.7	0.6	0.5	0.5	0.4	0.0				

Initially after the UCD collapse the main right-wing party, the *Aliánza Popular* (AP), also managed to increase its share of the vote. Although the party claimed to be a mainstream conservative party, its continued affiliation with the conservative elements in Franco regime appears to have prevented it from winning more than a quarter of the popular vote. This is partly because its leader, Manuel Fraga, had been a key part of the regime itself (although he had been one of the reformers in the regime). In 1977–8, for instance, about 70 per cent of the electorate saw the AP as a Francoist party, and only 33 per cent believed that it was democratic (Heywood 1995: Chapter 8).

The party spent the next ten years trying to reposition itself to gain a large enough proportion of the right-of-centre votes to form a government. Part of this included adding the *Coalición Democrática* (Democratic Coalition), which included some Christian Democrats who had not joined the UCD, but this did not help and in 1979, the party won only 6 per cent of the vote and only nine seats in the Congress (and three in the Senate).

In addition to the problem of the UCD having initially taken over much of the centre of the political spectrum, the AP was also seen as too far to the right, in that it was still hostile toward the idea of autonomous communities and devolution to the regions and was in favour of the death penalty. In 1979, after its miserable electoral performance, the party tried to remake itself and its leaders advertised it as 'reformist, popular and democratic'; however, it continued to emphasize traditional values, like respect for authority, public order, and the importance of religion in society.

The party's founder eventually stood down in the midst of internal dissension, and a youthful lawyer, Antonio Hernandez Mancha, was selected to replace him. The party still could not rise above the 25 per cent ceiling and began to experience more internal dissent. Fraga came back to lead the party and tried to re-launch it again, this time as a broad coalition of conservative, liberal, and Christian Democratic forces. The party was renamed the *Partido Popular* (People's Party).

The party finally made headway by winning the regional election of Galicia, which was Fraga's homeland, and he went back to serve in government there. The new party leader who was selected was José María Aznar (selected in 1990), and he aimed to distance the party from its Francoist past and chose to do this by adopting a Christian Democratic identity and joining the European People's Party, which is the EU-wide Christian Democratic party grouping.

Aznar also used the media quite effectively and slowly the party started gaining popularity first in municipal elections, then in European elections, and finally in 1996, it won the most seats in the Parliament. Importantly, his party relied on the support of a Catalonian party to govern, thus finally dispelling any notion that the party was still a foe of regional devolution. In the 2000 general elections, the PP won an outright majority of seats in the national parliament. The party looked set to win another victory in the 2004 parliamentary elections, but the Madrid train bombings in March of that same year made the governing People's Party appear both incompetent and deceitful, so it became immediately unpopular.[10] Thus, the Socialist party returned to win the plurality of seats in the parliament.

As with the Italian experience with organized interests and party representation, the Spanish experience produced mixed results. In the Spanish Second Republic, many of the organized interests (e.g. anarchists and communists) refused to take part in the democratic regime and waged open warfare on its institutions as well as the group's opponents on the right. Moreover, there is little evidence to indicate that the parties that were in parliament were able or willing to cooperate to maintain the institutions of the regime. Given the fundamental disagreements over the nature of these institutions, this is not surprising. At the end of the Franco regime, many of these same groupings on both the left and the right remained, other than the anarchists, and it is these political groups that negotiated Spain's transition to democracy and its new democratic constitution. Despite the animosity of the Civil War and repression of the Franco years, these groups proved able and willing to work together after his death in 1975. Also of potential importance is that – other than the Basques and a few minor left-wing groups – Spanish society had been largely depoliticized by Franco's encouragement of greater interest in material goods. Thus, there were fewer individuals interested in engaging in militant activities than had been the case in the Second Republic.

Turkey: the failure of electoral institutions?

The first completely free elections in Turkey are thought to have been held in 1950.[11] Immediately prior to this, Turkey was ruled in a mildly totalitarian manner and regime leaders had prevented the development of an organized opposition. Even before the rise of Mustafa Kemal, however, Turkish political parties were still in relatively fledgling states. The largest and most influential of these was the Committee of Union and Progress which had emerged in the constitutional period of 1909–11 as a civilian party. It was a strongly secularist party and favoured a fairly elitist version of democracy, with only indirect elections and the vote being given to male subjects over the age of 20 who possessed some property. The party generally favoured freedom of assembly and press, but also preferred some restrictions on these as well. It also contained some somewhat socialist preferences: free public primary school education, regulation of relations between workers and employers, and tax reform to reflect economic and social needs (Shaw and Shaw 1977: 282–3). There were several break-away parties from this one, and other parties that formed weak opposition. The Ottoman Socialist Party was formed in Istanbul in 1910, for instance, but appears to have mostly contained Bulgarians and Armenians. However, all political parties were suppressed by the military and had very little influence on politics within the empire during this time (see Shaw and Shaw 1977: 283).

During the civil war in Turkey and the Turkish War of Independence in the early 1920s, there were also multiple small groups of militias forming. In addition, many of the Ottoman Communists were in Russia but sent propaganda literature into the Anatolian portion of the empire. During the War of Independence Mustafa Kemal's response was to try to incorporate the Communists into a joint Communist–Unionist organization called the People's Communist Party, enabling the Communists to emerge to the Turkish public for the first time. Kemal also allowed the formation of a Turkish Communist Party in October 1920, but insisted that it be run by associates of his from within the National Assembly. Some of the party's groupings became active in places like Ankara and Eskişehir, but were criticized by the regime for operating outside of the parliament and were ultimately crushed – along with the Communists more generally – by Kemal's forces (see Shaw and Shaw 1977: 353–4).

At the end of the Turkish War of Independence, therefore, there was very little in the way of organized opposition in Turkey. Much of the opposition was destroyed during the war, and the major groups that might have formed bourgeois parties – the Greeks and Armenians – had already been either deported or disappeared. For the entirety of his reign, Kemal was thus able to prevent the rise of political parties that might have represented interests outside of those of the new ruling class – i.e. strong secularism and state-led economic development.[12] The tight reign on organized opposition continued until 1946, when Kemal's successor, İsmet İnönü, unexpectedly announced that the elections held in that year would be open to opposition parties. This left very little time for any opposition groups to become organized and it is also believed that the elections were rigged by the governing party. However, the latter made it clear that subsequent elections would be free and fair, and so opposition groups had four years in which to become organized to contest the next elections, to be held in 1950.

It is important to note that the electoral system in place was one which had the effect of discouraging small groups or parties. It was a multi-member system inherited from the first Ottoman electoral regulations of 1876, in which the electorate had the right to vote for one or more candidates, depending on the number of MPs to be elected in a particular district. While some members of the electorate did split their tickets between parties, in practice, the system generally functioned like a plurality system with multi-member districts; the party that won the plurality of the vote in a district tended to win all (or most) of the seats in that district (see Shaw and Shaw 1977: 405; Hale 1980: 402). Thus, the opposition behaved rationally and created a single party, the Democratic Party, to contest the 1946 election. This party was formed by groups that were opposed to government policy. Because there were vastly differing reasons for opposition to government, the party became a patchwork of interests. Some of those opposed to the ruling party were moral and religious traditionalists who were strongly opposed to the secularizing measures taken by Kemal in the 1920s. Others were opposed to the strong state intervention in the economy and wanted a party that would represent bourgeois interests. Thus, in some ways, the Democratic Party in Turkey in the 1950s resembled the Christian Democrats in Italy in the same period. Recall that the latter was also a broad coalition of interests emphasizing moral conservatism, and that many within its fold were also opposed to Socialist proposals for state intervention in the economy (although it must be noted that many others in the party were in favour of socioeconomic reforms that were consistent with Socialist Party demands, as was the case with the Turkish Democratic Party).

Also recall that the Christian Democrats enacted measures that would have given them a clear majority of seats in parliament, just as the Democratic Party was able to achieve between 1950 and 1960. Given the ease with which such authority was used to convert a new democracy into a non-democracy, it seems that Italian democracy might have been saved from the same sort-of events that transpired in Turkey in the 1950s. Although this made governance difficult in Italy (see the next chapter), it also meant that governance was generally fairly democratic.

After the 1960 military coup, constitutional designers (see Chapter 5) had the clear aim of converting Turkish institutions from majoritarian to consensual institutions. Included in these changes were vast changes to the electoral law. Indeed, the 1960s witnessed a great deal of tinkering with the electoral system (Hale 1980). Initially, the system adopted was similar to the current Spanish electoral law – a system of proportional representation with a d'Hondt quota system that tended to favour larger parties and penalize small parties. However, in 1965, the governing party decided to try to increase the proportionality of the results by adopting a largest remainder system in addition to the d'Hondt quota; essentially, parties that were penalized at the district level could capture seats at the national level, depending on their overall popular vote. The law was again changed for the 1969 election such that this remainder system was scrapped, but the formula used to determine seats at the district level was a more proportional one. Thus, beginning in 1961, we start to see the fragmentation of the two main parties; as the electoral formulas became more proportional, the components within these groups perhaps behaved as would be predicted by rational choice institutionalists and split off to form their own parties. Most electoral engineers would have likely hailed this as a positive achievement, in that it meant for the first time that major groupings in Turkish society could gain access to the political system via coherent organized political parties. However, in practice, it helped to create government instability, and prolonged periods in which parliament could not agree on any coalition formula (Hale 1980), a topic to which we will return in Chapter 7.

Importantly, though, it seems that the new electoral system revealed deep-seated cleavages which were already in existence but had been previously subsumed within the two major parties. The different social classes and political groups that had been united under each of the two parties began to split in 1961 (see Shaw and Shaw 1977: 424).

Accounting for all of the break-away parties during this period is beyond the scope of this text, but some of the major divisions that were developing will be examined. During the 1960s, the strongest left-wing group was the Turkish Workers' Party which was formed in 1961 by union leaders in Istanbul and in 1962 was converted into a fully fledged Socialist party. The party was hostile to the US's role in Turkey (see Chapter 10) and advocated closer links to the Soviet Union. Domestically, it took a typically socialist line, such as a return to state control of heavy industry, the nationalization of banks and insurance companies, land reform, and the notion that private enterprise would slowly disappear as a result of its uselessness in a Socialist State. The party was alone in demanding a five-day, 40-hour work week (see Shaw and Shaw 1977: 423–4). At the same time, the Republican People's Party began to adopt rhetoric that rivalled that of the other left-leaning groups. The party's roots were in the strong state-led policies developed by Kemal, and so it was no stretch for the party leaders to begin to speak in terms of nationalization of industry, improved working conditions, etc., thereby co-opting the rhetoric of the socialists. Indeed, despite the existence of break-away parties, the RPP consistently received more votes than any of the other leftist parties (see Dodd 1976 on parties and voting in 1960s and 1970s Turkey).

The right also split, with groups like the New Turkey Party forming with an ideology that accepted the notion of private enterprise and rapid industrialization, with some government intervention to help promote economic development. Although religious education would be encouraged, secularism and freedom for all religions was to be accepted and even encouraged. Another break-away party that formed on the right was the Republican Peasant's National Party which emphasized social and religious aims similar to those of the National Socialist Movements in pre-war Germany and Italy; the economic aims were fairly socialist in nature – prevention of excessive profits and exploitation of capitalism (without abolishing it, though), planning, etc. Also, though, Turkish nationalism and Islam were to be emphasized, and it was believed that people should be educated and directed through their entire lives (Shaw and Shaw 1977: 422). This party eventually became the Nationalist Action Party. A more moderate party, the Nation Party, also formed out of the right.

Also in existence on the right during the 1970s were religiously oriented parties. The first of these was the National Order Party, formed in 1970 but closed by the Turkish Constitutional Court for using religion for political purposes in 1971. The Nationalist Salvation Party formed shortly thereafter, using a very similar religiously oriented platform, and was allowed to remain open until 1981. In the 1970s, the party was relatively small, gaining 5–10 per cent of the seats in the parliament, but as will be seen below, its successors have become even more popular, indicating the increased importance of the religious cleavage in Turkish politics.

The largest party of the right, however, in the 1960s and 1970s was the successor to the Democratic Party, the Justice Party. The party continued to emphasize liberalism and private enterprise. There were also some social-democratic aspects to the party's platform: workers would be allowed to strike and would be given social security, health care, etc. More autonomy for villages and towns, and encouragement of foreign capital were also part of the platform (Shaw and Shaw 1977: 423; see also Dodd 1976).

Despite the continued existence of the two large parties – the Republican People's Party and the Justice Party – in most elections in the 1960s and 1970s, neither of these managed to win enough seats in parliament to govern alone and were thus forced to form coalitions. The most common coalition pattern was a centre-right one between the Justice Party and the religious and/or nationalist party. However, there were also times when the left-wing Republican People's Party approached the small right-wing parties to form coalitions. Not surprisingly, these were very short-lived, as disputes over policy differences broke out (see Chapter 7). The continued failure to find workable coalitions, along with accusations that many of the parties were fostering violence amongst their active supporters, led to another military intervention in 1980.

Although all of the parties and politicians who had been in parliament and government were banned from politics for some time after the 1980 coup, in the 1980s, successor parties began to form. For instance, the key parties on the right became the True Path Party and the Motherland Party. The ideological approaches of these parties were very similar to one another and to that of the outlawed Justice Party, emphasizing privatization, liberalism, etc., along with some mild critique of extreme secularism. The main reason that two different parties with very similar ideologies formed appears to be related to the personalities of the party leaders themselves and the inability of leaders to cooperate with one another. Indeed, even forming a coalition between these two like-minded parties proved extremely difficult due to personal conflicts between leaders (see Chapter 7).

It should also be noted that the electoral formula chosen in the post-1980 period represents a return to conservatism and an attempt to push the political system back toward a majoritarian formula. The system is still technically a proportional representation system, but with a minimum 10 per cent nationwide threshold and a maximum district size of 7; both rules tend to favour larger parties and penalize small parties (see US Library Congress 1995; see also Finkel and Hale 1990). It was hoped that this threshold would keep the small extremist parties like the religious parties and the Nationalist Action Party out of parliament and make it unnecessary for large mainstream parties to turn to the extremes for coalition partners. However, with regard to the parties on the right, the new formula has generally failed to produce the expected consequences. As indicated above, the centre-right formed two separate parties. Moreover, the Nationalist Action Party continued to exist and even managed to win a significant portion of seats in the

1990s and eventually became a governing party. Perhaps even more perplexing for the designers of the electoral law, the religious parties have also managed to win an impressive number of parliamentary seats: 28.7 per cent in 1995, and 20.2 per cent in 1999. The leader of one of these (the Welfare Party) even managed to secure the post of prime minister until a military intervention forced him to step down. Finally, in the 2002 parliamentary elections, a religious successor party (the Justice and Development Party) to one of those previously closed down won a majority of parliamentary seats with only 34.3 per cent of the popular vote and again won a majority of seats in parliament with 46.7 per cent of the vote in 2007. The party has been in government since 2002. Thus, the Turkish electoral system may have eventually produced a more majoritarian system in the long run, but this was only after the established secular parties were completely disgraced by an inability to address a major economic crisis at the start of the twenty-first century.

The left also experienced considerable splintering after the 1980 coup. The Republican People's Party was dissolved in 1980 and the subsequent leftist parties that formed were the Populist Party and the Social Democracy Party; these two parties merged to form the Social Democratic Populist Party in 1984 and eventually returned the party to its original name, the Republican People's Party, in 1992. The other leftist party that formed during this time was the Democratic Left Party (formed in 1985). As with the mainstream right, the ideologies of these two – the Democratic Left Party and the Republican People's Party – were very similar, and after the collapse of communism in Central and Eastern Europe, the RPP and DLP both began to migrate further toward the centre.

While the post-1980 electoral system has failed to keep the number of parties in the national parliament low, it *has* succeeded in preventing any overtly Kurdish-oriented parties from gaining representation in the national parliament. Such parties (see Chapter 8) have won seats in municipal elections and representatives from the parties have won seats in the national parliament under the banner of another party or as independents, but they have generally then been closed down for threatening the territorial integrity of the Turkish state and nation (see Kogacioğlu 2003, 2004 on party closures in Turkey).[13]

What about organized social groups in Turkey? As with our discussion of Italy and Spain, we focus here on organized labour. Chapter 3 illustrated that Turkish industrialization, much like that in Spain, got off to a relatively late start and was generally dominated by foreign industrialists who were better able than domestic entrepreneurs to take advantage of Ottoman provisions that had been adopted for the encouragement of industrialization. Along with the development of nascent industry in the Ottoman Empire and particularly with the *Tanzimat* liberalization in the 1800s, workers began to use strikes to try to gain concessions from the industrialists. It must be noted that these were not generally organized by unions (which did not yet exist in the Ottoman Empire) but were instead fairly spontaneous events (see Karakisla 1995). The state's approach to this activism was that it was disruptive and troublesome and so laws were passed making unions and strikes illegal.[14]

The Committee for Union and Progress – the organization that eventually overthrew the Ottoman regime and established the Turkish Republic – while it was an underground organization had no solid plan for how to govern, and so its approach to unions was initially ambiguous. At first, in 1908–9 some of its leaders attempted to mediate between strikers and employers, but they soon came to take a repressive approach (Karakisla 1995). This continued with the regime of Mustafa Kemal, whose government feared socialists and socialism in part because they represented a competing ideology to the one being developed by the regime, the latter consisting of an ideology which saw the state and citizens in organic terms very similar to the fascist ideologies of Italy and Spain. That is, different sectors of the economy were perceived to be working together to achieve goals that would benefit the nation, and so these sectors should not be in conflict. Eventually, Kemal adopted corporatism in the 1930s, modelled on Italian corporatism, which looked favourably on workers associations or corporations, but not unions. In addition, the penal code of the Republican era – also adopted from the Italian penal code in 1936 – was designed to prevent the discussion of class and class struggle. In fact these laws remained on the books until the early 1990s (Ahmad 1995).

Thus, the development of this form of civil society was severely curbed by government policy. However, by 1923 while the regime was still in flux, labour unions *had* formed. Some of these were Marxist, but not all of them were (Yavuz 1995). The regime's approach to unions was one of repression, and most of the Marxist-oriented union organizers were either jailed or went into exile in Europe and the Soviet Union. The repressive laws were solidified with the passage of a new Law of Associations in 1938; this law stipulated that associations could be founded only with the permission of the government and that associations based on classes were illegal; further, all associations were prohibited from engaging in political activities (Yavuz 1995: 99–100).

During World War II, martial law was instituted, and the right to gather, organize, and demonstrate were restricted; restrictions were also placed on press freedom. Thus, the transition to multi-party politics occurred during a period of martial law; indeed, even as late as December 1946, two socialist parties and their trade-union affiliates were closed by the military authorities (Guzel 1995: 127–8). The Trade Union Act of 1947 did finally permit the establishment of unions of workers and of employers but still prohibited the use of strikes and lockouts. The next government elected in 1950 made no attempt to change the laws until 1957 when the right to strike was conceded, and so prior to this point the regime continued to operate on the basis of promotion of social order and solidarity (Hershlag 1959: 289–94).

Proponents of civil society approaches to democratic consolidation would likely point to this as a prime explanation for the failure of Turkish democracy in the 1950–60 period. Namely, the lack of such organizations – for whatever reason – meant that a democratically elected government could become just as oppressive as the authoritarian government that had preceded it because there were no civil society organizations that could call the government to task. However, as noted with the examples of Spain and Italy, the existence of organized labour may have little impact on whether democracy fails or not. In addition, as shown above, the electoral institutions that were still in use in the 1950s – left over from the Ottoman electoral law – appear to be the key factor giving a single party the overwhelming majority it needed to rule unchecked.

Developments in the 1960s and 1970s in Turkey – much like the events in 1920s Italy and Spain – point to the conclusion that organized civil society, at least in the form of trade unions, simply cannot guarantee continued existence of democratic institutions. The 1960 constitution created the framework whereby new legislation establishing trade-union freedom and the right to strike could be passed (Tuna 1964). Although far from overwhelming, union membership figures show an eight-fold increase in membership between 1948 to 1963 (Tuna 1964: 425). Between 1963 and 1978, the number of workers unions almost doubled (T.C. Çalişma ve Sosyal Güvenlik Bakanlyğy 1983). Parties which had been seen as elitist, particularly the Republican People's Party, began to transform into mass-based parties. The RPP specifically encouraged the creation of civil society organizations and cooperative networks. Also important is that the party appears to have created clientelistic networks in the 1970s, most of which survived into the 1980s. As argued by Güneş-Ayata, '... in a society where resources are scarce and the state is a crucial factor in resource allocation, clientelism is used as a participative strategy by certain social classes and groups to operate an exclusive allocation system in their own interests' (1990: 181; see also Özbudun 1981).

At the same time that 'civil society' began to form, however, many members of these groups – again, as in Italy and Spain – began to use militant, and at times, violent, techniques. Specifically, leftist trade unionists formed a political party, the Turkish Workers' Party in 1961, thus providing a potentially important connection between the growing civil society organizations and the state. Initially, the party contended that it would push for socialist reforms via the ballot box and criticized the Soviet invasion of Czechoslovakia in 1968. Thus, it was following a path similar to the 'Italian way to socialism'. However, shortly after this the moderate leadership was replaced by leaders who took a pro-Soviet line. These hardliners became convinced that if they could not win power by constitutional means, they would have to do so by violent revolution. This led to the proliferation of violent leftist urban guerrilla groups in the late 1960s (Hale 1994: 176).

At the same time, the 1960s saw a revitalization of the Turkist movement mentioned in Chapter 2. Recall that this was a nationalist movement that began in the late 1800s in an attempt to create a new identity in the midst of a crumbling empire. In the 1960s and 1970s new groups such as the Association of Turkists formed to revitalize these ideas. By the time of the 1980 coup, the movement had grown and had several trade unions and other occupational groups organized under its banner. These groups were connected initially to the Republican Peasants' and Nation Party which renamed itself the Nationalist Action Party in 1969 (see Landau 1981: 148). Interestingly, Islam had increased its appeal and the Turkist movement had begun to incorporate it into the Turkist ideology. However, this movement had a very violent side and began to form 'commando' units in the late 1960s in order to fight off the 'internal enemy', namely the leftists (Çağlar 1990: 85). In addition, much of the conflict in the 1970s was motivated by disputes between the industrialists and business elites in urbanized areas and the petit bourgeoisie, represented by the newly founded National Salvation Party (Shambayati 1994). The regime eventually collapsed in 1980, in part because of government inability to control the violence and alleged collusion between some of the parties and the violent activists (see Chapter 9 for further discussion of these events).

In short, Turks were becoming extremely active in politics in the 1960s and 1970s, although some might contend that many of the activities carried out could hardly be referred to as 'civil'. At the same time, it must be noted that observers tend to lay much of the blame for these activities on party leaders and activists, who managed to stoke the flames of violence. As a result of all of this activity, in the 1982 constitution, citizen activities and activism were severely restricted. Provisions within that constitution allow for restrictions on activities (as well as speech) which threatens the public order or the indivisibility of the state 'with its territory and nation' (Article 14). Perhaps most importantly, young people – in particular, students – are restricted from joining political parties. This constitutional provision was a result of the fact that much of the political violence in the 1960s and 1970s was waged by university students. The effect of this restriction has, however, been de-politicization of the Turkish youth, which then has considerable implications for their politicization in later life. In many ways, modern Turkey resembles modern Spain in the realm of political activism. As was seen with the Spanish example, however, the lack of organized activism does not appear to have harmed Spain's consolidation of democracy, and as shown with the contrasting Italian case, a low level of activism may help to promote a speedier consolidation.

Part of the problem for Turkish democracy has been a result of the banning of certain parties. On multiple occasions, both the religiously oriented parties and parties that were thought by the authorities to be designed to represent Kurdish interests have been banned after winning seats in the national parliament or in municipal elections. The latter of these parties has never been large and never became powerful enough to win seats on its own in the national parliament, in part because of the 10 per cent national threshold required to obtain parliamentary seats. The ban on them is the equivalent of the Catalonian or Basque parties being banned from the Spanish parliament or municipal elections, and as would be the case in Spain, it creates a political system in which a fairly key group that has traditionally been concentrated in a clearly defined region of the country feels alienated from the polity. As has been the case with the Basques, it has, in turn, meant that groups of activists have been carrying out violent terrorist attacks in order to bring attention to the fact that they are a minority group that is not adequately represented – or rather, not represented at all – in Turkish politics. The response of the Turkish government to the violent attacks was an all-out war against the population in the east and southeastern parts of the country, legislation allowing for lengthy detention periods for those in the region suspected of terrorism, the use of military courts to try such individuals, etc. Indeed much of the criticism of Turkish democracy – and particularly the human rights aspect of it – has been connected to the battle being waged in the Kurdish regions. Ultimately, the reason for government unwillingness to consider the option of representation rather than repression has been tied to a constitutional provision protecting the territorial integrity of the Turkish state (see Chapter 8). Based on the assumption that all Kurds want separation, they have been perceived as a threat to this provision. However, no published analysis has been conducted on the goals and aims of the Kurdish portion of the public on the part of the government, and so it is difficult to know whether these concerns of government have been valid. At the very least, the failure to acknowledge this group at any level as has been the case with threatening groups in Spain, such as the Basques, or in Italy, such as the Communists, has very likely impeded the consolidation of Turkish democracy.

Similarly, religiously oriented parties have been perceived as a threat to other constitutional provisions protecting the secular nature of the Turkish Republic. Not surprisingly, given Turkey's proximity to Iran, there is clear concern about some groups trying to transform Turkey into a religiously based regime and perhaps return Turkey to the days of *sharia* law. In fact, religious groups appeared to be becoming more active in the 1990s. The obstinate refusal to consider parties that have religious leanings as legitimate has thus traditionally also created a pool of citizens who are potentially unsupportive of the regime itself. Although these groups have made no attempts to actively undermine Turkish democracy, neither have they traditionally had any reason to actively support it when times have become difficult. The experience of both Spain and Italy, however, would indicate that the only real way forward for a fledgling democracy may be to acknowledge groups like this as legitimate parts of the political system. In Spain, for instance, the former Franquists were allowed to form their own party and compete in elections; in Italy, the Communists also competed freely in elections, despite alleged fears about a Communist takeover in Italy; the neo-fascist MSI was also allowed to compete, despite being illegal. Without such incorporation into the democratic system, groups like this may have the potential to serve as an organized system of opposition to the regime itself.

It is important to note that the recent years in Turkey have witnessed vast changes in the treatment of groups like the Kurds and religious parties. Kurds will be discussed further in Chapter 8, but here the issue of religious parties will be addressed. The tension over religious issues in Turkey, particularly issues like attire in public places, had reached a boiling point in the late 1990s and in 2000–2. Moreover, religious parties that had received 15–25 per cent of seats in parliament were being banned, posing a real threat to the very legitimacy of the regime itself. In 2002, however, the religiously oriented party, the Justice and Development Party, won the majority of seats in the Turkish parliament (with only a minority of the popular vote), as discussed above. This created an unprecedented situation in which a party that would normally be banned very shortly after the election was in a position to form a single-party government. Although there is no doubt that the party and its policies are under close scrutiny by the military (see Chapter 9) and the 'establishment', the party has managed to govern with relatively minimal interference. It is argued here that this has created a situation in which consolidation of democracy in the country seems far more possible than in previous times.

In fact, this is true by definition. Whereas before the 2002 election, the country existed in a state of quasi-authoritarianism, in which all parties could compete in elections, but then some of them would be thrown out of parliament, leaving their constituents feeling inadequately represented, the system is now far less authoritarian. That is, previously, it was clear that only those groups of certain ideological leanings could ever participate in government, whereas now this seems no longer to be the case. Moreover, this potentially important group which had been previously excluded may be in the process of being co-opted into the regime itself, as was the case with the Communists in Italy. Importantly, much of the constitutional and penal reform in recent years has been led by this party, perhaps giving it a stronger stake in the constantly changing republic.

Conclusions

What has been the role of citizens and parties in consolidating democracy in Italy, Spain and Turkey? Let us consider first the political landscape at the time of the start of the most recent transitions to democracy in each of the three – 1946–8 in Italy, 1975 in Spain, and 1983 in Turkey. In the case of Italy, the transition began after more than two decades of authoritarian rule. Even after this lengthy dictatorship and the successful 'taming' of the working classes discussed in Chapter 3, one of the major dividing lines in Italy was still that of class. Moreover, working-class interests still generally preferred the extreme left Communists rather than the more moderate

Socialists. Set against this secularly oriented group were Catholic interests, and a few hard-line fascists also still remained. As discussed above, many scholars would contend that one of the reasons that Italian democracy did survive these early tenuous days was precisely because all of these interests gained legitimate representation in the political system. The pre-Mussolini breakdown of democracy, however, would point us to the conclusion that representation alone is clearly not enough to guarantee democracy. In that period very similar groups were represented – although the Catholic groups were weakly represented at this stage compared to their post-war presence – but it is perhaps the extreme ideology particularly of the leftist parties that made them unwilling to work with other parties in parliament or in government. Clearly in the post-war period, the leadership of these parties had changed its approach and became far more conciliatory, a point which will be discussed further in the next chapter. While representation alone may not have been a sufficient cause of consolidation of democracy in Italy, if we consider the counterfactual situation in which a major group like the Communists was outlawed, banned, etc., it seems likely that this group *would* have engaged in behaviour that would have destabilized the new democracy. As discussed above, much of the workforce in Italy was unionized and tended to affiliate with the left, and such a high level of organization would indicate that these groups could have played a major part in destabilization; indeed, many would contend that their willingness to forgo wage increases and avoid strike activity for a short period while the Italian economy recovered (see Chapter 4) gave the regime the breathing space it needed to establish solid democratic institutions.

In the case of Spain, at the time of its transition to democracy and shortly thereafter, citizens themselves were not all that active, at least in terms of union membership. In fact, Riley (2005) indicates that Spaniards have never been as active in unions as Italians. Thus, there appear to have been no major potentially divisive societal cleavages to represent in the new Spanish democracy. On the other hand, there *were* powerful elites who claimed to represent key interests, and it is thought to be important that all of these did gain representation in the new democratically elected Constituent Assembly and later the Cortes proper. This is unlike the situation at the start of Spanish Second Republic where the right failed to organize itself to contest elections to the Constituent Assembly and subsequently played a limited role in the design of that democratic constitution. Leonardo Morlino's research indicates that while representation may be important in a new democracy in which the democratic institutions are of questionable legitimacy, as in Italy in 1946–8, in countries where the institutions are widely accepted as legitimate – as in Spain – the party system is less of an important factor in consolidating democracy (Morlino 1995). The analysis of this chapter tends to confirm this argument.

This leads us to our final case, Turkey. This case would initially seem to point us to the conclusion that parties and party systems may indeed be crucial for consolidating democracy. First of all, after the most recent transition to democracy in 1983, it is clear that some of the key groups that have been persistently excluded from the representational scheme have worked to destabilize the regime itself. Most prominent amongst these are Kurdish groups. The violent activism of these groups resulting from the state's unwillingness to allow them legitimate representation has produced a situation in which the Turkish military (discussed in Chapter 9) has been able to continue to amass and control a large budget ostensibly for the purpose of maintaining the territorial integrity of the state. This, along with its pursuit of war against the Kurds, has allowed it to continue to maintain its strength and independence from elected civilians. Other groups that could have destabilized the regime were those with religious inclinations; the refusal of the regime to incorporate these interests, along with the closure of parties that represent them (until relatively recently), presented the regime with clear legitimacy problems that were likely to eventually create problems that would undermine the regime itself. Indeed, the refusal to allow the representation of particular groups has directly led to breakdown of democracy, for instance in 1997 (see Chapter 7). Perhaps most importantly, as discussed in the previous chapter, is the fact that institutions themselves have been designed by a very limited range of representatives, leaving the unrepresented opposition in the position of consistently arguing that these institutions are illegitimate. This, in turn, has led politicians to promote or sympathize with extra-parliamentary means, including violent behaviour, which eventually results in military intervention. Ultimately, then, it may be the failure of elites to understand the importance of representation and to guarantee it that has produced the unstable democracy that is Turkey. At the same time, the uncompromising behaviour of these elites in the 1960s and 1970s – as was the case in Italy in the early 1920s – may equally explain the periods of destabilization of Turkish democracy. The next chapter explores this possibility further.

7   The functioning of government
Executive and parliament

The manner in which key governing institutions are organized and operate may be relevant for the creation of consolidated democracy. The main dividing lines in this respect are between presidential and parliamentary systems and between majoritarian and consensual forms of government. Here it is also contended that the clarity of powers and rules and procedures may be important as well – failure to specify these clearly in written, authoritative documents creates a situation in which it may be unclear regarding which governmental body has ultimate law-making ability. This situation can, in turn, produce at least three negative outcomes.

First, and most relevant for the analysis of this book, it can create the opportunity for a slow migration toward authoritarianism on the part of the democratically elected government itself. That is, without clear regulations limiting the power of the executive and clear enforcement mechanisms, the danger is that the executive can exercise unlimited authority and adopt undemocratic policies such as persecution of minorities and/or opposition groups.

Second, a lack of clarity and agreement regarding the rules may create a situation in which non-democratic actors have a clear, valid excuse for moving the system abruptly toward authoritarianism (e.g. via a military coup). This is because disputes over the distribution of power are likely to surface in the form of open conflict between the Head of State and Head of Government, between the Head of State and parliament, or the Head of Government and Parliament. Such disruptions increase the odds of authoritarian interventions, especially if there is a body already poised for such intervention.

Finally, lack of clarity of powers, rules, and procedures interferes with the ability to provide responsible government: if power is shared in an ambiguous manner, for instance, it means that all government institutions can potentially shirk responsibility for policy-making, leaving important decisions on economic and social policy in limbo. Although this problem is in great part one of the *quality* of democracy, it also creates an opening whereby non-democratic forces can easily contend that the democratic institutions and participants are an utter failure, and ultimately provides the situation whereby such forces can validly intervene.

Along with clarity of rules, the type of rules chosen are also thought to be relevant for democratic consolidation. As mentioned above, one of the key dividing lines is that between presidential and parliamentary systems. Using Latin American countries as examples of failed presidential systems, Juan Linz argues that new democracies should avoid this type of political system (Linz 1990). Later analyses have confirmed that presidential political systems on average have a higher likelihood of breakdown into authoritarianism (Mainwaring 1993; Stepan and Skach 1993; Lijphart 1996). This dividing line is not entirely relevant to the analysis here, as none of the three countries under investigation has ever had a presidential system: Italy and Turkey currently have a president as head of state, and Spain's Second Republic also contained a president, but in none of these cases was the president popularly elected. The popular election of the president, along with a constitutional division of powers, is what is thought to give presidents in presidential systems like that of the US their power and legitimacy, and having a popularly elected parliament and president then creates problems in which it is unclear as to which body is responsible for various aspects of policy-making. However, it is also the case that if a president is chosen by the parliament – and presidents chosen in this way are often chosen by a super-majority of parliament – and the parliament cannot then remove the president except in very unusual circumstances, the president also gains a certain degree of independent legitimacy and can claim to be the choice of a broad coalition of interests and to be 'above politics'. It seems that being in this position has just as much potential to create ambiguity regarding power and responsibility as the situation where the president is popularly elected. And indeed, all three of the political systems studied here have at various times experienced difficulties over the exercise of presidential power, creating disputes over whether the government (i.e. the prime minister and cabinet) or the president has ultimate decision-making authority in certain policy areas. Again, such a situation creates the possibility for non-democratic actors to step in, claiming to resolve such disputes or to step in to solve other problems while the president and government are fighting over power distribution.

The other major dividing line in terms of types of democratic institutions is between consensual and majoritarian institutions. Arend Lijphart has consistently argued that consensual political institutions work better in countries where there are deep societal-level cleavages. Lijphart generally refers to ethnic, linguistic and religious pluralism, pointing to cases like Switzerland and the Netherlands as democracies that simply would not work if majoritarianism was the model that had been adopted in these countries. What is the difference between majoritarian and consensual? Conceptually, the difference lies in whether it is believed by constitutional designers that policy-making should be based on majority rule or whether policies should satisfy the greatest number of interests possible. It is generally thought that institutions can be developed that will help to produce one or the other of these types of systems. Namely, electoral rules that fail to produce a clear majority in parliament – i.e. proportional representation systems – are more likely to produce consensualism, as parties must adopt a compromising approach in order to form governing coalitions. On the other hand, coalition formation and cabinet stability may present a new democracy with considerable difficulty because maintaining a governing coalition across disparate ideological groupings and individual personalities can be a major challenge. As argued by Pasquino (1995), cabinet stability can have an important impact on democratic consolidation because it has an effect on whether the new rules of the regime become institutionalized:

> cabinet stability will create conditions favoring institutionalization of rules and regulations devised during the transition. Conversely, cabinet instability and continuing uncertainty over the prospects and capacity of the government to act authoritatively and to make binding decisions will impede the institutionalization of these rules. In doing so, such instability may impede the consolidation process.
>
> (Pasquino 1995: 264)

Executive–parliamentary rules can also be designed such that parliament is more or less powerful; an executive with almost absolute power that controls a majority in parliament can easily enforce a majoritarian system, whereas when rules are such that parliament has a great deal of decision-making authority, the political system becomes more consensual, as government is forced to negotiate with parliamentarians (as in the US political system for instance). Other rules can also contribute to the overall nature of the political regime, such as the organization of interest groups; many of these other rules do not appear to be overly relevant to the analysis here, but in addition to addressing executives and parliaments, we will be addressing another consensual institution – devolved power – in the next chapter. Moreover, the previous chapter briefly discussed electoral laws that are thought to have impacted the functioning of the regimes of Italy, Spain, and Turkey. Some of this will be reviewed here, as it has had an impact on the nature of executives and executive power in all three countries, but generally the focus of this chapter is on the latter, along with the power and functioning of parliaments.

It has also been argued that parliaments often have a key role to play in consolidating democracy. First, they may play an important role in drafting the democratic constitution. As seen in previous chapters, if this is done with the representatives of major socio-political groups taking an active part in the construction of the new rules, then it is more likely that these groups – or at the very least, their leaders – will cooperate with the new democratic institutions. Second, parliament may contribute to consolidation or failed consolidation by illustrating – or failing to illustrate – that conflict resolution can occur peacefully within this institution. Chapter 3 of this book provided an example of the failure of parliament to serve as a body of peaceful conflict resolution during the Spanish Second Republic. Creating a consensual parliament which can be used for conflict resolution may, in part, be accomplished by drafting parliamentary rules that allow for a more consensual approach to conflict resolution. Another of the main functions of parliament is to represent the interests and cleavages present in society. As discussed in the previous chapter, failure to do so necessarily means that the very legitimacy of the regime is reduced and that groups that are consistently excluded from parliament have strong incentives to undermine the new democratic regime (see Liebert 1990).

This chapter therefore addresses the main aspects of the functioning of government discussed above. Namely, it investigates parliamentary–executive relationships, the clarity and institutionalization of rules governing relations between these bodies and between the Head of State and Head of Government, and also examines the role of parliament specifically in consolidating democracy in the three countries under investigation.

Italian parliament and executive: order in chaos?

This section begins by briefly discussing the role that the Italian parliament played in the early days of post-World War II democratization and the role that it played in Italian politics in later years. We will then turn to a discussion of the Italian executive.

After the collapse of Mussolini's regime, it was not immediately clear that any assembly would necessarily be formed; the bureaucracy and many of the pre-fascist era politicians who favoured the monarchy were pushing for a minimalist form of regime change, and were hoping to lead the transition away from fascism, although it was not clear as to specifically what they had in mind: a pure monarchy, a return to constitutional monarchy, or what? However, the Committee of National Liberation (discussed in Chapter 5) had gained a great deal of legitimacy and authority as a result of its assistance in driving Germany out of the country. It thus became apparent that the main parties of the CNL were simply too powerful and too vocal to be excluded, and their preference was for the creation of a Constituent Assembly for the purpose of designing a new constitution.

This assembly took key decisions that would then have a subsequent impact on the functioning of the new Italian democracy. For instance, the CNL decided to use a relatively pure form of proportional representation to elect the Constituent Assembly. As mentioned in previous chapters, all of the groups in the CNL had doubts about how well they would perform in elections held under FPP and so had an incentive to opt for PR. Those favouring a more majoritarian solution like the one of pre-fascist Italy (which used a single member district plurality electoral system) were willing to give in to PR because of the stipulation that the electoral system chosen was only for the Constituent Assembly elections and would not necessarily be the electoral system used to select the first parliament. A system of preference voting, wherein voters could rank order candidates for elections in their parliamentary districts, was offered as a way of compensating those who favoured FPP. In fact, this was the electoral system that was eventually chosen for the selection of parliament, and so this first negotiation within the CNL was in hindsight rather important in shaping the nature of the Italian parliament and thus Italian government, and the Assembly continued to use this electoral system until 1993 (see Cotta 1990; Ginsborg 1990; Hine 1993).

Another important decision taken by the Assembly was the agreement to leave the decision regarding the monarchy in the hands of citizens in the form of a referendum. If the Assembly itself had attempted to tackle this issue, it would have been extremely divisive and would have very likely split the major party, the Christian Democrats, which would, in turn, have created regime legitimacy problems, as some factions within the DC would have inevitably come out in favour of the monarchy and others opposed, thereby having lasting consequences for the positions of these various DC factions regarding the fundamental nature of the regime. As mentioned in Chapter 5, the popular vote in the referendum was extremely close, with only 54 per cent favouring a republic, but was decisive and managed to depoliticize a potentially divisive issue.

The Assembly also played a major role in the design of the constitution. Despite the fact that the government that was selected out of the Assembly appointed technicians such as constitutional law professors to write various articles of the Constitution, once they were turned over to the plenary session of the Assembly, significant alterations were made by the Assembly itself. One example of this was the decision to have a bicameral parliament in which both chambers are popularly elected in roughly similar ways. In most other countries with bicameral legislatures, representation in the second chamber is specifically designed to be different from that in the first. For instance, state or regional governments might be represented in the second chamber, or the upper chamber might be designed to include elites who are above the fray of day-to-day politics, as with the UK's House of Lords. The only reason to have a perfectly bicameral system – as Italy is – is to (a) increase the number of seats that can be won by all groups and (b) reduce government power by requiring that legislation pass in identical forms in both chambers.[1]

Overall, the fact that the constitution was designed by a parliament as opposed to a government meant that every effort was made to increase the power of parliament. The above-mentioned constitutional provision is one that has helped make the Italian parliament extremely powerful: the fact that all legislation must be approved by both chambers in identical forms and that both houses have real constitutional authority means that the parliament as a whole can have a major impact on altering and delaying government legislation.

In addition, certain constitutional provisions have been used in the legislature to allow the parliament to make laws in standing committees. Article 72 of the Constitution gives each chamber the power to decide how it will approve legislation, which made it possible for both chambers to adopt rules allowing them to simply pass legislation in committee without having it considered on the floor of the house. As of 1994, roughly about 75 per cent of all legislation approved by the Chamber of Deputies across the lifespan of the institution was approved in this way. At times the figure exceeded 90 per cent (as in 1994).[2] Note that much of the legislation approved in this way are what are known as '*leggini*', or little laws, meaning that they are not major policy initiatives and instead tend to deal with specific constituency interests or needs (Hine 1993: Chapter 6; Della Sala 1997; Capano and Giuliani 2001).

There have been other factors making the Italian parliament stronger than most other European parliaments as well. First, the parliamentary standing orders adopted in 1971 gave no special treatment to government-initiated bills; the parliamentary calendar is designed by a conference of leaders of parliamentary groups – which includes most parties – by unanimous vote. Government traditionally had no input, other than sending an observer with no voting power. These standing orders also included a mandatory right of secret ballot within the parliament if requested at any stage in the law-making process; the only way this could be stopped was with a request from the government for a vote of confidence. This meant that in cases when the right of secret ballot was invoked, legislators did not necessarily have to support government proposals even if their parties were in the governing coalition. Note that the rules were changed in 1988 and the use of the secret ballot was restricted to civil liberties legislation only, but that during the key transitional period, the secret ballot was used extensively, with consequences that will be discussed further below.

Overall, then, the Italian parliament is usually said to be one of the strongest, if not *the* strongest, in Europe. What impact has this had on policy outputs, though? A great deal of legislation comes out of the Italian parliament – much more than in other European parliaments – but as mentioned above, much of this is in the form of *leggini*. That is, the parliament has not been all that effective in passing major reforms, which perhaps calls into question just how powerful it really is (Della Sala 1997).

Returning to the general theme of this book, the key role that the Italian parliament is likely to have played in consolidation was its integration of the main opposition party, the PCI, into the new democratic institutions (Cotta 1990). At the governmental level, the PCI was completely excluded, even though it often supported the government, either by abstaining on votes of confidence or by approving specific government legislation. The fact that the party was never rewarded with formal governing posts might have served to anger its leaders and supporters, had it not been for the influence it was clearly able to have via the national parliament. For instance, the PCI was given many of the deputy chair positions on legislative committees. Beginning in 1976, it was also given many of the chair positions, although it lost this privilege again after 1979 with the collapse of the 'historic compromise' (see Chapter 6). The party was even given the presidency of the Chamber of Deputies periodically. After 1979, the DC in particular became much less consensual and the PCI was incorporated less and less, but by this time, it had already been co-opted into the system. However, throughout much of post-war Italian history, one indication of the degree of accommodation being made to the PCI was that the vast majority of all legislation passed in the Italian parliament was approved by super-majorities of at least 85 per cent, and sometimes 95 per cent (Della Sala 1997; Capano and Giuliani 2001).

We now turn to a discussion of the Italian executive. The Italian political system is very much a parliamentary one in that the government (the Prime Minister and Cabinet) must be supported by a majority of the Parliament, which includes both the Senate and the Chamber of Deputies. In Italy, this requires a vote of investiture by both chambers of parliament. That is, an Italian government cannot begin functioning until it is formally approved by majority vote (of all of those voting, that is).

Given that the electoral system and political cleavages helped to ensure that no party won a majority of seats in the Italian parliament, coalition governments have been necessary. How have coalitions formed, though? In general terms, there are two main concerns that parties might have when going into coalition: spoils of office and policy-making (see Laver and Schofield 1991). In the Italian case, the emphasis has traditionally been on spoils, but since the collapse of fascism, coalition formation included the implicit stipulation that neither the extreme left nor extreme right could become part of the coalition. Thus, coalitions were almost always led by the largest party in parliament, the Christian Democrats, and much of the time were kept to a minimum. At times, the coalition became larger and larger as it became clear that the government was having difficulty maintaining the support of the parliament for its policy proposals. Also, there were times when there has been a minority government, in which one party or a small coalition that did not command a majority of support in parliament took control of government alone but had the support of parties that did not formally participate in the coalition. The most noteworthy of these was the case discussed in Chapter 6 when the PCI provided support to a DC government during 1976–9 in the historic compromise.

The most notable point about Italian coalitions that has now become common knowledge is that they have tended to be very fragile. The average life span of governments up until the early 1990s was ten months. The constant threat of collapse and the long periods of 'caretaker' governments (governments temporarily in place until a new government can be selected) have meant that taking major policy initiatives has been almost impossible. But why did governments traditionally collapse so often in Italy?

First, the secret ballot system that was used in both the Chamber of Deputies and Senate meant that proposed government policies were often not getting through, thereby calling into question the government's abilities to govern. Governments became frustrated over time at the level of difficulty they were having at getting policies through and this would precipitate a collapse of government. Similarly, lack of control over the parliamentary agenda further frustrated government objectives. In addition, the executive traditionally had no control over which individuals were able to run for seats in parliament, as this was in the hands of party leaders; in the case of the largest party, the DC, these leaders chose to not occupy government positions and often were not even sitting members of parliament. Thus, even if there was no secret ballot, it would have been very difficult for a government to punish party members for not supporting legislation. Further, the lack of government control over candidacies meant that MPs were able to build up their own electoral followings, as is the case with members of congress in the US; Italian MPs thus felt like they could behave independently of government wishes if their constituency interests were in opposition to government proposals. Some argue also that main reason cohesiveness could not be maintained was because of the lack of possibility for alternation of government and opposition resulting from the permanent exclusion of both the extreme left and the extreme right – even if the governing parties defected from coalitions, most likely a similar coalition formula would result anyway (see DiPalma 1977; Hine 1993).

Why did coalition partners defect then? Sometimes defections were related to policy disputes. More often, however, they were a result of squabbling over patronage and distribution of posts. Also, if the constitutional period of the parliament was coming to an end, it might make sense for one of the coalition partners, or even one of the factions within the largest party, the DC, to openly claim to no longer support government policies in order to gain a larger percentage of the vote in the election (and thus a larger number of parliamentary seats, and potentially a larger share of the spoils of office) (see DiPalma 1977; Spotts and Weiser 1986: Chapter 6; Hine 1993: Chapter 7).

However, collapse of a coalition did not mean what it would mean in most other European democracies because there was tremendous stability in terms of both the parties in the coalition and the specific individuals that were appointed to cabinet posts.

For instance, the first government led by Prime Minister Aldo Moro lasted seven months (December 1963–July 1964) before collapsing, but the subsequent government that was formed was again headed by Moro and contained exactly the same political party configuration. This government lasted for approximately a year and a half (from July 1964 to February 1966); the Moro government then collapsed again and re-formed itself, again with the same Prime Minister and same parties. This government then lasted until June 1968 (that is, until shortly after the parliamentary elections held in May 1968). (See Hine 1993: Appendix 1.) Similarly, the governments led by Prime Minister Giovanni Spadolini (of the Republican Party) had identical party compositions and lasted from July 1981 to December 1982 but with a government collapse during this period. As mentioned in Chapter 3, this is very similar to the situation that prevailed in the Liberal era in Italy. Unlike the Liberal era, however, during 1945–1993, the DC was *always* one of the coalition partners, and except for Spadolini and Socialist Prime Minister Bettino Craxi, the DC always took the post of Prime Minister. Thus, despite the apparent constant government collapse, government was, in fact, fairly stable during the post-war consolidation (DiPalma 1977; Hine 1993: Chapter 7). Moreover, while the constant collapse and reformation of coalitions resembled the Liberal era to a great extent, the difference in the post-war period was that the extremes were not considered to be acceptable coalition partners.

Besides the constitutional provisions that strengthen the parliament, there are also constitutional and legal regulations that limit the power of the government in Italy. The prime minister in particular is extraordinarily weak. In other parliamentary systems, the head of government is usually the strongest person in his/her party. This has not traditionally been true in the case in Italy; instead, as mentioned above, non-office holding party leaders tended make the decision of who gets to run for office, and particularly, who should be put forward as a candidate for prime minister. Moreover, the prime minister was not traditionally free to hire or fire his cabinet ministers. Even the ministers from the same party (the DC usually) were selected by that party's leaders, and those from other parties were selected by their party leaders. Thus, again, the head of government had no power whatsoever to punish cabinet members who no longer supported the prime minister. In addition, the constitution left it to parliament to spell out how the prime minister's office should be organized and to determine the number, responsibilities, and structure of the ministries. The required enabling legislation for creating the prime minister's office was not enacted for a very long time, and thus the prime minister had no staff to control the government or coordinate its various parts. Moreover, there are still legal restrictions on the ability of the prime minister to hire and fire cabinet ministers without the approval of parliament.

Thus, the political system in place during the early days of the new Italian democracy was one which consisted of a weak government which required the support of multiple parties and a parliament which apparently worked to build consensual legislation, even if most of these were *leggini*. As stated above, it may have been this institutional set-up which allowed for the integration of the extremes – particularly the sizeable PCI.

It must be noted that since the 1980s, governments and reformers have attempted to push the Italian political system toward being one with greater government control over policy-making and generally toward a more majoritarian system. One way that government has been able to increase its strength has been through the use of decree laws. Provisions for decree laws are included in the constitution and according to the latter are only supposed to be used during times of emergency. Once enacted by government, they become law immediately but last for only 60 days unless the parliament converts them into full law before the end of the 60 days. Otherwise, they expire. However, a government can simply pass the decree again until parliament does finally address it. Parliament does have the power to amend such laws before approving them, and tends to do so around 90 per cent of the time. Thus, this has been one method that the government has used to get important legislation onto the parliamentary agenda, as indicated by its increased use. In fact, it appeared that until 1970, no government had really thought to use this technique, but then in the following two years, 69 decrees had been issued; during 1972–6, the number was 124, and during 1976–9, it was 167, and then 274 during 1979–83. Another way that government has gained greater power has been through the restriction on the use of secret ballots in the parliament (as of 1988) for civil liberties legislation only. In addition, prior to 1988, as mentioned above, parliament had not enacted the enabling legislation to allow the prime minister to have anything resembling an office – that is, support staff, advisors, etc. This had been one of the ways the Constituent Assembly had allowed the parliament to keep control over the prime minister – the parliament must give the government the power to reorganize his office. In 1988, such provisions were finally passed (Hine 1993: Chapter 7; Della Sala 1997).

As mentioned in Chapter 6, in 1993, a referendum was held on the electoral system in Italy. The purpose of the proposed reform was to move the country toward a more majoritarian style of government, with clear government and clear opposition which would alternate periodically. As a result of the referendum, the electoral law was changed. The new electoral system was a mixed system, with 75 per cent of parliamentary seats being decided by single-member-district-plurality elections and the remaining 25 per cent selected by proportional representation. In fact, 1996 saw the first clear switch of governing party blocks from the centre-right to the centre-left. However, instability persisted and government appeared to fail to gain any additional control over the legislative agenda, nor did the functioning of parliament itself become more majoritarian. For instance, the number of private member bills introduced actually doubled in the 1990s, indicating that government had not gained control over the legislative process. The number of decrees issued in the 1994–6 parliament was an overwhelming 538. Moreover, the percentage of decrees that were passed with amendments increased, indicating that the legislature was keeping control over policy-making this way as well. Finally, bills continued to be submitted by MPs belonging to the opposition coalition and bills were still approved by abundant majorities. For instance, since 1987, two-thirds of laws have been supported by 95 per cent of members of parliament and four-fifths of them by no less than 85 per cent of MPs (Capano and Giuliani 2001).[3]

As a result of the failure of the 1993 reforms to the electoral system and the continued government instability, the electoral law was changed again for the 2006 general election. For elections to the Chamber of Deputies, each elector now casts one vote for a party list. These lists are now closed, so electors cannot choose individual candidates in or alter the order of such lists. Six hundred and seventeen out of 630 Chamber seats are distributed at the national level by the largest remainder method of PR among: coalitions that obtain at least 10 per cent of the vote and which include at least one party that obtains 2 per cent of the vote or more; political parties that obtain at least 4 per cent of the vote, running individually or as part of a coalition that obtains less than 10 per cent of the vote; and parties representing recognized linguistic minorities that obtain at least 20 per cent of the vote in their corresponding regions. Chamber seats awarded to a coalition are in turn proportionally allocated among constituent parties that have obtained at least 2 per cent of the vote; however, this requirement is waived for the coalition party with the largest number of votes among those polling fewer than 2 per cent.

The new Chamber system provides for a nationwide majority prize: if the coalition that obtains a majority of votes initially receives less than 55 per cent of the seats filled in Italy proper (340 out of 618), its number of seats is increased to 340. In this case the remaining 277 seats are apportioned among the other qualifying coalitions and individual parties.[4]

Under the new electoral system, for elections to the Senate, electors vote for a closed party list in 18 of Italy's 20 regions. Senate seats in these regions are apportioned by the largest remainder method of PR among coalitions that receive at least 20 per cent of the vote and which include at least one party that receives 3 per cent of the vote or more, as well as parties that receive at least 8 per cent of the vote, running individually or within a coalition that receives less than 20 per cent of the vote. Senate seats awarded to a coalition are in turn proportionally allocated among constituent parties that have received at least 3 per cent of the vote.

The new Senate system also features a regional majority prize: if the coalition that obtains a majority of votes in a given region is initially allocated less than 55 per cent of the seats filled in the region, its number of seats is increased to no less than 55 per cent of the region's total, and the remaining seats are distributed among the other qualifying coalitions and individual parties[5] (www.electionresources.org/it/).

Thus, the new rules have been designed to guarantee a clear majority in parliament for governing parties, thereby increasing the strength of the government. Recently Silvio Berlusconi (before his party's electoral defeat in 2006) proposed constitutional reforms to increase the power of the government as well. Under the proposed reforms, the prime minister would have been granted powers to dissolve parliament, appoint and dismiss ministers and determine the general direction of government policy. The proposed reforms were presented as a referendum and were rejected by a vote of 62 per cent in June 2006.[6] Thus, the nature of policy-making and of executive–parliamentary relations does not appear to have changed a great deal since the early days of the Italian democracy.

We now turn to a discussion of the other portion of the executive – the Italian presidency. Recall that at the end of World War II, considerable ambiguity remained regarding the future nature of the Italian polity. The monarch appeared to envision a return to pre-Mussolini style regime with a monarch and weak parliament. In fact, world leaders such as Winston Churchill recognized the king as the official diplomatic leader of the immediate post-war regime. At the same time, many participants in the CNL were aghast at the possibility of allowing a return to monarchy, given the events of the 1920s and the monarch's continued support for – or acceptance of – Mussolini's fascist regime. Thus, potentially explosive divisions remained amongst key players in the post-war regime that – with the aid of various wings of the military – could have resulted in civil war along the lines witnessed in Spain in the 1930s. As mentioned in previous chapters, a major step toward resolving these difficulties was eventually taken after a six-month stand-off between the CNL and the monarch, when the PCI – the strongest opponent of the monarchy – agreed to cooperate with the monarch. The decision about whether Italy was to remain a monarchy of some sort or switch to some other form of government was ultimately placed in the hands of Italian citizens by the CNL, and the slim majority supporting the establishment of a republic indicates the wide variation in public opinion on this issue. Still, the major actors of the day accepted the result and the monarch went into exile.

Resolving the question of this portion of the executive thus may have been one of the major steps in setting Italy along the path of consolidated democracy. As will be shown below in the case of Turkey, failure to adequately resolve the issue of executive power may produce difficulties in consolidation, however.

It is important to note that once the issue of the monarchy was addressed via referendum in Italy, it was left to constitutional designers to then consider the role of the head of state, which was to be a president. As Spotts and Weiser (1987) point out, there is some constitutional ambiguity surrounding the Italian presidency. We now turn to a discussion of the selection of the president, the role holders' constitutional powers, and then to a discussion of the functioning of the Italian presidency.

Italian presidents are selected for a term of seven years by an electoral college composed of all members of the Chamber of Deputies and Senate, along with delegates from the 20 regions (see Chapter 8). This is a highly partisan contest and has taken anywhere from one vote (which is rare) to 23 to finally select a candidate that a majority is willing to support. The president's constitutional powers include the power to select the prime minister. This power has traditionally been somewhat limited, in that most presidents felt obligated to select a Christian Democrat for the role since this party tended to win the most seats in parliament. However, given the large number of factions in this party, the president has had the power to set the tone and direction of government. Also, one president – Alessandro Pertini (a Socialist) – took the unprecedented step of selecting a non-DC Prime Minister (Craxi) in 1983.

The president also has the authority to dissolve one or both houses of parliament and can also refuse to do so (for instance, with the intent of forcing the parties to form a viable government without calling new elections). Before deciding on dissolution, the president must consult with the presidents of the Chamber and Senate, but it is unclear as to whether he[7] is bound to follow their advice. The president also has the authority to summon parliament into special sessions and appoints one-third of the members of the Constitutional Court. Laws and regulations are valid only if signed by him and he may refuse to authorize the government to present bills to parliament. Legislation may be sent back to parliament, but whether he may veto it is a matter of controversy. The president is also commander in chief of the armed forces. The greatest limit on presidential powers is the highly ambiguous constitutional requirement that his official acts must be approved by the appropriate minister. In some cases, like the nomination of the prime minister and dissolution of the parliament, approval would not make much sense, though. The president's acts as commander-in-chief, however, could presumably be exercised only with cabinet approval. As stated by Spotts and Weiser, 'Between these two extremes lies a legal no-man's land' (Spotts and Weiser 1987: 125).

Because the constitution is unclear as to how independent the president is and how much of a role he is to play in policy-making, it was also unclear as to what the nature of the Italian presidency was to be. This appears to have mostly been determined by the people who have held the office. The first two presidents, Enrique De Nicola and Luigi Einaudi, were very well respected and it is argued that they brought moral stature to the presidency. De Nicola was from the liberal wing of the pre-fascist period, and Einaudi was an internationally renowned economist, governor of the Bank of Italy, and the architect of the country's post-war economic recovery. The third president, however, Giovanni Gronchi, tried to claim a stronger role in guiding the country's domestic and international policy, but his attempts to do so, particularly his efforts at foreign policy, were seen as inept. Subsequent presidents established the convention of limited presidential authority, and a president who attempted to do too much after this convention had been established would be likely provoke a difficult political and constitutional crisis (Spotts and Weiser 1987: Chapter 6).

In general terms in post-war Italy, the strength of the parliament, especially the lack of clear provision for government-initiated legislation and the existence of the secret ballot, meant that major policy initiatives have been sorely lacking and that the country has had tremendous difficulty dealing with problems, especially economic and budgetary ones (DiPalma 1977). In fact, it might be expected that in other countries, where regimes rest on rules that allow for ineffective governments that are constantly on the verge of collapse and a parliament that precipitates such collapses, those regimes would itself not survive very long. On the other hand, the fact that (a) major interests were aggregated into parliament and (b) leaders representing all of these interests were keen not to undermine the fundamental rules of the democratic game seems to mean that the Italian republic has indeed survived without having been governed very much (Di Palma 1977).

Spain: from consensualism to majoritarianism

Italy represented a case of democratic consolidation in which most parliamentary groups were accommodated, even by the late 1990s when consolidation was no longer in question. Thus, it appears that a practice that began primarily out of concern about returning to authoritarianism has continued, at least in part because the constitution and other rules have continued to keep parliament strong and the political executive weak. As discussed above, this has meant that major policy initiatives have been minimal but it has also meant that organized groups which could have had the power to collude to undermine the democratic regime did not do so. Spain also represents a case in which consensualism was presumably one of the keys to guaranteeing regime stability; however, this approach broke down fairly shortly after the Spanish transition to democracy. This section discusses these themes in the context of the Spanish parliament (the Cortes), the political executive, as well as the head of state.

The Law for Political Reform of 1976 provided for the creation of the new transitional Spanish parliament, which would consist of the Congress of Deputies and the Senate. According to this law, the Cortes could, after its first elections, agree to be a constituent assembly for the purpose of writing a new Spanish constitution, and it did so. As mentioned in Chapter 5, the subsequent stability of the regime is often said to be a result of the compromises that were made in that constitution. In this sense, the parliament served as the arena in which differences in constitutional preferences could be ironed out via a series of negotiations. Amongst the key negotiating groups were: (a) the Alianza Popular, composed primarily of the Franquist supporters; (b) the UCD, the broad coalition of Franco regime members who favoured reform; (c) the Socialist Party; (d) the Communist Party; and (e) a Catalonian party, Minoria Catalana. A small committee of seven consisting of representatives from these parties was formed to write the first draft of the constitution, and this committee continued to monitor revisions to the constitution to make sure that it was consistent with the general design they had developed. The fact that the constitution received almost unanimous support within the assembly indicates the degree to which the parliament was used to design rules that would be acceptable to all (Giol *et al.* 1990).

Parliamentary rules were designed in these early days to encourage a 'pactist' style of decision-making and promote dialogue between a majority and opposition, safeguarding negotiation between the basic interests of society (Giol *et al*. 1990: 101). In fact, under the first UCD government (1979–82), because of divisions within this party and because it did not have an outright majority support in parliament, negotiations would occur between the UCD and various parliamentary parties; that is, there was no single party that gave the UCD its permanent support. However, parliament and executive–parliamentary relations became far less consensual from 1982, when the Socialist party won an outright majority of seats in the parliamentary elections (see Field 2005). At this point, parliamentary rules that had been designed to bolster a weak minority government could be used to create a strong executive with little or no need to consult opposition parties. For instance, bills drafted by the government are discussed in parliament by the minister responsible and members of parliament of the governing party who are specialists on the subject of the bill. If there is disagreement regarding amendments, the opinion of the prime minister and deputy prime minister is decisive (Giol *et al*. 1990: 110). Another procedure that can serve to favour a majority government is *toma en consideracion* (prior consideration): during this procedure, the Congress debates in a plenary session whether it is appropriate to commence formal discussion of a bill or not. With this procedure, the parliamentary majority can limit the ability of non-majority parties to get legislation passed (Giol *et al*. 1990: 111–12).

Other indicators that the parliamentary process has moved from consensus to majority-rule is in the role of sub-committees (*ponencia*). In the 1979–82 Cortes, the subcommittee phase was generally the longest part of the legislative procedure, and bills were significantly revised and amended by these committees which included wide parliamentary representation. Beginning in 1982, however, this was no longer the case, as the party with the parliamentary majority no longer needed to negotiate with other parties (Giol *et al*. 1990: 113).

Like Italy, Spain also has a bicameral legislature; however, unlike Italy, the upper chamber in Spain is extremely weak and thus Spain is a case of asymmetrical bicameralism. The second chamber of the Spanish parliament, the Senate, was designed to provide territorial representation: each of the 47 peninsular provinces is assigned four seats, while the larger islands on Balears (Baleares) and Canarias – Mallorca, Gran Canaria, and Tenerife – are assigned three seats each, and the smaller islands – Menorca, Ibiza-Formentera, Fuerteventura, Gomera, Hierro, Lanzarote, and La Palma – one each; Ceuta and Melilla are assigned two seats each, for a total of 208 directly elected seats. In constituencies with four Senators, electors may vote for up to three candidates; in those with two or three Senators, for up to two candidates; and for one candidate in single-member constituencies. Electors vote for individual candidates: those attaining the largest number of votes in each constituency are elected for a four-year term of office. In addition, the legislative assemblies of the self-governing or autonomous communities into which the provinces of Spain are grouped (see Chapter 8) are entitled to appoint at least one Senator each, as well as one Senator for every million inhabitants.

However, as mentioned above, Spain represents a case of weak bicameralism, with the second chamber having very little power. If the Senate wishes to initiate legislation, the consent of the entire body is required to do so. In responsive mode, it is only allowed two months to review, modify, and approve bills passed to it by the Congress. If the Senate does modify the legislation, the bill is sent back to the Congress, which can either accept the revisions or not. In addition, the two-month period can be further restricted to 20 days if the Congress decides that the legislation is urgent (Giol *et al.* 1990: 114–15; see also Newton 1997: Chapters 4 and 5 on the Spanish parliament and executive; see also Heywood 1995: Chapter 4).

According to Article 72 of the Constitution, as in Italy, each house is free to draw up its own standing orders or rules of procedure governing its internal organization and mode of functioning, including its own budget and offices to administer affairs. Thus, in theory, like the Italian parliament, it should be able to exercise considerable power; however, it generally does not do so. Much like the situation in the 1930s, then, the role of the Spanish parliament nowadays is relatively small; to quote one set of authors, 'Parliament has become a mere formality' (Giol *et al.* 1990: 117; see also Soto 1997). The reasons for this will be outlined below.

Each chamber is organized into parliamentary groups: each group consists of the deputies or senators within the House belonging to one political party or coalition; each group must have at least 15 members, although provisions are made for smaller groups of no less than five deputies. These groups are important because members of parliament are placed on committees in proportion to the size of their party grouping, and the size of the parliamentary group also determines the amount of time granted for speeches and questions, as well as the order in which individuals are called to speak. Thus, these rules favour large parties, and particularly governing parties over all others.

Parliamentary sessions run from September to December and from February to June; outside of these times, there is a Standing Council that includes 21 MPs and the president of the chamber; this Council has the power to approve or reject decree laws submitted to it by the Council of Ministers (the cabinet) and to act in the name of the House as a whole in between sessions. Composition is based on the size of party group, so again, it favours government parties.

With regard to the parliamentary agenda, this is set by the president of the chamber in consultation with the Board of Party Spokesmen (a board representing each party group), but according to parliamentary rules, the government has the right to insert in the agenda any matter that it believes deserves priority treatment. In addition, the members of the government present in the Congress may request the right to speak at any time, whereas other members must request and obtain the permission of the president in advance.

The rules governing initiation of legislation also tend to favour the government over the parliament. Constitutionally, the government, the Congress, the Senate, and the assemblies of the autonomous communities all have the right of initiation. Legislation can also be initiated by a direct popular initiative with 500,000 signatures, although these cannot deal with tax affairs, international affairs, or pardons. Thus, it appears that in constitutional terms, legislative power is dispersed and there is no priority for any particular kind of legislation. However, according to the parliamentary rules, *proyectos de ley* (government bills) are automatically introduced into the legislative process; while *proposiciones de ley* (parliament-initiated bills) initiated in the Congress can only be introduced by a deputy with the signatures of 14 other members of the House, or by a parliamentary group with the signature of the group's spokesman. However, on budget bills, if parliament proposes increases in spending, these must correspond to reductions in other areas. The government then has the right to decide whether to take the bill into consideration and/or whether its approval would imply an increase in borrowing or reduction in budgetary income. If, within 30 days, the government presents no objection to the bill, it is submitted to the full Congress for a special debate to decide whether or not to accept it for parliamentary processing. If the outcome is positive, the bill is passed on to the appropriate committee and processed the same way as a *proyecto de ley*. There is a similar procedure for initiating in the Senate, but initiative must come from a parliamentary group or 25 senators (rather than 15) and a detailed explanation of the rationale of the bill must be provided. Again, government bills have priority over *proposiciones*, and the vast majority of laws are *proyectos* (see Heywood 1995: Chapter 4).

Parliament does have some powers, but they are fairly limited. Other than having the right to use votes of confidence and censure motions, parliament also has the right to demand that the government and any authorities from the state or autonomous communities provide them with help or information that they may require for the exercise of their duties. Both houses and their committees also have the right to demand that members of the government appear before them. However, Prime Ministers are absolved from this obligation, and often take advantage of this provision. On the other hand, the government has the right to attend all sessions of the Houses and their committees, and has the right to be heard in them. In addition, there is a fairly limited PM question time (15–20 minutes per week), and questions must be submitted in advance. In addition, the right of vote of no confidence is restricted to a *constructive* vote of no confidence. That is, parliament must present an alternative government that will command majority support in parliament at the same time as issuing the vote of no confidence. The opposition did attempt to use this procedure twice in the 1980s, but it failed both times, indicating to successors that the constructive vote of no confidence is a very blunt instrument indeed.

Also problematical for parliament is that having closed party lists means that MPs cannot build up independent bases of support within their constituencies. This is unlike the case of Italy, where elections until the 1990s were conducted using preferential voting, in which voters could rank order the candidates on a party's list.

Interestingly, as in Italy, Spanish parliamentary committees can carry out full legislative functions in limited areas of law. This apparently has its roots in the Franco regime in Spain (Soto 1997: 412). Unlike in Italy, however, it does not seem to have increased the power of the parliament, most likely because of the weakness of mass political parties (and corresponding strength of party leadership) and the priority of government legislation on the parliamentary calendar. Indeed, this procedure (which appears in the Rules of Procedure) tends to be used mostly by the *government* to get large amounts of legislation through parliament quickly. Because the opposition has such little opportunity to change legislation in the Spanish legislative process, it tends to rely extensively on the Constitutional Court (which can consider legislation, or parts of legislation before it is enacted) as a delay or check on the government.

Moreover, although the monarchy played an instrumental role in the transition to democracy and in its consolidation (see Chapter 9) and the maintenance of the monarchy rather than opting for a republic was also important (see Chapter 5), the powers of the monarchy in policy-making in modern-day Spain are limited. Thus, this institution also fails to serve as a realistic check on the government's power (see Powell 1996 on Juan Carlos's monarchy).

In sum, although government and party leaders in the mid-1970s believed consensualism to be necessary for making a smooth and effective transition to democracy, they also designed parliamentary rules that would help a weak government to get its legislation considered in parliament, thereby avoiding the problems of governance experienced in Italy. Once a single party was able to win a majority of seats in the Cortes, as was the case with the Socialist victory in 1982, the rules then made it possible for a strong majority party to govern with limited parliamentary input. While a single party does not always win a majority of seats in parliament, generally one party comes close to doing so and only tends to have to negotiate with one of the smaller parties to build a majority-support coalition. Thus, the system has come to resemble the majoritarianism of the UK political system far more than the early consensual system that appeared to be forming (Giol *et al.* 1990; Heywood 1999; Capano and Giuliani 2001; Hopkin 2005). As argued by Richard Gunther, 'while it can be argued that the successful conclusion of the transition to and consolidation of democracy in Spain was largely the product of consensual decision-making principles, once that consolidation had been achieved consensualism was no longer a necessary feature of Spanish politics' (1997: 289–90).

Turkey: the failure of consensualism

Toward the end of the Turkish War of Independence, the rebels who eventually established the Turkish Republic created a new parliament in Ankara. This parliament passed a Law of Basic Organization (adopted in 1921) making parliament supreme. According to this law, ministers were to be mere agents charged temporarily with executive responsibilities. The law was designed to build consensus amongst the spokesmen of various groups within the parliament.

By 1924, the modernist-republican wing was clearly in the majority in the parliament and was able eliminate other groups from political competition. The Basic Law was then changed to give the executive more autonomy and parliament was no longer to be the arena where major policy decisions were debated and consensus achieved. Instead, it was to be a forum where decisions reached by the government would be popularized and support for them mobilized (Turan 1985; Kolaycioğlu 1990). The model of parliamentary consensus building was thus one that was rejected early on in the Turkish republic, and even once the regime opened up to multi-party elections, parliament continued to function in a majoritarian and conflictual manner.

Legislative power in modern-day Turkey is exercised by a 550-member parliament (Grand National Assembly) elected every five years on the basis of universal suffrage (Art.75, as amended and Art.77 TC). Recall from the previous chapter that since 1982, in order to participate in the distribution of seats a political party must obtain at least 10 per cent of votes cast at a national level, as well as a certain percentage of votes in the contested district (calculated by means of a fairly complex formula).

However, even during times of fairer representation (e.g. the 1960s and 1970s), the Turkish parliament has not traditionally served the function of resolving conflict and developing a consensus because:

a   Government parties dominate committees and the opposition has very little influence over policy-making – nor do ordinary MPs because of strong party discipline; thus, multiparty support for legislation is rare.

b   There have at many times been instances of unruly behaviour, including fist-fights in parliament, as had been the case in the early democratic experiences of Italy and Spain (see Chapter 3). Part of the problem in Turkey may be that the rules of procedure have tended to be adopted by the majority party or parties and were not acceptable to all parties. Indeed, the number of incidents of unruly behaviour increased between the years 1946 and 1980. Current rules were also adopted by governing parties, and up until the 2002 general elections, there were still regular incidents of fights breaking out in parliament. While recent years have witnessed a far more conciliatory approach of the main parliamentary parties, unruly behaviour persists. (See Kolaycioğlu 1990; Aslan-Akman 2005.)

The power of ordinary members of parliament is quite limited because parliament is organized around party groups (in terms of the amount of floor time given). Individual members of parliament have the power to initiate legislation, but private member bills are not nearly as successful as government bills becoming law. In addition, governments starting in the 1980s increasingly began to use decree laws; note, however, that governments do not appear to be overwhelmingly successful in getting these transposed into permanent law.

There are other problems that have served to reduce the power and professionalism of the Turkish parliament. First, recall that most politicians who had participated in the pre-1980-coup regime were banned from participating in politics during the first few post-coup elections. This meant that those coming into the legislature had no experience at writing laws, nor were there older MPs who could help to socialize the younger ones. The same problem has occurred after recent parliamentary elections, as many members of parliament from the governing party have had very little prior experience legislating. Such inexperience means ordinary members of parliament are dependent on government and party leaders for information and support. In addition, although Turkey experienced asymmetrical bicameralism under the 1960 constitution, with an appointed Senate and a popularly elected Chamber of Deputies, the country has had a unicameral legislature since 1982, thus reducing the potential power of the legislature as a whole. Moreover, despite the strength of party leaders, parties in parliament at times do not behave coherently and there is considerable switching from one party to another (see Turan 1985; Kalaycıoğlu 1988, 1990).

Thus, parliament clearly has not served as a central place for conflict resolution and consensus building in Turkey. Given the conflictive behaviour of backbench members of parliament, it is not surprising to find that governments themselves have also taken a conflict-dominated approach to governance. In the first ten years of multiparty politics (during 1950–60), one party – the Democratic Party – held an overwhelming majority of seats in the parliament. The only other party with seats in parliament at the time was the Republican People's Party, the successor to the party founded by Mustafa Kemal. As discussed in Chapter 6, the Democratic Party was generally established to oppose the Republican People's Party and most of its rhetoric and policies did just this – the party was opposed to the extreme secularism of the RPP and claimed to also oppose the policy of strong state-led economic development (although in practice, the DP did little to change this policy). Thus, it is not surprising that the DP was far from conciliatory toward the RPP and indeed took repressive measures against the latter, eventually provoking a military coup.

It was after the 1960 coup and the introduction of a PR electoral system that Turkey first experienced the need for coalition governments. As in Italy, these coalitions tended to be extremely unstable. Unlike the case of Italy, however, the government leaders and coalition formulas were not stable, nor was there any consensus across centrist parties regarding what approach to take to the extremes of the political spectrum. Coalition difficulties began in the first few months after the 1961 elections. The problems partly stemmed from the fact that the military insisted that the Republican People's Party must lead any government that formed. The problem was that none of the other parties wanted to join the RPP in coalition: the successor to the Democratic Party, the Justice Party, was extremely hostile toward the RPP, given that the latter was perceived to have been complicit in the collapse of the Democratic Party government and the party itself, as well as the execution of the party's top-level leadership. The other parties were also wary of the RPP because they perceived it as being the party of the state apparatus and as being too close to the military (Heper and Başkan 2001).

The initial coalition that was pursued in 1961 was between the ultra-conservative Republican Peasant Nation Party and the RPP. Talks failed, and the military pushed the Democratic Party and Republican People's Party into forming a grand coalition between themselves, which lasted for seven months (from November 1961 to June 1962). After this, two of the smaller parties were coaxed into joining the RPP, and this included the neo-fascist Republican Peasant Nation Party. There was much fighting over the distribution of ministries and wide policy differences, and the coalition collapsed after 18 months (June 1962–November 1963).

When this coalition collapsed, the leader of the RPP (İsmet İnönü) refused to try again, and so the president of the republic approached the leader of the Justice Party. Initially, it was expected that the JP – a centre-right party – would form a coalition with two of the smaller right-wing parties, including the Republican Peasant Nation Party. However, these two smaller parties refused to join the coalition because they worried that they were too close to the JP ideologically and that they would lose their identity (and presumably votes) by joining the coalition (Heper and Başkan 2001; see also Dodd 1969 on the 1960–5 governing period in Turkey).

The problems in coalition formation in Turkey have persisted along these lines since the 1960s. For instance, after the October 1973 general elections, which followed a coup-by-memorandum (to be discussed in Chapter 9), there was still no conciliatory approach between the two main parties, and the leader of the Justice Party refused to join a grand coalition because he thought his party would perform better in the next round of general elections if it remained in the opposition. Other parties were also resistant for similar reasons, and eventually after more than four months of a caretaker government, a coalition between RPP and the religious party, the National Salvation Party, was formed. Given the extreme secularism of the RPP, this was a particularly unusual coalition. Eventually, in the mid-to-late 1970s, the leader of the Justice Party managed to convince two of the right-wing parties to join a coalition. One of these was the religious National Salvation Party, and the other was the Nationalist Action Party, the newly renamed neo-fascist party. In fact, as a result of the second of these coalitions to form, some members of the Justice Party resigned because the party appeared to be moving toward a neo-fascist line itself. The rest of the 1970s then saw considerable switching back and forth between short-lived RPP-led governments followed by governments led by the Justice Party which generally included both the religious right and the neo-fascist right.

In general, therefore, it appears that there was no consensus across the mainstream parties that preservation of the democratic system was to be the first and foremost concern of parties and clearly no consensus that the extremes needed to be excluded from government. In fact, as argued in Chapter 5, this may have in part been due to the fact that only a limited range of elites were allowed to participate in the design of the democratic institutions, leaving the opposition to constantly challenge their legitimacy.

Somewhat surprisingly, the post-1980-coup era has revealed similar difficulties. Initially, there was no need to form a coalition government, as a new party, the Motherland Party, won a majority of seats in parliament up until the general elections of October 1991. Between 1991 and 2002, no party managed to win a majority of seats, however, and so the problem of coalition formation occurred once again. And once again, party elites often formed extremely counter-intuitive coalitions. For instance, by this time there were two mainstream centre-right parties in parliament, the Motherland Party and the True Path Party. These two were virtually indistinguishable in terms of party platform and so collaboration between the two might have been expected. However, the leader of the Motherland Party worried that in such a coalition, his party would be dominated by the larger party, the TPP, and that the latter would reap all the benefits if the government performed well. Thus, the TPP turned to a centre-left party instead (the Social Democratic Populist Party, one of the successors to and offshoots of the RPP).

In the next round of elections in 1995, the religiously oriented Welfare Party (successor to the National Salvation Party) won a plurality of votes and seats, with the Motherland Party coming in second and the TPP in third place. Initially, the two centre-right parties formed a united front against the Islamic party, but bitter personal conflict between the party leaders over the leadership of this coalition brought it to an end within three months. Thus, once again, we see a failure on the part of the party leaders to join together to keep out the extremes. In fact, the TPP then formed a coalition with the religious Welfare Party, until the military forced the coalition to split in 1997.

In the April 1999 elections, once again, no party won a clear majority of seats in the parliament, and a broad-based coalition formed between the centre-left Democratic Party of the Left (a successor to and offshoot of the RPP), the centre-right Motherland Party, and the formerly neo-fascist Nationalist Action Party. Again, this was an unusual coalition, but party leaders at this stage agreed to put national interests ahead of partisan interests and personal gain. Despite the fact that militant groups close to these parties had engaged in bloody clashes in the 1960s and 1970s (see Chapter 6 and Chapter 9), by the late 1990s, things had changed considerably. Generally, there were far more policy affinities across the three: the centre-left DSP was tinged with nationalism; the Nationalist Action Party was now moderately nationalist (rather than extremely nationalist); the left had also become less extremist in its views on economic policy, allowing for collaboration with the centre-right Motherland Party. Finally, the 2002 election produced a clear majority in parliament as did the 2007 election, and so there has been no need to form a coalition since 2002.

Despite the continued difficulty with coalition formation, one change made in the 1982 constitution at least made it easier to prevent the sort of no-win situation that had occurred before 1980. Under the 1961 constitution, the only way that early elections could be called was if a majority in parliament voted in favour of dissolution or if a government (i.e. the same government) was unseated twice within an 18-month period and a third vote of no confidence was then passed. This constitutional rule became particularly problematical in the 1970s when parties were having difficulty finding reasonable coalition formulae (see Hale 1994: 219–20). Under the 1982 constitutional provisions, the president was given the right to call early elections if the government lost a vote of no confidence and a successor could not be formed within 45 days (Hale 1994: 257).

The above account leads to the question of why coalition government has been so problematical in Turkey. Heper and Başkan indicate that it starts with the original purpose for which the main opposition party, the Democratic party, was established, which was to challenge the power of the state elites (the bureaucracy and military), and much of the 'platform' of that party was about this contest for power rather than about clear policy goals. Ideologies that were outlined by the party were chosen because they were in opposition to state elite ideology (e.g. opposition to secularism). The RPP was associated with the state elites and so this is why parties trying to increase the power of the *political* elite refused to participate in coalition with it: 'the CHP [Republican People's Party] and AP [Justice Party] could be persuaded to work together only at gunpoint' (Heper and Başkan 2001: 83). In addition, is clear that political parties often pursued office for its own sake rather than for the sake of implementing policy. This is clear in the behaviour of mainstream centre-right parties, for instance, whose leaders refused to participate in coalitions with one another. Indeed, eight out of the 12 coalitions formed between 1961 and 1996 were minimum-winning and many of these were not set up to minimize policy compromises but to win the spoils of office. None of them could make substantial policy shifts. Of the four surplus coalitions, two of these were set up at gunpoint, and the remaining two were cross-ideology. So far, secular political parties on the left or on the right could not cooperate among themselves to ward off a religious threat from the right (from Heper and Çinar 1996) – although the coalition government established in the late 1990s was finally doing this to some degree.

Another potentially important part of the Turkish executive to consider is the Turkish presidency, a position that was originally created with the founding of the new Turkish Republic. Indeed, the first president of Turkey was the founder of the republic, Mustafa Kemal. Given the authoritarian manner in which the republic operated during his presidency (from 1923 to 1938), the role itself was also seen as a powerful one. As indicated in previous chapters, when the Democratic Party eventually won the majority of seats in parliament in 1950, they used the same political institutions in a largely authoritarian manner. This included the presidency, which was occupied by one of the founding members of the Democratic Party, Celal Bayer.

Given the problems created by the strong presidency, and by the electoral system, and the lack of separation of powers, measures were taken in the 1961 Constitution to resolve these problems of governance. Accordingly, the presidency of the Turkish Republic was to be clearly ceremonial and symbolic. Like other parliamentary systems in which the head of state is a president, the Turkish president was to represent the entirety of the Turkish republic and the unity of the Turkish nation and was thus clearly to be above the fray of political disputes. In fact, all three presidents who served from 1960–80 (Gemal Gürsel, Cevdet Sunay, and Fahri Korutürk) had military backgrounds and were chosen because of their acceptability to high-ranking military officers.[8] At the same time, despite the constitutional limitations on presidential power, Hale (1994) contends that the president actually wielded more power than a strict reading of the constitution would imply. Specifically, the president's power to choose the prime minister became vital when normal parliamentary procedures were disrupted, when no party had a majority of seats in parliament, or when parties were having difficulty finding a workable coalition formula. In addition, the president's role as National Security Council chair gave him considerable power, particularly given that this body was expected to be consulted on a wide range of policy issues (see Chapter 9 for further discussion).

According to the 1982 Constitution, the president is elected for a single seven-year term and it is generally expected that he/she will come from within the parliament. However, there is a provision for allowing the president to be selected from outside parliament if one-fifth of the total membership of the parliament can present a written proposal for this. The president is elected by two-thirds majority of the full membership of the assembly; if two-thirds cannot agree on a candidate, another ballot is held, and the two-third rule applies again; if a third ballot must be held, only a majority of all members is necessary to elect the president; if no one wins a majority, there is a run-off between the top two candidates and whoever gets the majority of all votes is elected. If no one can get a majority of votes (e.g. if there are many abstentions), new parliamentary elections must be held. Thus, the process is designed to force parliament into building a consensus and finding a candidate that is suitable to an overwhelming majority of parties. Once the president takes office, he/she must sever relations with his/her party and his/her status in the parliament ends. All of this is quite similar to the 1961 constitutional provisions for the selection of the president, which also attempted to produce consensus and presidents who were above the fray of politics; the new part of the procedure appears to be the fourth ballot and the provision allowing for the dissolution of the parliament if there is a deadlock – deadlock is indeed what happened in 1980 and without the threat of dissolution, it was simply difficult to get the parties to agree to a presidential candidate.

The 1982 Constitution introduced some ambiguity regarding the role and powers of the president, however. In terms of constitutional powers, the president has the power to preside over Council of Ministers meetings when he deems it necessary. This appears to have been designed as more of a symbolic role than one of real power and influence. This is very much like the Italian president and Spanish king, who are brought into Council of Ministers meetings to try to promote compromise. At the same time, this constitutional role clearly has the potential to give the president a great deal of power over policymaking. The Turkish president has emergency powers, but these are limited and a state of emergency cannot be declared by the president alone, but by the Council of Ministers meeting under the chairmanship of the president. Although the president seems to have vast appointment powers – for instance, he can appoint the Chief of General Staff of the armed forces, the Chief Public Prosecutor (who has been the key player in party closure cases), and members of the Constitutional Court – later articles of the constitution indicate that these appointments are to be made based on candidates nominated by another body, normally the Council of Ministers.

There are some actions the president can take alone. These include summoning the parliament during recess, returning laws to the GNA for reconsideration, submitting constitutional amendments to referendum as he sees fit (constitutional amendments do not normally need to be approved by referendum), appealing to the Constitutional Court for the annulment of laws, law-amending ordinances and the Standing Orders of the Assembly on grounds of unconstitutionality, dissolving the Assembly in cases specified by the constitution, appointing the prime minister and accepting his resignation, and preparing the agenda for and chairing meetings of the National Security Council. There are no circumstances in which the president can carry out executive functions, like issuing decrees, without the signature of the Council of Ministers, however.

The major sources of strength of the Turkish presidency have traditionally included preparation of the agenda and chairing meetings of the National Security Council. The NSC will be discussed further in Chapter 9, but it is important to note here that it has had a key role in directing policymaking in Turkey, including both domestic and international policy. The president's constitutional role of setting the agenda and chairing the meetings of the NSC thus gives the officeholder a strong institutional place from which to pressure the Council of Ministers regarding policy-making (Heper and Çinar 1996). Other potentially powerful roles including signing decree laws adopted by Council of Ministers, refering laws to Constitutional Court, and determining who the PM will be (from within the parliament, that is) (Heper and Çinar 1996).

Constitutionally, it therefore seems that the Turkish presidency was to be a relatively weak, symbolic position, but with some strong powers that can be used at times when the government is faltering. However, different presidents have interpreted their roles and functions differently and, as has been the case with the Italian presidency, the power of the president has depended in great part on the interpretation of the president's role by the person occupying the office. Since there have only been three civilian presidents selected according to those new constitutional provisions since 1982, it is worth describing how each of those individuals have considered their roles as president in order to provide a clearer idea as to how the Turkish presidency operates.

The first president under the new constitution was Kenan Evren, who had been the leader of the 1980 coup. Included in the 1982 constitution was a provisional article indicating that upon the ratification of the constitution, Evren would be elected president. The first civilian to be elected, however, was Turgut Özal in 1989. Özal was the leader of one of the parties that was allowed to form to contest the 1983 parliamentary elections, and his party, the Motherland Party, won a clear majority of seats in that election. Özal had a clear vision about the party's goals and was considered to be a powerful party leader and powerful prime minister. Based on the constitutional provisions regarding the issue of non-partisanship of the presidency, Özal should have given up control over party affairs and the day-to-day running of government. However, although he did officially give up leadership of the Motherland Party, he managed to get a fairly subservient party member elected as its new leader (Yildirim Akbulut), and then appointed this person as prime minister when he (Özal) became president in 1989. Prime Minister Akbulut was clear about wanting to work in harmony with the president, and allowed Özal to suggest names for members of the Council of Ministers and to advise the government on policy, particularly economic issues. Özal also continued to intervene in the internal affairs of his former party. In the realm of foreign policy, Özal generally acted alone, negotiating critical problems with other countries without consulting the Ministry of Foreign Affairs. His contention was that he was constitutionally empowered to do this because he was president and head of the NSC, making him responsible for the external security of the Turkish Republic.

Things changed, however, when Akbulut's term came to an end. Özal tried once again to influence the outcome of the party convention but this time he failed and a new leader who was not prepared to be subservient to Özal was elected (Mesut Yilmaz). Yilmaz's approach was that relations with the president would function according to the rules outlined in the constitution. Because Özal continued trying to influence policy by inviting deputies and ministers to the presidential palace for briefings, Yilmaz eventually adopted a policy of asking ministers and bureaucrats not to see the president without first obtaining his permission.

In the 1991 general elections, Özal's Motherland Party came behind the True Path Party, which then went on to lead a government (a TPP–Social Democratic Populist Party coalition) that excluded the Motherland Party. The True Path Party leader at the time (Demirel) was hostile to Özal and to the Motherland Party, which he accused of stealing votes from the old Justice Party (which had been banned from participating in the first few general elections after the 1980 coup). Things were so tense between the two initially that Demirel threatened to bring down Özal's presidency as soon as he could control enough votes in parliament to do so. Özal attempted to alleviate some of the tension by announcing that the elected government should be free to rule but that he would continue to express his own views. Although the two made some conciliatory statements, they also continued to make other statements indicating that the hostility and tension were still present. Özal tried to get Demirel to schedule weekly meetings with the president, and Demirel refused, saying they were unnecessary; in order to get information, Özal began inviting bureaucrats to the Presidential Palace. He even created his own staff of experts and used their help to come up with alternative policy proposals. Özal was also having difficulty with his former party's leader (Yilmaz), who simply did not think he could be an effective leader if he allowed Özal to continue influencing party affairs behind the scenes. In the midst of all of this, Özal suddenly died of a heart attack in April 1993, bringing his presidency to an abrupt end. Özal's presidency obviously led to debates about the role of the presidency and his expansionist interpretation of his role, as well as general questions regarding the legitimacy of the office.

Given the unhappiness of the major parties, including Özal's own former party, with Özal's behaviour as president, it is not surprising that someone who took a less expansionist approach was next selected as president. President Süleyman Demirel (1993–2000) was clear from the start that he was going to be a 'constitutional president' and would act within the bounds set by the constitution. He did indeed sever party ties and did not appear to try to meddle in party affairs after taking the presidency. He had no interest in trying to influence economic policy, which had been a major preoccupation of Özal's. The only executive function in which he took a strong interest was in the realm of the military. He contended that he had the discretion to approve or disapprove the candidate for chief of general staff nominated by the government, which constitutionally is correct, and he was victorious in winning this right for the presidency. Demirel also tried to avoid openly criticizing the government, but did do so on a few occasions (Heper and Çınar 1996; Özbudun 1988).

At the end of Demirel's term, the idea behind selecting the next president was to further de-politicize the presidency by choosing someone who would allow government to make policy without interference and who would behave in a statesman-like fashion, giving Turkey a respectable frontman. The person selected was Ahmet Necdet Sezer (2000–2007), who was chief justice of the Constitutional Court, a fairly widely respected body among many Turkish elites, and a somewhat meek character, especially compared to Özal and Demirel. There were several ballots before Sezer was selected, and government leaders eventually pushed for him as the ideal de-politicized candidate.

However, it appears that the government got far more than it bargained for, and Sezer was, in fact, fairly activist. The president took on the role of protectorate of the people, especially when it comes to corruption issues, and refused to sign government decrees on the appointment of civil servants because these were going to be based on party patronage and included the sacking of many civil servants who allegedly had ties to Islamist or separatist groups (September 2000). He also adopted measures that would allow the State Inspection Board, which is affiliated to the presidency, to investigate bankrupt banks. The issue here is that many of the bankrupt banks had links to political parties, and it seems that Sezer suspected that there had been some underhand, corrupt actions taken by party leaders using their affiliated banks.

Things peaked when the prime minister at the time (Bülent Ecevit) and president exchanged harsh words in a February 2001 National Security Council meeting; the president attempted to toss a copy of the constitution to the prime minister so he could see the appropriate constitutional provisions related to the powers of the president over banking issues, and the Constitution apparently hit the prime minister in the face, after which the prime minister left the meeting claiming there was a serious state crisis, an event which then plunged the country into a serious economic crisis.

Since the 2002 elections which produced a majority government for the Justice and Development Party, President Sezer continued vetoing laws and stalling government proposals by refusing to approve appointments of high-ranking bureaucrats to important state posts. The president also refused to promulgate a law passed by parliament allowing Prime-Minister-in-waiting Erdoğan to return to politics, but this was passed over his head.[9] By-elections were then held, with a Justice and Development Party deputy giving up his district seat so Erdoğan could run for it.

Thus, the relations between the president and government in Turkey are still very much contested and do not appear to have been institutionalized yet. This may be because of the lack of clarity of the constitution, but it also may have a great deal to do with the interpretation of the office's functions on the part of the office holder at the time.

Conclusions

This chapter began by arguing that three aspects of the functioning of government are likely to have an impact on democratic consolidation: (1) the degree to which the institutions are designed to function in a consensual manner; (2) the degree to which parliament is able to serve as a central site for conflict resolution; and (3) the clarity of rules regarding the powers of the Head of State, Head of Government, and the parliament. What do the findings from our three case studies indicate about the importance of these variables in consolidating democracy?

As discussed in Chapter 5, the cases of Italy and Spain as examples of successful democratic consolidation and the case of Turkey as a thus-far unconsolidated democracy point to the potential importance of consensualism in the process of designing new democratic rules. These cases also point to the conclusion that it may be helpful for the institutions themselves to function consensually, at least for the first few years of the fledgling democracy. Moreover, in situations where one or more 'extremist' groups (e.g. Communists, neo-fascists, religiously oriented parties, etc.) are to be excluded from participation in government, incorporation of these groups into policy-making decisions via the national parliament may be crucial to maintaining their commitment to the new regime. Thus, beyond the failure to design rules consensually in the first place, Turkish democracy may have also stumbled because of its failure to control the extremes via consensual rules and norms in the national parliament. Such failure has at times had the effect of prompting the military to intervene and impose control by force.

Similarly, unlike the cases of Italy and Spain it is clear that the Turkish parliament has been unable to serve as the central site for conflict resolution in the country in part because certain groups have been more or less permanently excluded from parliament. Given that these groups have severe grievances with the rules of governance (e.g. in the case of Kurds and religiously oriented parties), it appears that these groups should have been incorporated via the 'legitimate' political institutions. Again, such incorporation might have prevented the need for military interventions and human-rights violations in the East and Southeast of the country, and the continued perceived need for a military presence to protect against the religious right.

Moreover, this chapter has illustrated the considerable difficulties of governance in the politically divisive societies of both Italy and Turkey. Both countries witnessed problems with coalition formation and government collapse, and this was particularly acute in the 1960s and 1970s when students, workers, and other groups were becoming more actively involved in politics and engaging in politically motivated violence. The chapter has also shown how the two cases differ. In Turkey, the failure of political parties to form coalitions and to quell the political violence resulted in a dramatic breakdown of democracy; in Italy, by contrast, constant government collapse did not spell the end of the democratic regime. One of the major reasons for this is that when the regime appeared close to breakdown in Italy, parties agreed to work together via the national parliament to continue to make policies, and to cooperate to try to end the social and political unrest. In Turkey, parties were extremely reluctant to cooperate with one another for various reasons, leaving an opening for unelected officials to step in to resolve the political crises. The most immediate of the reasons for failure to cooperate included electoral opportunism, particularly on the part of smaller parties, as well as hostility toward the main left-wing party, the Republican People's Party. Another potential explanation for the unwillingness to cooperate lies in the fact that elites had little reason to do so. In Italy, cooperation was achieved for the sake of protecting the system of democracy that was created consensually by the post-war leadership from collapse. In Turkey, elites who had no say in creating the democracy in the first place – and indeed whose predecessors had been brutally overthrown by those who did subsequently design the new democracy – had very little reason to support it when it reached the point of collapse (on the role of consualism amongst political elites, see Higley and Burton 2006). This is a problem that has continued to trouble Turkish democracy in the post-1980-coup era.

Finally, it is clear that Head of State–Head of Government relations have been more-or-less institutionalized in Spain and Italy; although Italy experienced a few problems early on in this regard, Italian presidents have come to interpret their roles in fairly minimalist terms, stepping in only to resolve severe governmental crises. This has clearly not been the case in Turkey, with Presidents Özal and Sezer taking on fairly activist roles. Thus, the rules regarding president–government relations are not yet institutionalized in Turkey. Although this has not directly provoked any return to authoritarian rule, it is argued here that its role is indirect. Namely, it has exacerbated the problem of authority and responsibility, at times contributing to the lack of clarity regarding which person or institution commands ultimate decision-making authority. This, in turn, leaves policy-making in limbo, creating an opening for non-democratic institutions to step in to 'save the day'. Thus, it appears that both the institutions and the interpretation of those institutions by the individuals who operate within them have an important impact on the consolidation of democracy.

8 The resolution of regional conflict

As discussed in Chapter 2, problems of stateness make the creation of stable democratic institutions difficult. This is because in contrast to authoritarian regimes, democracies may have more difficulty legitimately using force to keep such disputes under control. If there are groups of citizens concentrated in particular geographical areas who identify themselves as being of a different nationality than those who control state institutions and these groups make separatist claims against the state, the state has several means for addressing such claims. One of these is forced assimilation or submission to the authority of the state. As mentioned above, though, this method is problematical for *democratic* states. Other methods available include separation and/or population exchanges. Scholars like Arend Lijphart advocate an alternative method, however, which is the use of federal institutions to incorporate regional groupings. Federal institutions generally include regional assemblies and representation of regional interests at the national level via the national parliament, along with sub-national public financial discretion and administrative autonomy (see Wheare 1964; Friedrich 1968; Duchacek 1970; Lijphart 1999; McKay 1999).

Academic research indicates that federal institutions are generally created for three main reasons. First, some scholars point to the importance of the ideas of constitutional scholars, political leaders, and the general public in shaping the structure of a new state: in some countries, at the particular time during which the nation-state was formed, the generally accepted political philosophy on state structures may be one which emphasizes decentralization and avoidance of over-centralization (see Burgess 1993). Another explanation offered for the adoption of federal institutions lies in cultural, ethnic, or historical territorial differences within a state: when such differences exist, federalism is likely to be the proposed solution when unifying the territory (see Umbach 2000). Finally, the approach offered by rational-choice scholars contends that federalism emerges because the new central government is not militarily powerful enough to establish a unitary state but at the same time the regions are not powerful enough to overthrow the central government; that is, federalism is chosen as an institutional structure that can manage and maintain the delicate balance of power between the centre and the regions (Riker 1964).[1]

However, it is not clear as to whether federal solutions or devolution actually do help to reduce conflict in multi-national or multi-ethnic states. On the one hand, the examples of Switzerland, Canada, India, and Malaysia indicate that states structured around multi-national or multi-ethnic federations can survive, and that these structures can go a long way toward managing conflict (Landau 1973; Forsyth 1989; Gagnon 1993; Wiessner 1993; Linz 1999; McKay 2001; Simeon and Conway 2001; Filippov Ordeshook and Shvetsova 2004). At the same time, examples such as Nigeria and Belgium point to the failure of such solutions in multi-national states (Elazar 1993). However, it must be recognized that short of allowing for secession, a multi-national state has very little choice but to attempt some form of devolution or federalism, as historical experience would indicate that repression of ethnic or sub-national cleavages is generally not a viable long-term option. This chapter discusses problems of regional conflict in the three countries analysed in the book and attempts to determine whether the differential handling of these conflicts may explain differences in democratic consolidation across the three. Specifically, the chapter briefly outlines the nature and sources of tension between the central state and regions in the three countries under study and then discusses the institutional and legal solutions chosen by these countries to address the potential problem of violent regional conflict or demands for regional secession. As shown in the chapter, the manner in which a transitional state addresses these conflicts is likely to be crucial for its future prospects for consolidating democracy.

Italy: delayed devolution

Chapter 2 discussed some of the early problems of state-building in Italy and contended that many of these problems were largely resolved by the turn of the twentieth century. At the very latest, potential stateness problems seem to have been resolved to a great extent with the Lateran Pacts of 1929. However, at the start of the post-war democratic transition, Italy was facing some new separatist movements across multiple regions. First, the Sicilian 'political class' had apparently been building grievances against the regime for decades and had formed secret 'autonomous associations' to struggle against the 'Continentals' of mainland Italy during World War II (Clark 1984: 292; Finkelstein 1999). Traditional forms of banditry flourished in the 1943–7 period, provoked primarily by government attempts to reintroduce conscription. Outlaws were signed up to an independent army being organized by conservative landowners in Sicily. In the words of Martin Clark, 'The Sicilian elite had little desire to be ruled from Rome at all, and even less to be governed by Northern Resistance partisans', who were trying to establish themselves as the post-war government (1984: 322).

In the Northeastern part of the country, discontent with Mussolini's regime had been growing amongst the 200,000 or so German speakers in the South Tyrol region. The fascist regime had, in fact, banned the use of foreign words in public places (Moss 2000: 106–7). During the war, many of those of German origin in the South Tyrol area apparently hoped Germany would annex the region. Also in the Northeastern part of the country were a significant number of Slavs. When Italy occupied and administered parts of Slovenia and the Croatian and Dalmatian coasts which border the Italian region of Venezia Giulia and share the same ethnic composition and history, the connection across these regions was re-established and the Italian government was soon facing a Slav revolt. The fascist government took strong measures to fight off the growing resistance movement, but by the summer of 1943, the resistance movements were – in effect – alternative governments and they had spread fairly far into the Italian region of Venezia Giulia itself (Clark 1984: 283, 293) Similarly, there was discontent amongst French speakers in the Valle d'Aosta in the Northwestern part of the country (see also Partridge 1998: Chapter 3).

Thus, at the end of the war, the country was facing revolt and demands for secession from these outlying regions at the same time that the Italian resistance leaders were attempting to make the transition from fascism and war to democracy (Clark 1984; Bull and Newell 2005: 156). The solution to these threatened revolts was to attempt to buy these peripheral regions off with regional autonomy. As discussed in Chapter 5, there were vast differences in approaches to the issue of regional autonomy amongst the main resistance groups in the CNL: the Christian Democrats preferred a decentralized system of government while the Socialists and Communists preferred a centralized system. (Note that over time these positions became reversed.)

The compromise that was agreed was that historic regions – Sicily, Sardinia, the Valle d'Aosta, and Trentino-Alto Adige – would become 'regions of special statute'.[2] These regions would be able to elect their own assemblies and were granted certain legislative and administrative powers; their regional autonomy statutes were given the status of constitutional legislation, that is, legislation that has been 'expressly provided for' by the Constitution, having the same legal status as the articles of the Constitution itself (Bull and Newell 2005: 155–6). In this way, it was hoped that the local elite would feel that they could preserve their languages, cultures, as well as economies, welfare systems, and – perhaps more importantly – their own jobs and power (Clark 1984: 322). Also included in the Constitution were concessions to non-Italian languages, with references to linguistic equality and the defence of linguistic minorities (Moss 2000: 107–8).

Thus, according the 1948 Constitution, the state would be decentralized within the framework of a unitary state. As discussed above, at the time, there were only a handful of peripheral territories that were pressing for greater autonomy, but the vast majority of the country was not. Thus, constitutional designers distinguished between 'special' regions mentioned above and 'ordinary' regions. As in the case of Spain (see below) the result was an ambiguous constitutional compromise. Constitutionally the two would have the same powers vis-à-vis the central government, but because there was little pressure from below to actually establish the ordinary regions and because the political parties were so divided on this issue, the enabling legislation for the 15 ordinary regions was not enacted until more than two decades after the ratification of the Constitution. Moreover, prior to 1999, the statutes of ordinary regions had to be sent to parliament for approval and were treated as ordinary legislation rather than having the same legal status as the Constitution (Bull and Newell 2005: 155–6).

The model outlined in the Constitution was not a federal one: Constitutional designers clearly wanted some degree of decentralization but not federalism. Thus, there are very few powers that are constitutionally devolved and almost no policy areas are exclusive to the regions; moreover, the regions were given very limited financial autonomy. According to Article 117 of the Constitution, regions may legislate in the areas of: municipal boundaries; urban and rural police forces; fairs and markets; public charities, health, and hospital assistance; vocational training and financial assistance to students; local museums and libraries; urban planning; tourism and the hotel industry; regional transport networks; regional roads, aqueducts, and other public works; lake navigation and ports; mineral and spa waters; extractive industries; hunting; inland fisheries; agriculture and forestry; and artisanship. However, if the regional government passes legislation in any of these areas, it must take into account any framework legislation that has already been passed at the national level. As Hine (1996) argues, much of the framework legislation is extremely detailed and seems to restrict the leeway actually granted to the regions even in policy areas outlined as being within the remit of the regions in the constitution. In addition, the regions have very limited ability to raise independent sources of funds: while regional governments are able to charge varying amounts for permits and regionally provided services, most of the revenue of the regional governments comes from the central government; moreover, while the regions themselves collect taxes, these go into a central government fund for redistribution (Bull and Newell 2005: 159).

Still, in addition to quelling the nascent separatist movements, regional institutions served another key function in the Italian democracy, which was the incorporation of the PCI into the polity whilst simultaneously preventing it from holding posts in the national government. Specifically, despite initial opposition to the idea of regional autonomy by the Communists in the 1940s, the PCI performed very well in local and regional elections, particularly in the northern part of the country, and managed to take control of several of the governments in these areas. Not only did they gain the reputation of being competent governors (e.g. in Turin), participation in regional and local governments gave the party the ability to further show beyond its actions at the national level that it was indeed committed to the new Italian democracy (see Hine 1993: Chapter 9).

Although it appeared that demands for separatism had been quelled with the 1948 constitution, in the early 1990s, the new quasi-nationalist/quasi-racist party, the Northern Leagues, began to argue for separation of the Northern part of Italy from the rest of the country; this was toned down fairly quickly, and the League began to press for federalist arrangements instead. Other parties joined the bandwagon, and so legislation and Constitutional reforms were passed to try to increase the power of the regional governments. These included measures to increase the power of the chief executives in the local, provincial, and regional governments as well as the introduction of the local property tax which allowed the local councils to increase their financial autonomy.

In 1999 the Constitution was changed and regions were given the authority to decide upon new statutes for themselves, as well as to choose their own electoral laws. The control over the content of these statues on the part of the central government was also greatly reduced. In addition, after 2001, ordinary regions were granted exclusive competences constitutionally, as had already been the case with special regions (Bull and Newell 2005: 156).

However, the conclusion still seems to be that Italy is far from a federalist model: for instance, the Senate still has not been transformed into a Chamber of Regions which would be necessary in order to achieve federalism. Also, the new constitutional clause conferring concurrent legislative powers fails to draw a clear-cut division among tasks and responsibilities. Finally, there are a large number of functions listed as falling within the purview of the central government which has left many observers wondering about the extent of the additional competences that the regions have actually acquired (Cento Bull 2002: 190–1).

Spain: between a unitary and federal solution

Spain – after the *reconquista*, that is – traditionally consisted of multiple kingdoms. Even after these were united under King Ferdinand in 1515, the territories generally still preserved their political organization; in particular, they held *fueros*, or statutes as privileges and rights that protected the integrity of customs and ways of life, which acted as vehicles for political relations with the monarchy. These *fueros* were codes dictating the norms pertaining to the administrative, civil, penal, and political life of the cities and territories under their jurisdiction and formed the basis of the idiosyncratic make-up of the modern Spanish state (Moreno 2001: 40). Thus, in stark contrast to Italy, the foundation of what we now recognize as the modern Spanish state was marked by only a qualified agreement by citizens of various kingdoms to yield authority to the central state. That is, recall that in the Italian case, plebiscites were held to allow the kingdoms to join a unified Italian state, and so at least at an elite level, there was agreement about the creation of a new centralized state. In contrast, local elites in Spain maintained their right of rule over most political life in their territories or provinces, ultimately creating problems for the development of a centralized modern state.

Certainly notions of centralization did become popular among liberal elites in the nineteenth and twentieth centuries in Spain (Domínguez Ortiz 1976). In particular, these elites were influenced by French Jacobin ideas, according to which the nation state would be defined in rational but not historical terms. The Jacobins argued that the prerequisite of the nation-state or people's community was the common desire to do things together and to achieve common glories (Renan 1947). However, the approach toward regimented centralization was not new in French history and in contrast with the Spanish case, since the eleventh century the aim of the French ruling classes was the establishment of a united nation under the central royal authority (Hyslop 1950; Castro, 1984; Moreno 2001: 26). Even by the 1800 and 1900s in Spain, however, these notions were extremely foreign, even to the elites who claimed to be proponents of them (Moreno 2001: 43).

When the Bourbon dynasty took the Spanish throne, the policies adopted mirrored those that were being adopted in France. In the process of attempting to develop a centralized state, monarch Philip V abolished the Catalan *fueros* in 1714. During the War of Independence with Napoleonic France, the territories of the Spanish peninsula fought separately but united in a common aim to free themselves from Bourbon rule (Moreno 2001: 43–4).

Ironically, however, the model adopted in the liberal Constitution of Cadiz (1812) designed a centralized unitary state and thus was very similar to the French Jacobin programme: it included a centralized bureaucracy, an internal market, common taxation, and judicial and cultural homogenization. For the liberals who promoted the Constitution of Cadiz and their political heirs, the provinces were territorial entities tied to a feudal past. These were judged to be the sources of backwardness and decline of Spain's foreign influence (Moreno 2001: 44–5; see also Nunez 2001). Moreno contends, however, that these ideals were 'more theoretical than practical' and that the 1812 Constitution actually failed to adopt a framework that would create a unitary Spanish state, in that the privileges of the old classes and estates remained untouched (Moreno 2001: 45). Moreover, the attempts at centralization provoked some regions, particularly Navarre, the Basque provinces, and Catalonia to assert their rights to autonomy (Moreno 2001: 46). The centralization process was then interrupted by the Carlist civil wars (1833–40, 1846–8, and 1872–5). The First Republic of 1873, established toward the end of the Carlist wars, was initially envisioned as a federal one. As discussed in previous chapters, however, this experiment with democracy was short-lived and a military coup restored the Bourbon monarchy with Alfonso XII as king of Spain (1874–85) (Moreno 2001: 47–8).

The nation-building and political modernization that took place in Spain during the nineteenth century (discussed in Chapter 2) did achieve some of its intended goals of centralization. For instance, formal education was extended throughout the country, as was the use of the Spanish language

(Castilian). The internal market was also consolidated, together with a centralized bureaucracy and judiciary; a national network of communication and transport was also created. Also important was the development of 'romantic historiography' – the reinterpretation of historical events that played down internal differences and supported the idea of a single unified nation-state. However, the problems of internal territorial accommodation would remain for years to come. With the Restoration of the monarchy during 1876–1923 and the centralizing dictatorship of Primo de Rivera (1923–30) which followed, there was a renewed attempt to impose uniformity on the country, but this ended in failure (Moreno 2001: 48–9).

During 1900–24, multiple regional parties began to form. Some of these appeared to be stimulated by the growing Catalan and Basque movements, but they were also the result of the legitimacy problems of the central government; during this period, it is argued that there was widespread distrust and hostility against the central government and this helped to fuel regional sentiments. The central government often resorted to brutality to repress popular demands. At the same time, some skilled workers and members of the middle classes saw state institutions as the main providers of political positions and stable jobs in the army and civil administration in their relatively poor territories; thus, inhabitants of large areas of Castile and Andalusia, and even of a whole historical nationality such as Galicia, regarded state institutions as the main source of life opportunities and eventually adopted a strong Spanish identity. As a consequence, administrative, juridical, military and political officers became increasingly hostile to the idea of Spanish plurality, something which was to have far-reaching effects in subsequent civil and political conflicts (Moreno 2001: 53).

The Second Republic initially made some attempt to resolve the issue of territorial conflict and territorial distribution of power. The most notable contribution was the constitutional design of the state as a regional model, situated somewhere between a unitary and federal state, which would influence later models of state power in Spain. The regional model during the Second Republic led to statutes of autonomy for Catalonia, the Basque Country and Galicia. In addition, several other regions had expressed autonomist claims by the time of the military uprising in 1936. Although many of them had not yet taken the legal steps required by the 1931 Republican Constitution to establish regional autonomy, a significant number had begun some part of the process (e.g. Aragon, Andalusia, Asturias, the Balearic Islands, the Canary Islands, both Castiles, Leon, and Valencia). This process of devolution played a major part in the polarization leading up to the Civil War. In fact, the issue of regionalism versus centralism created controversies within the Republican forces themselves, as a large proportion of these had inherited the Jacobin ideas of the nineteenth century. As discussed in previous chapters, the Franco regime tried to resolve this question of centralization versus regional autonomy by creating Spanish national cultural uniformity by force. In reality, the linguistic and cultural oppression during Franco's reign appeared to have stimulated peripheral regionalism and nationalism in Spain (Moreno 2001: 54–8; see also Gilmour 1985: Chapter 6).

Although there is evidence to indicate that there has been a regional contagion effect (to be discussed further below), with many regions 'discovering' regional identities in the twentieth century, the strongest of the regional identities have tended to be in Catalonia and the Basque country. Galician national identity is also relatively strong, but as shown in Chapter 2, most residents of this region prefer to remain part of the Spanish state, and separatism has generally not been a problem in this region.[3]

Given that the potentially problematical sub-national groupings in terms of Spanish state-building processes have generally been the Basques and Catalans, it is worth elaborating further on the nature of identities in these regions and the threat of national identity in these two regions to Spanish democracy. Both of these nations use indigenous languages other than Castilian (see Shabad and Gunther 1982). However, nationalism in the two regions has very different roots. Modern Catalan nationalism was created by the industrial bourgeoisie in the region and initially rather than promoting separation from the Spanish state, these bourgeois elites tended to argue that the advanced capitalism found in Catalonia should be used as a model for the rest of Spain; that is, Spain should be reshaped in the image of Catalonia (see Balcells 1996). These ideas eventually evolved and leaders of the nationalist movement began to promote regionalism. In contrast, Basque nationalism was a result of reaction *against* rapid industrialization, as the latter was perceived as being a threat to the region's Catholic values, its social system, and 'the integrity of the Basque race' (Greenwood 1977; Conversi 1990, 1993; Grugel 1990; Esenwein and Shubert 1995: 49).

The Catalonian nationalist movement remained largely within the realm of the intellectual classes until Spain lost the last of the American colonies to the US in 1898. For Catalan industrialists, this represented a significant loss of markets, particularly for Catalan textiles; some of the industrialists in the region joined forces to create the first Catalonian political movement, the *Lliga Regionalista* during this time; the latter even went so far as to attempt to wage a political revolution against the monarchy in 1916 as a result of an announced increase in taxes on industrial profits. However, this antagonistic approach to the Spanish state ended when the working classes began to organize themselves. Recall from Chapter 6 that the working classes in Spain tended to affiliate with the anarcho-syndicalist CNT, which was an extremely militant organization. Catalonian industrialists realized that they would need the help of the Spanish central government and military to protect their position against revolution by the workers. This 'led to the virtual abandonment of their regionalist demands' (Esenwein and Shubert 1995: 52). Instead, regional demands began to be organized by Republican regionalists who held close ties to the working classes and the peasantry (Esenwein and Shubert 1995: 52; see also Heywood 1995: Chapter 1).

As discussed above, Basque nationalism was also stimulated by industrialization. However, rather than being led by the industrial bourgeois classes, it was aimed at the peasantry, the artisanate, and the petty bourgeoisie and was hostile to the industrial bourgeoisie. The Basque nationalist movement formed and remained most prominent in the region of Vizcaya, which experienced rapid industrialization. The movement was partly a result large-scale immigration from the rest of Spain which threatened traditional life and stimulated some (e.g. Sabino Arana Goiri) to begin creating Basque nationalism. The movement took on a political bent in 1894 with the formation of the Centro Vasco, and then in 1895, the Vizcayan Provincial Council, which was the predecessor to the Basque Nationalist Party (PNV). Very much unlike the Catalonian counterpart, Basque nationalism was built upon notions of the need to maintain the purity of the Basque race, particularly by avoiding marriage with the *maketo* (slang for non-Basque Spaniard); also emphasized were factors like common language, laws, customs, and historical figures (see Heywood 1995: Chapter 1). The early stages of the movement witnessed only weak support, largely because it excluded industrialists and financiers, who were loyal to the constitutional monarchy (Esenwein and Shubert 1995: 53). Around the turn of the twentieth century, some industrialists, particularly from the shipbuilding industry, joined the movement, and this marked the beginning of the split between those who took a more liberal approach to nationalism and dropped independence as a goal and those who wanted to create a confederation of Basque regions. Eventually, the main leader of the idea of Basque nationalism (Arana) stated that autonomy within Spain was an acceptable goal, but the mass movement continued to remain divided on this issue (Esenwein and Shubert 1995: 54; see also Gilmour 1985: Chapter 6; Heywood 1995: Chapter 1; for a discussion of regional identity in Spain see Medhurst 1977; Shabad and Gunther 1982; Newton 1983; Giner 1984; Pi-sunyer 1985; Heiberg 1989; Conversi 1997; Río del Luelmo and Williams 1999; Guibernau 2001).

As discussed in previous chapters, one aspect of the conflict that stimulated the start of the Spanish Civil War was fundamental disagreement over the issue of centralization versus decentralization (on the positions of politicians and parties regarding the Basque and Catalonian regions, see Payne 1993: 201–6). The Republican left supported the idea of regional autonomy, particularly for 'historic' regions like Catalonia and the Basque Country, while much of the right supported the idea of building a centralized state and common national identity. Franco's coalition of forces supported the latter. Indeed, the general notions of an organic state, which served as the ideological backbone of the regime, seemed to rule out the possibility of regional autonomy. Thus, the regime attempted to keep a tight rein on regional movements, restricting the use of language other than Castilian in public places and churches, and used brutal repression, particularly to control those even suspected of having separatist inclinations. The repression utterly failed: in Catalonia, Catalan is still the first language of the majority (see Shabad and Gunther 1992) and the brutal repression of the Franco years appeared to have initially won much sympathy and support for Basque separatism (Gilmour 1985: Chapter 6; Heywood 1995: Chapter 1; Perez-Agote 2006).

Given these past conflicts between differing ideas about the structure of the state, the 1978 Constitution needed to address the historically conflicting conceptions of Spain: the idea of an indivisible Spanish nation-state versus the notion of Spain as an ensemble of diverse peoples, historic nations and regions. As discussed in Chapter 5, the result was an open model of decentralization (Moreno 2001: 60–1; see also Gibbons 1999: Chapter 2; Requejo 2005). Somewhat surprisingly, shortly after the Constitution was approved, even the regions that had shown only weak aspirations for home rule suddenly found reasons to claim these rights; that is, regions of Spain 'discovered' regional identities and the attractions of self-government (Moreno 2001: 58).

The starting point for the process of decentralization can be found in the provisions of Article 2 and Title VIII of the 1978 Constitution. In fact, the autonomy issue was easily the most controversial issue that arose during the drafting of the constitution. Given the history of the Second Republic and its ultimate collapse into civil war, along with growing unrest on the part of the regime 'ultras' regarding the increased ETA terrorist activities during the transition (see Chapter 9), some balance would need to be achieved between the regional interests and the parties of the right who feared the former would threaten national unity (Newton 1997: 117–18; see also Gibbons 1999: Chapter 2). The compromises are evident in the working of various provisions in the Constitution. For instance, as mentioned in Chapter 5, Article 2 states that

> The Constitution is based on the indissoluble unity of the Spanish Nation, the common and indivisible motherland of all Spaniards, and recognizes and guarantees the right to autonomy of the nationalities and regions of which it is composed and the common links that bind them together.

However, Title VIII states that

1   In the exercise of the right to autonomy recognized in Article 2, bordering provinces with common historical, cultural, and economic characteristics, the island territories, and the provinces with a historical regional unity may accede to self-government and constitute themselves into autonomous communities in accordance with the provisions of that Title and the respective statutes.

2   The initiative for the autonomous process belongs to all the interested deputations or to the pertinent inter-island body and to two-thirds of the municipalities whose population represents at least the majority of

the electorate of each province or island. These requirements must be fulfilled within a period of six months from the first agreement adopted on the subject by one of the interested local corporations.

3   The initiative, in case it does not prosper, can only be repeated after the passage of five years.

The Constitution then established multiple routes to autonomy, a fast route envisioned for the historical communities of Catalonia and the Basque Country, as well as Galicia, and a slow route, presumably for the rest of Spain. However, constitutional designers also incorporated an 'exceptional route' or accelerated procedure for regions that were not historical but wished to gain autonomy quickly. The three historical communities did indeed use the fast route, and Andalusia managed to use the exceptional route to establish its autonomy quickly. Given the attempted coup in February 1981 (see Chapter 9), however, the government decided to keep a tighter rein on the process and other regions were forced to take the slow route to autonomy. Still, their statutes of autonomy were in place by early 1983 (whereas the Basque Country and Catalonia had such statutes in 1979).

The case of Andalusia is instructive of the post-1978 drive for regional autonomy. In 1982 political leaders and the population at large in Andalusia opted for the same 'fast route' procedure and degree of home rule previously pursued by the three historical nationalities of Catalonia, the Basque Country, and Galicia, despite the fact that there is little evidence to suggest that Andalusia previously had any desire for regional self-rule. The popular referendum held in Andalusia ratified these wishes and a demonstration effect appears to have sparked off a sense of ethno-territorial identification in other regions. Thus, various provisions within the rather vague Constitution have been used to demand regional autonomy. For instance, the *Comunidades Autónomas* were constituted on historical nationalities (Catalonia, Galicia, and the Basque Country), nationality according to Article 151 (Andalusia), nationality according to 143 (Valencia), regions under 143, *fuero* community (Navarre), and provinces with *fuero* status, provincial *diputaciones*, *cabildos*, island councils, and municipalities (see Newton 1997: Chapter 7).

Among those granted autonomy through Article 143, some define themselves as *historical regional entities* (the Balearic Islands, Cantabria, Extremadura, La Rioja, Murcia). In other autonomy statutes there are concepts such as *historical entity* (Aragon) or references to a historical and cultural origin of the provinces constituting the region (Castile and Leon). Regions like Valencia have referred to *nacionalidad* in their autonomy statutes (and also use Article 143). The rest have simply avoided categorization (Asturias, Castile-La Mancha, Madrid).

All of this was in contrast to the original idea of many constitutional designers that only the historical nationalities would gain home rule while the other regions would merely gain administrative decentralization (or deconcentration). This, in turn, has produced a movement in the historical nationalities to try to establish a 'political differential' with respect to the rest of the *Comunidades Autónomas* and one idea that has been proposed is the creation of a confederal model of 'shared sovereignty' (Moreno 2001: 64–5).

The autonomy statutes for each region – approved by the national parliament – all vary in terms of the type of autonomy specified. For instance, the Basque Country statute included provisions regarding tax-raising privileges; the Catalan statute included provisions granting considerable freedom in matters related to education, culture, and language.

The Constitution also specified that regions taking the fast route system would be allowed to have the following institutions: a parliament, an executive (consisting of the president, vice-president(s), and ministers who perform the executive and administrative functions of the autonomous community), a president (who holds powers similar to a prime minister but is also the symbolic head of the region), and a high court of justice; for the slow-route regions, no institutions are specified. However, the latter have, in practice, adopted the same institutional structure.

The Spanish system of territorial division of powers is an extremely unusual one. Unlike a federal structure, in which the rights and responsibilities of the different levels of government would be specified constitutionally and would be the same across all the territorial sub-units, in the Spanish case, just as each region was free to decide whether to request autonomous status or not, they were also free to decide upon the level of autonomy desired and the timescale of progression to full autonomy.

The Constitution does, however, specify 'exclusive powers of the state', including foreign affairs, defence, customs, and international affairs. The Constitution also enumerated the powers that the slow-route regions could initially be granted. These include: the organization of their own institutions of self-government, town planning, housing, public works, forestry, environmental protection, museums, libraries, cultural affairs, the regional language, tourism, sport and leisure, social welfare, health and hygiene, and non-commercial ports and airports. Thus, communities were given power in areas that are often devolved even in unitary states.

However, the Constitution also mentions some 'devolveable' powers that are normally exclusive to national governments in unitary states. These include justice, fiscal affairs, public security and international affairs. For instance, autonomous communities can create regional police forces, and appear to have the right to raise their own taxes (although most regions other than the Basque Country and Navarre have avoided this option). International-affairs provisions are – as might be expected – fairly limited and include the right to request information on treaties that are likely to affect them directly and to make proposals on international matters and participate in decisions that might affect them via their regional representatives in the Senate (see Newton 1997: Chapter 7; see also Heywood 1995: Chapter 1).

There are two basic systems of finance for the *Comunidades Autónomas*: the special regime and the common regime. The special regime applies to Navarre and the Basque Country; these two communities enjoy a fiscal 'independence' in which they collect their own taxes for personal income, companies, and VAT. A previously agreed quota is transferred by the Navarran and Basque executives to the central state Treasury. These transfers represent a compensation for Spanish common expenditure and to cover the costs of running state administrative bodies in these two regions (Newton 1997: 131–2).

The constitutional provisions regarding territorial autonomy permitted any number of the *Comunidades Autónomas* to be self-governing, depending on the will expressed by either the inhabitants of each nationality or region, or their political representatives. The Constitution also made it possible for the degree of self-government to be wide or restricted, according to the wishes of each nationality and/or region. Thus, the accepted solution to the issue of territorial autonomy was essentially an unwritten pledge to extend the procedures of political dialogue and consociationalism into the future; the formulation of a clear division of powers based upon 'orthodox' federalism was avoided, however (Moreno 2001: 61; García de Añoveros 1984), as this could provoke the hardliners in the regime to attempt to return the regime to some form of authoritarian rule.

Overall, in terms of public satisfaction with the regional devolution process, it appears that Spain's experiment has been a success. Public spending figures indicate that the regional governments have gained considerable power over decisions regarding spending (Moreno 2001; see also Agranoff and Gallarin 1997; Agranoff 1996; Banon and Tamayo 1997). In addition, even in the short period between 1994 and 1996, Spanish survey respondents became far more positive about the process of setting up the Autonomous Communities, with 67 per cent claiming to feel positively about the process (Moreno 2001: 67). Furthermore, when we examine the numbers still wishing for regional independence from the Spanish state, it is apparent that even in the Basque Country and Catalonia, the percentages holding this preference are small (19 per cent in the former and 17 per cent in the latter). Naturally, activists of separatist parties like *Herri Batasuna* in the Basque Country and *Esquerra Republicana de Catalunya* in Catalonia clearly still want these regions to be independent of Spain, but this appears to represent a very small minority (Moreno 2001: 69). Finally, it is estimated that only approximately 27 per cent in the Basque Country and 12.5 per cent in Catalonia feel exclusively Basque or Catalonian; that is, the rest also feel some identity with Spain (Moreno 2001: 115). Thus, although the problems of terrorism on the part of ETA should not be discounted, for the majority of the population it appears that the ambiguous compromise regarding regional devolution has been a success and that separatist activities have not been strong enough to undermine the legitimacy of Spanish democracy (see also Martinez-Herrera 2002).

Turkey: failed solutions to regional conflict

As with most cases of regional conflict, Turkey's main problem of regional conflict resulted from its state-building processes. The conflict itself centres around the eastern and southeastern parts of the country where the population is predominantly of Kurdish origin. It is important to note that – as outlined in Chapter 2 – other potential domestic regional conflicts, particularly with Greeks and Armenians, were generally settled with population exchanges in the case of the former and by the repression of an insurgency in the case of the latter. Thus, the population of the Turkish state is thought to be predominantly of Turkish origin except for those living in the eastern and southeastern regions of the country.

Given that the key minority group in Turkey is actually one that is spread across five countries and that the leadership of this group has often claimed to wish to unite the group into one state, it is worth considering how they became separated to begin with. We are concerned with regional conflict in Turkey here, and so the main focus will be on how the boundaries between Turkey and its neighbours were established in such a way that individuals of Kurdish ethnicity were divided from one another.

As discussed in Chapter 2, the boundaries of the Turkish state were only established in the 1920s. The original settlement that was agreed between the Ottoman government and the victors in World War I provided for a relatively small, mostly land-locked territory. The initial agreement was that the allies would control the western portion of what is now Turkey, as well as the eastern portions of the territory. Specifically, Greece was to take control of the west, and Britain, France, and Russia would take the east. Russia then gave up its claims after the Bolshevik Revolution. The new Soviet government held a plebiscite in the area that it was to control, and those voting in the plebiscite preferred to stay with the Ottoman Empire; France was then given the right of control over these areas. Of potential importance is that the original treaty signed between the Ottoman government and the Allies (the Sèvres Treaty) referred specifically to the possibility of independence for the Kurds (Howard 1931). However, the treaty was never ratified.

A resistance movement – often referring to itself as societies for the defence or preservation of national rights – began to form in the spring of 1919, and it is important to note that it included both Turks and Kurds. For instance, at one of the congresses held amongst resistance groups (in Erzurum in 1919), 22 of the 56 attending delegates were of Kurdish origin. Kurds were also represented on the executive committee of the resistance movement. Further, in response to one particular Kurdish nationalist's attempt to negotiate a deal with France that would grant Kurdish independence in a small part of eastern Anatolia, ten Kurdish tribal leaders sent a telegram to the French High Commissioner in Istanbul protesting the actions of this particular individual and declaring that Turks and Kurds were 'brothers in terms of race and religion'. A few months later, 22 Kurdish tribal leaders signed a declaration emphasizing Islamic solidarity and opposition to efforts to separate Kurds and Turks (Kirisci and Winrow 1997: 75–9). By gaining the cooperation of Russia – the resistance agreed to respect the eastern boundaries Russia was establishing in the Caucasus in exchange for military equipment – and managing to control several domestic rebellions and push the Greek army out, the resistance movement appeared strong enough that the allies realized they would be forced to negotiate with them over the issue of boundaries.

Both Britain and France wanted to maintain a strong presence in the area and thus proceeded to take the lead in establishing the boundaries of neighbouring states – Iraq and Syria. For the resistance in Anatolia, the key area of contestation in this process was the area north of Mosul.[4] The Lausanne Treaty, signed in 1923, established the boundaries in the region, but the new Turkish government pressed for an alteration of the Iraqi boundary (i.e. moving it further south toward Mosul) by attempting to convince the allies that Turkey would be better able to control the area. However, a Kurdish rebellion broke out during this time that made it difficult for Turkey to make its case. Thus, the boundaries remained unchanged. In fact, this appears to have been a pivotal point at which many Kurds who had participated in the resistance began to have a change of heart with regard to cooperating with the Turks in the resistance. However, the group itself was too divided to be able to press for an alternative solution (see Kreyenbroek and Sperl 1991; Izady 1992; Gunter 1997; Barkey and Fuller 1998; Ergil 2000; Natali 2005).[5]

Equally important in distancing Kurds from the newly forming Turkish state was the modernization process discussed in previous chapters. Recall that the perception on the part of the Turkish leadership at the time was that modernization was associated with secularism, and that a state built on religion and religious laws could by definition not be modern. Amongst the defining moments for the new state were the abolition of the Caliphate and the abolition of sharia law and adoption of a civil code in its place. Given that much of the collaboration that occurred during the resistance was built upon notions of religious connections and that many Kurdish tribal leaders were still deeply conservative and religious, it was inevitable that the abrupt attempt at creating a secular state would produce difficulties.

Decisions regarding the creation and promotion of a common nationality created further problems for the state. Even the decision to name the state the *Turkish* Republic was potentially problematic from the perspective of ethnic Kurds. However, state leaders attempted to define the people living in the republic in terms of a common civic national identity. For instance, Mustafa Kemal came to define a nation as consisting of 'a group of people who inhabited the same piece of land, who were bound by the same laws, and shared a common morality and language' (quoted in Kirisci and Winrow 1997: 97). Thus, ethnicity and race were not initially considered to be elements of a nation. Perhaps this strategy could have created a civic nationalism similar to the one that France has managed if the government had consistently pursued it. However, emphasis quickly came to be placed on the factors that Kemal and his associates were trying to discount, namely religion and language. For instance despite official commitment to avoid using religion as a defining characteristic of Turkish nationalism, Christians and Jews were excluded from military schools and academies. In addition, in 1930 all the non-Muslim personnel of Turkish Railways (a nationally owned enterprise) except for a handful of experts were laid off. In a similar situation, Jewish employees of the Anatolian Press Agency were dismissed with only one day's notice in 1942. The notorious wealth tax that was introduced during World War II tended to be most heavily used to tax non-Muslims, and non-payment resulted in many people being sent to labour camps in the eastern part of the country. Moreover, Turkish ethnicity began to be emphasized and began to take on racist overtones (Çağlar 1990; Kirisci and Winrow 1997: 97–8).

The above policies were directed specifically at a relatively small group of citizens – Greek and Armenian Christians and Jews, of which there were very few remaining by this time – and so their potential for inciting regional conflict was extremely limited. The policy which did appear to spark conflict, however, was the introduction of a unified education system which attempted to instil common cultural identity and teach the common language of the state, Turkish. This led to a wave of rebellions in the 1920s and 1930s – almost all of these in the eastern part of the country – and it is argued that the first of these (February–March 1925) was more costly than the war of independence, both in human and financial terms. The rebellion had been immediately preceded by calls for the restoration of sharia courts, which were closed down the previous year. The rebellions were led – not surprisingly – by many of the disillusioned deputies from the parliament who had been part of the resistance movement. The state responded by introducing new legislation that further emphasized Turkish ethnicity and language, as well as taking a hard-line military approach to the rebellions (Kreyenbroek and Sperl 1991; Izady 1992; Kirisci and Winrow 1997: 100–1; Gunter 1997; Barkey and Fuller 1998; Ergil 2000; Natali 2005).[6] It is important to note that many Kurdish tribes actually assisted the Turkish government in controlling the rebellions.

Thus, by 1930, the preferred solution to the growing regional conflict was a combination of military-enforced repression and stepped up efforts to create a common identity based on ethnicity, history, and language. So, for instance, the Turkish Institutes of History and Language were created, the former to develop common myths about the origins of Turks and the latter to 'purify the language' (Kirisci and Winrow 1997: 102). This then led to attempts to prove that Kurds were Turks who had simply adopted a different language at some point, and it was also during this period that the infamous 'mountain Turks' phrase was used by an Army General (Adullah

Alpdoğan) in referring to the population in the East and Southeast. Thus, the emphasis was now clearly on ethnic nationalism rather than civic nationalism (Kirisci and Winrow 1997: 103).

The rebellions that occurred in the 1920s and 1930s in the eastern region of Turkey appear to have been motivated by opposition to modernization and particularly to the attempt to convert the country into a secular society. That is, they do not appear to have been motivated by ethnic or nationalistic solidarity. Kirisci and Winrow (1997: 105) contend that by 1950 there was little evidence of Kurdish nationalism in the country. After this, however, such nationalism clearly did emerge (Kreyenbroek and Sperl 1991; Izady 1992; Gunter 1997; Barkey and Fuller 1998; Ergil 2000; Natali 2005).

The modernization of Turkey appears to have opened the way for the creation of consciousness, and it was the urbanized and better educated amongst the Kurds who transformed the issue of identity into one related to ethnic identity and self-determination. Kurdish nationalism began as an analysis known as 'Eastism' which contended that the problems of the eastern regions were due to exploitation and lack of development. Essentially, the thinkers behind this were inspired by leftist, class-based analyses that were increasingly prominent in the 1960s in Turkey. Indeed, these groups were closely connected to Turkish leftist groups, and these groups combined forces to use violence to support the 'struggle against fascism and imperialism, for ideological independence and the liberation of peoples, including that of Turks and Kurds' (quoted in Kirisci and Winrow 1997: 109) The group began holding meetings in 1967 ostensibly to draw attention to the problems of the eastern regions, and it does not appear that they were designed to promote Kurdish nationalism or separatism. Still, the government accused the organizers of being traitors because they were trying to divide the country.

Although the initial meetings themselves were focussed on developmental issues, they also appear to have raised public consciousness and subsequently organizations began to form to promote Kurdish ethnicity. At first, the aim of most of these was to persuade the Turkish government to recognize the language and cultural rights of Kurds. Eventually the rhetoric became more radical, taking a revolutionary approach. The collaboration with Turkish leftists ended, as the latter perceived that the Kurdish leftists were losing the Marxist plot and focusing too much on ethnicity issues. The number of radical Kurdish leftist groups multiplied, and one of these was the PKK (the Kurdistan Workers Party), the most radical and the most influential of them all.

The PKK adopted radical separatism as its stated goal, and engaged in terrorism and armed conflict to pursue the goal. Small military outposts and military personnel became targets, as did tourist destinations, and key government economic operations, such as transport and communication. Teachers and schools – the disseminators of the common language and culture – were also targeted. The reaction was a major military backlash, and a re-emphasis on the unity and territorial integrity of the state. Even a former Republican People's Party deputy was imprisoned by a military court for one year for having said in an interview, 'There are Kurds in Turkey. I am a Kurd' (Kirisci and Winrow 1997: 111).

The approach of the military to the Kurdish issue was also apparent in the 1982 constitution, which stipulated that the state must protect the 'independence and integrity of the Turkish Nation, the indivisibility of the country, the Republic' (Article 5). This effectively made it illegal to express any idea that could be interpreted as amounting to a recognition of a separate, Kurdish, ethnic identity. Another article of the Constitution stated: 'No language prohibited by the State shall be used in the expression and dissemination of thought' (Article 26); subsequently, a law was passed in October 1983 banning the use of Kurdish for the dissemination of information. Political parties which supported activities 'in conflict with the indivisible integrity of the state' were also banned (Article 68). The 1982 Constitution also revitalized the History and Language Societies of the 1930s, which resulted in articles and books being published once again claiming that Kurds and Turks shared a common ancestry.

The separatist violence continued, however, and was stepped up. The military continued to pursue a military-led solution to the problem, co-opting Kurds to help put down the rebellions and fight PKK terrorism. Simultaneously, the PKK was putting pressure on Kurds to decide where their loyalties lay, and if they sided with the Turkish government, they ran the risk of having their villages burned down. This period thus saw a significant deterioration of democracy, as a state of emergency was declared in ten eastern provinces; in these places, civilian governors were given the right to exercise martial law powers, including restricting the press and removal of persons whose activities were believed to have threatened public order; this also meant suspension of the application of human-rights agreements and the trial of suspects in these regions in military courts (Kirisci and Winrow 1997: 128).

During this time, it would have thus been difficult for civilian leaders to propose a political solution to the crisis. A few did begin to discuss such possibilities. Notably, President Özal openly claimed to be of Kurdish origin and began to discuss the possibility of allowing radio and television broadcasts in Kurdish, as well as allowing Kurdish to be taught as a second language at school. Again, this was during a time when making such suggestions could land a politician in prison for threatening the territorial integrity of the state and nation. Members of his party became increasingly critical of Özal's position, and his successor tended to fluctuate over the handling of the Kurdish question. Eventually in 1996, the government surprisingly announced that a political solution should be sought. However, no real moves were made in this regard.

One of the other key parties at the time, the True Path Party, initially mentioned the idea of pursuing a political solution to the Kurdish question in its campaign propaganda but instead became absorbed in constitutional battles over executive powers (see Chapter 7). Once President Özal died, the National Security Council became increasingly powerful in dictating policy on the Kurdish problem (Hale 1994). Another subsequent party leader, Tansu Çiller, toyed very briefly with the idea of a 'Basque model' for Turkey but was criticized by her party and by the military and backed down from this idea quickly. Other key parties were also very opposed to the idea of language rights or autonomy (e.g. Nationalist Action Party and Democratic Party of the Left). In fact, by the mid-1990s, the only parties that claimed to want to grant cultural rights to the Kurds were the Republican People's Party and the Virtue Party. There was, however, little discussion of autonomy or a federal model.

The international community has been critical of the Turkish government's handling of the 'problem in the Southeastern part of the country', with many European governments and the European Parliament passing resolutions in protest against policies such as the use of local village guards and violence which has produced large-scale migration away from the region. As was the case with the Spanish government, Kurdish separatism was largely treated by the Turkish government and military as a threat to territorial integrity and separatists were seen as terrorists. Under pressure from the international community and particularly the European Union (see Chapter 10), the Turkish government's approach to the 'problem in the Southeast' has begun to change.

For instance, in June 2004, Turkey allowed the first Kurdish-language broadcasts on state radio and television.[7] Nationally owned TRT became the first Turkish broadcaster to broadcast in Kurdish. In 2004, TRT decided to show Kurdish programmes amounting to approximately 35 minutes of broadcasting twice a week.[8] Although critics contend that this is fairly minimal in the general context of state repression against the use of the Kurdish language, it may also be seen as fairly revolutionary. Equally impressive is that the Turkish government allowed a literary conference to use Kurdish in its proceedings in November 2003.[9] While these steps are somewhat limited and there is still no realistic discussion of the establishment of regional government or federal arrangements, they may be the first steps toward such a process.

Conclusions

All three of the countries under investigation here have experienced difficulties related to regional identity and separatism. Somewhat amazingly, Italy appears to have resolved many of these problems swiftly after World War II when newly formed separatist movements were threatening secession. Italy's solution to this potential state crisis was to grant constitutional guarantees of use of language and guarantees of influence over regional policy for elites who had become deeply dissatisfied with the Italian state.

Like Turkey, Spain has struggled to strike an acceptable balance between desires for unity and centralization and desires on the part of regional groups to maintain their own language and sovereignty over policies that directly affect them. Some of the Spanish governments over the nineteenth and twentieth centuries attempted to grant varying degrees of autonomy, but often this was reversed by authoritarian leaders wishing to impose a common language and culture. The most extreme of these was the lengthy Franco dictatorship. By the time Franco died, however, it was clear that forced assimilation was unsuccessful and may have had the reverse effect: various wings of ETA had formed in the last few years of Franco's life and had begun to wage war on the Spanish state. As mentioned above, many in the region appeared to begin to sympathize with the terrorist movement because the treatment of suspected separatists was extremely brutal. The threat posed by separatism is thus one that threatened to undermine the fledgling democracy, in that it was one of the main causes of the 1981 coup attempt, as will be discussed in the next chapter. However, the regime appears to have found a reasonable, albeit ambiguous, constitutional balance, and all but the most determined separatists have been brought into the democratic system.

The Turkish response to its growing separatist problem resembles – and perhaps exceeds – Franco's response to such problems. Groups speaking languages other than those accepted as foreign languages (with foreign languages generally referring to French, German, English, etc.) were denied the right to use those languages in public places such as courts of law and denied the right to openly teach or broadcast in the language. The policy being pursued was one of centralization and forced assimilation. As was the case with the Franco regime, this policy was a dismal failure and appears to have provoked increased sympathy for the movement, both within the region and internationally. The Spanish and Italian cases would seem to point to the conclusion that the only way to move past these problems of separatism is with the establishment of an institutional apparatus that allows for some degree of regional autonomy. As both of these cases indicate, federalism as a model may not be necessary – aspects of the federal model, particularly representation of the regions in the national parliament, render these regimes somewhat different from 'ideal types' of federalism. Still, their versions of quasi-federalism, devolution, etc. appear to have gone a long way toward reconciling disputes over the territorial division of power. This may be the route that Turkish democratizers will be forced to take as well. Such an approach may then reduce the temptation to use non-democratic means to halt separatist activity and may also reduce the perceived need for military independence.

9 The professionalization of the military

The definition of democratic consolidation outlined in Chapter 1 of this book included the notion that democratically elected civilians hold ultimate decision-making authority within the political system. In many areas of policy-making, this stipulation becomes somewhat ambiguous. For instance, civilian governments in many western democracies have delegated a considerable amount of policy-making and oversight capabilities to regulatory agencies which are not directly accountable to the public, particularly in realms deemed to be of a fairly technical nature, such as telecommunications and transportation (see Majone 1996). Although the democratic nature of decision-making in these policy areas can be called into question, it is still very much the case that civilians make the initial decision to create the regulatory body and that elected civilians continue to provide policy-making direction to such agencies, as well as some parliamentary oversight.

The topic to be discussed in this chapter is one which concerns government agencies that usurp – or threaten to usurp – power from elected governments without the consent of the latter. In most countries, there is one key institution that has the power to do this, and that is the military. While the state may have the monopoly on the use of force, it is the military that has direct control over the mechanisms of force – the tanks, bombs, aircraft equipped with weaponry, etc. Given the vast resources available to them, it is a wonder that military leaders do not intervene more than they do (Finer 1988).

By definition, in democratic political systems military officials do not intervene in politics and instead take their orders from elected civilian leaders. When they do not derive their authority from democratically elected civilians, the implication is that policy-making has transferred from individuals and groups who can be held accountable at the next round of elections (e.g. political parties) to individuals or groups who are unaccountable. Thus, one of the most important issues for countries in the midst of a democratic transition is that of establishing or ensuring the supremacy of civilian institutions and leaders over the military. Drawing upon the work of Felipe Agüero, we can define civilian supremacy as 'the ability of a civilian, democratically elected government to conduct general policy without interferences from the military, to define the goals and general organization of national defence, to formulate and conduct defence policy, and to monitor the implementation of military policy' (1995: 19). That is, elected civilians must be in control of both non-military and military-related policies. The key question is how civilians go about gaining such control.

Academic literature on the role of the military in politics tends to point to the process of professionalization in converting politically active militaries into non-political bodies. Professionalism implies that the military is politically neutral and is politically subordinate to constitutionally designated authorities. It further implies that elected officials have supreme authority over policy decisions that concern the armed forces such as defining the security threats, deciding when military force is necessary and will be used, resource allocation through the defence budget, the structure of the armed forces, and promotions particularly at senior levels (see Born *et al.* 2006: 7). According to Huntington, in order to gain civilian control over the military, the latter must be rendered 'politically sterile and neutral' but must also be treated as a professional body and not used, for instance, by the civilian government for internal party-political purposes (1957: 83–4). Thus, where these elements are lacking, professionalization implies that civilians will begin a process of systematically altering policy and decision making such that these criteria are met.

Under what conditions do militaries intervene in the political process? There are several factors that could trigger a military intervention. If military leaders feel that the civilian government is failing to take the institutional needs and interests of the military seriously, this could provoke an uprising. Also important is the perception of the effectiveness of civilian governments. In circumstances where the civilian government is perceived as ineffective, inefficient or corrupt, the likelihood of military intervention increases (Kadt 2002: 320). In justifying interventions, military leaders often emphasize the identification of the armed forces with the fate of the nation and its core values, the need to maintain order and especially the integrity of the state. Thus, the destiny of the state and the interests of its people are linked to 'the historic mission of the military' (Kooninngs and Kruijt 2002: 10; see Janowitz 1964, 1977; Finer 1988).

Political armies generally perceive that they are best placed to understand the essence of the nation by birthright. That is, they perceive that the military was there at the birth of the nation and that without the sacrifices made by the armed forces, the nation would not have formed or survived. This myth may or may not be historically correct, but it is often believed to be so by political armies. The latter also believe that they are best placed to take care of national interests because of their organization and resources: they are hierarchically structured, with unity of command; they are goal-oriented; efficient; and they have control over the means of force. They may also see themselves as able to overcome sub-national particularism which may become a threat to national interests. In the face of seemingly incompetent or inadequate civilian leaders, the military may regard civilian ability to protect national interests and affairs with suspicion (Kooninngs and Kruijt 2002: 19–21)

The techniques used to gain control over militaries are generally thought to include removing military personnel from power positions outside of the area of defence, such as regional governorships. In addition, civilian political superiors are appointed and acknowledged as being the ultimate decision-makers on policies carried out by the military (see Welch 1976). To this end, the establishment of a department of defence which is headed by a civilian is likely to help in gaining control over the military, although it is no guarantee that this will happen. Civilians must also have control over the defence budget, force levels, and promotion of senior grades of officers. As argued by Agüero, this transformation of civil–military relations may not happen quickly and probably will not happen by way of force, but instead involves a process of negotiation between civilian leaders and top military personnel, and importantly, a recognition that the military's key institutional interests must be accommodated (Agüero 1995a: 20; Agüero 1995b: 126–7). Moreover, civilian consensus across both the government and opposition on the fundamentals of the regime itself will render resistance on the part of the military less likely, as does overwhelming citizen support for the new civilian institutions, structures, leaders, and policies (see Agüero 1995a: 31–2; Agüero 1995b: 126). Alternatively, if the military is to resist reforms and/or engage in political matters, the military will have to be unified behind the same position in order for these actions to be successful. That is, the actions of a few lone military personnel with only a portion of the military leadership's backing are unlikely to halt civilian attempts at consolidating democracy (Agüero 1995: 101); again, however, if the civilians are not, in fact, unified themselves, a less-than-unified military may still effectively resist civilian control. Also of potential relevance is the role occupied by the military in the outgoing authoritarian regime. Where the military held core leadership positions in the authoritarian regime, the military was better able to set the transition agenda and impose protective preconditions. When the outgoing regime is steered primarily by civilians, the military has a more difficult time influencing change (Agüero 1995b: 140).

In terms of our three case studies, the military dimension represents one of the most important for consolidating democracy. Namely, one of the main factors keeping Turkey out of the realm of democratic consolidation is the continued military intervention in ordinary political processes, whether this occurs by direct intervention – or 'hard' coup – or meddling behind the scenes by making public statements regarding public policy. As will be shown in this chapter, the Turkish military has a very long history of interventionism and political activism which appears to make professionalization difficult. At the same time, Spain is another case in which the military has had a long history of interventionism and indeed coup attempts and plots against the new democratic regime continued into the mid-1980s. Nowadays a successful military intervention in Spain is unthinkable, however, raising the question of how the Spanish military's role was altered to such a great extent. Although the Italian military has been far less active in politics than the militaries in Spain or Turkey in the modern day, there were still aspects of the regime that made military intervention likely, including the ineffectiveness and corruption of politicians and political parties. Indeed, there was at least one major plot on the regime in the 1960s. This chapter thus provides an overview of military interventionism in these countries and ultimately tries to answer the question of why the cases differ in their levels of military activism. The chapter includes summaries of the major plots on the democratic regimes and the subsequent actions (if any) taken by civilian leaders to prevent future interventionism by the military.

Italy: the case of minimal military interference

Compared to the two case studies to follow, Italy has had very little experience with outright military intervention in politics in the form of *pronunciamientos* or *coup d'etats*. In many ways it is unclear as to why this might be. Italian governments from the time of the founding of the new state have been extraordinarily unstable (see Chapters 3 and 7), and the state has at various times faced threats from the extreme left and the fascist right. Moreover, prior to World War II the Italian military's role was primarily domestic in nature – it was sent to repress domestic uprisings, to defend the state against internal enemies (Clark 1984: 49; Bosworth 2004: 61).[1] In addition, civilians traditionally were very rarely in charge of the war ministries in the Liberal period of Italy; that is, the War Minister and Navy Minister were almost always military men (Bosworth 2004: 62). Finally, according to military historian Giorgio Rochat, by the 1940s the size of the officer corps was extremely inflated (Rochat 1967: 586). As will be shown below in the case of Spain, the combination of all of these factors would appear to place Italy in a prime position for military coups.

Up until around 1919, three main factors are likely to have prevented such coups from occurring. One is that military personnel were extremely loyal to the monarch, who was himself of military background. Thus, the fact that their commander in chief was a military officer himself made it unlikely that military personnel would disobey his orders. Indeed, loyalty to the king remained a feature of the Italian military even throughout the Mussolini years (Mack Smith 1959: 367 and 436; Clark 1984: 296). Second, although potentially problematical, the military leadership adopted a policy of moving regiments around the country on a regular basis so that troops could not become too connected to the local domestic population; this approach was taken because of fear that such connections would provide the military with the social basis and reason for interventionism (Clark 1984: 49–50).[2] Third, unlike the cases to be considered below, despite government instability in the Liberal era, the extremes were kept out or stayed out of government by choice. Of particular importance is that the fairly militant Socialist party remained out of government, which meant that the key sub-versive group in the political system was not in charge of state institutions. Given that the parties running the government, along with the monarch, were not thought to be a threat to the state itself, there was little reason for a strike at the state.

At the end of World War I, though, military personnel began to display unprecedented levels of political activism: ordinary soldiers were taking part in street protests and street fighting and many officers began to act more independently than before the war. Mondini (2006: 447) contends that this was in great part a result of the fact that the military had been given free rein in military administered areas, particularly the Governorates of Dalma-tia, Venezia Giulia, and Trentino. Dissatisfaction over the post-war settle-ment and particularly the government's lack of willingness to insist that regions like Fiume – where the vast majority of the population are Italian – remain part of Italy sparked rumours of a military coup d'état. In fact, one general, General Gabriele D'Annunzio, agreed to lead such a coup organized by Nationalists, army officers, and a handful of industrialists. D'Annunzio and his troops marched into Fiume and stayed there for 15 months. Finally, on Christmas Day 1920, the new prime minister, Giovanni Giolitti, took control of the situation and sent the Italian navy to Fiume to put the coup down. There was little resistance and D'Annunzio surrendered almost immediately (Clark 1984: 205).

This event did not put an end to military activism, however. As the country descended into chaos in 1919, some of the generals did become involved with Mussolini's movement and eventually helped to lead the 'March on Rome'. However, the fascist squads were mostly non-military, and while Mussolini had served briefly in World War I, he was no longer in the military at the time that the fascist squads began to form, and so it is difficult to refer to the March 1921 uprising as a military coup. Moreover, the evidence generally indicates that if the king had commanded the mili-tary to put down the uprising and to find and destroy the fascist squads, they would have very likely done so (Mack Smith 1959: 367).

During the fascist era, Mussolini kept his paramilitary fascist squads as a counterforce to the military, thereby preventing any coup attempts on the part of the latter; in essence, a strike at the state would have very likely pushed the country into civil war because the fascists and the king's forces were both armed and very loyal to their respective causes. It is also con-tended that there was a sort-of alliance between fascism and the army, with fascism assuring the armed forces of respect and privilege, as well as some autonomy in their own internal operations, and the army in turn giving the regime substantial assurance of support (Rochat 2005). Mondini contends that 'the political presence of Fascism, even before October 1922, allowed most of the officer corps to consider the case for a direct intervention to be unnecessary' (2006: 458).

By the end of World War II, the military's role had been changed from repressing domestic uprisings to fighting external conflicts, and it was seen as generally incompetent in this area. Moreover, 'the most important single factor governing the Italian military apparatus in the postwar period has been its integration into NATO – its role, organization, weaponry and activity – flows from that' (Allum 1973: 172). Thus, the US dominance over the Italian military through NATO and control over Italian military bases via the latter appears to have restricted any potential military inclination to become involved in politics, and the main reason the US was able to maintain such a strong presence was that the Italian military was severely weakened and discredited by defeat in World War II. At the same time, given the post-war abolition of the monarchy, which appeared to be the key government institution maintaining ultimate control over the military, military intervention would seem very likely had NATO not kept strict control over the Italian forces.

Government instability has continued to be a problem in Italy and the perceived threat from the left has remained a problem in the post-war era; these are conditions that would otherwise seem likely to provoke a military intervention (see Chapter 6). Although the externally oriented portion of the armed forces do not appear to have become active in trying to independently fight off these threats to the regime, there is one component of the Italian military from which such a coup *was* waged. In addition to a regular domestic police force, the Italian military contains a branch known as the *carabinieri*, which functions like a domestic police force but consists of individuals who are essentially soldiers – they received military training and are subject to military discipline. Organizationally, this body fits within the Ministry of War (Clark 1984: 51). This component of the military remained a part of the post-war configuration, as it was thought that internal enemies still posed enough of a threat to warrant military force. Moreover, this branch does not appear to have been subjected to American control via NATO.

It is this branch that became a source of conspiracy to carry out a coup. Namely, in 1962, General Giovanni De Lorenzo was appointed to the post of commander-in-chief of the *carabinieri* after spending several years in the top command of the military intelligence. Shortly after he was appointed to the post he began to amass a modern mechanized brigade – apparently prior to this, the *carabinieri* mostly consisted of ill-equipped mobile and horse-mounted battalions. In the words of former Prime Minister Ferruccio Parri, De Lorenzo had formed 'his own little personal army, superior in discipline and efficiency to the rest of the armed forces' (quoted in Ginsborg 1990: 276).

In the midst of a government crisis in the 1960s in which a centre-left coalition had collapsed and the leader of the Christian Democrats, Aldo Moro, was unable to form a government for several weeks, De Lorenzo developed his 'Solo' plan: lists of individuals who presented a danger for public security would be drawn up and provision made for their arrest and detention. In addition, television and radio stations, telephone and telegraph offices, as well as the offices of certain political parties were to be occupied by his forces. In the midst of the coalition formation problems, De Lorenzo gave orders for the Solo plan to be prepared at the local level (Ginsborg 1991: 276–7). However, the other *carabinieri* generals ignored De Lorenzo's instructions, and the *carabinieri* troops remained in their barracks (Clark 1984: 342). The plan was for the *carabinieri* to carry out the plot alone because De Lorenzo did not believe the rest of the armed forces would support him (Ginsborg 1991: 276–7). Thus, the plot failed in great part because of lack of support from almost all elements in the armed forces. It was not discovered until some years later, though, after De Lorenzo had been promoted to Chief of the Staff of the Army. De Lorenzo was never punished, except by removal from office for other issues related to his former role as chief of military intelligence, and eventually he became a member of parliament, first as a Monarchist and then transferring to the neo-fascist National Social Movement (Ginsborg 1990: 278).

Although the left had been refusing to participate again in government during the 'Solo' plot because of the slow progress in the realm of socialist reforms, the Socialist leader appeared to realize that danger was in the air and decided to stop arguing and support the Christian Democrats in coalition again (Ginsborg 1990: 278). Indeed, the continued willingness of the left to cooperate with the centre against multiple threats to the regime may have helped to avert future such plots.

The De Lorenzo affair seems to indicate that civilian control over the Italian military may be weak. As discussed above, prior to the fascist era, it was common for the war ministries to be run by generals. In the absence of any problem of coups being waged by top-level officers in the Italian military there seems to have been far less impetus to ensure civilian control over the military than in countries like Spain (see below). In the post-World War II era, there have in fact been civilian bodies that interact with the military. The most important of these is the Supreme Defence Council, which consists of the President of the Republic (chairman), the Prime Minister (Vice-Chairman), and the Ministers of Foreign Affairs, Interior, Treasury, Defence, Industry, and the Head of the General Defence Staff. Thus, it is mostly a civilian-led body. However, according to Allum, it acts 'more as a pressure group for certain policies than as a constitutional consultative body' (Allum 1973: 174).

Apparently the Higher Council of the Armed Forces is the key military decision-making body in Italy. It includes the four Heads of the General Staffs and the Secretary-General of Defence, which is a political appointment and also requires the confidence of the military. The Head of the Defence General Staff is the chief of all of the Heads of the General Staff and thus commands all of the levers of military power. He, in turn, is responsible to the Minister of Defence, which is a civilian post (Adams and Barile 1966).

However, the Defence Minister is obliged to consult the Head of the Defence General Staff on top-level appointments, and the latter also determines the military's scientific research programmes and supervises military information services (Allum 1973: 174–6). In essence, the military has almost complete control over the armed forces but is still subordinated to civil power. Given the large number of apparent government collapses in the post-war period, it seems unlikely that elected civilians have been able to exercise a great deal of control over military decision-making, though (see Spotts and Weiser 1986: Chapter 13, on the effect of this problem particularly on foreign policy).

It is also important to note that there are too many field officers (e.g. generals) in the Italian armed forces. For instance, in 1970 there were 1016, whereas the Armed Forces had provided for 321. The same was true of colonels and staff officers. In addition, promotion has tended to be slow and driven in great part by seniority (Allum 1973: 177). Again, these are problems that have been mentioned in the context of the Spanish army leading up the 1981 coup attempt, but these problems did not lead to a similar level of plotting in Italy. As argued above and in the sections to follow, it is thus highly likely that the response of the civilian leaders to perceived threat to the regime itself, along with NATO control over the externally oriented forces, made it very difficult for military officers to plot in the same ways the Spanish officers did.

Spain: from *golpismo* to professionalization

According to historian Paul Preston, Spain experienced more than 50 *pronunciamientos*, or military interventions in politics, between 1814 and 1981. Initially, these interventions were generally for the purpose of pushing the regime toward political liberalism. Beyond this early period, interventions tended to be more authoritarian in their intent. Civilian governments came to be viewed within the military with distrust, and interventions occurred for the purpose of 'saving Spain' (Preston 1990: 131).[3]

Indeed, the Franco regime itself had been the result of a military uprising against a popularly elected government. Supporters of this uprising included groups that were particularly threatened by the left-wing governments of the Second Republic: monarchists, authoritarian Catholics (CEDA), and the small fascist Falange Española (Preston 1990: 111; Rees and Grugel 1997: Chapter 1). Sections of the officer corps, with the support of these groups, thus rose against the Spanish Second Republic to save their country from a breakdown of law and order, the disintegration of national unity, and 'proletarian godlessness' (Preston 1990: 3). The officers thought they were acting out of patriotism, to save Spain from these threats (Cardona 1983: 197–247).

Given the lengthy history of military plots, it is not surprising that the Franco regime itself also faced some fairly serious discontent from within the military. Potentially the most significant of these was dissatisfaction that Franco was not making moves toward restoring the monarchy, which is precisely what many soldiers and officers believed they had been fighting for in the Civil War. Related to this, many were hostile toward the fascist wing of the Franco regime and were offended by having to use the fascist solute and by having to be members of the Movimiento (see Rees and Grugel, Chapters 2 and 3). However, during the early part of Franco's regime only a dozen or so senior officers attempted to stand up to him, and this was done very hesitantly (Preston 1990: 86–91).

After this initial period, multiple factors helped to keep Franco's regime relatively free from major plots. First, many of the monarchists amongst the military generals eventually retired or died. In the case of less senior officers, Franco assigned many of these who were suspected of having the potential to undermine the regime to high-ranking posts with little or no power to mobilize troops.[4] He also periodically granted very high pay rises across the board, and importantly, even during times of scarcity, he made certain that the soldiers' shops were stocked with food and medicines that were available at subsidized prices. He also turned a blind eye to corruption, including the use of rank-and-file troops and Republican prisoners of war as cheap or free labour on the part of officers with business interests, as well as the use of army vehicles for private purposes, etc. (Busquets 1984: 214; Gilmour 1985: Chapters 2 and 12; Preston 1990: 105, 137).

At the senior level, Franco used the strategy of divide-and-rule to keep the military from becoming too powerful. The Ministry of Defence was divided into three separate army, navy, and air force ministries, with coordination across the three provided by his own advisory board. Franco was the supreme commander and the three military ministers were to serve as administrators. Similarly, the eighteenth-century practice of distributing the army across nine military regions was revived under Franco, as was another layer of hierarchy within the military. This system is argued to have enhanced Franco's ability to play different officers off against each other (Preston 1990: 135). The system generally appears to have worked to keep senior officers from plotting any serious overthrow. With regard to middle-ranking officers, which in many countries have also been the source of plots (including Turkey, as will be shown below), these officers tended to be loyal to Franco. Many of them had been trained by Franco during their time at the military academy (Preston 1990: 136). It was the generation after this one that eventually became more problematic: many of the officers amongst this generation were far more concerned with professionalism than their predecessors and were especially appalled by the corruption and the inefficiency of the military, which by the 1950s and 1960s was also severely under-funded (Preston 1990: 139). However, 'in the late 1950s and early 1960s, with the stability of the regime as yet unquestioned and ... with no officers prepared to stand up to Franco, internal conflict within the army was virtually indiscernible' (Preston 1990: 150; on the Franco regime, see also Payne 1987).

However, as discussed in Chapter 3, the country began to face strikes by workers in the 1960s, and the latter managed to obtain concessions on wages and working conditions. Many amongst the army and the Falange were concerned about the revival of working-class militancy, which they saw as being a result of the rush toward modernization under way in Spain. The conclusion drawn was that there needed to be a return to the hardline Francoism – traditionalism and autarky – of the post-Civil War period. This was confirmed by the rise of ETA and the subsequent violence wreaked by that organization (Preston 1986, chapter 1).

Toward the end of the Franco regime, as the left (Communists and Socialists) began to press for a transition to democracy led by the workers and the regime was becoming ever more repressive, the ranks of the opposition to the regime grew. Equally problematic for the regime was that the Catholic Church had withdrawn its support. At the same time, the army and the Falange became increasingly intransigent and the army resented the fact that it was being turned into a target for popular discontent as a result of having to clean up messes which officers perceived to be a consequence of political weakness. As the regime stepped up its repression of ETA and leftist organizations, hardliners continued to be preferred when it came to army promotions and they continued to influence Franco's choice of political leaders as well (Preston 1986: Chapter 2). Ultimately, the dominance of the top of the military hierarchy by hardliners was to create problems for leaders wishing to introduce political liberalization as a solution to the increasing political violence.

Evidence that hardliners were still very much in control of the regime in the mid-1970s can be found in the policies of Arias Navarro, appointed after Prime Minister Carrero Blanco was killed by an ETA car bomb. Arias put forward a programme in early 1974 promising a small amount of opening in the form of election of mayors and other local officials, and election of deputies to the Cortes, although suffrage would be limited to regime elites. Over the course of the next two years, even this small *apertura* was whittled down by the 'bunker', though. Particularly worrisome for the latter was the Portuguese revolution and the sudden crumbling of 45 years of authoritarian rule in that country, as well as the fact that the Greek military regime was crumbling. The hard-right (ultras) in the regime claimed the *apertura* was 'an opening to subversion' and implied that they would appeal to the armed forces to protect the regime. When Arias announced that he was going through with the *apertura* and would introduce political associations before the start of 1975, the ultras began a fierce attack on the regime, preparing dossiers for Franco revealing the scale of 'pornography' permitted by the regime. The resignation of several government ministers seemed to indicate the triumph of the bunker in preventing any political liberalization (Preston 1986: Chapter 3).

At the same time, however, prominent industrialists and financiers had been meeting with members of the opposition, and the size of the opposition to the regime grew. In addition, there was also evidence of opposition to the regime increasing within the armed forces. Specifically, in late 1974 the intelligence services had discovered that groups of young officers were meeting to discuss the future of the regime. Some of these then formed a small organization, *Unión Militar Democrática* (Preston 1986: Chapter 3), which consisted primarily of captains and included a total of 100–200 officers. This group preferred a *ruptura democrática* and the stated purpose of the organization was to provide the neutralization of any attempts by military leaders to interrupt this process. By the time several members of the group were arrested, they had already been holding national and regional meetings and meetings with opposition leaders. Although there was disagreement as to what to do about the group once it was discovered, the hardliners decided to have members arrested and tried in military courts. Nine of the officers were sentenced to terms ranging from three to eight years in March 1976 for conspiracy to create a military rebellion. Prime Minister Suárez granted them amnesty after being sworn in as president of the government later in the year but they were still restricted from returning to their posts in the armed forces (Agüero 1995: 104–6).

In the three weeks before Franco died (after suffering a heart attack), his designated successor, King Juan Carlos, began to make contacts that suggested he was likely to steer the regime towards democracy. However, there were enormous problems: the 'bunker' was still powerful and was entrenched in the army, the police, and the Civil Guard. The army was still very much an important pillar of the regime and many of the regime's ministers had, in fact, come from within the army (Carr 1980: 166; Gilmour 1985: 30). Moreover, at least 100,000 Falangists were authorized to carry guns. Importantly, some of the king's first acts were designed, therefore, to consolidate his position with the army. For instance, shortly after Franco's heart attack, he visited Spanish garrisons in Morocco. The day after Franco's death, he sent a message to the armed forces renewing his oath of fidelity to the flag and acknowledging their position as defenders of Franco's Fundamental Laws. A few days later, he issued a royal decree making Franco a senior officer for eternity (Preston 1986: Chapter 3).

By the end of 1975, the opposition both within and outside of the regime was growing, but there was still a significant, powerful group of ultras within the Falange and the military, with the latter in particular taking the view that they had been instrumental in creating the regime and fighting off instability and immorality, and that they would also be the ones to continue to defend the regime from subversives. Initially the military was 'delighted' at the appointment of Adolfo Suárez as President of the Government because of his strong Francoist credentials. However, soon after taking office, Suárez announced his programme for reform, which included a promised referendum on political reform and elections before 30 June 1977. Also announced was a royal pardon for political offences, thereby freeing many of the leaders of the leftist parties. During this time Suárez was meeting with the leaders of both the Socialist party and the Communist party. There were 'constant rumours of military subversion ... the military capacity to invigilate the political process had been maintained by the continued presence of ultra generals at the head of the service ministries' (Preston 1986: 96). The king had actually wanted to appoint a liberal general to the ministerial cabinet, but the ultras managed to put together a dossier implying that this person had been head of the *Unión Militar Democrática* and prevented the king from making the appointment (Preston 1986: 96). Throughout 1976, it is clear that leading generals and Francoist ultras had been in contact with one another about bolstering opposition to democratic reform (Fernández 1982: 63; Preston 1986: Chapter 4).

In order to garner support amongst the armed forces, Suárez presented his programme for reform to a group of officers in September 1976; since the plans had the backing of the King, they were reluctantly accepted by the officers, but with a demand that the Communist Party be excluded from any future reform. Suárez assured them that the international loyalties enshrined in the Communist Party's statutes would make legalization impossible. In fact, Suárez was in talks with the PCE's leader, Santiago Carrillo, about changing those statutes. When he eventually legalized the PCE, the army saw him as breaking his word to them, which provoked considerable dissatisfaction among the officer corps (Preston 1986: Chapter 4).

Moreover, trade-union reform also provoked extreme dissatisfaction and opposition from the Minister of Defence, General de Santiago. Suárez forced this defence minister to resign because of his disobedience, but in Santiago's letter of resignation he implied that he was resigning voluntarily because of the growing militancy of the unions and because of the PCE being legalized. He and another senior officer were punished by being placed on the reserve list. Both of their cases were adjudicated by another general, who declared that the government's decree had been improper and that the conduct of both officers had been blameless, thus undermining Suárez's ability to gain control over the armed forces. In the next few years, the articles of these officers published in the ultra press, particularly *El Alcázar*, came to reflect and promote anti-democratic sentiment within the armed forces, or *golpismo* (Preston 1986: Chapter 4).

It must be remembered that the generals and admirals who were in power throughout much of the transition had a political outlook that was very much determined by their experiences during the civil war:

> They had fought in the victor army, which defeated Republicans and 'reds' and which remained sworn to defend *Franquist* institutions and ideals against the forces of 'anti-Spain.' As members of 'the *Movimiento*,' the official *Franquist* organization, it was the duty of top military officers to preserve the fundamental principles of 'the Crusade,' which was victorious in 1939.
>
> (Agüero 1995: 6)

However, the resignation of the above-mentioned hardline defence minister gave the king the opportunity to promote someone to the post who was more supportive of the reforms being proposed, General Gutiérrez Mellado. Thus, this appeared to be a first major step toward gaining civilian control over the armed forces on the part of the transitional regime. Mellado then proceeded to replace ultra officers with staff who were more loyal to himself. This at times meant expediting an officer through the promotion system, which was strictly based on seniority, and so meant that Gutiérrez Mellado came to be resented by many of the remaining senior officers. When the government finally legalized the PCE in April 1977, the Minister of the Navy resigned, and a number of civilian ministers threatened to do so as well. The army also issued a communiqué referring to the general revulsion that legalization of the PCE had caused. Propaganda within the military barracks was increased and emphasized Suárez's 'treachery'. Fake military-based organizations were invented to provide the propaganda, which gave the impression that many sectors of the army had come to the conclusion that an intervention in politics was necessary. This was also echoed in the ultra press (Preston 1986: Chapter 4).

Also problematic was the government's treatment of ETA. Initially Suárez treated it as a terrorist organization and continued to use violent methods to quash it. However, ETA violence became more brutal and increasingly targeted government and military officials. Suárez was anxious not to hold national elections in the midst of regional violence, and so after a spate of terrorist violence, his government negotiated a ceasefire with ETA and conceded total amnesty to prisoners being held on suspicion of terrorist activity. To the hard right, this was an intolerable capitulation in the face of armed violence (Preston 1986: Chapter 4). In addition, it appears that the opening up of the political system during this time produced a brief increase in the amount of pornography available, fuelling the fury of the ultras even further. For them, democracy was associated with pornography and disorder, both of which were becoming ever more apparent (Preston 1986: 123).

While the hardliners in the military and ultras outside were pressing for a military intervention, the government appears to have been oblivious to much of it. Preston contends that this was a result of the intelligence services preventing this information from getting to the government, either because of disloyalty or inefficiency (1986: 129). Suárez had actually begun to try to gain control over the intelligence services, which were divided into 11 different agencies, most of which were under the control of the military. In November 1977 Suárez created a central information service that was to control intelligence collection and processing. However, it kept the same personnel and managed to build up a power structure that was virtually independent of the king and the defence minister. The government appears to have ignored or missed this fact, and it was one of the key players in the intelligence services, Lieutenant Colonel José Ignacio San Martín López, who was to later be involved in a coup attempt (Fernandez 1982; see also Morales and Celada 1981).

In addition to the problems caused by the legalization of the PCE, the failure of the government to deal effectively with ETA, and concerns about increased pornography, rumours had spread that the government was planning to ask for the resignations of older officers, thereby preventing them from completing their full career and pension prospects. In September 1977, General Fernando de Santiago – the former Minister of Defence – held a meeting at his home which was attended by three ex-Army Ministers and two hardline generals. They wrote a memorandum which called upon the King to appoint a government of national salvation to be presided over by Santiago. The Ministry of Defence unofficially denied that such a memorandum had been presented to the King, but evidence points to the conclusion that high-ranking military officials were calling for a bloodless coup and that there was a clear threat of military intervention (Fernandez 1982: 181–3). Surprisingly, nothing was done to the officers who had participated in the meeting (Preston 1986: 131).

The Minister of Defence, General Gutiérrez Mallado, continued to try to gain control over the armed forces with strategic postings and promotions. One of the key postings for the waging of a coup was likely to be the Brunete Armoured Division, which controlled an armoured brigade in the Madrid area and a mechanized brigade farther to the southwest near Badajoz. Initially, an ultra, General Jaime Milans del Bosch, was Commander of this division, but General Gutiérrez Mallado replaced Milans del Bosch with someone more trusted. However, in order to soften the blow, Milans del Bosch was promoted to Captain General of the military region centred around Valencia. According to Preston, 'this merely placed a determined enemy of the regime in a powerful position without breaking his influence' (1986: 131).

Other signs of problems with military loyalty included the resignation of the Chief of the General Staff, General José Vega Rodríguez, who the government had regarded as a reliable moderate. He had apparently been in contact with an ultra who was editor of one of the ultra newspapers, and was increasingly concerned about ETA terrorism and unhappy with the government promoting officers out of turn, thereby ignoring the strict seniority system. His resignation provided the government with the opportunity to replace him with a professional apolitical Chief of the General Staff, and they chose General Tomás Liniers Pidal. Despite belief that he was indeed apolitical, Pidal delivered a speech in Buenos Aires praising the Argentine military's use of violence against the opposition and implied that similar methods would be appropriate in Spain. Surprisingly, no action was taken against him (Morales and Celada 1981: 39–41; Fernandez: 218–20).

ETA violence continued to escalate in 1978, and ETA particularly stepped up attacks on senior officers, policemen, and Civil Guards. As a result, many neutral officers were coming around to the ultra side, but many of these also realized that the government's continued approach of using strategic promotions was undermining their position and so action needed to be taken quickly if it was to be taken at all. Several officers agreed to the date of 17 November 1978 for a coup, a plan called 'Operation Galaxia' after the cafe in which it was plotted. The plan was to seize Suárez and his cabinet, convince other units to become involved, impose law and order, impose a government of national salvation, suspend parliament and launch a 'dirty war' against ETA. However, the plot was discovered. The two key leaders, Lieutenant Colonel Antonio Tejero Molina of the Civil Guard and Captain Ricardo Sáenz de Ynestrillas of the police, had apparently contacted almost 200 officers about the plan. One senior intelligence expert found out about the plot and informed his head of division, who dismissed it as a 'mad fantasy'. Later investigations indicate that Tejero and Ynestrillas had taken things further than most realized: the units in Burgos, Valladolid, Seville, and Valencia were involved and were placed on alert the night before the coup was to occur. Tejero and Ynestrillas only served seven months of detention, and Tejero was then posted to Madrid as head of a transport unit. Both the government and the left-wing opposition parties seemed to assume that the plot was simply the wild scheme of a few officers who did not represent the majority view, and so the whole affair was treated relatively lightly. At the same time, as ETA attacks continued, the ultra press stepped up its calls for a military intervention, and it had become clear that military officers could attack the democratic regime with very little in the way of punishment (Preston 1986: 146–51).

The government continued to try to use promotions to gain control over the military, however. Hostility toward the liberal defence minister, General Mellado, had grown, and so Suárez decided to move him out of the firing line by promoting him to Vice President of the Government with responsibility for Defence and Security. The new Minister of Defence began to make concessions to the military hardliners to appease them, but dissatisfaction was still high. When the post of Chief of the General Staff of the Army became vacant, promotion by strict seniority would have placed a hardliner into the post. Most favoured by the supreme advisory council was Milans del Bosch. Instead, the government appointed General José Gabeiras Montero, who was an associate of Mellado. Effectively, Montero had surpassed five other generals to be promoted to this post. The liberal position was further reinforced with the promotion of another relatively liberal general to be Captain-General of the Madrid forces (Morales and Celada 1981: 51–3).

In May 1979, after further attacks by both ETA and the left-wing group GRAPO, two generals met to discuss the need for a military intervention (Urbano 1982: 26). In addition, the three most senior ultras still on active duty by September were making open statements to the press condemning the government and threatening military action against ETA (Preston 1986: 165).

The government made further attempts to gain control over the ultras. Since the middle of 1979, the Brunete Armoured Division had been under the command of an ultra, and other hardliners had been requesting and obtaining postings to this unit. Within a month of the ultra General Luis Torres Rojas taking command of the division in mid-1979, a series of unauthorized manoeuvres had begun. It was later discovered that Torres Rojas was part of a planned coup to take place just before the Basque autonomy statute was to be considered in a referendum. The coup included a plan for a parachute brigade to seize the prime minister's palace with helicopter support; control would then be taken of Madrid with the units of the Brunete Armoured Division. The government would be forced to resign, and a military directorate would be formed under the former Defence Minister, General Santiago, or another general, Vega Rodríguez; the Cortes would be dissolved, the PCE would be banned, and the regional autonomy process would be reversed. However, the government was suspicious that a plot was under way and kept fuel and ammunition in short supply. Eventually Torres Rojas was removed from his post at the Brunete Armoured Division and sent to be military governor of La Coruña (Preston 1986: 166–7).

By the end of 1980, plots were still being discussed. In the summer of that year, the government developed a draft plan to grant amnesty to military officers who had fought with the side of the Republic during the Civil War and to members of the *Unión Militar Democrática*. Assassinations and attempted assassinations of senior generals by ETA-M (ETA had by this time split into more and less militant wings) and GRAPO continued in the spring and summer of that year as well, and the decline in participation in elections and referenda was taken by the right to mean that the public rejected the 'politics of intrigue' of the civilian government and was looking to the army to save Spain. The Turkish coup of 12 September 1980 (see below) prompted many colonels to consider a similar possibility for Spain. On 17 October 1980, 26 of the most prominent hardliners met in Madrid to discuss financial and civilian support for a coup. During this year, the Military Governor of Lérida, General Alfonso Armada had been developing a plan to establish a government of national salvation under his own presidency by using non-violent techniques. Armada had actually been one of Juan Carlos's tutors and the Secretary-General of the Royal Household until he was dismissed in July 1977 for alleged political meddling. On 17 November 1980, he met with Milans del Bosch, who was still Captain-General of the Valencia military region, to discuss the plan. He insinuated that he was acting under the discreet orders of the King. On 23 January 1981, 17 senior generals met again to discuss the need for military intervention (Preston 1986: 179–97).

In the midst of growing difficulties for the UCD government, Prime Minister (i.e. President of the Government) Adolfo Suárez resigned on 29 January 1981. During the second vote on the investiture of the proposed new prime minister, Leopoldo Calvo Sotelo, a group of civil guards under the command of Colonel Tejero arrived at the Cortes. Members of parliament were ordered to lie under their seats and the ceiling and TV cameras were shot with machine guns. 'Super-hostages' Felipe Gonzalez, Santiago

Carrillo, Gutierrez Mellado, Suárez, and a few others were locked in separate rooms and the rest of the Cortes was held hostage as well. Tejero contacted Milans del Bosch who was still Captain-General of the Valencia region and then announced to the Cortes that a senior military person would arrive shortly to take control. Milans del Bosch declared a state of emergency in Valencia and posted tanks near important buildings. Against the advice of Suárez, Armada had been brought back to Madrid on 12 February 1981 to the post of deputy chief of staff of the army. During the occupation of the Cortes, Armada was pretending to work toward making Tejero release the Cortes deputies; he was trying to implement his solution as a 'patriotic sacrifice' and would offer to form a government without ever appearing to have played any role in the coup (Preston 1986: 192–7).

The king took over the job of dismantling the coup with the support of his Secretary-General of the Royal Household and the new Director-General of Security. They were supported by the Chief of the Army General Staff and the Captain-General of Madrid. The Inspector-General of the Police and the Director-General of the Civil Guard also directed local operations. Police were placed around the parliament building in order to prevent any further subversives from entering. Thus, the police, despite doubts about their loyalty, made a fairly important contribution to blocking the coup.

When the king and his aides phoned the Captains-General of the other military regions, several of these hesitated and contacted Milans del Bosch. According to Paul Preston, 'If the King had been prepared to abandon the Constitution, there is little doubt that the Captains-General would have happily brought their troops out into the streets' (1986: 199). While Milans was the only one of 11 Captains-General to rebel openly, only three of the others appeared unequivocally loyal to the Constitution; the rest had, however, expressed hesitation (Agüero 1995: 164): 'The fact that a good number of captains general hesitated the night of the coup is a good indication of the uncertainty with which the outcome was perceived that night' (Agüero, 1995: 167).

Importantly, the Brunete Division came very close to intervening decisively. Torres Rojas, one of the key conspirators, had previously managed to get himself into a post through which he could take control of the division while the commanding officer was out inspecting some division units. When the Brunete Division commanding officer, General Juste, was informed of what was going on, he telephoned the king's residence expecting to find General Armada directing operations on behalf of the king. When he found out that Armada was not there and seemed to not be acting on behalf of the king, he took command over the division and ordered Torres Rojas to return to his posting at La Coruña (Preston 1986: 199–200).

Armada was sent into the Cortes as a mediator, and at this stage, he presented his solution of a government of cross-party national salvation to Tejero. Tejero rejected Armada's idea of including Communists and Socialists in a government and instead wanted a Pinochet-style junta to crush the left and to reverse regional autonomy. By this time, the king already suspected Armada's deceit. In a broadcast at 1.15am on 24 February, it was announced that the monarchy would not tolerate actions that attempted to interrupt the democratic process by force. The king contacted Milans and said he would not abdicate nor leave Spain and that if he and his co-conspirators were to prevail, they would have to shoot him. He sent a telex confirming this message. Milans realized that the pretence of the king's support could no longer be sustained and that the other Captains-General had not supported him either, and he withdrew his troops from the streets. Tejero negotiated his surrender with Armada, and the latter was arrested the following day. In all, it took 18 hours to dismantle the coup (Preston 1986: 201).

Agüero contends that the coup was a failure because of the divisions among the hardliners and co-conspirators. Things had clearly progressed to a point where a coup was realistically possible, but the hardliners had no clear alternative political vision, nor any plans for government policy after the coup. Some of the conspirators, mostly colonels and lieutenants, wanted to completely replace democracy; another group, consisting of loosely coordinated retired lieutenant generals who had connections to those on active duty, along with the extreme right civilians and press, wanted to see the establishment of a military junta. They had no clear platform, other than opposition to democracy, but claimed to be loyal to the monarchy. Finally, the group connected to the proposed 'Armada solution' did not want to completely destroy the parliamentary monarchy but wanted to create a stronger sense of governmental authority and to limit decentralization, halt the problems with terrorism using a hardline approach, and 'to enhance the institutional position of the armed forces' (Agüero 1995: 167–8).

After the attempted coup, Calvo Sotelo was confirmed as prime minister, and clearly one of his key tasks would have been to get *golpismo* under control. He appointed attorney Alberto Oliart Saussol as Minister of Defence. However, the latter was fairly malleable to the military's desires. As 1981 progressed, there was a growing conviction that the coup attempt was in many ways a success. Even the king's statement to the leaders of the parliamentary groups the day after the attempted coup indicated that the government was not going to react decisively: the king said that 'an open and tough reaction by the political parties against those who committed acts of subversion in the last few hours would be most unadvisable' (quoted in Preston 1986: 203).

After the coup attempt, all of the main party leaders made offers to support Sotelo in the Cortes, and ETA-PM (the less militant wing of ETA) released three kidnapped foreign consuls and announced an indefinite cease-fire. Additionally, three days after the attempted coup, mass demonstrations in support of democracy were held across Spanish cities. In the Madrid demonstrations, leaders included the party leaders of the right-wing Alianza Popular, the PSOE, and Communist Party, the UCD, as well as national labour union leaders. This sent a clear signal that civilians were unified behind democracy (Agüero 1995: 175).

Still, the unity of parties and the backing down of ETA-PM was interpreted by the hardline press as indicators that the coup attempt (the *Tejerazo*) had been successful. In addition, minor participants in the attempted coup were released in March and April, and Tejero was able to publish an article defending the coup. In April, the liberal officers of the *Unión Militar Democrática* were again refused re-admission into the military. Furthermore, only 30 of the nearly 300 officers who had been involved in the attempted coup were to be tried. Only Milans and Tejero were given harsh penalties of 30 years in prison each and the loss of military employment; even Armada was given only a six-year prison term (Agüero 1995: 172–3).

In June, it was revealed that several right-wing colonels had tried to organize another coup in which the king would be seized and forced to abdicate, and a military junta established, with blacklists of democrats to be 'liquidated' already having been drawn up. Equally shocking was that the general who had been military governor of Valencia on the night of 23 February and had acted in an ambiguous manner was made Captain-General of a fairly important military region, Zaragoza, and General Milans del Bosch was awarded a medal for 'sufferings for the Fatherland'. Further military indiscipline was revealed with the resurrection of *Unión Militar Español* and the publication of an anti-constitutional manifesto signed by 100 army officers, most of whom were from the Brunete division (Preston 1986: 204–16; see also Gilmour 1985: Chapter 12; Agüero 1995: 168–74).

The government and the king began to act more authoritatively, though. In March 1981, Sotelo presented the Cortes with a law which would allow the government to take action against the press networks of both the bunker and ETA-M. In addition, in January 1982, the king held a meeting with his Joint Chiefs of Staff. After this meeting, the decision was made to replace all of these officials. The explanation provided was that many of the members of the Joint Chiefs were coming up for retirement and that a total replacement was the only way to guarantee a coherent team to oversee the upcoming entry into NATO. In this way, the government was able to appoint constitutionalists to the top military posts (Preston 1986: 206–16). Furthermore, those who had plotted the 23 February coup attempt were on trial in early 1982, and the behaviour of these individuals shocked and repelled both the public and many officers. After the trials, pro-constitutionalist officers began to write articles and to appear on television. In addition, the president of the Joint Chiefs of Staff continued to implement changes to the promotion system and to transfer Francoist generals to the reserve list (Preston 1986: 218–19; also see Agüero 1995: Chapters 6 and 7 on the 1981 coup attempt; other sources include Busquets 1981; Cañaveral *et al.* 1981; Oneto 1982, Urbano 1982). Moreover, President (Prime Minister) Sotelo decided to not include any military officers in his cabinet, and his defence minister managed to appoint a few more civilians to the defence ministry than had his predecessors. The president also decided to appeal the sentences of the 23-F conspirators in the Supreme Court, symbolizing that the ultimate decisions on crimes of such national importance would be taken in a civilian court, not a military court (Agüero 1995: 176–7).

Still, the reforms were modest, hardline opposition remained, and the UCD and government were still in considerable difficulty. On 3 October 1982, news broke of another projected coup scheduled for 27 October, the day before general elections were to be held. Clearly, large sectors in the army continued to be hostile to the democratic transition, and this was partly fuelled by government's apparent inability to control ETA violence, which was increasingly targeting senior-level officers, including officers directly in the service of the king. Also of considerable concern was the fact that, with the UCD disintegrating, and the PSOE becoming increasingly popular, the latter was very likely to gain control of the government in the forthcoming election. Although the PSOE had become a far more moderate party (see Chapter 6), the prospect of a PSOE-led government still produced anxiety amongst business groups, the church, and the military (Agüero 1995: 168–9).

In the 27 October plan, both the King's and Prime Minister's palaces were to be taken over, along with the headquarters of the Joint Chiefs of Staff, several government ministries and other public buildings. The political elite was to be 'neutralized' in their homes, and the king was to be deposed for having betrayed his oath of loyalty to the *Movimiento*. In contrast to 23 February 1981, the central military intelligence authority acted swiftly once the plot was discovered. In addition, the plans for the physical elimination of the Chiefs of Staff produced outrage and isolated the *golpistas*. Still, only the three main instigators were arrested despite the discovery of documents implicating at least 200 more (Preston 1986: 224–5).

One point of importance to the transition process was that the military was not actually included in the core decision-making process at the time of the regime's demise, and it therefore had little influence over the agenda of the transition (Agüero 1995a: 11; Agüero 1995b: 140). On the other hand, it was potentially problematical for the transitional regime that officers had been allowed to have input into political affairs under Franco, and that officers had participated in the Franquist structures and political associations (Porras Nadales 1983).

Another point to consider is that the military was divided between the liberals, the conservatives, and the hardliners, plus the bulk who were indifferent. The conservatives shared the view of the hardliners that the Franquist regime should continue but did not see a forceful military intervention as a realistic option; this group was aware of limits imposed by law and held discipline and obedience in high esteem. In addition, the conservatives and hardliners did not appear to have any unifying leaders; alternative, charismatic leadership had, in fact, been suppressed by Franco. There were also differences amongst officers and soldiers in terms of their affiliations – some were Falangists, others were monarchists (but not necessarily behind Juan Carlos), and still others were liberals (Agüero 1995: 108–9).

During the transition to democracy, the government tried to gain control over the armed forces by substituting a single defence ministry for the previous three ministries created by Franco. In addition, the military was removed from other participatory positions during the dismantling of other Franquist institutions. Furthermore, the Constitution excluded the maintenance of public order from the functions of the armed forces and instead placed it with the Civil Guard. Participation in political organizations was banned for officers, and the internal rules of the military were redesigned. This did not, however, necessarily mean that the government's power increased over the armed forces, as indicated by the high degree of independence discussed above. In fact, while three branches were lost by the military, they were given a potentially more powerful institution, the newly created Joints Chiefs of Staff which provided an institutional means for communication and coordination across all the branches of the armed forces. Of most concern to hardliners was that the civilians did not encroach too much on military affairs and so this meant maintaining control over the defence ministry. During the transition, they were apparently successful in doing this. Also of importance is that the 'service ministries' were seen more as the provider of military support rather than as superior to the military. The relatively small, new defence ministry was thus up against an established, potentially cohesive group of officers who had just been given an even more powerful institutional connection to one another via the newly created Joint Chiefs (Agüero 1995: 147–51).

Also problematic was that the military chiefs believed that the Joint Chiefs was entitled to a direct, regular connection with the supreme commander, the King, without needing to approach the defence ministry (Agüero 1995: 151). The military was given special deference in the Constitution, with the definition of its mission being mentioned in the preamble – Manuel Fraga had argued in drafting this part of the constitution that 'The Armed Forces are not the same as the Treasury' (quoted in Agüero 1995: 152). This helped to legitimate the above interpretation of the connection between the king and the armed forces.

Agüero contends that the failed coup in February 1981 really marks the beginning of the end of military opposition to democracy in Spain, and allowed the democratization process to advance by disarming a significant threat that could have remained in place for many years to come. The failed coup made it clear to the military as a whole that there were no possibilities for the advancement of personal, professional, or institutional interests outside of the democratic regime (Agüero 1995b: 138) and created conditions that would allow the hard-line opposition to be dismantled (1995b: 161–2). It was to be under the new PSOE Minister of Defence, Narcis Serra, that the government 'would inaugurate a programme of military modernisation, redeployment, professionalization and de-politicization which would finally undermine the Third World *golpista* mentality of the armed forces' (Preston 1986: 226).

The Socialists had, in fact, already provided a clear indication in the documents for their 27th Congress in 1976 that they wanted to give the military and defence issues serious consideration. In these documents, they emphasized the need for coordination and integration of the armed forces, and the latter's withdrawal from areas of civil administration, as well as reforms in their territorial organization. The proposals in the documents also emphasized organizational reforms, with explicit mention of the need to gain parliamentary control over the military via the creation of a defence ministry which expresses government (and thus presumably parliamentary) thinking on topics related to defence. The party also criticized the backward conditions in which Franquism had left the armed forces and claimed to favour modernization and higher levels of spending on the military. At their 29th Congress in 1981, the Socialists proposed lowering the retirement age for top-level officers and changing the promotion criteria in order to improve the qualifications of officers. By this time, the ministry of defence had already been created, and now the Socialists called for a less inept handling of it than had been the case with the UCD.

Once the Socialists were in office, the Defence Minister, Narcis Serra, spent the next year studying the problems of his department and learning how command structures work in countries like the US, Germany, and other parts of Europe. The 1984 Organic Law on National Defence thus transformed the Joint Chiefs from a command organ into an advisory body for the president and defence minister. The National Defence Board, which had previously included the king, the government, and the Joint Chiefs sharing the formulation of military policy, was transformed into an advisory board for the king and the government. The chiefs of staff retained individual command of their respective services, but these were placed explicitly under the authority and 'direct dependence' of the minister of defence. The latter was to be given the responsibility of formulating and implementing military policy, strategic planning, military administration, and monitoring military preparedness. He could also assume the functions of the president of the government (prime minister) and direct defence policy on behalf of the president. In the legislation, the president (prime minister) was charged with determining grand strategic goals, the general distribution of forces, and the direction of war. Thus, the bill established a clear chain of command, with the president (prime minister) and defence ministers at the top. The king was included as chair of the National Defence Board, but the new legislation was unambiguous in moving the leading role of policy-making into the hands of the government. A new post was also created, the post of chief of defence staff; this person would be the 'principal collaborator' of the defence minister in formulating and implementing the operational aspects of military policy. In the case of war, he would be appointed as chief of operational command, operating under the authority of the president. The person was to be assigned a joint staff for defence as his own working group and would chair the Council of the Joint Chiefs if the Defence Minister was absent. Agüero (1995) contends that the creation of this role was crucial in the modernization of the Spanish military. Most importantly was that the person in the post could, according to reforms of 1984, be placed by the government in the position of general chief of the operation command of the armed forces. In this instance, each of the services' chiefs of staff would become his advisors. The person would hold the senior most ranking in the military but would be appointed by the government. Given that the individual would need to command the logistics of war for the entire military, it was important that he be ready to do so. The first person to take up this post, Admiral Angel Liberal Lucini, created working groups to help design strategic planning, logistical coordination, coordination of maneuvers, etc. (Agüero 1995: 198–200).

Because of the previous difficulty of the chiefs of different military bodies coming to agreements on policy-making and the subsequent ineffectiveness at coordination, the chiefs of the various branches were not, in fact, opposed to the increased coordination. They were, however, surprised by the element of control introduced over sensitive areas such as personnel policy and the supervision of military education, which they regarded as being internal to the military.

Three weeks after the Organic Law was passed, a Royal Decree was issued which further regulated the internal structure and functions related to the defence ministry. The decree created the secretary of state for defence who would manage and coordinate the financial resources, as well as determine policy on armament, materials, and infrastructure. The agency was also to take over the agencies that each armed service had for these functions, which were scattered across the various branches of the armed forces. The subsecretary for defence was to direct policy related to personnel – reductions, promotions criteria, career structures and paths. Each armed service was also to be incorporated into the structure of the ministry. Eventually, in 1985, the ministry also finally took possession of its own building. While there were problems in implementation of the reforms and clear evidence of bureaucratic resistance, ultimately, the power of the purse, controlled by the secretary of state for defence, meant that the military chiefs had little choice but to adopt the reforms. Also, despite persistent bureaucratic resistance in part of the forces, the government continued to issue decrees making the structure more hierarchical. In addition, the number of civilians in top-ranking positions increased considerably.

In terms of promotions, importantly, a ministerial order of March 1986 required that when the post of general became vacant, the supreme councils of the army, navy and air force must submit the entire list of those qualified, and the defence minister could select anyone from it, whereas previously the council had only submitted three names from which the minister would select one. The minister also gained the power to appoint officers in the grade of colonel or navy captain to posts of divisional chiefs of staff, regiment or ship commanders, and as directors of the military schools. Also granted was the right to select professors for military schools; this was one way that the government hoped to try to modernize the training given to trainees, but was another major point of contention for the officers. Various other measures were adopted through which civilians attempted to wrest control over the military, including the decision in November 1986 to finally grant the former members of the *Unión Militar Democrática* the right of reincorporation into the army (Agüero 1995: 185–98). In addition, the 1989 Law on Military Personnel represented a further step toward civilian control by changing military career structures, salary scales, and the length of time that an individual could serve in the military, and in 1993, plans were agreed on the abolition of military governorships (Heywood 1995: 64).

As mentioned above, also important in terms of reorganization of the armed forces was the removal of the 'forces of public order' from the military defence structure. This began with the 1978 Constitution, which separated the forces to be used for domestic security from the armed forces (Article 8). The 1986 Organic Law of Security Corps and Forces went further in promoting the demilitarization of domestic security forces, and by 1987 all of these were led by civilians.

In addition, the military judicial system was reformed and integrated into a single national judicial system. The Supreme Council of Military Justice was disposed of and replaced with a unit dealing with military affairs housed within the Supreme Court structure. Further reforms removed the jurisdiction of military courts over civilians and also expanded civilian court jurisdiction over military personnel (Agüero 1995: 202–3).

Most scholars on the topic of the Spanish military mention the importance of Spain joining NATO in reforming the Spanish armed forces. Particularly hard-hit by this was the army: the new definitions of threat identified the Canary Islands, the Strait of Gibraltar, and the Balearic Islands to be of key strategic importance, and the requirements for defending these areas tended to lie more in the areas of naval and air forces and high-tech air defence weapons. Thus, entry into NATO further undermined the strength of the Spanish army by reducing its budget and thus ultimately the size of its personnel (Heywood 1995: 63). To achieve the reduction in personnel, a 1984 law set targets for the reduction of the number of generals, majors, colonels, and lieutenant colonels, as well as the rest of the officer corps. Targets were set for general troop level reductions (Agüero 1995: 203–8; Heywood 1995: 63).

Also of importance is that the defence minister imposed a policy prohibiting top military officers from stating openly critical views on controversial political or defence issues (including complaints about the changes in promotions policy); this was backed by the removal of those who violated the policy. For instance in September 1983, Lieutenant General Fernando Soteras was removed from his post of Captain General in Valladolid for making statements about the 1981 coup and other statements to the press.

In July 1984, the director of the naval war school was removed from his post for circulating a memo that was critical of the promotions policy. Other officers were removed from posts during 1984–7 for criticizing the US policy in the Mediterranean, for praising Franco, for criticizing politicians, judges, and journalists, for making controversial statements on regional independence and federalism, and so on (Agüero 1995: 212).

Obviously measures taken by the government to appoint constitutionalists to top posts are likely to have had a powerful effect on ending interventionism on the part of the Spanish military. At the same time, the government's unwillingness to take harsh action against conspirators during the early years of the transition indicated some concern about the reaction this would provoke, and it seems that it was more likely to have been widespread agreement amongst elites – including the monarch – along with widespread popular support for the civilian government, that played the crucial role in halting *golpismo* in Spain. Namely, the coherent reaction of elites and the mass public to the 1981 coup attempt appeared to pave the way for the establishment of institutional mechanisms of control that could be used by future governments to prevent military interventionism (on the importance of elite consensus in the maintenance of stable democratic regimes, see Higley and Burton 2006).

Turkey: from *golpismo* to institutionalized interference

Military interventionism in politics in Turkey can be traced as far back as the sixteenth and seventeenth centuries. One of the crucial components of the Ottoman military was a standing army known as the Janissaries. This institution was established in the fourteenth century when it was decided that children would be selected from amongst the conquered nations to serve in the Ottoman army. These children would be taken away for education and training at a very early age, and when they began service in the military would receive regular salaries. The basic idea was that rather than relying on local tribal leaders whose loyalty could not be trusted for military support, the monarch (sultan) would create a force whose loyalty would be exclusively to the monarch. Thus, the children chosen for this task were treated extremely well by the regime. The problem was that these individuals were eventually allowed to integrate into Turkish-Muslim society and their loyalties changed as a result. Thus, the Janissaries were able to establish something resembling an unstable corporate military dictatorship during the late sixteenth and seventeenth centuries. For instance, during 1618–1730, six sultans were overthrown by the Janissaries and in two of these cases, the sultan was murdered. In addition to overt cases of deposition, Janissaries also began to play an important role in determining which particular heir would succeed to the throne (Hale 1994: 8–9; see also Lybyer 1913; Gibb and Bowen 1950; Itzkowitz 1972; Cook 1976; Shaw and Shaw 1977; Ahmad 1993; Zürcher 2004).

In the late 1700s, the Ottoman state began to attempt to reform and modernize the military, which was becoming technologically obsolete. The government also began to try to trim down the size of the Janissary corps, but the latter – assisted by clerical leaders – managed to resist and waged multiple revolts. Finally, by the early 1800s, the government had won over the clerical leaders and crushed the Janissaries in an attack on their barracks. The corps was then abolished by decree and the new military system was modeled on the French system (Hale 1994: 13–18; Shaw and Shaw 1977).[5]

In the late 1800s new military schools were created to teach modern military techniques. However, these also had the effect of creating a group of officers and soldiers who saw themselves as being the vanguard of enlightenment. The result was the overthrow of Sultan Abdülaziz and the introduction of the Ottoman Empire's first constitution in 1876. Despite the fact that the constitution was abrogated shortly after its creation, this coup is argued to be particularly important in providing a source of inspiration and historical legitimacy for officers in later years (see Hale 1990: 55; Hale 1994: 26).

The next major insurrection began as a result of professional demoralization in the army. While the Empire was attempting to modernize and improve the military technologically, the monarch reigning during the 1876–1909 period (Abdulhamid II) simultaneously engaged in policies to debilitate the army because he feared the possibility of conspiracies forming amongst military officials. For instance, troops were never allowed to fire live ammunition and shells were kept in storage in Istanbul rather than distributed across the territory. New rifles purchased from Germany remained packed in their boxes for several years, and soldiers' uniforms were in tatters; pay was generally months overdue (Hale 1994: 29). Plots for a coup d'état were clearly beginning to form in 1896. However, there were serious disagreements amongst the plotters as to what the nature of the new regime ought to be. Some favoured a strong central government (and became known as Unionists) while others thought that given the wide range of nationalities living within the Empire at the time (this was prior to the World War I massacres and post-war population exchanges), a decentralized system ought to be adopted (this group came to be known as Liberals). It must be noted that there were also conservatives who opposed these plots as well as independents within the armed forces. However, within the upper ranks of the army, the officers supporting revolution appear to have been in the majority. They managed to force the sultan to capitulate and promise to reconvene parliament.

The Unionists – those favouring a strong centralized government – won all but one seat in the Chamber of Deputies elections held in 1908 and voted the next year to depose the sultan and appoint his brother to replace him. In addition, the powers of the sultan were drastically reduced in 1911: the first minister (the Grand Vizier) and cabinet were made responsible to the parliament rather than the monarch. The sultan could be deposed by the parliament, and royal prerogatives in most government functions were removed. Civil liberties were more clearly defined, but this was nullified almost immediately by laws providing for the suppression of strikes, meetings, and associations, as well as the press.

It was not until the 1913–14 period that leaders of the insurrection (the Committee of Union and Progress) finally managed to get themselves appointed to top-level cabinet posts in the government. During 1914–1918, the Ottoman government became a mix between a personal dictatorship of CUP member Enver Pasha, a single-party state under the Union and Progress Party, and a military regime. It appears that government was being run from the General Headquarters of the Union and Progress Party which was functioning as a self-appointed politburo. Throughout the period, the regime was under continuous threat by attempted counter-coups and there were proposed side deals between potential regime successors and foreign powers. The Empire ended up on the losing side of World War I and the Unionist regime collapsed in 1918. The Committee of Union and Progress leaders fled to Germany and the committee closed down. As argued by Hale:

> Political involvement had fatally weakened the army and almost ended national independence. The need to avoid a repetition of this process, but equally to reconcile it with the army's continued perception of itself as the bedrock of the state, was to prove one of the dominating themes of Turkish politics for the rest of the century.
>
> (Hale 1994: 55; see also Shaw and Shaw 1977; Zürcher 1984)[6]

Thus, because of this history of military involvement in politics, after the founding of the Turkish Republic, Ataturk took measures to try to exclude the army from open involvement in the political process. For instance, officers who were elected to the parliament had to resign from their military posts before their election as deputies could be validated. In addition, the Military Penal Code restricted soldiers from joining any political organization, participating in demonstrations, or writing or speaking in public on political topics. Later governments also disenfranchised all soldiers (Hale 1990: 56; Hale 1994: 72). Finally, potential rivals to Ataturk were moved to various army corps outposts or their positions were simply eliminated. These changes 'served to restore the government's control over the army and to distance Ataturk's most important rivals from the centre of the political stage' (quoted in Hale 1994: 71). Ataturk later used suspected plots – sometimes contrived, sometimes genuine – to destroy any further potential sources of coups; in several cases, the plotters were executed (Hale 1994: 73–6). Thus, it is argued that Ataturk made considerable progress in reducing the military's inclination toward political involvement. As Hale contends 'Under the Young Turks, constant army interventions had reduced the empire to ruin; under the new republic, Turkey achieved a degree of political stability which it had not known for decades' (Hale 1994: 76).

Hale also contends that these attempts at removing the army from politics were never complete, however. Particularly problematical was Article 35 of the Turkish Armed Services Internal Service Code (adopted in 1935) which stated that 'the duty of the armed forces is to protect and safeguard Turkish territory and the Turkish Republic as stipulated by the Constitution' (cited in Hale 1990: 56). Moreover, Ataturk himself encouraged officers to think of themselves as the standard bearers of Ataturkism and as the ultimate guardians of its principles (Rustow 1959; Harris 1965a, 1965b; Dodd 1976).

In addition, Ataturk's long-serving Chief of the General Staff, Fevzi Çakmak, had been given considerable free reign over military decisions during Ataturk's presidency. Ataturk's successor, İnönü, did attempt to reduce the power of the Chief of the General Staff after Çakmak was retired in 1944. Specifically, the government attempted to adopt a policy whereby the Chief of the General Staff would be responsible to the Minister of Defence rather than directly to the president. That is, İnönü and his advisers were attempting to gain further institutional control over the army. Top-level generals opposed this change and forced a compromise whereby the Chief of the General Staff was placed under the direction of the prime minister with instructions to deal directly with other ministries as necessary. In practice, the Chief of the General Staff was to continue to operate with a considerable amount of independence in determining defence policy for many years to come (Hale 1994: 83).

Eventually, the government did manage to pass legislation in 1949 whereby the Chief of the General Staff was made responsible to the Ministry of Defence, making the system more compatible with western democratic practices. The Ministry of Defence was given the responsibility of carrying out army business connected to personnel, intelligence gathering, manoeuvres, education, etc. However, the control over the Chief of the General Staff and defence making policy was to continue to be extremely contentious in years to come (Hale 1994: 93–4).

When the Democratic Party came to power in 1950, it made further attempts to gain control over the military by removing all top-level commanders, several generals, as well as the Chief of the General Staff (Hale 1994: 93). Prior to this, it is clear that during the transition to multi-party politics, there were multiple plots and counter-plots. For instance, one group of officers was determined to see that the transition to multi-party politics occurred and that elections were not rigged in 1950 as they had been in 1946. These officers agreed amongst themselves that if the elections were indeed unfair, they would force the regime to hold new elections. They even contacted one of the leaders of the Democratic Party, Celal Bayar, to assure him that the army would oppose any rigging of elections. On the other hand, other groups of officers were less than thrilled about the prospect of multi-party politics and after the 1950 elections, four senior-level officers went to the leader of the Republican People's Party, İnönü, to suggest that they launch a coup to annul the results, a plan which İnönü rejected (Hale 1994: 92).

The 1960 coup actually began with a small group of young middle-ranking officers (colonels) meeting in Ankara and Istanbul to discuss their dissatisfaction with the lack of modernization in the approach taken to military planning and strategy by senior officers. As in the late 1800s, these younger officers were receiving training in the use of modern military techniques and equipment, particularly as a result of the influx of resources from NATO, and they perceived the senior officers as still using backward approaches to military strategy (Hale 1994: 96–7). The discussions eventually turned to politics, particularly what appeared to be the total breakdown of parliamentary democracy, as the ruling Democratic Party began to seize the opposition party's property, close down its newspapers, and plant its own supporters at public events given by the opposition in order to harass and bully the opposition leader (Hale 1994: 95); at one point, it even began to look like the government or some of its supporters were planning to murder the leader of the opposition and to re-establish a single-party regime (Hale 1994: 104).

Thus, plans for a coup had already begun in 1957 amongst these junior officers. They realized that they would need senior officers in order to carry out the coup, and recruited the commander of the land forces, General Cemal Gürsel, a little over year before the coup was carried out. Other generals were recruited only four weeks prior to the coup, which was carried out on 27 May 1960 (Hale 1990: 58).

Importantly, groups of officers approached the leader of the opposition, İnönü, as well as individuals within the government who were perceived to be opposed to the ruling party's leadership to discuss a military takeover. They were rebuffed by both of these, but importantly, no one made any attempt to remove these officers from their posts, arrest them for plotting to overthrow the regime, etc. (Hale 1994: 101). The plot was eventually uncovered because of other unrelated events, and the government arrested several of the officers. However, there were many others involved in the plot and they simply regrouped (Hale 1994: 102).

Thus, the coup was instigated by radical revolutionary officers (see Shaw and Shaw 1977). Several of these believed that the army should create a long-term military government and also create a new political party to fill the gap that would be left by the party that was to be overthrown, the Democratic Party (Hale 1990: 59–60). They also believed that the military regime ought to carry out economic and social reforms to promote development and particularly to eradicate the growing inequality in the country. The senior commanders disagreed with this approach and wanted to return the country to civilian rule very quickly after the coup; this was the approach taken, and the radical members of the organizing group (the National Unity Committee) were expelled from the group (Hale 1990: 59–60).

The final breaking point came in the spring of 1960 when a parliamentary session broke out into fistfights, with one Democratic Party MP going so far as to threaten the opposition with a pistol in parliament. The fight was the result of a proposed motion to establish a Committee to Investigate the Activities of the Republican People's Party and a Section of the Press. The motion passed, and nine days later, further legislation gave the committee the powers of search and arrest. It appeared that the government was trying to close down the opposition party and hold elections in which it would be the only contender. In addition, fighting had spread to the streets, with violent demonstrations becoming the norm in Ankara and Istanbul (Hale 1994: 106–7; see also Ahmad 1977; Karpat 1959; Lerner and Robinson 1960; Robinson 1963; Weiker 1963; Dodd 1976).

The coup began on 27 May 1960 and considerable evidence indicates that at the time the coup was carried out, there was little in the way of a plan regarding how the military regime would function nor how long it would remain in place. Once the senior commanders had made the decision that the regime would be short-lived, they set about creating a Constituent Assembly that proceeded to write a new constitution and overhaul the electoral system, as discussed in Chapters 5 and 6 (see Hale 1994: 121–2).

In what is now seen as the worst decision made by the military junta, the overthrown Prime Minister, Adnan Menderes, and two of his cabinet ministers were executed. In fact, the National Unity Committee (NUC) had the power to commute these sentences and did indeed commute the sentences of other party officials. However, it appears that senior officers within the NUC were worried that if all of the death sentences were commuted, the radical junior officers would rebel, and this created the potential for civil war within the armed forces. The problem, however, was that the executed prime minister became a martyr and the treatment of all Democratic Party members became the primary issue of government attention after this (Hale 1994: 128, 143–5).

At the time of the 1961 general elections there were still several army colonels who were dissatisfied with the results of the coup. Apparently not all of these individuals had not been purged from the armed forces[7] and indeed had formed a secret organization, the Armed Forces Union (Hale 1994: 139–42). As discussed in Chapter 7, the 1961 elections themselves produced a parliament from which most coalition formulae would have been problematical. The left-leaning Republican People's Party won 173 seats while the successor to the Democratic Party, the Justice Party, won 158 seats, out of a total of 450 seats. No other party that could have served as an ideologically reasonable coalition partner to the Republican People's Party won any seats, whereas a small centre-right party, the New Turkey Party, did manage to win 65 seats; however, even combined with the Justice Party's 158 seats, this would not have been enough to form a centre-right coalition. Moreover, it seemed rather unthinkable that the successor to the party that had only just been overthrown in the military coup would then form a government yet again immediately after the coup.

Basically, the election results – which had been produced using the new system of proportional representation – produced a hung parliament, and the Armed Forces Union came to the conclusion that the elections had not 'completely realised the National Will' (quoted in Hale 1990: 65) and that an intervention would be necessary. There was disagreement as to whether this ought to occur immediately or whether the army should wait until the civilian government had demonstrated its incompetence. The former of these positions won the day, and initially officers signed a protocol demanding that the assembly be dissolved, that all party activities would be ended, and that government would be handed over to 'the authentic and qualified representatives of the nation' (quoted in Hale 1990: 65). However, another, less radical protocol was eventually adopted. This one demanded that the General who had been invited to lead the 1960 coup, General Cemal Gürsel, be elected president of the Republic by the assembly and that the leader of the Republican People's Party, Ismet İnönü, should be appointed prime minister. In compliance with this protocol, Gürsel was elected president and İnönü formed a 'shotgun coalition' with the Justice Party (Hale 1990: 65; Hale 1994: 145–7).

In yet another instance of coup plotting, in February 1962, a group of officers met in Istanbul and signed another protocol threatening a second coup to enact the reforms 'which the 27 revolution failed to realize' (quoted in Hale 1990: 66). The group agreed that they would only carry out the plan if senior commanders agreed. The latter refused, however, and began removing these individuals from crucial positions in the armed forces, although apparently still not purging them completely from the armed forces.

Several of these officers feared that they would be arrested and began a coup on the afternoon of 22 February 1962. There was a brief stand-off between this group, their supporters, and the rest of the military, and this was eventually resolved when the prime minister, Ismet İnönü, sent a message to the officers stating that they would not be court-martialled if they dropped their action immediately. The group surrendered on the morning of 23 February 1962. In an extremely bizarre turn of events, one of these colonels, Talat Aydemir, who had been dismissed from the army but still maintained support and connections with War College cadets in Ankara, attempted a second coup in May 1963. He had even less support during this attempt, and the coup collapsed. Aydemir and his chief supporting officer were both executed. These executions appeared to send a message that potential coup-makers faced very serious potential consequences if they attempted a coup on their own without the support of either the high command or the government. At the same time, however, many of the coup supporters then were allowed to enter politics as private citizens. For instance, one of those who had supported the notion of a long-term military junta, Alparslan Türkeş, took over the leadership of the Republican Peasant's Nation Party (which was eventually renamed 'Nationalist Action

Party' in 1969) in July 1965 and regenerated it using ultra-nationalist right-wing radicalism; six of the other plotters also entered parliament in the 1960s under different party names (Hale 1990: 66–8; Hale 1994: 156–69).

Although the 1961 constitution appeared to be far more democratic than the one in place prior to this (the 1924 constitution), it created a new institution that fundamentally and institutionally undermined the authority of elected governments. That institution was the National Security Council. According to Article 111 of the 1961 Constitution, the National Security Council would consist of the president of the republic or the prime minister, along with other ministers as provided by law, plus the Chief of the General Staff, and the commanders of the army, air force, navy, and gendarmerie. Constitutionally, the council was to 'assist the Council of Ministers in reaching decisions related to national security and coordination'. However, in practice it tended to function as a second cabinet and became the means by which the military could exert influence in politics without resulting to overt interventions (Hale 1990: 68–9; Shaw and Shaw 1977).

The 1965 and 1969 elections produced an outright majority in parliament for the Justice Party, and the leader of the party took a fairly conciliatory approach to the military at the time. However, the right began to splinter after the 1969 election – several members of the Justice Party left the party to join the smaller right-wing parties and others broke away to form entirely new parties. Thus, as discussed in previous chapters, it appears that the proportional electoral system might have created incentives that produced a major splintering of the party system.

At the same time, public order was breaking down, as outlined in Chapter 6. Leftist urban guerrilla groups had formed and in response, the extreme right set up squads of armed commandos. In addition, there were still many young officers who felt that the government had failed to carry out the social reforms that had been demanded in the 1960 coup. Thus, in March of 1971, the Chief of the General Staff, and the commanders of the army, air force, and navy, issued a memorandum which forced the prime minister (Demirel) to resign. He was then succeeded by a 'supra-party' government led by a member of the Republican People's Party who was seen as being one of the least political members of any of the parties. Senior officers appeared to have acted out of fear of revolt by their subordinates or because of dangerous divisions within the senior command itself (Hale 1990: 70).

Once again, there is clear evidence that many of those supporting the intervention actually wanted the military to take over policy-making by coup. This was again overruled by senior officers but the memorandum did threaten direct intervention if the government failed to 'neutralise the current anarchical situation and ... implement the reformist laws envisaged by the constitution' (quoted in Hale 1990: 72; Hale 1994: 184–93).

Also apparently as a result of the intervention by memorandum, a series of constitutional amendments was passed limiting the independence of the universities (where a great deal of the political violence had occurred), as well as that of the press and radio, and also limiting civil liberties in general (Hale 1990: 72). Moreover, there were more than 2000 arrests, including some distinguished university professors (Hale 1994: 197–8).

Shortly after this, it appears that the elected civilians began to try to re-establish their supremacy over the military in what became a fairly tense showdown. After the government had been forced to elect General Gürsel president in 1961, the military again forced the hand of the government at the end of Gürsel's term and pushed for another military official, General Cevdet Sunay, to be elected in 1966. Towards the end of Sunay's term, the showdown between the civilians and the military began. The latter was once again pressing for the Chief of General Staff at the time to be elected. Before the election of the president was held, the top military commanders held meetings with all of the party leaders to put pressure on them regarding the election and regarding restoration of law and order and other unspecified reforms. Importantly, the leader of the Justice Party, Demirel, refused to attend these meetings. In addition, the sitting president – himself a former Chief of the General Staff – stated publicly that he expected the current Chief of General Staff to be elected and that he would be extremely displeased if this did not happen (Hale 1994: 205). Thus, the military and supporters were making overtly threatening statements to the civilian leadership. In what would now be seen as a rare turn of events, the leaders of the two largest parties in parliament, Demirel (leader of the Justice Party) and Ecevit (leader of the Republican People's Party), both opposed the idea of setting the precedent that a Chief of General Staff would automatically succeed to the presidency and absolutely refused to comply with the military leadership's demands. Eventually the Grand National Assembly selected a neutral candidate, an ex-admiral who had left the navy in 1960 to join the Senate (Hale 1990: 73–4; Hale 1994: 204–7; see also Nye 1977).

Hale contends that as a result of these events, 'the days of the 12 March memorandum were numbered' (1994: 208); that is, the 1971 intervention by memorandum came to be seen as one of abject failure. By the spring of 1973, none of the commanders who had written the memo remained in their posts and those who followed had little interest in upholding it (Hale 1994: 208–9). The ultimate effect of this failed coup by memorandum was that it made military officials reluctant to take similar measures – only an outright military takeover or remaining on the sidelines were the remaining options. In addition, it is argued that 'the retreat of the generals in the presidential election created a fatal disjunction between the real power of the military establishment and the illusion that it could be confronted with impunity by civilian politicians' (Harris 1988: 191).

The next few years of Turkish politics continued to experience similar, more intensified difficulties. Coalition formation became even more difficult, and there were long periods of caretaker governments. Even when a seemingly solid centre-right coalition managed to form in the mid-1970s, it barely managed to survive and was simply unable to adopt policies to address the two key issues of the day, which were a growing economic crisis and a drastic decline in law and order (Hale 1994: 216–22).

Both sides in the political dispute apparently received equipment and other support from foreign governments and militant groups. Kidnappings, murders, and armed robberies increased, with an average of eight people dying every day in political violence in the 1979–80 period (Hale 1994: 224). In the face of what many perceived as movement toward civil war, the main political parties appeared helpless. Indeed, it is argued that they had contributed to the whole situation by appointing police officers with openly political leanings – leftist police were arresting the leaders of right-wing violence but not those from leftist groups and vice versa. Moreover, left-leaning police officers would simply release leftists who had been arrested by the right-leaning police, and the latter would release extreme right guerrillas as well (Hale 1994: 227–8).

With regard to the economy, the OPEC oil crisis appears to have hit Turkey extremely hard. Deficits and inflation increased as governments refused to limit expenditures in the face of upcoming general elections. By 1980, there was a chronic shortage of fuel, daily power cuts, shortages of cooking oil, light bulbs, and medicines (Hale 1994: 223–4). Ultimately as the country descended into anarchy, with politicians squabbling amongst themselves regarding who was to blame, the next military coup on 12 September 1980 was greeted with general relief (Hale 1994: 231–2).

The 1980 takeover was quite different from the 1960 and 1971 interventions. This time, the planning of the coup was concentrated amongst the top level military leadership and this group maintained full control over subordinates. That is, there is no evidence to indicate that middle-ranking officers were involved in the planning nor that there were disagreements regarding how the coup would be conducted and what type of regime would be established afterward. In addition, the Chief of the General Staff, Kenan Evren, waited until there appeared to be no other alternative but intervention so that the legitimacy of the coup would be unquestioned. Rather perplexingly Evren and his colleagues did send a warning letter to the president of the republic in December 1979 suggesting that the Justice Party and Republican People's Party form a grand coalition and that they adopt new legislation and administrative measures to strengthen the powers of martial law commanders, who had been given the responsibility for law and order. The letter was even broadcast to the nation in January 1980. Oddly, in his discussions with the leader of the Justice Party (Demirel), the president of the Turkish Republic gave the impression that there was no real danger of a coup, presumably because the president himself was advising the military against it. Thus, Justice Party leader Demirel refused to go into a grand coalition and began to push instead for early elections (Hale 1994: 234–5). With somewhat unfortunate timing, the president's regular term came to an end in April 1980, and this time, the two main party leaders, Ecevit and Demirel, were unable to agree on a compromise candidate. There were 115 rounds of voting over five months but still no candidate could receive an absolute majority in both chambers of the parliament. Ecevit pressed Demirel to form a grand coalition but the latter refused and was still pushing for early general elections. Ecevit, however, refused to go along with early elections while the country was in chaos. As Hale argues, 'The last chance for a reconciliation between the two leaders had thus slipped away' (1994: 236; see also, Dodd 1983; Harris 1985; Briand 1987).

In addition to the military takeover being planned amongst top generals who were generally in agreement about the aims of the coup, a key difference between this takeover and previous interventions was that there was also a clear plan regarding how the regime would function after the takeover and what would transpire with regard to handing power back to elected civilians. A transitional government was established with an ex-admiral as prime minister and non-party technocrats as cabinet ministers. The only person in the cabinet who had been affiliated with a political party was Turgut Özal, who was seen as a fairly technocratic member of the previous Justice Party coalition. Özal was kept on to continue with the economic reforms thought necessary to stabilize the economy.

Rather than turning the party leaders into martyrs as had been the case in 1961, party leaders this time were shipped off to an army holiday resort, and all political activities were banned. Charges were eventually brought against two party leaders – neo-fascist Turkeş and religious party leader Erbakan – but one of these individuals was eventually released from prison on medical grounds and the other was acquitted on appeal.

As in 1960, after the 1980 coup, a Constituent Assembly was established and a constitution written, as described in Chapter 5. The Constitution passed in a referendum in 1982 and parliamentary elections were to be held in 1983. Despite having banned previous party leaders and members from political activity under Provisional Article 4 of the Constitution, the military had considerable difficulty keeping a lid on party formation. Friends and supporters of banned political parties attempted to re-establish those parties under different names. However, the military had reserved the right to veto proposed party leadership lists. Moreover, if a party did not have a certain minimum number of leaders, it would not be allowed to take part in the 1983 elections. Thus, it was by repeatedly rejecting most of the individuals on party lists that the military managed to keep the old parties from reforming themselves. In addition, all criticism of the National Security Council's decisions was banned during the election.

Still, by 1987, the prime minister – Özal – realized that it would be impossible to keep leaders like Demirel from finding a way to reform their old parties and so he tabled a package of constitutional amendments which included the withdrawal of Provisional Article 4 of the Constitution. The amendments were then put to a referendum, and passed with a bare majority of popular support (50.2 per cent to 49.8 per cent) (see Hale 1994: 232–90 on the 1980 coup and its aftermath).

Thus, despite an overt, well-planned takeover and revision of the Turkish constitution, the military was still unable to maintain absolute control over the situation or of ordinary politicians. In addition, constitutional provisions restricting activities of trade unions began to be challenged, as did provisions regarding the use of Kurdish (or rather, the use of a language not recognized as the official language of another country). Hale argues that 'Turkey moved away not only from the possibility of an outright military takeover of the state but also from the involvement of the army in the day-to-day running of the country within a formally civilian regime. There was a gradual shift towards a new balance, in which the generals would become the servants of an elected government, as in Western democracies' (1994: 290).

On the other hand, the 1982 constitution retained the institution whereby the military would have direct input into government policymaking, the National Security Council. In addition, now the government was obliged 'to give priority consideration' to its decisions in matters that the NSC 'deems necessary for the preservation of the existence and independence of the state' (Hale 1994: 258). Note that the composition of the NSC remained as it had been under the 1961 constitution; that is, it was a fairly military-heavy institution. Importantly, it was believed that this was the institution through which the military continued to pressure governments regarding a wide range of issues such as coalition formation, internal security, as well as economic policy-making.

In addition to the formal constitutional role granted to the military via the NSC, legislation that had been passed in 1970 further contributed to the independence of the military from civilian control. Namely, the Chief of the General Staff was given autonomy in determining defence policy, the military budget which was not subject to parliamentary debate, and future weapons systems, production and procurement of arms, intelligence gathering, internal security, and all internal promotions would exclusively be in the hands of the military. In 1970, the Minister of Defence claimed that he was the only civilian in the entire ministry. Moreover, the Chief of the General Staff has generally influenced the decision as to who would be his successor (Cizre 1997). These policies continued after the 1980 coup and military activism in politics has continued. One of the most prominent examples of this was the forced collapse of a Welfare Party–True Path Party coalition in 1997, a coalition which saw a religiously oriented party leader selected as prime minister for the first time since the founding of the republic. Another was the threat of a coup posted on the Chief of the General Staff's website in 2007 in reaction to the Turkish parliament's choice of President of the Republic.

Since Turkey was granted candidacy status for the EU in 1999, changes have been made which are designed to comply with European Union requirements that aim to ultimately remove the military from politics. For instance, the composition of the NSC was altered such that civilians are in the majority; the current composition (set by law) includes seven civilian members and five military members. In addition, the reforms made it possible to appoint a civilian as Secretary General of the NSC, and this occurred for the first time in August 2004; the size of the staff of the Secretary General was also reduced somewhat. This reform on its own was seen as relatively minimal, but the roles and functions of the body have also been altered. It no longer has the authority to monitor other bodies or to follow up on the implementation of NSC 'recommendations', and it no longer has unlimited access to all civilian institutions. In addition, according to amendments to the Law on Public Financial Mangement and Control of December 2003, which came into force in January 2005, there will be greater transparency regarding military and defence expenditures. Extra-budgetary funds were scheduled to be dissolved by the end of 2007. More-over, the Court of Auditors has been authorized to audit defence expenditures on behalf of parliament. The amendment to Article 160 of the Constitution means that state property owned by the Turkish armed forces will also be subject to audits. The auditing process still requires enabling legislation, however. Other significant reforms have been the removal of the ability of military courts to try civilians, unless crimes have been committed by military personnel and civilians acting together (Commission of the European Communities 2006: 7–8).

Despite these changes, civilians appear to be fairly far away from gaining control over the Turkish military's political role. Article 2a of the National Security Council Law still includes a broad definition of national security: 'National Security means the protection of the constitutional order of the State, its nation and integrity, all of its interests in the international sphere including political, social, cultural and economic interests, as well as the protection of its constitutional law against all internal and external threats.' Thus, the military still has the legal right to interpret its role to include a wide range of domestic political problems. This is in contrast to the Spanish military, for instance, whose remit has changed and become the provision of security against external threats as defined by civilian leaders. In addition, parliament still has only very limited monitoring ability. The Parliamentary Planning and Budget Committee only reviews the military budget in a very general manner but does not examine programmes and projects, and extra-budgetary funds, from which most procurement projects are funded, are completely excluded from parliamentary scrutiny. Additionally, evidence still exists to indicate that military operations are being conducted for internal security matters without request from the civilian authorities (Commission of the European Communities 2006).

Also, in contrast to the Spanish case, as well as most other members of the EU and NATO, the Chief of the General staff is still accountable not to the Defence Minister but to the Prime Minister; this implies privileged access to the head of government on the part of the top military leader. Given the history of coalition government (and problems therein), some contend that the alternative arrangement of making the military directly accountable to the defence ministry could become extremely problematical. Equally important, though, is that the Defence Minister's department does not incorporate the General Staff in the same way that modern Spain's does, nor does it control the armed forces; instead, its function is to support the armed forces, as was the case in Spain prior to the reforms made by the Socialist government in the 1980s. Thus, currently the Chief of the General Staff and the Ministry of National Defence coordinate between themselves, but they are not directly linked in institutional terms. Moreover, decision making on security issues occurs mainly in the office of the General Staff. The head of this body is the Chief of the General Staff, and the person in this role (always a military general) has command of the armed forces. The commanders of the land, naval, and air forces report directly to him. In addition, he commands the Gendarmerie and the Coast Guard. With regard to the latter two forces, during peacetime they are affiliated with the Ministry of the Interior Affairs, but in wartime, they come under the control of the Land Forces Command and the Naval Forces Command, respectively.

Again, responsibility for the policies, plans and programmes of the armed forces, including roles and missions, size, shape, equipment and deployment, rests with the General Staff, as does the responsibility for initiating policy-making. Political direction comes directly from the Prime Minister. The staff of the General Staff is dominated by military personnel and civilians only provide social service and technical support. The Ministry of Defence essentially manages the military estate, handling the procurement of weapons, equipment, etc., and recruitment and other personnel-related work.

In terms of the organization of the Ministry of Defence, the two most senior posts below the minister are the Undersecretariat of the Ministry for National Defence and the Undersecretariat for the Defence Industry. The former is headed by a general, and the latter by a civilian. At the same time, it appears that the limited role played by civilians in defence policymaking is not due to the numbers of civilians in the Defence Ministry – more than half of those working in the ministry are civilians – but due to the status that the non-military staff occupy and the very limited scope that exists for the contribution of civilian expertise and perspectives (CESS/IPC 2005).

Perhaps most important is that the armed forces continue to openly exercise political influence, often making pronouncements on issues of the day. These have included issues such as Cyprus, terrorism, secularism, and EU–Turkey relations. As mentioned above, most recently the Chief of the General Staff stated its intention to 'openly display its position and attitudes when it becomes necessary' (on the Chief of the General Staff's website) after the Turkish parliament elected a head of state from within the ruling Islamic-leaning party (see, for instance, 'Military steps in presidential election debate', *Today's Zaman* 04/05/2007, consulted 4 May 2007). Subsequently, the issue was taken to the Constitutional Court, which ruled that the vote in parliament was invalid because the necessary two-thirds majority of the entire parliament was not reached on the first vote. Constitutionally, the ruling party could have simply held further rounds of voting, and in the third round, only a majority of parliamentary support would have been necessary to elect a candidate the government's choosing. Given the military's openly stated position on the selection of the president, however, the ruling party decided to hold early parliamentary elections.

Ultimately, the historical legacies which have had an impact on the self-defined role of the Turkish military included the Ottoman legacy, the legacy of the independence war, the legacy of Mustafa Kemal and Kemalist ideology (Güney 2002: 162). Overall, the problems related to military involvement in politics might best be summarized by an ex-officer (and ex-politician):

> The method of training for Turkish officers is not at all like that in other armies. Being an officer in other armies is just a professional job, like any other form of state service. With us, however, it is much more than just a job, it is a national duty, it is the Guardianship of the State.
>
> (Quoted in Hale 1994: 83)

Compounded with this role profile is the fact that many elites and many amongst the ordinary citizenry are supportive of this role for the military. According to public opinion polls like the World Values Survey,[8] for instance, the Turkish military is clearly one of the most trusted state institutions. Thus, it appears that the general will to alter the military's role in politics is lacking, making such an alteration extremely unlikely.

Conclusions

What conclusions can be drawn from these case studies about the role of professionalization of the military in consolidating democracy? As discussed in the introduction to this chapter, it is often argued that the process of professionalization implies the establishment of institutional structures and mechanisms that guarantee civilian control over virtually all aspects of the military, including planning and considering strategic imperatives. Until such control is gained, the threat of military intervention is always present – so the argument goes. The case of Italy indicates that perhaps this is not as crucial for stabilizing democracy as is generally argued: civilian leaders in that country made very few attempts to control military decision-making and planning, and in the 1960s in the midst of growing strike activity and the failure to form a governing coalition, a coup was indeed being planned. It was perhaps the continued cooperation with one another on the part of the political parties that prevented further plots from developing.

Moreover, the case of Spain indicates that government attempts to encroach upon the areas that military officers have traditionally considered to be within their remit, including organization, strategy, promotions, and other personnel issues, are likely to be met with hostility. Thus, professionalization is a potentially dangerous activity which may result in plotting against the civilian regime, particularly if the latter is struggling in other areas as well. The idea of a *Socialist* government leading the professionalization process in Spain would have seemed extremely unlikely in 1975, and it appears that the events prior to the Socialist victory are what made it possible for that government to adopt drastic professionalization policies. Namely, almost all political elites including the monarch had expressed their commitment to the new democratic institutions, as had the mass public in rallies held after the 1981 coup attempt. The near-unity of the public and elites in support of the regime was extremely important for guaranteeing that further plots would be warded off, thus making it possible for the Socialist government to carry out reforms in the knowledge that they would be supported by other elites. Such unity was, in turn, guaranteed by the fact that there was agreement on the institutions themselves at the outset.

In Turkey, on the other hand, civilian elites have generally had little reason to protect the rules, which most of them had no say in designing in the first place. Many of these rules, particularly in the post-1980 period have been seen as fundamentally flawed. Moreover, there does not appear to be any basic agreement amongst civilian elites as to what the role of the military ought to be. As discussed above, the 1980 coup was, in fact, welcomed by many civilians as an end to the growing political and economic chaos of the previous decades. Thus it seems that in the absence of civilian agreement about the general rules of the game and about civilianizing control over the military as had been the case in Spain, it is impossible for Turkish democracy to become consolidated.

As argued by Agüero (1995: 13):

A unified civilian coalition with persistent and substantial electoral backing will find it easier to promote reforms that weaken military resistance to civilian control ... a cohesive military facing a divided government lacking public support may be better able to deter civilian initiatives or even to strengthen military prerogatives altogether.

10 External influences and democratic consolidation

Much of the research on democratic transition and consolidation has tended to focus on factors within the country undergoing regime change that are likely to have an impact on whether the country becomes a consolidated democracy – the social structural aspects of the economic system (and its subsequent impact on things like party systems), the agency effects of key actors during and after a transition, and institutional design within the regime itself. Thus far these have served as the core points of comparison and explanation across the three cases studied in this book. This chapter alters the focus somewhat and considers the potential impact of factors outside of the national polity, namely the impact of the international environment and international organizations on democratic consolidation. As will be seen below, the evidence on the effect of international factors on democratic consolidation is extremely mixed, and at best, it is the interrelationship between these international factors and domestic structures and actors that might help to provide a more holistic explanation of differences in outcomes of regime transitions. The chapter begins by providing an overview of the external factors that are likely to affect a democratic transition and then analyses the effect of these in our three case studies.

Contagion, dominoes, and democratization

One fairly well-established 'fact' of comparative politics is that location tends to matter considerably for what type of political system will govern a particular country (see Gleditsch and Ward 2006). Thus, as regimes in a region switch from authoritarianism to democracy, this increases the likelihood that other regimes in the region will do the same. Some of the causal mechanisms outlined in this approach include factors like the mass media conveying images of happy citizens dancing in the streets, tearing down walls, and so on; such images may subsequently trigger pro-democracy protests and opposition to authoritarian rule in neighbouring countries. More substantively, a transition to democracy in a neighbouring country may give opposition groups ideas as to how to go about making similar transitions in their own countries. Moreover, the fact that a climate of change is in the air may boost the courage of the opposition to try to emulate opposition forces in other countries.

Of course, the reverse logic may apply as well. Military coups may be contagious, for instance (Li and Thompson 1975). Indeed, as Chapter 9 indicated, there is evidence to indicate that the plotters of the early 1980s military interventions in Spain looked to the Turkish example of 1980 – although it is equally clear that they failed to follow the calculated, structured approach taken by the Turkish military leadership.

Other examples of negative effects of contagion may include the collapse of democracy and subsequent rise of fascism in Germany and Italy in the interwar years, along with the control of countries like France by the Nazis: these factors may have made the likelihood of success of Spain's Second Republic far lower than if neighbouring countries were also democratic. Similarly, at the time of the establishment of the Turkish Republic, the country was far from flush with European democracies which could be emulated. Indeed, if Mustafa Kemal's goal was the modernization of Turkey, many of the European examples at the time might have easily led him to the conclusion that a fascist approach to this process was not unusual and could very well deliver the benefits to Turkey that he desired. In short, according to the contagion argument, all three of the cases analysed here were very unlikely to be democratic prior to the start of World War II because democracy was so very rare in the region.

While contagion may impact whether a country makes a transition to authoritarianism or democracy, it must be recognized that 'democracy is not just like a virus which happens to spread from one organism to another without intentionality' (Whitehead 2001: 8). Both the intentionality of international actors and domestic actors must be considered. First, most of the post-war democratic regimes in Europe which might show signs of contagion were actually established intentionally by occupying forces. Democracy was established both in the western part of Germany and in Italy under the supervision of occupying Allied forces. Under the influence of the Allies, neighbouring countries were also able to (re-)establish democratic rule. At the same time, by agreement amongst the Allies, other geographical areas of Europe were allowed to make transitions to a totalitarian model. Thus, while the geographical concentration of regime type cannot be denied, it is not something that necessarily occurs simply because of media coverage, the travel of ideas, etc. (see Whitehead 1986).

In addition, it is clear that not all regimes give way to democracy or authoritarianism even if transitions are occurring in neighbouring regimes. This is because domestic actors are extremely important in the process as well. Moreover, even if a *transition* occurs by pure contagion, this in no way guarantees that democratic *consolidation* will occur. If domestic conditions and actors are not overly favourable and the regime is unable to withstand the difficult times of a transition, contagion is unlikely to carry it through to consolidation.

International climate and international political economy

In addition to the potential effects of localized contagion, it is thought that the international climate more generally can effect both democratic transitions and consolidations. According to Whitehead, by and large, the international context 'made a significant difference both in generally promoting trends of democratisation and in loading the dice in favour of successful transition to liberal democracy' (1991: 26; see also Panebianco 1986). As discussed above, at times foreign regimes have a political or economic interest in promoting democracy in a given country, but it is also likely to be the case that the overall international context is important as well. For instance, at the end of World War II many regimes fell into one sphere or the other in the bipolar world, and those in the US sphere of influence were expected to become liberal democracies while those under the Soviet sphere were expected to become communist totalitarian regimes, and each of these two sides used heavy-handed intervention to ensure that the appropriate transitions were made. The change in international climate in the late 1980s and 1990s as a result of the collapse of the Soviet Union provided pressure for non-democratic regimes to become democratic, as democracy appeared to be the only acceptable game in town. Given the continued existence of authoritarian regimes, including Russia, at the start of the twenty-first century, however, it appears that democracy is *not* the only game in town and that the general context of international environment may be less important to guaranteeing stable democracy than first believed.

Another international dimension that deserves mention is the international economy. Chapter 4 discussed the economic situations at the time of the three transitions to democracy studied in this book. In all three cases, the international economic situation was not overly promising – both Italy and Turkey made transitions to democracy in the early post-World War II period of extreme poverty, and Spain's transition occurred in the midst of the 1970s oil crises. However, what should be clear from Chapter 4 is that the international financial community was instrumental in helping to stabilize the economies of Italy and Spain, and in the case of the latter, made it possible for government to 'buy off' potential sources of violent protest with generous social-welfare benefits and wage increases which would not have been possible without the influx of foreign funds (see Pridham 1991: 16). Chapter 4 also indicated that Turkey may not have received nearly as much assistance from the US as did Italy and Spain, but Turkey *has* had a steady influx of foreign capital and clearly still struggled to fully consolidate democracy.

International organizations

International organizations (IOs) may have a role to play both in transitions and consolidation. International relations literature has long pointed to the likelihood of international regimes (i.e. rules, norms, etc.) affecting state behaviour, limiting what state leaders may consider to be viable courses of action with regard to their international ventures. Similarly, it may be argued that international rules and norms influence what states can do domestically. For instance, international conventions on human rights appear to be making it more and more difficult for regimes to violate human rights and discriminate against minorities with impunity (Soysal 1994). Formal organizations may put even more direct pressure on states to enact certain policies and ultimately to enact policies that place them within the realm of democratic rule.

Not all organizations have an equal amount of power in this regard, however. Clearly, the influence of IOs like the United Nations on altering regime type is extremely limited, and many would argue the same is true for most regional IOs. Jon Pevehouse (2002a, 2002b, 2005) contends that it is actually the nature of the regimes within the organization which has the most impact on a member state. When a transitional country joins an organization that is a wide mix of liberal democracies, 'illiberal' democracies, nondemocracies, etc., that organization is likely to have very little influence on whether the country sticks to a democratic path or returns to authoritarianism. If, on the other hand, all of the other member states of the IO are democratic, the likelihood of transitioning away from democracy is significantly reduced.

Although all IOs may serve as a forum in which member states may air concerns about a regime and place pressure on the regime to (continue to) democratize, IOs may have additional mechanisms at their disposal. The previous chapter mentioned the importance of NATO in assisting the Spanish civilian government in its attempt to gain control over the military. Military organizations such as NATO are argued to have two main effects on democratic consolidation. First, the funds and equipment promised by these IOs may help to assuage the fears of officers regarding funding cuts and neglect on the part of the new civilian government. Second, and more importantly, is the role of socialization: 'Regional alliances and military organizations, especially those that conduct joint training operations or maintain permanent institutions (such as NATO), can help to socialize military leaders in member states as to the role of the military in domestic society' (Pevehouse 2002b: 528). More to the point, membership of such organizations puts officers into contact with officers of other states where the military's role is completely professional; doctrines of professionalism may then be internalized by the officers of the transitional state (Pevehouse 2002b: 528–9).

Non-military IOs such as the Council of Europe and the European Union (EU) can use the lure of membership alone (Vachudová 2005) as well as the threat of expulsion to prevent a return to authoritarianism (Pevehouse 2002a, 2002b; Vachudová 2005). In addition, the EU has developed further steps and mechanisms which allow it to pressure transitional governments into continuing with democratizing reforms. Conditionality is one of the key aspects of the EU's influence, and research points to the conclusion that this is far more effective at promoting both policy change and democratic stability than the lure of membership or incentives which are provided before a country makes the change being demanded of it (see Schmitter 2001; Ethier 2003); on the other hand, it is likely that incentives such as aid, credit, and investment can help with the economic aspects of a transition while a clear timetable for entry to the IO may help with the political transition (see Yilmaz 2002: 73).

Milada Vachudová (2005: Chapters 3 and 4) refers to the 'passive leverage' that organizations like the European Union and the Council of Europe have over transitional countries. This sort of leverage may be operative in countries where leaders (and citizens) desire membership in the IO, but no promise of entry or any clear entry strategy has been granted by the latter. The Council of Europe and the European Union are generally seen in Europe as *the* key organizations to join to secure the stamp of democratic credibility. To gain entry into these IOs, a country must be European and must be democratic. A European country that is deemed ineligible for membership invites criticism and there are reputation costs both within the country and on the world stage (Pevehouse 2002b). Moreover, the prospect of being left out of an organization like the EU carries potentially heavy economic costs: those excluded from the organization stand to lose out on aid, foreign direct investment, and trade as each of these is diverted to countries that are in the organization (Mattli 1999).

However, as Vachudová's analysis indicates, the general lure of membership as such is likely to mostly serve as an additional motivating force for leaders already making transitions to democracy for other reasons, e.g. to modernize the economic and political system, to become wealthy like the West, etc. For countries that are not pursuing liberalization in earnest, however, the vague lure of membership or exclusion from membership is unlikely to have much impact on the transitional process or outcome. Moreover, while membership of the Council of Europe (and NATO) is often seen as an initial stamp of approval for new European democracies, the standards of acceptance to that IO are relatively low and there are no real mechanisms to enforce compliance with European standards of democracy. Thus, the lure of membership and membership itself appear to have no discernible effect on regimes (Vachudová 2005).

On the other hand, *expulsion* or the realistic threat of expulsion from an IO may have significant effects. For instance, in 1967 the European Economic Community suspended its Association Agreement with Greece after a military coup in that country. The Association Agreement is thought to have facilitated trade between Greece and the EEC – although with considerable limitations which will be discussed below – and when the agreement was suspended, Greece suffered financially (the Greece–EEC Financial Protocol was also frozen). Some scholars claim that this action served to keep pressure on the military regime, both in terms of its economic costs and because of the political embarrassment of having the agreement suspended and the subsequent criticism directed against the regime by EEC governments (see Verney and Couloumbis 1991 and Coufoudakis 1977).

Thus, IOs may exercise 'active leverage' (Vachudová 2005: Chapters 5 and 6), either in the form of expulsion or through believable threats of exclusion from the organization. In this sense, the Council of Europe has been considerably weaker in leveraging prospective member states and current member states into reforming relatively poor democratic institutions. The European Union, on the other hand, has come to have considerably more influence.

Nowadays, the EU has a relatively wide range of tools that can be used as leverage to push transitional regimes toward consolidation. This process appears to have begun in 1962 when an explicit link between democracy and accession to the EEC was established in the Birkelbach Report, approved by the European Parliament in January 1962 just before Spain lodged an application for associate membership of the European Economic Community (EEC), to be discussed further below. The report outlined the political conditions that must be met by applicant countries, and democratic government was established as a precondition for membership of the EEC. Countries wishing to join the EEC were required to recognize the principles for membership outlined by the Council of Europe: democracy, respect for human rights, and the rule of law. Associate status of the EEC was specified as a future possibility for countries that fulfilled these political conditions for membership but were not economically ready for full membership (MacLennan 2000: 53; Closa and Heywood 2004: 10).

The entry process designed by the EC/EU leaders and the European Commission includes multiple steps, and at any of these, the EU could theoretically stop the process. The first step in the process is usually the signing of trade agreements with potential candidate countries; nowadays this also includes aid agreements. The EU could very well refuse to even begin this process with a country until it reaches a certain level of political development, but in practice, conditionality has not been used at this stage. Nor has it always been used at the next stage – the signing of an association agreement with the potential candidate.[1] Again, historically the EU/EC/EEC has not imposed strict conditionality requirements to get to this particular stage either. That is, although a candidate must show signs of adopting democratic institutions and practices, these do not appear to need to be stable and fully functioning prior to the granting of associate status. This is very similar to the requirement for gaining entry to the Council of Europe.

At the next stage, the EU will screen a candidate to determine whether it is eligible to become a member of the IO; the member states will generally ask the European Commission to draw up a report indicating its opinion on whether a potential candidate is eligible for membership. This does not necessarily mean that the candidate must have already implemented all elements of the *acquis communitaire* (the body of EU law accumulated up to the point of accession), but tends to be an opinion on the fitness and compatibility of the country's political, economic, and administrative institutions with those of the EU. Thus, at this stage, the EU can put a brake on a potential candidate's ambitions for membership by indicating that it is far from being ready for entry – that is, it has not met the basic conditionality of having stable democratic institutions, the rule of law, respect for human rights and respect for and protection of minorities (see Grabbe 2002: 256–7). This, for instance, was the initial result of Turkey's application for EC membership in 1987, although other reasons were also mentioned (see below). As indicated above, however, the EU does not always use this tool: accession negotiations were started with Greece before the country was deemed by the European Commission to be fully ready for entry into the EU. In more recent enlargements, though, the EU was faced with the prospect of taking on several new member states, most of which were far larger than Greece, and could not risk opening negotiations before candidates had met the basic criteria of having democratic institutions and a fully functioning market economy.

Even if a country passes the initial screening and makes it to the negotiation stage (thus becoming a fully fledged candidate), this is no guarantee that the country will get to the next stage of opening and closing all elements of the *acquis*. Again, Turkey finally made it to the candidacy stage, but negotiations over some aspects of the *acquis* are now stalled indefinitely (more on this below). If all aspects of the *acquis* are not adopted, the EU can refuse to take the process to the next stage, the signing of the accession treaty. In addition, conditionality can be used after candidacy is granted. For instance, in 1997 Slovakia was excluded from the first round of negotiations for entry to the EU that were already being conducted with other candidates because it was deemed to have not met the democracy criteria (Grabbe 2002: 257).

Thus, at any step in the process, candidates face the possibility of exclusion from the EU. Again, such an eventuality has severe economic implications (trade, aid, and investment), but it is also likely to have severe political implications domestically. A government that continues to fail to deliver the EU goods to its citizens may face problems during elections. On the other hand, this depends on how domestic leaders present these issues to their publics. Prior to the formalization of the process, potential candidates may pretend to have a cosy relationship with the EU, or may claim that the EU was treating the country unfairly for one reason or another, both of which reduce the EU's leverage over that country's political process. As Vachudová (2005) contends, the fact that the process is now formalized and that all candidates appear to receive the same treatment has increased the EU's leverage.

This point was especially driven home with the treatment of Bulgaria and Romania. Initially, the European Commission reports issued on these countries were very unfavourable and it was clear that they were not going to gain entry at the same time as the frontrunners – countries like Hungary, Czechoslovakia, and Poland (the so-called Visegrad Three). It would have been very easy for leaders in these countries to claim that certain countries like the Visegrad Three were given special treatment because of their geopolitical significance and that the process was fundamentally unfair. The fact that the Visegrad Three were subjected to the same regular reports and the same overall process, however, ultimately made this an inappropriate argument and also meant that reports on the defects in the political and economic systems in Bulgaria and Romania had to be taken seriously by the domestic audience. It is argued that negative reports provided one of the main points of consensus for the opposition parties in these two countries, around which they developed an election strategy that helped them defeat parties that were seen as carrying out extremely questionable (i.e. non-democratic) practices (Vachudová 2005: Chapter 6).

The potential effect of membership of the European Union is of obvious importance to this analysis, as our two consolidated democracies – Spain and Italy – are EU members while Turkey is not. Moreover, many researchers argue for the likely importance of the EU in stabilizing democracy in countries like Greece, Spain, and Portugal (Sobles Mira 1990; Powell 1996; Ethier 1997). Before turning to a discussion of the impact of the EU in our three case studies, we must reconsider the issue of causality. Empirically, there is clearly a link between EU membership and democratic consolidation: a country has never joined the EU and then transited away from democracy. However, this may be because the EU has not accepted as a full member any country that was deemed to be on very shaky ground. Certainly countries like Greece, Spain, and Portugal were in the early days of their transitions when accession negotiations began, but by the time they were finally admitted into the EU there were very few threats to the democratic regimes anyway. As we have seen with Spain, the main threat – the military – discredited itself in the 1981 attempted coup and the subsequent trial of participants, and Spanish elites had cooperated to ward off this potential threat to democracy. In Portugal, it was the military itself that initiated the transition to democracy but by the time the country entered the EC as a full member, civilian control over the military had been achieved (Morlino 1998: 72). In Greece, the regime of the colonels was largely discredited by the crisis in Cyprus in 1974,[2] and very shortly after the transition to democracy, the civilian government was able to gain control over the military, even resisting coup attempts in 1975 (Morlino 1998: 73–4). Thus, by the time the country joined the EC in 1981, it could be argued that civilians were already consolidating the new democratic regime. As Whitehead argues, 'in practice it was not until the evidence had accumulated that all three democratic regimes were pretty well consolidated that enlargement eventually occurred' (1991: 50).

Generally, the findings on the relationship between the EU and democratic transition and consolidation point to the conclusion that at best, when the EU can specify clear requirements and link these directly to a reward, it can make a difference in the policies a non-member state enacts (Schimmelfennig and Sedelmeier 2005); in the case of the most recent CEE transitions, apparently the EU's potential influence was 'constrained by diffuseness and uncertainty' (Grabbe 2006: 3). Moreover, it appears that the EU is far more effective at getting governments to change the language and content of a policy than in the area of policy implementation (Haughton 2007: 242) and that it is only effective at all when the domestic political circumstances are amenable to the changes being suggested by the EU (Schimmelfennig *et al.* 2003). At the same time, Vachudová's (2005) research indicates that the EU may play a significant role in unifying normally divisive elites around the goal of EU membership, and these coalitions of odd bedfellows can help push through reforms that lead the country toward greater political liberalism. Thus, in general terms, it appears that the international environment and international actors can have an impact on events, but the main sources of a democratic transition and consolidation are domestic (Whitehead 1986, 1991, 2001; Pasquino 1986: 70; Segal 1991). We now turn to a discussion of the impact of these factors on the three case studies analysed in this book.

Italy: under the influence of the Cold War

The potential importance of the fact that Italy fell within the sphere of influence of the US has been mentioned in previous chapters, as has the importance of the influx of cash from the US and other allies. Here two other key international factors that are likely to have contributed to producing stable democracy in Italy are briefly discussed as well: direct intervention on the part of the US and USSR, and the impact of the EEC.

Although Italy was clearly in the British and American camp as a result of agreements made with the Soviet Union at the Yalta conference of 1945, this was no guarantee whatsoever that democracy would survive in Italy. Of particular concern to the US was that Italy would become a communist regime – a general preoccupation of the US until the early 1990s. Despite the *Svolta di Salerno* on the part of the Communist Party of Italy in 1944 (when the party's leader announced that the party would put aside the long-standing hostility to the monarchy and join the royal government in an act of national unity against the Nazis and the Fascists (Ginsborg 1990: 43)), the US was still fearful of the possibility that the Communist Party would win enough votes to form a government in Italy. Thus, despite having very little previous contact with Italy before World War II, the US took an active interest in preventing the country from collapsing to communism and made every effort to help ensure that the left did not win the first post-war elections in Italy to be held in April 1948. The leader of the main centre-right party, Christian Democrat de Gasperi, 'played his anti-Communist card quite well' with the United States (Leonardi 1991: 72), informing US officials that pressure was being exerted to bring Italy within the Soviet sphere of influence via the Italian Communist Party. In essence, a case was presented to the US for continued funding of economic development in Italy, and in exchange the Christian Democrats would make every effort to keep the left from holding power. The US government agreed with this strategy and made it clear that all US aid would be suspended if the leftist slate of candidates was successful in the 1948 elections; these views were communicated publicly by the ambassadors to Italy and to the Vatican in public appearances (Leonardi 1991: 76–7). In addition, despite opinion polls indicating that the Christian Democrats were likely to win the elections, the US had already begun to plan for different outcomes, and planned to use force in the eventuality of a Communist coup resulting from the elections (Leonardi 1991: 76–8). According to Ginsborg, US warships were anchored in the waters of the main Italian ports in the weeks leading up to the election (Ginsborg 1990: 115–16). Similarly, prior to the 1953 elections the US ambassador issued 'dire warnings of the consequences if the Christian Democrats lost' (Leonardi 1991: 143).

At the same time, the Soviet Union was clearly intervening to assist the PCI. It was in great part thanks to Soviet assistance that the PCI had survived the fascist period: the PCI leader, Togliatti, lived in exile in the Soviet Union and with the financial assistance of the Soviet government – particularly Stalin's government – the party survived and was able to re-build its membership rolls quickly after the end of the war. The Union Fund of Assistance to Worker Organizations of the Left in the West was created to formalize Soviet support for Communist parties in other countries. Even into the early 1970s, the PCI leader (Berlinguer) was cooperating with the Soviet Union in the training of Italian Communists by the KGB. It was only in 1975 when new laws were passed changing government policy on the public financing of political parties that the PCI began to try to disengage financially from the Soviet Union (see Cervetti 1999; Drake 2004; Riva 1999).

With regard to the impact of international organizations on the consolidation of democracy in Italy, it is difficult to find any research indicating that these were key. Recall that much of the modern research on the effect of the EU points to conclusion that the EU can use conditionality in order to help a transitional country achieve stable democracy. At the time that Italy's democracy was consolidating, however, the EU's predecessor, the European Coal and Steel Community was clearly not used in this way. Indeed, most accounts of the ECSC indicate that it was a trade agreement that functioned poorly even in the realm of trade. As a founding member of the ECSC, Italy was also included in the Treaties of Rome in 1957, and the key one of these, the treaty founding the European Economic Community, was very much an economic agreement and included no mention of the need for member states to be democratic – although this may be seen as implicit in the treaty, as mention is made of political parties and European elections in the treaty.

Clearly there was no explicit attempt to push member states into democracy, except indirectly through economic development (see Clark 1984: 345 on the limited importance of the EEC to Italy's political system).

In terms of the effects of the EEC on the economy in Italy, according to Hine (1993), Italy's economic miracle may not have been primarily attributable to the EC, but for business leaders Community membership was a guarantee that the open-market-economy path would be adhered to by Italian leaders and in the 1970s community loans helped the country through its external-payments difficulties. Also, participation in the Exchange Rate Mechanism helped to keep inflation under better control than previously was the case (Hine 1993: 285).

In addition, NATO membership may have also had some impact on developing professionalism amongst the Italian military, but as shown in Chapter 9, a more important factor may have been direct US administration of the Italian military via NATO. Still, as discussed in Chapter 9, one branch of the Italian military was able to plan a coup despite US involvement in the Italian military. Overall, however, 'it was the USA which emerged as the most important and consistent outside influence on the Italian transition' (Leonardi 1991: 64).

Spain: the effect of international organizations

If we consider the case of Spain within the context of dominoes, contagion, etc., during the country's first attempt to establish democracy in the twentieth century, the international context for such a transition was not promising at all. Fascism and communism were serious ideological contenders in many of the countries nearest to Spain. That is, there was no sense at all that democracy was the only game in Europe. Moreover, the international economy was still in the midst of depression, and although the effects of global depression were less in countries like Spain which were not as strongly tied into global markets, they were still fairly negative.

Thus, the international context certainly did not help to promote the survival of democracy in the 1936–39 period in Spain. Perhaps more importantly, though was that western democracies opted against intervention as the country descended into civil war, while the Soviet Union, Fascist Italy, and Nazi Germany provided military aid in support of the causes of communism or fascism (MacLennon 2000: 13; see also Payne 1993: 374–5). If anything, then, international factors made democracy less likely and fascism or communism more likely at the time.

Many would argue that the international context would eventually come to play an important role in pushing Spain toward democratization and consolidation, though, and much of this effect began in the 1960s when Spain attempted to establish linkages with the EEC. First, though, in terms of the US's effect on Spanish regime type, it is clear that the US had very little interest in fostering democracy in Spain. Of key concern to the US during the Franco years was that it was able to gain a military ally in a strategically important area of the world. As discussed in Chapter 4, US aid is likely to have been important in bringing Spain's economy out of the doldrums in the 1950s, but the only condition the US placed on this aid was that it could have access to Spanish military bases for its own strategic purposes. Moreover, when Franco died the main concern of the US was keeping the country as an ally (Powell 2001: 289–90), and assisting with a democratic transition appears to have been a secondary concern. In order to achieve both of these goals, in June 1976, the US began to lay the groundwork for a one billion dollar loan to Spain (Story and Pollack 1991: 132).

By the early 1960s it had become clear that the Spanish economy was going to need more than aid to keep it going, and many within the Franco regime wanted to establish stronger trade links with European countries. The newly formed European Economic Community and European Free Trade Area meant that Spanish products – particularly agricultural products – were being subjected to high quotas and tariffs, and removing these would improve the Spanish economy tremendously. With Greece being granted association status for the EEC in 1961, Turkey looking like it would gain such status, the British application to join the EEC, and the adoption of the Common Agricultural Policy in the EEC, the Spanish government decided that it must apply for membership of the EEC itself (MacLennon 2000: 47–8). Franco perceived the EEC as an economic organization and was convinced that membership was unrelated to domestic political arrangements (MacLennon 2000: 52). Even when the Birkelbach report was issued in January 1962, this did not appear to alter Spain's strategy, which was to continue pursuing the idea of applying for associate status of the EEC; the Spanish Foreign Ministry had reached the conclusion that the political obstacles were not as serious as they seemed and implied that cosmetic changes to the Franco regime would be all that was necessary (MacLennon: 53–4).

Thus in February 1962, Spain applied for association with the EEC. Given that the EEC had yet to develop a clear policy regarding applications from non-democratic members and that the member states were divided on whether Spain should be granted associate status at this stage, it seems that this period was quite important in terms of whether the EEC/EU would ultimately become an IO with significant power to influence domestic reform or not. In fact, France and Germany were somewhat positive about Spain's application while the other member states were hostile to the idea; the European Parliament was divided on the issue as well (Preston and Smyth 1984; MacLennon 2000: 59; Closa and Heywood 2004: 9–13).

Events in Spain – particularly the confiscation of passports of individuals believed to be leaders of the opposition to the Franco regime and then giving these individuals the choice of exile or confinement in the Canary Islands – brought home the extent to which the Franco regime was incompatible with the general 'cause of Europe' (MacLennon 2000: 70). In Italy all of the political parties unanimously condemned the Franco regime; in

Germany, the Social Democrats requested that the German government adopt a more distant attitude toward the Franco regime; and the Dutch parliament passed a resolution against Spanish entry into the Community. Franco tried to give the appearance of change by reshuffling his cabinet, and one of the new cabinet ministers (Manuel Fraga) made a decision that was to be of fairly major importance, the relaxation of censorship which enabled anti-Francoist literature to be published (Preston and Smyth 1984; MacLennon 2000: 68–71).

Two years after Spain's application for associate status, the EC Council of Ministers finally responded to Spain's application by stating that they were authorizing the European Commission to initiate discussions with the Spanish government to study the economic problems that the EEC had caused Spain and to develop a solution. Both sides had by this time dropped any mention of associate membership (MacLennon 2000: 75).

Events within the EEC, including the continued discussion and rejection of the British application for EEC membership and the Empty Chair Crisis,[3] distracted attention from EEC–Spanish relations, and it was only in 1970 that a new arrangement was made with Spain – a preferential trade agreement. The Franco regime presented this as political victory, but after this 'relations with Europe emerged as the recurrent excuse for criticizing the political system: for the sake of Europe, the business and economic sectors demanded liberalization...' (MacLennon 2000: 82); the issue of Europe also created dissent within the regime, and Franco supporters began to transfer to the opposition as a result of their disagreement over the necessity to implement political reform in order to obtain a better arrangement with Europe. Supporters of the regime continued to believe, though, that the EC would eventually admit Spain even while the regime maintained its 'political peculiarities' (Preston and Smyth 1984; MacLennon 2000: 86–90).

Thus, rejection by the EEC became a major rallying point for opposition groups and for members of the regime itself. It implied an inferiority to Europe which had plagued Spanish identity since the 1898 war with the US in which the last of the Spanish colonies in the Americas was lost. That is, rejection was a blow to national pride (MacLennon 2000): 'the EC came to be seen as the embodiment of European values, notably liberal democracy, and an antidote to the regime's authoritarianism. It was thus widely accepted that the democratizing process would be incomplete until it had been formally sanctioned by Brussels, while Spain's continued exclusion from the EC would represent an insult to national pride as well as a negation of democratic credibility' (Powell 2001: 297). As argued by Closa and Heywood: 'EC rejection of the Franco regime transformed Europe into a symbol of democracy.... The aspiration to identify with Europe and the EC became a central element of the political culture and discourse on democratization.... Membership was viewed as an anchor for democracy...' (Closa and Heywood 2004: 15; see also Ortega 1994; Bassols 1995; Closa 1995; Morata 1998; Barbé 1999). Failure to achieve full EC membership was also perceived by business elites and economic ministers within the regime as having extremely negative consequences for the Spanish economy, particularly after the enlargement in 1973 which meant – amongst other things – that the British market would suddenly be closed to Spanish goods (Preston and Smyth 1984; MacLennon 2000; Powell 2001; Closa and Heywood 2004).

Other international organizations may have also played a role in pushing Spain toward democracy. In particular, the Socialist International provided the financial means for the survival of the PSOE and eventually stepped in to help resolve a highly contentious issue regarding whether the party should be led by individuals who were in exile or who had remained in Spain (resolving the issue in favour of the latter) (MacLennon 2000: 105–7). Toward the end of the regime, European institutions began to organize events in which Spanish opposition groups could discuss Spain's future. For instance, one of these took place at the European Commission's premises in Brussels (MacLennon 2000: 111); the Council of Europe and European Parliament also provided forums for opposition groups (MacLennon 2000: 128). Although many of the meetings of opposition groups took place in Spain as well, it seems that European institutions helped to foster agreement amongst these regarding the approach to take toward the regime – e.g. agreement to not insist on the dissolution of the monarchy.

By the time of Franco's death, the international political climate had clearly changed: Spain's neighbours and trading partners were democratic and were increasingly coming to the view the authoritarian regime as anachronistic (Powell 2001: 286). Moreover, it was clear that Spain would not be able to achieve the desired EC membership without adopting political reform. Governments before Suárez's realized this as well, and when Prime Minister Arias Navarro began to adopt political reforms, he made it clear that his government would apply for EEC membership; the government managed to convince all of the EEC member state governments that the reforms were genuine and gained the support of each member state government. However, this was to turn to disappointment soon as the government began to arrest members of the opposition. After Suárez was selected as president of the government, it was announced that Spain would apply for membership of the EC once further political reform had been carried out. Initial responses from the EC were positive, but economic issues would soon break the unanimous political will to see Spain join the EC (MacLennon 2000: Chapter 5).

On 15 June 1977 elections were held in Spain, and on 28 July 1977 Spain officially applied for EC membership; at the end of the year, the Council of Ministers announced itself to be in favour of Spain's application and agreed that exploratory talks should be completed to allow negotiations for entry to start in February 1979 (MacLennon 2000: 154). While the carrot of EC membership may have indeed helped to unify varying groups around democratic reform, it is not clear that it was necessarily the same incentive that kept Spain on the track of democratic consolidation. This is because the promise of membership of the EC began to lose some credibility in the early 1980s. Although negotiations for Spain's entry into the EEC had already begun as scheduled in February 1980, in June 1980 French president Valery Giscard d'Estaing announced that the EEC had enough problems without considering the ones that new candidates would pose. It became clear that Giscard's remarks were directed at Spain and it seemed entirely possible that the smaller Southern European applicants, Greece and Portugal, could be allowed to enter the EC but Spain's application could be vetoed by France. Of specific concern to the French government was that the EEC needed to reform its agricultural and budget policies (MacLennon 2000: 161–2). French President François Mitterand continued this approach, stating that it would not be possible to negotiate chapters on agriculture or fisheries until the Community's problems in these sectors had been resolved (MacLennon 2000: 168).

Despite the coup attempt in February 1981 in Spain and even after the PSOE had won the 1982 elections in October, France continued to insist that it had not changed its opinion on the issue of Spain's entry to the EC. It was only in January 1983 when discussions were held between the French and Spanish foreign and economic ministries in parallel with negotiations for internal Community reforms and enlargement that the French government announced that it would help Spain with entry to the EC (MacLennon 2000: 166–74). Once the budget issue (i.e. Britain's demand for a rebate from the EC budget) was resolved in June 1984, the Spanish candidacy received unanimous approval. It was agreed that negotiations for entry would finish in September 1984 and that in 1985 the national parliaments would ratify the accession treaty. The final negotiations actually took place in March 1985, and Spain compromised considerably on issues like fisheries and free movement of labour (only a minuscule proportion of Spain's fishing fleet would be allowed in the Community's territorial seas, and Spaniards would have a seven-year waiting period before being allowed to participate in the free circulation of labour), but the country entered the EC as a full member 1 January 1986 (MacLennon 2000: 175–6). Again, although EC membership clearly served to unify opposition to the Franco regime, by the time the country was finally approved for full EC membership, democracy was already consolidated.

Another important IO to mention in the context of Spanish democracy is NATO. As discussed in Chapter 9, NATO provided the funds and technological capabilities that allowed the Spanish government to redirect the Spanish military's attention to external threats. At the same time, as Chapter 9 contended, it was more likely to have been the unification of elites against military intervention that paved the way for a Socialist government to completely revamp the civilian mechanisms of control over the Spanish forces. This issue is returned to below in the context of Turkish democratization.

Turkey: the limits of international organizations

Turkey began to democratize during the same period as Italy, in an international climate that was moving toward increased preference for democracy and protection of human rights. Given that Turkish elites had aligned themselves with the West since the founding of the Turkish Republic, it is perhaps not surprising that like the countries in western Europe, Turkey attempted to adopt similar principles of governance after World War II. Unlike much of Western Europe, however, Turkey's immediate neighbours were far from democratic themselves; neighbours to the north were coming under the Iron Curtain and even Greece was struggling to prevent a communist coup in the late 1940s; to the east and south were the authoritarian regimes of Iran, Iraq, and Syria. Thus, the basic notions of contagion and geographical proximity would have pointed to the likelihood of Turkish democracy struggling in these early years (Karaosmanoğlu 1991: 161).

Also of importance is that Turkey's geographical location meant that the country was of key strategic significance to both the Soviet Union and the United States. Thus, in the face of communist threats in Greece, the United States decided to assist both Greece and Turkey, providing $300 million to Greece and $100 million to Turkey in military and economic aid (this aid was announced in the Truman Doctrine). It must be noted that as in the case of Spain and Italy, the United States was far less concerned with helping Greece and Turkey to establish stable democracies per se but with helping them to keep communism out (see Leffler 1985 for an account of the reasoning behind the Truman Doctrine as applied to Turkey).

Also, as discussed in Chapter 6, because of Turkey's geographical position, aid was given to leftists by neighbouring countries: the Soviet Union, Bulgaria, Syria, as well as the PLO, who provided funds and arms to leftist militants. According to Karaosmanoğlu: 'The total spending of terrorists from 1977 to 1980 was estimated to be one billion dollars. This is the equivalent of US and other NATO military aid to Turkey during the same period' (Karaosmanoğlu 1991: 164). As discussed in Chapters 6 and 9, armed violence on the part of the left and the right in Turkey – and the government's inability to control it – was the main factor that destabilized the system and provoked the 1980 military coup. In addition, Syria and parts of Lebanon have been used by PKK terrorists for training, helping to create another extremely problematical situation that provoked government to suspend normal constitutional rights in some parts of the country in the name of fighting PKK terrorism (Karaosmanoğlu 1991: 165).

In addition, it appears that membership of international organizations had little impact on helping to create stable democracy in Turkey. The Council of Europe was seen by Turkish leaders as one of the key European IOs to which Turkey should become affiliated (see Karaosmanoğlu 1991: 161–2). Thus, only three months after the Council of Europe was founded in May 1949, Turkey was admitted to this organization, which takes as its goals the protection of democracy, human rights, and the rule of law. It is generally expected that members profess a commitment to democratic norms and institutions, but it is clear that a country does not necessarily have to be considered to be a fully functioning stable democracy prior to entry. Almost all of the founding countries were transitioning to democracy, for instance, when the Council of Europe was created, and countries like Greece, Spain, and Portugal were admitted in the early stages of their transitions to democracy as well. (For instance, Spain was admitted on 24 November 1977.) The vast majority of members of the Council of Europe have become stable democracies, and work by scholars like Pevehouse (2002a, 2002b, 2005) would indicate that this bodes well for each member state maintaining a democratic regime; however, despite being a member since 1949, Turkey has suffered from multiple military interventions and problems with human rights violations.[4]

Similarly, while considerable credit is given to NATO membership for helping to professionalize the Spanish military and to remove the Spanish army's predilection for political involvement, it is difficult to argue that this is as important as is generally argued to be the case. This is because Turkey has been a long-standing member of this organization, joining in February 1952 (while Portugal, incidentally, was a founding member in 1949). And while Turkish officers have had similar experiences of working with counterparts in other member states, it does not appear to have had the same socialization effect. In the words of Ali Karaosmanoğlu, 'Most of Turkey's high-ranking officers have either visited or served in various NATO headquarters and the United States. Such experiences abroad have given them an international outlook and contributed to their sense of professionalism' (Karaosmanoğlu 1991: 170–1; see also Duman and Tsarouhas 2006). Again, despite these experiences, middle-ranking and top-level generals appear to continue to see involvement in political matters as falling within their remit at times.

Previous sections have discussed the importance of transnational linkages across political parties and other groups in a newly democratising country. For instance, the Spanish Socialists appear to have been assisted considerably by the Socialist International, and Spanish trade unions began to establish linkages with international trade-union associations toward the end of the Franco regime. In Turkey, political parties do not appear to have benefited as much from such transnational linkages: in the early days of multi-party politics in Turkey there was not a great deal of natural ideological affinity between Turkish parties and those in other European countries because the nature of the political cleavages was different. On the other hand, when the Turkish Republican People's Party converted itself into a party of social democracy in 1965 its leadership did establish close links to other Social Democratic parties and with Socialist International. Moreover, trade unions such as DISK and TURK-IS have been fairly effective at establishing and using transnational linkages to pressure the Turkish government for trade union freedom (Karaosmanoğlu 1991: 168–9).[5]

As discussed above, it appears that there is one IO which may have clear and effective power to help a country to achieve stable democracy, and that is the European Union. Recall that it was Spain's failed application for associate status of the EEC that seems to have marked the turning point for the EEC to use things like conditionality to produce regime change because it was at this time that the member states decided to restrict membership to fully functioning democracies. This decision was to ultimately impact on many other candidates, including Turkey.

In 1959 Turkey applied for associate status with the EEC. In contrast to Spain's motivations in the 1960s, which appeared to be mostly economic in nature, the reason for Turkey's application was primarily political and strategic: Greece had applied for associate status and Turkey needed to avoid becoming isolated from a potentially key west European IO and allowing Greek interests to gain footing in that IO (Müftüler-Baç 1997; Erdoğdu 2002[6]).[7]

Discussions on Turkey's application were stalled by the same problems mentioned above for Spain, mostly connected to the British application for membership, but they also became stalled because of the military coup in Turkey in 1960. Once the new constitution was adopted in Turkey and elections were held in 1961, the country was in a very different position than was Franco's Spain, in that its leadership appeared to be committed to democratic institutions. Thus, the member states of the EEC agreed to grant Turkey associate status, and the agreement came into force in 1964.

The Association Agreement signed with Turkey stipulated three stages for Turkey–EC relations: preparatory, transitional and final. The preparatory stage was intended to be a period in which the Community would provide unilateral concessions and financial aid to Turkey while Turkey would take appropriate measures to develop its economy and to prepare itself for the transitional stage. A transitional stage of between 12 and 22 years would create a customs union between the EC and Turkey. The agreement also included the possibility of a final stage, full membership of the EEC. However, no timetable was provided for this (Müftüler-Baç 1997; Erdoğdu 2002[8]).

At one level, it may be argued that the EEC missed an opportunity to stipulate what would have been necessary *politically* for Turkey to obtain full EEC membership. At the time that the Association Agreement was signed, the constitution in place in Turkey was one that had been designed with considerable military influence and gave the military power over civilian policy-making via the National Security Council. Such an approach to policy-making was clearly inconsistent with the functioning of the political systems of the existing member states, and the EEC could have used conditionality prior to progressing to each stage to influence domestic politics in Turkey and to create a similar rallying point amongst Turkish politicians as was the case in Spain in the 1970s. In fact, the impression given by the EEC at the time was that the key problem keeping Turkey out of the Community was its relatively backward economy, although some concern was expressed over the level of democracy and the political structure (Müftüler-Baç 1997: 55).[9]

EC policy toward Turkey in the 1970s indicated that a conciliatory approach was to continue. For instance, an Additional Protocol outlining the process by which the customs union between Turkey and the EC would be established was signed on 13 November 1970 and came into force 1 January 1973 (Müftüler-Baç 1997: 58–60). Again, the fact that the agreement came into force is particularly surprising, given the military intervention by memorandum in 1971. Thus, as with the CEE candidates later, the EC was prepared to enter into such trade agreements prior to reform of the political system in Turkey; in the case of the latter, there still did not appear to have been a clear stipulation of what would have been necessary politically for Turkey to gain entry to the EC as a full member at this stage.

Because of political and economic crises in the 1970s and the military coup of 1980, the Ankara Agreement was in effect frozen. Turkey's membership of the Council of Europe Assembly was suspended, as was aid from the EEC (Karaosmanoğlu 1991: 162). After the major economic reforms and the return to civilian government in the early 1980s, Turkish Prime Minister Turgut Özal decided it was time to apply for full membership of the EC, and the application was lodged 14 April 1987. It was at this time that the EC flagged up political (and economic) problems in Turkey, pointing out that there were still problems of political instability and human-rights violations; however, the Commission's report on Turkey also emphasized other factors that prevented it from acting on the application: the fact that the EC was in the midst of trying to complete the Common Market and could not take on new member states at that time, and 'the negative consequences of the dispute between Turkey and one Member State of the Community, and also the situation in Cyprus' (quoted on www.etuc.org/a/241, consulted 25 June 2007; see also Müftüler-Baç 1997: 64).

Thus, the message given in this response was fairly mixed, in terms of whether and how Turkey might go about preparing for full EC membership. Without clearer direction from the EC, politicians could focus upon any of these aspects, and it became particularly easy to blame the EC's response on the fact that Turkey's key geopolitical enemy, Greece, was a full member state and very likely lobbied strongly against opening up accession talks to Turkey (see Müftüler-Baç 1997: 65). In essence, the EC's response made it easy to avoid politically difficult reforms such as restricting human-rights abuses in the fight against Kurdish separatism and removing the military's constitutional role in political affairs.

Evidence that a more systematic outline of reforms provided by the EC might have had the ability to alter the Turkish political system in the late 1980s can perhaps be gleaned from more recent events. As discussed in earlier sections of this chapter the EU was faced with multiple applications for membership from the CEE countries in the early 1990s. By the mid-

1990s, it appeared that only three to five applicants would be allowed to start negotiations because the rest were not deemed to be ready, either politically or economically (or both). This policy was changed drastically at the 1997 Luxembourg European Council meeting when it was decided that negotiations would be opened with all ten of the CEE applicant countries, as well as Cyprus and Malta. This decision came as a major blow in Turkey. Particularly surprising was that countries like Bulgaria and Romania were included in this decision since the economy of former was even less developed than Turkey's and the latter was still experiencing problems establishing stable democracy.

After considerable protest and lobbying by the Turkish government, the EU decided in December 1999 at its Helsinki European Council meeting that Turkey would be made an official candidate for entry to the EU and that discussions would commence to determine when Turkey would be in a position to begin accession negotiation. The Turkish government at the time was one that had tremendous potential for instability: the top vote-getters in the 18 April 1999 elections had been the Democratic Left Party, with almost 25 per cent of the seats in parliament, the reformed neo-fascist Nationalist Action Party, with 23.5 per cent of the parliamentary seats, and the religiously oriented Virtue Party, holding 20 per cent of the seats in parliament. Forming a coalition with the latter of these would have been extremely problematic, given that the military had already forced a coalition collapse in 1997 because it had included the Virtue Party's predecessor, the Welfare Party. A coalition between the two top vote-getters also seemed improbable because of the historical animosity and violence between them in the 1970s. Two mainstream centre-right parties managed to win about 15 per cent of the seats in parliament each, but as discussed in Chapter 6, a coalition between the two (along with another party) was impossible because of severe personality conflicts between the leaders of these two parties.

The coalition formula that was chosen was an extremely unlikely Democratic Left Party–Nationalist Action Party–Motherland Party (one of the centre-right parties) combination. As mentioned above given the ideological differences across these parties and their historical relations, and Turkish political instability more generally, it seemed highly unlikely that this coalition would survive. However, it did survive until the next elections were held (albeit early) in November 2002. Moreover, as a result of the European Council decision in Helsinki in December 1999, this particular government was able to coalesce around the goal of making reforms to prepare for accession talks. Although the reforms were relatively minor – abolition of the use of the death penalty except for offences of terrorism and war crimes,[10] reducing the number of military personnel represented in the National Security Council,[11] and agreeing to allow broadcasting in the Kurdish language – the fact that such a disparate group of parties stayed together, partly in the hope of taking Turkey into the EU perhaps attests to the ability of the latter to impact domestic politics even in a country that has struggled for decades to stabilize.

Moreover, further constitutional and political reforms have been carried out by the governing party since 2002 (the Justice and Development Party). For instance, the death penalty was completely abolished in May 2004, and further legislation has been passed related to the right to broadcast in languages other than Turkish as well as receiving language lessons in Kurdish (Müftüler Baç 2005).[12] In addition, the role of the NSC has been downgraded to 'advisory', and the number of required NSC meetings reduced. While the new policies regarding the Kurdish language have been judged to be fairly minimal by Kurds pressing for more drastic changes in Turkish policy toward this minority, they should still be seen as landmark decisions. At the turn of the twenty-first century, it was still politically difficult for officials to even refer to Kurds as 'Kurds' and instead referred to 'the population in the Southeast'. Continual criticism from the EU and Council of Europe finally appear to have driven home the fact that recognition of this group and better protection of their human rights is necessary for EU membership and ultimately for Turkey's political development into a fully functioning democracy.

On the other hand, there have been some serious setbacks since Turkey was granted EU candidacy status. For instance, Article 301 of the Turkish Penal Code which took effect in June 2005 makes it punishable by imprisonment for a person to publicly denigrate Turkishness, the Turkish Republic, the Grand National Assembly of Turkey, the Turkish government, the judicial institutions, or the military or security organizations. Although high-profile individuals who have been brought to court on charges connected to this part of the penal code have generally been acquitted, the fact that this code exists is particularly ominous. The adoption of this legislation would seem to indicate the limits of the EU's ability to impact democratization. Moreover, the continued role of the military in influencing decisions and its continued activism outlined in Chapter 9 also point to limitations on the EU's influence.

Conclusions

Although many scholars believe that the impact of IOs, and particularly the EU, is crucial in creating stable democratic institutions in transitional countries (Powell 2001), comparative research indicates that the effect is likely to be indirect, in that IOs may help politicians to rally around the goal of political reform in a way that would otherwise be extremely difficult (Vachudová 2005). However, it appears that if the domestic reforms are too costly politically for politicians, they will not make the reforms, no matter how IOs like the EU try to use conditionality or incentives to push reform along (Schimmelfenig *et al.* 2003). The findings of this chapter would appear to support these conclusions.

Reform-minded politicians and opposition leaders in Spain were able to use the prospect of EC membership – and the prospect of being excluded permanently because of the country's nondemocratic regime – to help promote political reform to those who were otherwise suspicious of liberalization. The general prospect of moving toward a more modern European political system was also likely to be important in the thinking of many of the reformers. However, Spain had already established fairly stable democratic institutions before it became clear that EC membership would be possible in the near future. Indeed, the new democracy faced its biggest threat in February 1981 at a time when the EC was hesitating on Spain's application and managed to fight that threat off regardless of what was happening with its application with the EC. Moreover, other international actors like the US were indifferent as to the type of regime that would be established, as long as it was not a communist regime. Ultimately, it seems likely that it was the clear agreement both of most major domestic political groupings and of the king that Spain would progress toward democracy that produced the transition and helped to consolidate Spanish democracy.

In the case of Italy it is extremely difficult to determine what impact the EC might have had on helping to stabilize democracy there. Any external influence appears to have mostly been by the US, which provided the funds to help stabilize the economy and actively kept the perceived Communist threat at bay by supporting the Christian Democrats. Moreover, in the words of Leonardi, 'in the transition to democracy in Italy a number of options were excluded due to the international and internal context within which the Italian postwar system emerged' (Leonardi 1991: 66). The fact that Italy was in the British and later the American camp as a result of the Yalta conference meant that the choice of political system was in many ways set by the outcome of World War II (Leonardi 1991: 66). The ECSC and the EEC thus seem somewhat peripheral to Italian domestic political reform.

Finally, while the EU is clearly having a strong impact on much of the legislation and reform process in Turkey in the modern day, there are clear limits to its influence, and the configuration of domestic political interests continues to be key in determining how the Turkish political system functions. Even now that the EU has opened accession talks and has specified clearly targets that must be met before Turkey can enter the EU, the country is only marginally closer to consolidating its democracy. In addition, despite the fact that many of Turkey's neighbours have moved much closer to stable democracy than was the case when Turkey first began her experiment with democratization and that the international context is even more positive than before, the country still struggles to consolidate. The chapter also calls into question the effectiveness of military organizations like NATO in professionalizing a country's armed forces. This is because Turkey's armed forces have participated in NATO since the 1950s and yet military interventionism has continued. While NATO funds and equipment might be used by civilians to try to help them in redirecting their military's attentions, this chapter and Chapter 9 indicate that there must be a consensus across the elected civilians that altering the military's role is essential for domestic reform. In the case of Turkey, the domestic political will has simply been lacking because elites are divided over the role of the Turkish armed forces in politics.

11 Conclusion

This book has analysed factors that produce democratic consolidation using the case studies of Italy, Spain, and Turkey. Of particular interest in the book has been the question of why – despite sharing many features with these two other Southern European countries – Turkey has failed to create a fully functioning democracy while the other two countries have managed to do so. As with most case-study analyses, the explanation for this difference is somewhat 'over-determined'. That is, there are too may potential explanatory factors and two few cases with which to analyse these potential causes of democratic consolidation.[1] This analysis has sacrificed the ability to provide a more definitive answer to the question of why consolidation varies across cases (e.g. by using large-N quantitative analyses) for the ability to instead say something about the historical processes in the three cases and to draw some inferences about which variables are and are not likely to have been connected to differences in democratic consolidation across the three. What does the analysis tell us about the answers to this question? Table 11.1 summarizes the factors investigated in this book and provides a rough numerical score representing the differences or similarities across the three cases for these variables. The findings for these variables are reviewed in this chapter.

The book began with an investigation into 'stateness' problems in the three countries. It was argued that a country simultaneously facing both a democratic transition and stateness problems was likely to struggle to consolidate democracy. That is, if large numbers of citizens concentrated in specific geographical regions of the country do not identify with the state and actively seek to undermine the state itself, the fledgling democracy will have difficulty stabilizing new institutions and fighting off separatist attacks at the same time. The investigation into stateness problems in this book revealed that all three countries have experienced problems in their attempts at creating a common nation-state. In Italy, there was initial rebellion in the South of the country shortly after the announcement that the Italian state had come into existence. It is generally believed that the rebellions were led by a few loosely connected groups with an interest in halting the state-building process, namely Catholic priests and a few local notables, but the vast majority of the participants held no real loyalty to the kingdom they

Table 11.1 Predictors of democratic consolidation

	Italy	Spain	Turkey
IV_1 Stateness problems: regional separatism (Chapter 2)	0.25	1	1
IV_2 Stateness problems: church/religion versus secularism (Chapter 2)	0	0	1
IV_3 Learning from experiments with democracy (Chapter 3)	1	1	1
IV_4 Long period of authoritarian rule after a breakdown of democracy (Chapter 3)	1	1	0
IV_5 Economic development (wealth) (Chapter 4)	0.5	0.5	0
IV_6 Industrialization (Chapter 4)	0.5	0.5	0
IV_7 Economic crisis (Chapter 4)	0	1	1
IV_8 Consensual constitution creation (Chapter 5)	1	1	0
IV_9 Party system adequately represented cleavages (Chapter 6)	1	1	0.5
IV_{10} Organized worker groups (Chapter 6)	1	1	0.5
IV_{11} Consensual parliament (Chapter 7)	1	0.5	0
IV_{12} Executive–parliamentary relations rules institutionalized (Chapter 7)	1	1	0
IV_{13} Regional conflict resolved via regional government (Chapter 8)	1	1	0
IV_{14} Professionalization of the military (Chapter 9)	1	1	0
IV_{15} External funding (Chapter 10)	1	1	0.5
IV_{16} NATO membership (Chapter 10)	1	1	1
IV_{17} European Union membership (Chapter 10)	1	1	0.5
DV Democratic consolidation	1	1	0

might have been asked to support and the rebellions were mostly acts of banditry. The large-scale violence was ended with the occupation of the South by the new state's army and stateness problems revolving around territorial identity were of little consequence until the end of World War II and then again in the 1990s. After World War II, the growing separatist movements on the periphery of Italian territory appear to have been assuaged by the granting of considerable policy-making autonomy to those particular regions, thereby protecting the power base of local notables, and by the time separatism began to flare up again in the 1990s – this time in the industrialized North of the country – the country's democracy was fully consolidated, although some would question its quality.

On the other hand, Spain and Turkey faced fairly severe problems with state-building by the time they began transitions to democracy. Spain was struggling with ETA violence that was directed at security forces and other key elites in the country at the time of Franco's death and during much of the initial transitional period. The state's repressive response appears to have attracted the sympathy of both the international community and citizens living in the northern regions of Spain, and the attacks on security forces helped to create the climate of hostility in which the 1981 coup was planned. Indeed, some argue that this was the intention of ETA activists – that is, essentially to provoke another civil war. Had the new regime continued to try to pursue Franquist policies of forced assimilation it is not difficult to imagine a similar revolt emerging in the neighbouring Catalonian regions. Likewise, shortly after the creation of the Turkish state leaders in the East and Southeastern regions began to organize rebellions against the state, partly in response to Mustafa Kemal's secularization policies but also partly in response to the threat to their power and authority in the region. This problem had not been resolved by the time the regime undertook a transition to democracy and it became increasingly problematic as the transition progressed.

Thus, the combination of evidence from the three countries indicates that stateness problems associated with regional identity and separatism in and of themselves do not necessarily constitute a major obstacle to democratic consolidation. Italy and Spain managed to consolidate their democracies despite small-scale separatism in the former and larger scale separatism in the latter, whereas Turkey has failed to consolidate democracy, despite having a separatist problem that is comparable to that of Spain. Therefore, the logic of comparative analysis would seem to dictate that it is not separatism itself that has created consolidation problems for Turkish democracy.

Chapter 8 of the book returned to this question and explored the manner in which state institutions address or incorporate potential stateness problems. In Spain, the Franco regime had tried and fundamentally failed to remove stateness problem by force – i.e. forced assimilation in the Basque and Catalonian regions. Despite the prospect of rebellion by the hardliners in the regime and the military during the transitional years, the leader of the transition, the UCD (representing the reformist element within the Franco regime), agreed to incorporate ambiguous provisions regarding regional autonomy and respect for regional languages into the new Spanish constitution. The effect of these provisions has been that citizens living in the Basque and Catalan regions, as well as those living in other regions, have considerable freedom to adopt and adjust policies that affect their regions, including sensitive policy areas like education in their native language. While this institutional arrangement has not completely removed the problem of ETA separatism and ended the periodic violent attacks, sympathy for this movement has declined and, as shown in the book, citizen satisfaction with the regional autonomy set-up is generally quite high in all of the Spanish regions. Thus, Spain appears to have made a successful transition to democracy while initially facing a severe stateness problem, and so stateness problems in and of themselves would not appear to be sufficient to cause a failure to consolidate democracy.

Similarly, as mentioned above, the Italian constitution included an institutional arrangement that provided for some autonomy over policy-making for 'historic' regions; such arrangements were also provided for the administrative regions but the enabling legislation for the latter was only adopted in the 1970s. The delay does not appear to have been overly problematic, however, as these regions were not demanding autonomy. At the same time, the regions that had been moving toward separatism at the end of World War II appear to have experienced few such demands after 1948 as a result of the institutional arrangement.

In Turkey, on the other hand, the structure of the state since its founding in the 1920s has been assumed to be unitary, and government policies regarding the provinces flow from this. Although there are local elections and local governors, policymaking is highly centralized, and there is no institutional mechanism that allows for variable regional policies, as in Spain and Italy. While it is in no way clear that adopting such an institutional arrangement would completely halt separatist violence – as was discussed in the case of Spain – based on the comparative analysis provided here, it seems that such arrangements increase the likelihood of reduced separatism and violence. In turn, this should reduce the use of government policies and techniques that have kept Turkey out of the realm of democratic consolidation – namely long periods of states of emergency, the use of state security courts to try civilians, and human-rights violations. Moreover, with reduced violence, the military would presumably have less reason to remain a powerful force to be used against the domestic population and civilians would have a greater chance of imposing civilian control over the Turkish military.

One of the stateness problems discussed in the book which may have had an impact on democratization experiences in the three countries relates to the role of religion in a new state. Chapter 2 indicated that for many years after its creation, the Italian state faced potentially severe legitimacy problems as a result of its hostile treatment of the Catholic Church (which included the confiscation of papal lands and general harassment of priests). Although the Church did not appear to take direct action to undermine the state after the initial 1860s rebellions in the South, its lack of support for the regime was argued to have had an indirect effect on the collapse of democracy in Italy in the 1920s. Namely, although the Church had reluctantly granted its approval to participation in elections in the early 1900s for the sake of fighting off the leftist threat, the Italian state still promoted secularism and had failed to incorporate religious interests and values into its institutional design. Thus, when those institutions began to falter a relatively large segment of the population lacked the loyalty to those institutions that may have helped to prevent collapse. Similarly, one of the major divisions that produced the Spanish Civil War revolved around the liberal state's approach to the Catholic Church. Thus, the problems surrounding church–state relations appear to have had a more direct impact on the breakdown of democracy in the Spanish Second Republic.

Both of these cases would seem to indicate that building a strictly secular state with policies that actively harm religious interests in a country that is still deeply religious is potentially problematical, and that the option of strict secularism may not be entirely appropriate in such societies. That is, a transitional state may need to strike a balance between secularism and support for (or acceptance of) religion that resonates with the majority of the population and their elite representatives. This may, indeed, be one of the main failings that has helped contribute to the collapse of Turkish democracy. In this case, the openly hostile treatment of religion has produced a group of citizens and elites who have very likely believed the Turkish state to be illegitimate, and when the institutions of the state have been on the verge of collapse, they have had little incentive to take action to support these institutions. As in Italy, there is no evidence to suggest that such groups have actively undermined the state and its institutions, but the impact is likely to have been indirect.

The book also reviewed experiences with the breakdown of democracy and the nature of authoritarianism immediately prior to the most recent transitions to democracy in each of the three countries. The cases of Spain and Italy indicate that there was a considerable amount of learning from the past in the post-war democratic transitions. Elites in Spain were keenly aware of the sorts of institutional arrangements that might spark a military-led revolt – particularly the dismantling of the monarchy and the creation of an outright federal state structure. While the Spanish state might be able to function well in the modern day under such institutional arrangements, during the transitional period attempts to establish a republic, and a *federal* one at that, would have been extremely unpopular with the armed forces and many hardliners within the regime. Reform leaders thus took their lessons from the Second Republic and avoided these sorts of institutional arrangements. Moreover, while the general atmosphere during the Second Republic had been acrimonious and violent even amongst elites, the lesson from this was clearly learned and a much more cooperative environment emerged after Franco's death.

Similarly in Italy, it was the inability of political parties and party leaders to cooperate that ultimately created a scenario in which centre-right party leaders and the monarch attempted to co-opt the fascist right in the 1920s. Post-war leaders recognized that the political violence and inability of elites to develop policies that would put a halt to this violence created a situation in which fascism, with its emphasis on order and tradition, would seem like a welcome solution. Thus, in both countries, elites – particularly those on the left of the political spectrum – seemed to have an understanding of where their predecessors had gone wrong and pursued vastly different policies as a result. At the same time, it must also be recognized that the designers of the Italian constitution and other founding rules still created institutional structures that would have the effect of producing weak governments and constant government collapse, indicating the limits of learning, particularly when individual or organized group power and representation may be at stake. The Italian experience would seem to imply that altering the institutions themselves may not necessarily be the learning experience that is most relevant to consolidating democracy.

When Turkey made its first transition to democracy in the 1940s, on the other hand, the country had had no real experience with the breakdown of democracy from which to build. However, even after a somewhat brutal end to the short experience with democracy in the 1950s, the 1960s experience failed to usher in a group of elites whose approaches had changed from acrimony to compromise; and after the 1970s intervention by the military which included a clear threat of more active intervention, elites continued to fail to work together to prevent the system from collapsing. Finally, much of the post-1980 coup period has also shown little evidence of elites learning from the past. All of this is despite the fact that institutional changes made over these decades indicate the existence of a great deal of learning, confirming again that it may not be the changing of the institutions themselves that matter for consolidating democracy.

It must also be recognized that the prior experiences with authoritarianism in the three countries was vastly different. All three leaned toward fascism under Franco, Mussolini, and Ataturk. Thus, all three had experienced considerable repression of the opposition to the regime by the time of their initial post-war transitions. The subsequent periods of outright authoritarian rule in Turkey, however, were generally very brief. The regime established by the military after the 1960 coup lasted only a few months until a new constitution could be written. Moreover, other than the execution of a handful of party elites, the brutality and repression of those months was relatively low. The period of military rule after the 1980 coup was longer and more citizens were affected by the military regime's use of torture and repression, but the numbers are still relatively small, particularly compared to the large-scale repression undertaken by the Franco regime in the years immediately following the Civil War. Thus, Turkey does not have the same experience of democracy, followed by a long period of authoritarian rule, and then a return to democracy that was witnessed in the other two countries. The experience of the latter would seem to indicate that if Turkey had faced a lengthy period of repressive dictatorship in the modern day, elite perspectives on cooperation and compromise might have changed considerably.

The case studies reveal that economic development may also help to explain the differential consolidation levels of the three countries. While all three were less well-off and less industrialized than their Northern European counterparts at the time of their transitions to democracy, it appears that there may have been substantial differences on both of these dimensions across the countries. In the 1960s, Spain experienced an economic miracle that had increased industrial output and overall wealth in the country. As a result of the increased industrialization, workers had become more concentrated than ever in the major cities of Spain and began to organize unofficial strikes even before Franco's death. These strikes could have had the effect of undermining the transition, but, in fact, the state managed to help fund wage increases despite a growing economic crisis resulting from the OPEC oil price increases. Italy, on the other hand, was economically devastated when it began its transition to democracy after World War II. It had been bombed and occupied by both the German forces and the Allies, and much of its industrial capacity was destroyed during the war. However, partly with the help of US funds, basic subsistence needs were met and industry subsequently began to thrive again in the 1950s and 1960s. Because of the increased atmosphere of cooperation during these years, left-wing parties and union leaders managed to keep a lid on worker protests for a number of years and by the time such protests began in earnest, the state and business were in a far better position to meet some of the workers' demands. In contrast, although Turkish industry has been increasing its capacity since the founding of the Turkish Republic, it appears that it has only been in the 1990s that industrial development has reached the level of that of 1950s Spain and Italy. Despite the lower level of economic development, the 1960s and 1970s still witnessed increased labour activism in the major cities. On the other hand, the lower level of overall wealth has meant that the government and industry have been harder-pressed to meet worker demands, and fighting between groups increased in the 1970s. Such protests died down in the 1980s, but this is in great part because union activity was severely restricted by the 1982 constitution.

Evidence related to economic crisis is mixed, however. Spain was suffering from high inflation and low growth during its transitional years, and these are conditions that could have destabilized the regime change process. Turkey has also faced economic crisis and the military interventions in the 1970s and 1980 were partly a result of the perceived inability of elected civilians to bring inflation and growth rates under control. Interestingly, Turkey has had one of its most stable economic periods since the election of 2002 (which produced a single-party government and thus no need for a potentially unstable coalition of governing parties). Indeed, periods of political instability have produced severe economic crisis in Turkey in previous years (e.g. 2001), indicating that it is likely to be the political situation which affects economic crisis rather than the reverse. At the very least, the fact that Spain produced a consolidated democracy despite major economic difficulties during the transitional period while Turkey has failed to consolidate democracy while also facing economic difficulties points to the possibility that economic crisis may not be the main explanation for differences in democratic consolidation.

One of the central points emphasized in this book is that the process of writing a constitution and designing other fundamental rules of the regime (e.g. how elections will be held) is likely to be amongst the chief factors explaining whether democratic consolidation occurs or not. This book has presented the argument primarily in terms of the interests of elites and the citizens they represent: all major – and potentially disruptive minor – groups must feel that they are getting their fair share out of the system, and importantly, that they will at some point have the opportunity to be winners in the system. Those who are excluded from the basic design process will very likely argue that the design itself is flawed because it works against them. This argument can also be presented in cultural terms, though. There are very few societies that are perfectly homogeneous, particularly if we consider differing socioeconomic interests or outlooks, differences in perspectives on religiosity versus secularism, and differing views on where state decision-making power ought to lie (e.g. in a monarch, a national parliament, with local governments). If representatives of some of these interests are excluded from the creation of democratic institutions themselves, as was the case in the Spanish Second Republic, then those institutions fail to represent the array of political-cultural values of the country as a whole. The problem therefore may not just be one of personal interests in retaining power, wealth, etc., but one of developing institutions that capture this vast array of perspectives on how politics ought to work. If institutions fail to capture this diversity, large minorities or even majorities have little incentive to work to protect the system, and may have tremendous incentive to undermine it instead. Thus, it is argued that one of the fundamental problems for consolidating democracy in Turkey has been the failure to try to create institutions that meet the cultural and interest-based perspectives of a wide range of elites who, in turn, represent differing views amongst the population. This is in contrast to Italy and Spain, where in both cases, their successful experiments with democracy, starting in 1948 in Italy and in 1975 in Spain, began with a representative Constituent Assembly that negotiated the basic rules of the game. As argued in the book, it becomes very difficult in such circumstances for the same elites to take action to undermine the regime or to fail to support it when they played a major role in designing its institutions in the first place. As also mentioned, it is unclear as to whether agreement would be reached amongst Turkish elites, particularly along the secular–religious divide, but no such compromise has been attempted and until very recently the system as a whole has not worked well because it has generally consisted of the imposition of the values of one group on another. In turn, this has left little will amongst elites to cooperate with one another to protect the system itself.

Similarly, representation via the party systems in the three countries has been extremely variable. The party systems of Italy and Spain have more-or-less been able to represent societal-level interests: in both countries, representatives of the left have been able to gain representation in national and regional governments; the conservative right has also been represented, as have regional interests. This has given these groups a voice in the legitimate political institutions of the state and has meant that they have not been permanently excluded from these institutions. Moreover, in the early years of the transition in Spain and throughout much of Italy's post-war history, the parties' main nationally representative institution, the national parliament, served to protect and incorporate these vastly differing perspectives, with policy output being consensually designed. This system changed in Spain once a single party won a majority of seats in the parliament, but it may be important that a consensual approach was taken in these first few years because it meant that no major group or set of elites felt that its interests were being neglected by the political system.

In Turkey, there have been times when the electoral system was designed in such a way as to make the party system more representative, and in turn, to promote more consensual behaviour on the part of party elites. The experiment appears to have failed to produce the desired outcome, though. Starting in the 1960s, a wider array of parties was indeed represented in the national parliament, and even neo-fascist and religiously oriented parties gained a foothold in national politics in this way. Part of the problem, however, was that the main centre-left party, the Republican People's Party, was perceived as colluding with the military in 1960 to bring down the Democratic Party government and causing the execution or imprisonment of much of its leadership. Moreover, recall that the only party that had representatives at the 1960 Constituent Assembly was the Republican People's Party. Thus, other parties – especially the DP's successor, the Justice Party – were able to criticize the constitution and institutional design and adamantly opposed cooperation with the RPP; the only cooperation that was achieved was done so at gunpoint, and the country descended into organized political violence that eventually prompted the 1980 military coup.

The post-1980 period exacerbated problems of representation by making both of these main parties illegal, as well as several others, and preventing them from taking part in the early days of the 1980 transition. Additionally, one of the larger parties of these decades, the religiously oriented party – was closed down on multiple occasions, thereby permanently excluding the interests it represented from national policy-making. Also important is that parties representing regional interests have been unable to win seats in the national parliament because of the high national threshold; such parties have won seats in municipal elections and in the national parliament by temporarily joining mainstream parties, but they have subsequently been closed down after the elections. Thus, unlike in Spain and Italy, both religious interests and regional ethno-nationalist interests have been excluded from the legitimate decision-making process. In the case of the religiously oriented parties, the implications are less obvious or direct. These groups have so far made no attempts to openly undermine the political system, and the effect of failed representation for these groups is likely to be in the realm of failure to support the system at times when it is in danger of collapse. In the case of the regional groups, the effects are more direct: some of their representatives have actively attacked various targets, and their actions are clearly designed to harm the Turkish state and its institutions, in great part because the state has refused to recognize their existence. As discussed in the book, such activity has provided the Turkish military with a seemingly valid excuse to expand its own power and to use extra-constitutional methods to address the problem. While the party closures themselves may be taken as an indicator of lack of consolidation of democracy, as discussed in this book, most countries that are considered to be stable democracies do have laws (or constitutional provisions) allowing them to exclude groups that threaten to destroy the regime itself. This has been the view taken by Turkish governments and the Turkish Constitutional Court toward religious parties and Kurdish-oriented parties. This book contends that in addition to the obvious point that such exclusions may be undemocratic in and of themselves, they create serious legitimacy problems for the regime that indirectly affect consolidation by promoting the growth of groups or parties that either openly and violently attack the state or fail to support the state in times of serious crisis.

Partly because of these representational issues, parliament has had a variable role in consolidating democracy in the three countries. In Italy and Spain, it has clearly served as a central site for consensus creation. For Spain, the consensual parliamentary approach ended a few years after the transition to democracy while in Italy parliamentary consensualism appears to have continued beyond the early transitional years. Parliament and parliamentary committees in these countries thus became places where different groups could hammer out policies that were acceptable to a wide range of interests during the transitional period. As discussed in the book, this created serious problems for large-scale policy design (or re-design) in Italy, in that grand policymaking was extremely difficult because of the way parliament functioned. However, the fact that parliament continued to serve as an effective vehicle for local representation and negotiation functions promoted continued cooperation amongst the parties. In Turkey, the failure of parliament to adequately represent interests because of the high electoral threshold and party closures in the post-1980 era has meant that it has been unable to serve as a site for consensus-building.

However, a comparison between 1960s–1970s Italy and Turkey may lead us to the conclusion that even adequate representation is not enough to produce consolidated democracy. Both countries witnessed a high level of representation for a wide range of groups in the national parliament via organized political parties. Both countries also witnessed a large number of strikes and organized political violence, as shown in Chapter 6, despite the high degree of representation in the legitimate political institutions. Thus, adequate representation alone cannot solve the puzzle of why organized violence produced a collapse of democracy in one case and not the other. The response of elected elites to this violence would appear to be of major importance to explaining differences in consolidation between these two cases. In Italy, elites remained committed to the democratic institutions and continued to work within the parliament and its consensual rules to develop policies that received overwhelming support, while in Turkey elites clearly were not very supportive of the military-designed institutions and behaved acrimoniously toward one another in parliament. Similarly, party elites generally refused to collaborate in government to prevent system collapse in Turkey. Once again, the lack of willingness to cooperate in making democracy work may be a result of the way the democratic institutions were designed. That is, having not been consulted in the first place on these, a very large segment of elected elites had no real reason to then protect them, leaving the group that had played a major role in designing them – the military – to step in once again. The Italian case seems to point to the conclusion that consensually designed and consensually functioning institutions may be used by willing elites in a politically mobilized society to strike the sorts of deals that will prevent the elites from opting out of these institutions.

Another source of difficulty for Turkish democracy is that parliamentary–executive relations, particularly in the realm of the power of the president, still have not been institutionalized. In the cases of Spain and Italy, there appears to be few open disputes regarding the power of the Head of State versus the power of the elected parliament and government. In Turkey, particularly since 1980, such problems have occurred partly because the 1982 Constitution was designed to give the presidency a few important powers that could be used when elected officials were perceived to be behaving incompetently. That is, the Constitution itself introduced ambiguity that has yet to be resolved by the Turkish political elites who have operated within its institutions. Such disputes have provoked considerable conflict between elected governments and the president, leading to a general appearance of incompetence and incoherence. These problems then perpetuate the military's view that it must at times protect the Turkish people from their incompetent, inefficient elected government. That is, the authority of the elected civilian elites is undermined, providing the military with the opening it needs to maintain its own power and influence in the political system. Recent proposals to change the selection process for Turkey's presidency are only likely to increase the problem of lack of institutionalization. Having a popularly elected president – as proposed by the Turkish government in 2007 – would serve to increase the authority of the president. Lack of clarity regarding authority would, in turn, increase the appearance of incompetence and keep the military in its supreme decision-making position; thus, recent proposals for reform have also included the possibility of weakening the presidency, although it is still far from clear as to how such a system might work in practice.

One of the main factors that – by definition – prevents Turkey from being counted as a consolidated democracy is the continued influence of the military over politics. Despite constitutional reforms that have tried to limit the military's influence, it is clear that such reforms have had very little effect and that high-ranking officers still perceive that they have a right and even a duty to intervene in political processes. The book has shown that such difficulties are not all that unusual, and both Italy and Spain also faced interventionism by colonels or generals. The problem was more acute in Spain, however, where – like Turkey – soldiers believed it to be their responsibility to protect national unity and the territorial integrity of the state. Indeed, such a duty was enshrined in the Spanish constitution. The implication is that in circumstances where civilians fail to protect these fundamental aspects of the state, the military has a duty to step in and do so themselves, with or without the help of the civilians. Moreover, the failure of civilians to provide such protection to the state from seemingly subversive forces may prompt officers to believe that the civilians are incompetent and must be overthrown by force. At the time of Franco's death, Spanish officers and soldiers were clearly divided over how the civilian government should be perceived and treated, and there was a risk of military overthrow as the civilian government proved unable to fight off separatist threats and threats from the left – the old sore spots that had produced the 1939 uprising. Given that the military was itself divided over the appropriateness of interventionism, it is important that the civilian elites took a unified approach to the coup attempt of February 1981. Had some civilian leaders taken a different view and supported the attempted coup, the outcome might have been very different: even if that particular attempt had failed, it would have sent a clear signal to officers that there were civilians with whom a coalition could be formed in the future to overthrow the democratic regime. The book has also described the measures taken after 1982 by the Socialist government to gain institutional control over the Spanish military. While such measures are important for the long-term protection of the democratic institutions in that they allow any group of elites to step in and retain similar levels of control over the military, it seems that it was the unification of elites on the issue of military involvement in politics that made it possible for such reforms to occur in the first place; that is, elite unification made it extremely difficult for military officials to resist the reforms.

The book also showed that the command and control structure of the Turkish military makes civilian control extremely difficult and that thus far institutional mechanisms giving civilians greater control have not yet been created. However, the reason such mechanisms have not been created is that there is not a unified approach to the military's role in Turkish politics. Many civilian elites have argued that more needs to be done to remove the military's influence over politics, but there are also many elites – and citizens – who would be fearful of taking such action. This is because they do not trust other elites – and citizens – to protect the political system itself and fear that these other individuals will produce a clear transition to long-term authoritarian rule (such as a theocracy). Again, in the absence of an opportunity to try to build agreement about the functioning of the regime and its institutions, it is difficult to know whether or not trust could be created through cross-party negotiations.

Finally, the book has considered external influences on democratic consolidation and argued that external funding – e.g. Marshall Plan or other aid – may indeed be crucial for a transitional country if it is experiencing severe economic difficulty. With very little in the way of resources to redistribute in the mid-1940s, the Italian government would have struggled to prevent large-scale hunger-driven uprisings, and the Spanish economic miracle would have been unlikely without external financial assistance. Turkey also began to rebuild its post-war economy with US assistance, but recall that the amounts granted to Turkey were considerably lower. This, in turn, may have had indirect effects on levels of wealth and industrialization in Turkey.

With regard to international organizations, it was argued that the effects of NATO membership have probably been overestimated by other researchers. All three of the countries discussed in this book are members of NATO; Italy is a founding member and Turkey joined only a few months after NATO was created. In Italy, the overwhelming defeat of the poorly equipped Italian forces in World War II and subsequent NATO membership have meant that the Italian military has been monitored and administered to a great extent by the US. Still, the early 1960s coup plot indicates that the US did not have total control over all branches of the Italian military. Also important is that the Turkish military has continued to engage in plots and overthrows of civilian governments despite NATO membership. Moreover, while membership in this IO may have given the Spanish government the opportunity to make personnel changes, redirect the interests of its military to external threats, and show that it was interested in helping to modernize the military via the provision of high-tech equipment and training, the same has not been true in Turkey, where the military's domestic role shows little signs of abating. Again, the important point seems to be that civilian governments chose to use NATO for the purpose of redirecting attention and resources, and this has altered the military's role in Spain.

The other IO discussed in this book is the European Union. The EU has been argued to have an impact on consolidation of democracy in that it serves as a rallying point for domestic elites to make the necessary reforms that will gain their countries' entry into this exclusive club of wealthy democracies. At the same time, the book has shown that there is very little that the EU can do to push such processes along if the domestic political will is lacking. With regard to our three case studies, Italy was a founding member of the European Coal and Steel Community, and at that time, the organization was not used to directly promote democracy. In addition, by the time Spain was finally admitted into the EU, civilian elites had already established new democratic institutions and had fought off their largest threat while the EU was wavering on whether to admit the country into the organization. In Turkey, the EU has clearly served to rally politicians around the reform process, but the book has shown that there is remarkable backsliding, both in terms of legislation passed by the government itself, and regarding the military's continued involvement in politics. This is despite the fact that accession negotiations have been opened with Turkey, and if it can make the necessary reforms, it seems very likely that it will finally achieve the long-desired membership in the club. Because of negative statements by the leaders of important EU countries like France and Germany, some question whether Turkey will indeed be admitted to the EU even if it meets the requirements specified in European Commission reports, but history has shown that governments in these countries can and do change (i.e. via elections), with significant consequences for Turkey's prospects for EU membership (see Müftüler-Baç and McLaren 2003); moreover, it seems that the path toward full EU membership has been institutionally set and reversing it would be extremely difficult at this point. Ultimately, it seems that democratic consolidation will be a result of large-scale political desire to make the necessary political reforms, and the prospect of EU membership may help to create incentives that will assist in this regard.

Thus overall this book has emphasized the importance of creating rules and institutions that resonate with the vast majority of the mass public and elites. The experience of the Spanish Second Republic and the Liberal Era of Italy both point to this conclusion. A political regime built on strict secularism in a society where a large portion of the mass public and their elite representatives still hold traditional religious values appears to be destined to struggle. In the case of the Spanish Second Republic, such policies contributed directly to the insurrection which led to the downfall of the Republic itself; in Italy, the failure of the regime to try to accommodate Catholic interests meant that the Church was openly hostile to the state and Catholic-oriented elites had little reason to take action to avert the regime's collapse. Indeed it is likely that fascism was seen as a way of preventing the rise of one of the Church's enemies – organized socialism. Although religious interests in Turkey have thus far not worked toward producing the downfall of the regime, it is clear that secularism has served as a fundamentally divisive issue since the founding of the Turkish Republic. The lack of attempt to accommodate and respect both of the main sides in this debate politically has meant that much attention is diverted to this issue, that many in the regime have had little interest in preventing its collapse, and that the military has been able to retain its strength and independence in the name of protecting secularism. It is clear that Turkish democracy cannot become consolidated until the latter element is changed and the military is brought under the control of elected civilians, and this particular situation is unlikely to change until civilians create basic institutions that accommodate and respect the fundamental interests of all sides. Importantly, since 2002, a religiously oriented party has led the way in institutional reform in Turkey, and this may help to resolve some of the legitimacy problems of the regime. The Italian experiences point to the conclusion that a complete overhaul of the Turkish constitution by a cross-party constituent assembly may, however, be necessary to finally put Turkey on a path toward consolidation.

The situation regarding regional interests is largely similar to that of reli-

gious interests: protection of the territorial integrity of the state has provided the Turkish military with yet another reason to retain its strength and
independence, as well as made large-scale human-rights abuses justifiable.
Clearly the military-led solution to separatism has not been entirely successful and the experience of Spain and to a lesser extent Italy would indicate
that a political solution may help to reduce terrorist activities, and in turn,
bring the military under civilian control and reduce the need for human-
rights violations as the threat to territorial integrity subsides.

This book has pointed to several factors that may have contributed to the
differing outcomes of the three countries. These have included wealth,
industrialization and economic crisis, institutionalization of rules regarding
power distribution at the national level, a consensual parliament, as well as
external factors. However, it is contended here that it is consensual rule-
making that would ultimately seem to be of utmost importance in explaining differential consolidation in Italy, Spain, and Turkey. In the face of
large-scale political violence in the case of Italy and military plotting in the
case of Spain, political elites unanimously protected the democratic institutions they had helped design. Thus, the failure of Turkish democracy, while
potentially connected to the wide range of factors discussed in this book, is
most likely to be a result of an unwillingness on the part of elites to protect
'their' institutions, and this, to a great extent, is a result of the fact that
these institutions are not really 'theirs' at all.

Appendix
Research design and case selection

Case selection in any analysis fundamentally depends on the goals of the research project. Thus, before proceeding with a discussion of the logic behind the cases selected for this study, it seems appropriate to briefly restate the particular aims of the book. As indicated in the introduction, the purpose of the book is twofold: it provides an elaboration and testing of theories of democratization *and* describes and explains the nature of the regimes being investigated. The implication of the latter is that the book can serve not only as a book on democratization but also a text on post-war politics in Italy, Spain, and Turkey. Moreover, the regimes themselves are assumed to be intrinsically interesting. Of particular interest in this project is the question of why Turkish democracy has faltered for so many decades despite facing many similar circumstances as other European regimes. This very question is thus what motivates – and fundamentally dictates – the choice of cases for the study. Ultimately, the project aims to identify the potential causal processes whereby seemingly similar situations in these countries led to differing outcomes. It must also be noted at the outset that because of the nature of many of the variables being investigated (see below) and the possibility for multiple, complicated linkages across these, large-N quantitative analyses have been deemed to be inappropriate for the study.

It should also be noted that the time-frame emphasized in all three cases is generally the post-World War II period, and specifically the period that begins when each country made its first post-war transition to democracy. For Turkey, this is 1946–50; for Italy, it is 1946–8; and for Spain, it is 1975. However, historical details from prior to these transitions which may be potentially crucial or relevant are also analysed. Furthermore, the years following each transition are also crucial in highlighting the explanations for consolidation or failed consolidation. Of particular importance for Italy will be the period between the post-war transition and the 1976–9 era of the 'historic compromise'. For Spain, this will be the period between the start of the transition in 1975 and the first subsequent change of government in 1982. In Turkey, because it is still considered to be an unconsolidated democracy, the era between its initial transition to democracy and the present is considered for analysis. However, as with the other two cases, the period up to 1982 is of special importance, as it is the decisions made during this time (1946–82) that are likely to have impacted the regime's ability to consolidate democracy. Further elaboration on the importance of these time-frames will be provided in the introductory chapter of the text.

Returning to the issue of the three cases chosen, case selection for small-N analyses always presents a basic conundrum. The conundrum begins with the need to select a small number of observations in the first place, and the need for this is fundamentally driven by human limitations in analysing vast amounts of historical detail. That is, because it is generally impossible for humans to know enough about the political and historical development of all countries (or other units) across all time points, we must often limit ourselves to small-N analyses.[1] Case selection is therefore fairly crucial in trying to draw conclusions and make generalizations about processes and phenomena. The conundrum thus is: given that we do not have unlimited knowledge about all cases and all time points, how can we go about selecting observations in the first place?

Drawing upon the logic of experimentation, there are two main methods for selecting observations within the comparative politics tradition (but see George and Bennett 2004): one is to select observations in which the phenomenon to be studied (e.g. democratic consolidation) is constant; in this case, if all observations carry the same value on the outcome, the goal is to find the explanatory variable that is also constant across the units of observation. Any variable that differs across the observations when the dependent variable is constant can be ruled out as a potential explanation for the phenomenon in question. This is generally known as John Stuart Mill's Method of Similarity (or Przeworski and Teune's (1970) Most Different Systems design).

Selecting observations in this way has come under great criticism (see King *et al.* 1994; Geddes 2003), however, because the analyst has no way of knowing whether the explanatory characteristic that is found to be present and potentially causal is also present for different outcomes on the dependent variable. Say, for instance, in the current analysis, we chose only unconsolidated democracies for analysis and we wanted to know why they were unconsolidated democracies. And for the sake of argument, let us say that we find that all of our unconsolidated democracies are using a fairly permissive form of proportional representation as their electoral formula for translating popular votes into seats. We would then conclude that proportional representation may be a cause of failed democratic consolidation. This seems like an unreasonable conclusion without also exploring cases of successful democratic consolidation – it may be (and indeed is) the case that many of these use proportional representation as well, and that the conclusion drawn from the Method of Similarity would be faulty. Although I recognize the potential uses of this technique for generating necessary causes (Collier and Mahoney 1996; Dion 1998), it must be remembered that the non-democratic observation chosen for analysis here was chosen not simply for the purpose of testing theoretical propositions about democratic consolidation but was also chosen because I – and presumably many others – find the issue of failed democratic consolidation in this case to be of interest. It is not clear that using the Method of Similarity to try to generate necessary causes for *failed* democratic consolidation would also generate explanations for why countries that faced similar potentially threatening circumstances to those faced in Turkey *did* achieve democratic consolidation.

The other main approach to case selection based on the logic of experimentation is Mill's Method of Difference, or Przeworski and Teune's (1970) Most Similar Systems. With this approach, the analyst chooses observations that do vary on the outcome but also tries to select cases in which variation on the predictor variables is limited. Thus, if the outcome varies but the potential predictors do not, those predictors can be ruled out as explanations of this variation. While this method also has its problems – for instance, the analyst may happen to select unusual observations that indicate a relationship when in fact for most other observations there is no relationship – the fundamental logic of the system is far more appropriate than the Method of Similarity to the questions posed in the research conducted in this book.

That said, it must be acknowledged that no small-N analysis is full-proof, and either design faces the criticism raised above – what if case A, B, or C was added to the analysis? Hypothetically, the only real way to address this criticism is to take on board the universe of cases. Practically speaking, this type of solution would mean either (a) we come to know very little about phenomena or processes because we simply cannot accumulate enough relevant knowledge about all cases or (b) we switch to large-N quantitative analyses. While the latter may be a reasonable solution, it is notoriously weak at incorporating historical linkages and analysis and ultimately requires a smaller-N approach to provide guidance regarding which historical phenomena to measure in the first place.

Ultimately, the small-N approach used in the proposed book cannot establish causality definitively, and realistic users of the approach in the modern day realize that this is the case. What we *can* hope to achieve is some ability to rule out potential explanations by using one of the systems of logic discussed above (or a combination of the two), and to provide some analytical guidance as to what might cause the phenomena or processes in question (see Savolainen 1994) and how these causal processes and mechanisms appear to work.

So how *have* the cases been selected for this study, then? The closest equivalent would be Mill's Method of Difference, or Przeworski and Teune's Most Similar Systems. Recall that the goal of the project is to explain the presence of Y (democratic consolidation) in some countries and the absence of Y in others, particularly the absence of democratic consolidation in Turkey. Thus, in terms of case selection, the goal is to find at least one observation for comparison which shares many similar characteristics to Turkey but which differs on the outcome variable – democratic consolidation. Again, it is for this reason that countries like 'another Muslim case', as suggested by one reader, would be inappropriate, as – to the author's knowledge – there are not examples of consolidated democracies amongst Muslim countries that would provide useful comparisons.

Moreover, Turkey's historical connections with Europe via its late incorporation into the European system of states (incorporation of the declining Ottoman Empire, that is), its inclusion in major European organizations like the OEEC (and later the OECD) and the Council of Europe, and finally the treatment of the country by the EEC and later the EU would indicate that it is at least equally close to Europe, if not closer, than it is to Muslim neighbours such as Iran, Iraq, and Syria. Amongst the important points to note here are (a) that the EEC signed an association agreement with Turkey in 1963 which was very similar to the one signed with Greece – a country whose European 'credentials' are usually not questioned and (b) when Turkey lodged its application for full EC membership in 1987, the response was very different than that given to Morocco, which had lodged an application for full EC membership in the same year. In the case of Morocco, the EC responded by indicating that the country was not eligible for full EC membership because it was not European. No such response was given to Turkey and indeed in 1999, Turkey was offered candidacy in the EU and negotiations for full membership are under way. While international recognition is certainly not the only way to define 'European', it is contended here that agreements with the EEC/EC/EU have brought Turkey further into the European geopolitical realm.[2] Moreover, as demonstrated in the book itself, Turkey has shared many similar experiences to other European countries, particularly the late- and incomplete-industrializers (see below).[3]

In an attempt to narrow the range of cases, then, we turn to Europe for potential comparison cases. The question then is how to choose amongst the many consolidated European democracies. At this point, it seems that academic literature on democratic consolidation can provide some useful starting points regarding case selection. Specifically, based on this literature, it seems reasonable to try to hold constant the level of economic development and industrialization, as well as the timing and problems of state-building processes.

First, quantitative literature on democratic consolidation has consistently found a strong connection between economic development and consolidation. There are multiple potential reasons for this connection outlined in the literature and in Chapter 4 of this book, and the two of these discussed extensively in the book are related to industrialization and to the ability of government to redistribute resources, thereby 'buying off' potentially undermining forces at the time of the transition to democracy. With regard to the former, it is thought by some that industrialization creates a large economic class with considerable power (the middle class in particular) that demands an increased say in the running of political institutions – which have an impact on economic institutions – and that in a highly industrial society, this class tends to be large enough and organized enough to then also prevent a breakdown of democracy (see Chapter 4 of the book). Although qualitative research has provided considerable evidence to counter the contention that it is the middle class that is important (see Rueschemeyer *et al.* 1992), such research does not necessarily counter the contention that industrialization matters. Thus, selecting observations that are similar on this variable allows us to investigate other potential causes of differences in democratic consolidation. Assuming that Turkey is a reasonable observation to have selected as a non-consolidated democracy, this leaves us with the problem of selecting similar observations that are consolidated democracies, again attempting to remain within the European context. In fact, the industrialization experienced by Turkey in the two decades leading up to its first transition to democracy was similar to that initially experienced by Spain and Italy. In both of these cases, industrial development was marked at the time of their transitions to democracy by (a) a slowly declining but still relatively large agricultural sector, (b) industrial development mostly being foreign-led, particularly by other European countries, rather than being led by domestic entrepreneurs (which has significant implications for the above-stated arguments regarding the middle class), and (c) prior failed attempts in all three cases at strong state-led development policies under fascist dictators (Mussolini, Franco, and Kemal). It is also important to point out that in contrast, for instance, to Northern European countries, the industrial development that did occur in these three countries was highly concentrated in a very limited number of cities. That is, it was not widespread across the three countries in question, with the Industrial Revolution passing by much of the territory of these countries (see Sapelli 1995). All of this implies the lack of existence of the large, organized middle class (or other class) that modernization theorists might argue to be important for maintaining a consolidated democracy.

Another potential economic explanation for democratic consolidation may lie in the actual resources that a state can distribute. Imagine a poor country that makes a transition to democracy and allows for universal suffrage (or at least universal male suffrage). Given that the country as a whole is relatively poor, this implies that the poor in the country represent a relatively large segment of the population. This, in turn, implies that – under a system of universal suffrage – these groups are going to gain representation in government. Naturally, their demands will relate to redistribution, but in a context in which there are not many resources to redistribute, such demands are likely to go unmet. There are many cases like this, in which strike action, riots, etc., increase, creating a situation in which a non-democratic force can offer proposed solutions to the economic difficulties and subsequent political chaos. If, however, the state had sufficient resources to redistribute at the time of the early fragile days of a transition, such difficulties might be avoided. Again, given that the non-democratic case selected here was relatively poor at the time of the transition to democracy in the 1946–50 period, it seems reasonable to select other relatively poor countries for comparison. In the case of Italy's post-war transition to democracy, the country was devastated by World War II and had very little left in the way of industrial capacity (which would then have presumably helped to fuel a rapid economic recovery). This was the context in which its democratic transition took place. Turkey was in a similar position. Although its industrial development had not been as strong as Italy's and although it stayed out of World War II until the very end, what industrial capacity it did have was – like Italy's – directed toward mobilizing for war (as the country was under threat of invasion from both the Soviet Union and Germany). Industry in both countries was, therefore, weak and directed toward providing for the military rather than for a civilian economy. Spain's democratic transition came at a later historical period, but also occurred in a relatively poor economy that at the time was struggling with economic crisis. In all three cases, US aid had been provided shortly after World War II to assist with economic development, but at the time of all three transitions, the economies were relatively poor and weak vis-à-vis Northern Europe (see Chapter 4 of the book). Thus, investigating these three countries allows us to hold this potential predictor as constant as possible and to investigate other hypotheses. In short, it provides the opportunity to explore the reasons for differences in consolidation amongst relatively poor countries and may also provide some useful information regarding the potential for consolidating democracy in the vast majority of unconsolidated democracies, most of which are neither wealthy nor industrialized.

Literature on consolidation is fairly emphatic about the necessary precondition of there being an uncontested state in which to launch democratic institutions. Thus, by the time democratic institutions began to be adopted in places like Britain and France, the creation of nation-states in these countries had long been under way. In stark contrast, such processes began relatively late in Turkey, and so given the potential importance of this independent variable, other observations that are also late-comers to the nation-state building process were selected for comparison. Spain provides a fairly obvious comparison for the Turkish case on this point: like the Ottomans, Spanish rulers made very little attempt to build any sort-of common national identity until after the loss of the last few pieces of its empire. In both countries, efforts at nation-building were stepped up in the 1920s, and in the case of Spain, stepped up considerably after the Spanish Civil War. Italian attempts at nation-state building were more concerted after the elite-led Italian unification in 1860, but were still relatively weak given the low levels of literacy, particularly in the South (see Chapter 2 of the book). Thus, all three cases represent latecomers to the process of nation-state building. Moreover, two of these – Turkey and Spain – represent cases in which significant portions of the citizenry question the very existence of the state. Some democratization researchers would contend that the latter factor does not bode well at all for creating a consolidated democracy.

However, one of these cases is indeed counted as a consolidated democracy (Spain), whereas the other (Turkey) is not.

The contemplation of this potentially important variable in the analysis provided in this book is the main reason that alternative cases such as Greece and Portugal were ruled out of consideration for inclusion in the analysis. Namely, neither of these countries at the time of their democratic transitions faced a situation in which stateness itself was in question. In Greece, this is primarily due to the population exchanges that occurred with Turkey in the 1920s after the conclusion of the Turkish War of Independence. In Portugal, this is because the territory itself is generally culturally and linguistically homogeneous. Some might therefore contend that consolidation has been possible in these countries partly because they were so culturally homogeneous at the time of their democratic transitions. This could indeed be the case, but Spain's experience indicates that this may not actually be a necessary condition for democracy and that drastic measures like partition may not be required for democratic consolidation.

Thus, the focus of the analysis here is on late and incomplete industrializers and late state-builders such that the observations in question are facing similar circumstances of poverty, weak industrialization, and the potentially severe problem of incomplete state-building. This then leaves other potential independent variables available for investigation. These include learning from early experiments with democracy and the breakdown of democracy, constitution building processes, social and political cleavages, electoral systems and parties, executive-parliamentary relations, functioning of parliament, the resolution of regional conflict (related to stateness problems discussed above), the professionalization of the military, and external influences on consolidation. The analysis is presented in Table 11.1 (see page 256).

The analysis is built upon the logic that if a potential independent variable does not co-vary with the dependent variable, that potential independent variable is ruled out as having been an unlikely cause of different outcomes on the dependent variable (although I recognize the potential problem of equifinality (see Ragin 1987)). Independent variables that vary in the same way as the dependent variable are ruled *in* as potential causes.

Some may contend at this point that a simpler two-case comparison between Spain and Turkey is appropriate and that the Italian case adds little to the analysis. However, it is argued here that the Italian case provides additional leverage for testing the multiple contending hypotheses under investigation. Particularly important here is the issue of political and social cleavage strength and representation. Older academic literature (Huntington 1968) and more modern approaches (Berman 1997) point to the importance of representation of major interests in government institutions such as parliament via political parties for maintaining stable, consolidated democracy. However, if we were to compare across the Spanish and Turkish cases only, the conclusion drawn would be that there is little hope for consolidated democracy in Turkey until the country reaches the point that Spain had reached in 1975, in which citizens had relatively little interest in politics and parties had started to become cartel-like parties. However, incorporating the post-war Italian case provides leverage by introducing a case which also had major, deep social cleavages that often found expression via radical, sometimes violent means, a similar situation that was faced by Turkey in the early days of its democratic transition. Given the potential importance of this variable in explaining the breakdown of Turkish democracy (and thus the failure to consolidate) it thus seems of prime importance to include a case that is similar on this variable to then determine what *does* explain democratic consolidation in instances of deep cleavages and violent expression of these. The incorporation of the Italian case then helps us to rule this potential variable out as the key explanation for differences in consolidation across the three cases studied, or at least to elaborate the processes whereby deep cleavages and violence do or do not result in the breakdown of democracy. In other words, adding the case of Italy allows us to thus rule out deep-seated cleavages and violence as a *sufficient* explanation on its own for failed consolidation.

Similarly, comparing the two cases of Spain and Turkey might lead us to the conclusion that the functioning of parliament and parliamentary-executive relations has little impact on democratic consolidation. Both countries have tended to use majoritarian approaches in parliament (in Spain this was the case after the 1982 elections), and one has achieved democratic consolidation while the other has not. However, this ignores the variable mentioned above – deep, unresolved political cleavages. As Morlino (1995) argues, majoritarianism would appear to be unproblematic when most major cleavages have worked themselves out and are no longer major points of contention. If, on the other hand, feelings about the distribution of resources and other values still run deeply in a country and are being organized by political elites or interest group leaders, then a more consensual approach to the running of parliament and parliamentary–executive relations may help to produce consolidated democracy. Again, this is a finding that might be missed if the focus was on a two-case Spain–Turkey comparison.

Equally, by comparing only Italy and Turkey, other conclusions drawn would be on shaky ground. For instance, given the lack of severe stateness problem in Italy – in that there were relatively minor separatist movements forming in Italy in the late 1940s – when it began its post-war transition to democracy, one might conclude that, as argued by Rustow (1970) as well as Linz and Stepan (1996), this is indeed a necessary pre-condition for achieving consolidated democracy. Thus, again, the prognosis for Turkish democracy is not good, in that until something is done to remove the separatists in the East and Southeast (something which has already been attempted, in fact) and the country no longer faces this stateness problem, fully consolidated democracy cannot be achieved. Introducing Spain to the analysis, once again, gives us leverage: Spain has managed to achieve full consolidation despite stateness problems, and so provides a reasonable comparison indicating how this might be accomplished in a case which faces similar difficulties and pointing to the conclusion that while stateness may produce *difficulties* for democratic consolidation, it is not necessarily the key factor producing failed consolidation. That is, it is certainly not *sufficient* on its own to do so.

Finally, an Italy–Turkey comparison would also lead us to the conclusion that unless a country's military is badly defeated and shamed – as in Italy's defeat in World War II – and as long as the military has not had a strong tradition of involvement in political matters, it appears that consolidation is unlikely. The Spanish comparison provides leverage by introducing an observation that has had a similar history of military independence and coup-plotting and a military with a similar initial self-devined remit to that of the Turkish military: to protect the territorial integrity of the state. Moreover, prior to the 1980s, very much like the modern Turkish military, the Spanish forces had been geared toward maintaining control of the domestic population rather than fighting external battles, thus providing Spanish officers with precisely the right equipment with which to stage a coup if the political or economic situation appeared to become out of control. And, indeed, some officers had such a perception in the early years of the Spanish transition and attempted to carry out a military coup. The perception of civilian governments being out of control and failing to protect the very nature and existence of the state has also permeated the Turkish military at times and has led to multiple military interventions since the initial transition to democracy in the 1946–50 period. Thus, Spain offers a reasonable comparison case for how a military with very similar predispositions and capabilities can be transformed into one that is no longer active in political decision-making, thereby paving the way for consolidating democracy. Thus, once again, a history of military independence and military involvement in politics can be shown to be *insufficient* on its own to explain failed democratic consolidation.

Thus I recognize that observations have been chosen both because of their variation on the dependent variable and out of a need to minimize variation on independent variables in order to eliminate causal explanations and to suggest explanations which are likely to be key. As with any selection method which either fails to use the universe of potential observations or fails to select randomly from these, the method chosen here clearly faces the potential of selection bias (see King *et al.* 1994; George and Bennett 2004). The implications of this bias are twofold: it is possible that for some of the factors that are found to be invariant across all three observations and thus eliminated as potential causal explanations, in fact, in a larger pool of observations, these might indeed be associated with democratic consolidation. Similarly, factors that *are* argued to be associated with democratic consolidation in these three observations may not be associated when a larger array of observations is analysed. This is a critique that any small-N study must face. Although one might be tempted to resort to using only large-N quantitative analyses, the point is that such analyses generally miss a wide range of events and processes. In fact, many such events and processes serve as the subject matter for this book. The main conclusions drawn from the research here – fortunately – are generally consistent with many other findings on democratic consolidation. For some, this may make the findings uninteresting; however, it is contended here that this provides confidence in the findings and arguments themselves. It is also contended that tracing the possible processes that lead countries to different outcomes is useful for exploring the cases themselves as well as general theoretical propositions (see George and Bennett 2004).

Notes

1 Introduction

1 For instance, the four-volume *Transitions From Authoritarian Rule* series edited by O'Donnell *et al.* (1986), Juan Linz and Alfred Stepan's *Problems of Democratic Transition and Consolidation* (1996), and *The Problems of Democratic Consolidation: Southern Europe in Comparative Perspective* (1995) edited by Nikiforos Diamandouros and Richard Gunther, to name a few.

2 Some scholars also argue that there are regimes that are simply quasi-democratic or electoral authoritarian regimes, and that rather than being in transition to democracy, the nature of the regimes is seemingly permanent quasi-democracy (see the special issue of *Journal of Democracy*, 'Elections without Democracy', 13(2): 21–80).

3 Other examples of relatively backward countries that began democratic transitions include France in 1870 and Sweden in 1890 (Rustow 1970).

4 Huntington (1991) finds that in the modern day (the 'third wave' of transitions) transitions tend to occur at middle levels of economic development; this is because countries at the higher levels have been democratic for a long time already and those at the lowest levels are not yet ready for democracy, with the citizenry and government presumably being preoccupied with basic necessities (and in many cases, dealing with civil war resulting from a shortage of such necessities).

5 The National Security Council was first established in the 1960 constitution, but its formal oversight powers were increased in the 1982 constitution (see Zurcher 2004).

6 According to Article 118 of the 1982 Constitution:

> The National Security Council shall submit to the Council of the Ministers its views on the advisory decisions that are taken and ensuring the necessary condition with regard to the formulation, establishment, and implementation of the national security policy of the state. The Council of Ministers shall evaluate decisions of the National Security Council concerning the measures that it deems necessary for the preservation of the existence and independence of the state, the integrity and indivisibility of the country and the peace and security of society.
>
> In addition, 'The agenda of the National Security Council shall be drawn up by the President of the Republic taking into account the proposals of the Prime Minister and the Chief of the General Staff'.

According to Article 26:

> Everyone has the right to express and disseminate his thoughts and opinion by speech, in writing or in pictures or through other media, individually or

collectively. This right includes the freedom to receive and impart information and ideas without interference from official authorities. This provision shall not preclude subjecting transmission by radio, television, cinema, and similar means to a system of licensing.

The exercise of these freedoms may be restricted for the purposes of protecting national security, public order and public safety, the basic characteristics of the Republic and safeguarding the indivisible integrity of the State with its territory and nation, preventing crime, punishing offenders, withholding information duly classified as a state secret, protecting the reputation and rights and private and family life of others, or protecting professional secrets as prescribed by law, or ensuring the proper functioning of the judiciary.

The formalities, conditions and procedures to be applied in exercising the right to expression and dissemination of thought shall be prescribed by law.

According to Article 28:

Anyone who writes or prints any news or articles which threaten the internal or external security of the state or the indivisible integrity of the state with its territory and nation, which tend to incite offence, riot or insurrection, or which refer to classified state secrets and anyone who prints or transmits such news or articles to others for the above purposes, shall be held responsible under the law relevant to these offences. Distribution may be suspended as a preventive measure by the decision of a judge, or in the event delay is deemed prejudicial, by the competent authority designated by law.

Finally, according to Article 68:

Judges and prosecutors, members of higher judicial organs including those of the Court of Accounts, civil servants in public institutions and organizations, other public servants who are not considered to be labourers by virtue of the services they perform, members of the armed forces and students who are not yet in higher education institutions, shall not become members of political parties.

The membership of the teaching staff at higher-education institutions in political parties is regulated by law. This law cannot allow those members to assume responsibilities outside the central organs of the political parties. It also sets forth the regulations which the teaching staff at higher-education institutions shall observe as members of political parties.

7 See Freedom House country report, 2005 at www.freedomhouse.org (consulted 16 August 2006).
8 Mehmet Yılmaz 'As Turkey turns to "police state", is it farewell to the Copenhagen Criteria?', *Hürriyet* daily newspaper, 13 June 2006; Tufan Türenç 'Some pleasure-reading for PM Erdoğan', *Hürriyet* daily newspaper, 22 May 2006. Cüneyt Arcayürek 'Blow to workers', *Cumhuriyet* daily newspaper, 21 April 2006; Oktay Ekşi 'Erdoğan and his idea of secularity', *Hürriyet* daily newspaper, 28 March 2006; Fatih Altayly 'Not appointing someone is a risk', *Sabah* daily newspaper, 28 March 2006; Mehmet Yılmaz 'Despicable is he who doesn't reveal what he knows!', *Hürriyet* daily newspaper, 27 March 2006; Güngör Mengi, 'A string of errors', *Vatan* daily newspaper, 20 March 2006.
9 For instance, in 1998, the largest party in parliament, the Islamist Welfare Party (RP) was closed for 'threatening the official secularist order by attempting to boost the role of Islam in public life'; see '...and they closed Refah: Court bans Necmettin Erbakan from political leadership for five years and strips

parliamentary membership of five more Refah deputies', *Turkish Daily News*, 17 January 1998. See also 'Refah closure goes into effect', *Turkish Daily News*, 23 February 1998. Parties representing Kurdish interests have also been closed; see 'HADEP closed, DEHAP in row', *Turkish Daily News*, 14 March 2003.

10 See, for instance, the Turkey report on www.freedomhouse.org or the European Commission's 2005 Progress Report on Turkey at ec.europa.eu/enlargement/key_documents/pdf/2005/package/sec_1426_final_en_progress_report_tr.pdf (consulted 16 August 2006).

11 According to Article 21(2) of the German Basic Law: 'Parties which, by reason of their aims or the behavior of their adherents, seek to impair or abolish the free democratic basic order or to endanger the existence of the Federal Republic of Germany are unconstitutional.'

12 Different variations of religious-oriented and Kurdish parties have been closed down multiple times. This will be discussed further in Chapter 6. See Kogacioğlu (2004) for an analysis of party closures in Turkey.

13 See 'Author's trial set to test Turkey by Sarah Rainsford, *BBC News*, 14 December 2005; 'Date set for Shafak trial in Turkey', *Guardian Unlimited*, 3 August 2006; also www.freemedia.at/cms/ipi/freedom_detail.html?country=/KW0001/KW0003/KW0085/ (consulted 16 August 2006); www.rsf.org/article.php3?id_article=13732 (consulted 16 August 2006).

14 'Turkey: journalist imprisoned for "insult to ataturk"', Rapid Action Network–10 June 2004–RAN 28/04 Network of Concerned Historians odur.let.rug.nl/~nch/action36.htm (consulted 11 August 2006); 'Turkey: Article 301: how the law on "denigrating Turkishness" is an insult to free expression', Amnesty International www.amnesty.org.ru/library/Index/ENGEUR440032006?open&of=ENG-2U5 (consulted 11 August 2006).

15 See www.freedomhouse.org Turkey country report; Amnesty International's report on Turkey at web.amnesty.org/report2006/tur-summary-eng; see also the EU's country report on Turkey at ec.europa.eu/enlargement/key_documents/pdf/2005/package/sec_1426_final_en_progress_report_tr.pdf (all consulted 16 August 2006).

16 See the European Commission's report at ec.europa.eu/enlargement/key_documents/pdf/2005/package/sec_1426_final_en_progress_report_tr.pdf (consulted 16 August 2006). See also 'Human Rights Association branch closed down', *Turkish Daily News*, 20 May 2000

17 www.freedomhouse.org/template.cfm?page=22&year=2005&country=6851 (consulted 16 August 2006); see also European Commission's Annual report on Turkey.

18 Note that others contend that ethnolinguistic fractionalization may pose a promising situation for the creation of stable democracy (Horowitz 1985; Hardgrave 1994; Reilly 2001).

19 As Przeworski *et al.* (1996) argue, however, it is not only democratic forces that learn, but so do antidemocratic forces. Moreover, countries often reuse old democratic constitutions in periods of redemocratisation even if those constitutions previously failed to protect against democratic breakdown.

20 Note that economic crisis can also produce a breakdown of authoritarian rule; essentially, whichever regime type in place at the time of the crisis is at risk of breaking down.

21 However, the Turkish government has recently proposed a constitutional amendment to alter the selection process whereby the Turkish president would be elected by the public rather than by parliament (see Chapter 7).

2 Problems in state building

1 There are, of course, exceptions to this generalization; the Swiss and Belgian states have been built upon the premise of linguistic and cultural diversity and governing institutions are designed to protect this distinctiveness. None of the states discussed in this book have adopted this as their guiding premise in state building, however.

2 This is in contrast to state building in the US, for instance, which from the start was forced to address the tension between centralization and retention of power for existing local governing units.

3 Some of the difficulties, particularly class conflict, did create considerable instability of government institutions, but they do not appear to have threatened the existence of the state itself. These conflicts will be discussed in the following chapter and in Chapter 6.

4 For histories of the creation of the modern Italian state, see Denis Mack Smith 1959 or Martin Clark 1984; Absalom 1995; also see Derek Beales 1971 or Harry Hearder 1983 on the *Risorgimento*; see Ziblatt 2006: Chapters 4 and 5 for a discussion of the issue of regional loyalty and state building in Italy.

5 Again, see Denis Mack Smith (1959), Absolom (1995), Beales (1971), and Hearder (1983).

6 According to Mack Smith (1959: 260–1), parents preferred that their children earn money rather than go to school and they also associated education with taxes. Sometimes protests against this perceived extra taxation took the form of assaults on school buildings. According to the 1911 census, almost half of the population was still illiterate.

7 It should be noted, however, that Italians do continue to use local dialects at relatively high rates (see Lepschy *et al.* 1996).

8 According to the 1931 census, only 20 per cent were still illiterate, although there were large regional differences; for instance, 48 per cent in Calabria were still illiterate in 1931 (see Mack Smith 1959: 416).

9 Note that some scholars argue that class and partisan organizations actually served to undermine any possibility for a cohesive national unity (Rusconi 1993; Gentile 1996; see review essays by Battente 2000, 2001).

10 Note that while the total size of the breakaway populations in question amount to similar levels to the percentages in Spain and Turkey discussed below (for instance, the Sicilian population currently represents almost 9 per cent of the overall Italian population, Friuli-Venezia Giulia, approximately 2 per cent, and Trentino-Alto Adige approximately 1.5 per cent, and Valle d'Aosta 0.2 per cent; see en.wikipedia.org/wiki/Ranked_lists_of_Italian_regions (consulted 17 August 2007), the post-war separatism in Italy appears to have been fairly temporary; for this reason, it is counted here as a minor problem of separatism vis-à-vis Spain and Turkey. Chapter 8 elaborates on the nature of the post-war separatism in Italy, however.

11 Moreover, state builders have been able to point to the marriage of Isabella I of Castile and Ferdinand II of Aragon in 1479 as the key starting point of the Spanish nation-state (although some historians trace it further back to the unitary kingdom created by the Visigothic monarchy in the late sixth and early seventh centuries; see Fernandez-Armesto 2000; Barton 2004: xv)

12 This hypothesis is also supported by the Spanish case of Galicia, where regional identity is strong and the use of Galician is still widespread (see US Library of Congress country studies: countrystudies.us/spain/38.htm), but resistance to the Spanish state in this region has been virtually non-existent, perhaps a result of the lack of industrial centres there.
  Olivares indicates that one of the results of increased industrialization in

Catalonia – which was ironically partly fuelled by Spanish government policies to help Catalonia to industrialize – was the development of nationalism, which was created primarily by the bourgeois classes. Again, as in Italy, it was the intellectuals and middle classes that began searching Catalan history for indications of the region's past greatness (1946: 377).

13 For instance, in 1931, a liberal–socialist alliance ended the Concordat and removed educational rights from the Church's realm.

14 It appears that some attempt had been made to define Ottomanism once the empire began to decline; see www.einaudi.cornell.edu/europe/initiatives/pdf/Morin_Paper.pdf (consulted 5 April 2006).

15 A thorough discussion of the caliphate is beyond the scope of this book. However, the word 'caliphate' comes from the Arabic word *khalifa*, which means successor. This was applied to the person who was chosen as the successor to Muhammed when he died. It implies someone who is a spiritual, political, and military leader of Muslims. Prior to 1517, the caliphate was controlled primarily by Arab leaders, but when the Ottoman Empire captured Egypt in 1517, it also captured the symbols of the caliphate and became the controller of Islamic holy places.

16 See www.uis.unesco.org/en/stats/statistics/UIS_Literacy_Country2002.xls (consulted 10 April 2006).

17 It should also be noted that unease with the most immediate past made the use of the accomplishments of the Ottoman Empire a difficult myth on which to build. Specifically, the founders of the new Turkish Republic were trying to make a clean break from the Ottoman past, and making such a break while also forging a new national identity on this past would have been extremely difficult.

18 The only officially recognized minorities in Turkey are religious minorities that are named in the Lausanne Treaty; since Kurds are Muslim, they have not been counted amongst the minority population of Turkey, and so no special category for this group has been included on census counts. Thus, the figure provided here is simply an estimate; see US Library of Congress, countrystudies.us/turkey/28.htm (consulted 10 April 2006).

3 Experiencing the breakdown of democracy

1 Although, there were pre-state experiences with parliamentary control, particularly during the medieval period (Mack Smith 1959: 30), this chapter focuses on the development of parliamentary democracy after the founding of the new Italian state (but prior to Italy's most recent, post-World War II transition from authoritarianism to democracy). As Mack Smith (1959) argues, these medieval practices would have largely been lost by the time of the creation of the new Italian state in any case.

2 Note that in addition to the Chamber of Deputies, there was a Senate which consisted of life peers appointed by the king on the recommendation of the prime minister (Clark 1984: 65).

3 Clark estimates that the Jewish population only represented about 0.1 per cent of the entire Italian population and had never been a target for popular resentment; Italy's new policies toward Italian Jews were embarrassing to many and many others thought it to be pathetic imitation of the more powerful German regime (Clark 1984: 257–8).

4 The party only won 56 per cent of the vote, but the electoral system was designed to create such distortions.

4 Pre-transition economic structures and economic development

1 But see Epstein *et al.* (2006).
2 Problems included destruction of forests which worsened the South's long-standing erosion problem, overpopulation of southern agriculture as a result of government's restrictive migration policies, and encouragement of high birth rate (Allen and Stevenson 1974: 6–7).
3 Daily caloric consumption of 1737 per person, compared to 2652 in 1936–40 (Allen and Stevenson 1974: 8).
4 According to one scholar amongst the vital resources for the Nationalists was the petroleum provided by US oil companies: Texas Oil Company provided the rebels with oil at the outbreak of the conflict, while Texaco, Shell, Standard of New Jersey and the Atlantic Refining Company extended credits of at least $20 million to purchase oil in the course of the conflict (Whealey 1977: 146; see also Herbert Feis 1948; Traina 1968).
5 The *sindicatos* degenerated into sham bureaucracies and laws attempting agrarian reform by breaking up the *latifundios* became dead letter laws (Harrison 1985: 120–2).
6 In 1956 inflation was 9.1 per cent and rose to 15.5 per cent in the following year (Harrison 1985: 137).
7 Opus Dei is an organization originally founded in Spain in 1928, and is built upon Catholic principles – although it was only recognized by the Catholic Church in 1950. In addition to promoting morality and holiness amongst its members, the doctrine of the organization also promotes the importance of work and to 'find God in daily life' and the excellent performance of work as a service to society and as an offering to God (see the writings of Opus Dei founder, Jose-maría Escrivá, at www.escrivaworks.org/). These individuals became influential in the Franco regime, both in terms of moral, social, and, importantly for this chapter, economic policy.
8 It must be noted that there is disagreement amongst economists over whether the Stabilization Plan and subsequent government plans were key to these developments or if it was more to do with increased tourism, emigrant remittances, and foreign investment or the general economic circumstances of boom (Harrison 1985: 145–6).
9 Note that the official title for a prime minister in Spain is 'President of the Government', but because the role is functionally equivalent to that of prime minister, this book tends to use the latter when referring to the Spanish head of government.
10 However, Linz and Stepan contend that in the case of Spain there is no direct connection between economic development and the onset of the *transition* to democracy because Spain had reached a level of development that should have led to a transition to democracy several years before Franco's death and there was little pressure from the business classes to democratise (1996: 112). On the other hand, it may be the case that the economic development that did occur created positive conditions that helped to prevent a return to authoritarian rule.
11 The manufacturing industry's share of GDP increased from 8.4 per cent to 13.4 per cent between 1927 and 1929. In 1927, 78 per cent of manufacturing enterprises were small scale or family run; by 1938, that percentage was 79 per cent (Hansen 1991: 330–1).
12 Hershlag indicates that in 1938, income per capita in Turkey was 75 dollars, while in Italy, it was 144 dollars. By way of comparison with more developed economies, France's income was 251 dollars, Britain's was 486 dollars, and the US was 519 dollars (Hershlag 1959: 165)

13 As Hershlag notes, however, the amount of aid to Turkey should not be overestimated (1959: 205).
14 That is, the economy was not converted to a full-scale market economy (Hansen 1991: 340).

5 Constitution building

1 As will be seen in the next chapter, however, given the nature of the cleavages and subsequent differences over the basic nature of the regime itself, along with the seemingly irresponsible behaviour of elected elites, it is also not clear that leaving the elected officials to sort out constitutional details would necessarily have put Turkey onto the path of stable democracy.
2 This is certainly how the British saw things; British Prime Minister Winston Churchill believed that the king, Victor Emanuel, and his choice of prime minister, Marshall Badoglio, were the best choices for helping Britain to guarantee its own interests in the region and saw no point in negotiating with the anti-Fascists (Ginsborg 1990: 40).
3 The closeness of the vote, however, should make it clear that a significant minority still wished to retain the monarchy. Moreover the differences across regions is striking: the vast majority in Northern regions voted to abolish the monarch while the vast majority in Southern regions voted to keep it (see Ginsborg 1990: 98–9). Thus, there was clearly the potential for conflict on the basis of the differences across these regions. As discussed in Chapter 2, however, the South has not tended to be all that strong at organized resistance, and this case was no different.
4 See Sassoon (1997: Chapter 12).
5 It is paradoxical that it was the DC that took so long to implement the constitutional provisions dealing with the regions and that the Communist party ended up performing very well in regional and local elections and came to advocate decentralization in order to experiment with new forms of local democracy (Sassoon 1997: 213–14).
6 The person who wrote the second paragraph was a socialist leader who represented the most radical wing of the non-communist socialist tradn in Italy (Sassoon 1997: 210–11).
7 For an excellent overview of the constitution-building process in Spain, see Heywood (1995: Chapter 2); also see Maravall and Santamaria (1985: 85–9); Gilmour 1985; Carr 1986; Preston 1986.
8 Earle (1925) also provides the full text of the 1924 Constitution.
9 'EU Report: Turkey Must Do More', *Turkish Daily News*, 15 November 2001.
10 'Turkey agrees to death penalty ban, BBC News online (9 January 2004); consulted 9 October 2006; see news.bbc.co.uk/1/hi/world/europe/3384667.stm.
11 'Turkey reform targets army power', BBC News online, 30 July 2003; consulted 9 October 2006; see news.bbc.co.uk/1/hi/world/europe/3110173.stm.
12 'CHP to block constitutional changes until elections', *Turkish Daily News*, 30 November 2006.

6 The representation of social and political cleavages

1 Clientelism can be thought of as 'the proferring of material goods in return for electoral support, where the criterion of distribution that the patron uses is simply: did you (will you) support me' (Stokes 2007: 2).
2 These included the creation of an independent Vatican city-state and giving the church sole possession of a number of churches and palaces in Rome, as well as other properties; the establishment of Catholicism as the sole religion of the

state; made Catholic religious instruction compulsory in both elementary and secondary schools; gave ecclesiastical courts sole power over marriage; the relegation to inferior status of non-Catholic religions and placement of these under certain restrictions; reimbursement to compensate for the property that had been lost during Italian unification. In return, the pope recognized the Italian state and the state was given the right to approve the appointment of bishops.

3 It must be noted, however, that the ability of the party to carry out such a revolution has been called into question (see Mack Smith 1959).

4 Almond and Verba (1963) did include Italy in their analysis of civic culture and their findings generally indicate a low level of civic culture in that country in the late 1950s; however, data from the 1980s and 1990s shows a marked increase in the indicators of social capital – participation in organizations and interpersonal trust (McLaren and Baird 2006).

5 In fact, it appears that the Vatican was pressing for this option as early as the 1950s (Ginsborg 1990: 142).

6 I am especially grateful to an astute student, Jarl Samuel Doveri Vesterbye, for reminding me of this particular incident in Italian electoral history.

7 Prior to this, other conservative parties had taken the role of advocating the church's interests. Note that a Spanish Christian democratic party did form in 1922, but it did not survive long (Payne 1993: 166).

8 Note that the government forced the party to change its name to *Acción Popular* in 1932 (Payne 1993: 167).

9 Franco's regime ultimately appears to have been based far more on this latter approach than on those of the fascist party, Falange Espanola, which Franco used as his own unifying party (Payne 1993: 173).

 Carlists also re-emerged with traditionalist, ultra-Catholic, monarchist goals (Payne 1993: 173–4).

10 Aznar's government attempted to pin the blame on the party's old enemy, ETA, despite the fact that the evidence did not support this accusation.

11 Recall that the political system was opened up to opposition parties in 1946, but the elections held in that year are widely believed to have been manipulated by the governing party.

12 Kemal himself did periodically experiment with creating an organized opposition, but would then destroy this when it appeared to be more popular than anticipated (Lewis 1968).

13 According to the 1982 Constitution, political party programmes shall not be in conflict with the territorial indivisibility of the state or with the democratic and secular nature of the republic (section IIIA).

14 These were the 1909 Law of Associations and Strike Law (see Yavus 1995).

7 The functioning of government: executive and parliament

1 Although the Italian constitution stipulates that the Senate is elected on a regional basis (Article 57), the chamber has generally not served to represent regional interests. Furthermore, although the exact formula used to elect the Senate is slightly different than that used for the Chamber of Deputies, the outcome – until 1993 – of both electoral systems was one of high proportionality. Also, those voting for the Senate must be 25 years or older while the minimum voting age for the Chamber is 18. Finally, senators must be at least 40 years old, while deputies must be at least 25 years old (Hine 1993: Chapter 6).

2 Note that there are restrictions on the use of this procedure, though. It cannot be used for changing the constitution, approving budgets, increasing taxes, or

ratifying treaties. Also, it is possible for 10 per cent of the house to call for the bill to be subject to the chamber's approval at any point.

3 For an overview of the functioning of Italian political institutions in the 1990s see Koff and Koff (1999).

4 Valle d'Aosta continues to elect one deputy in a single-member constituency.

5 However, no regional majority prize is awarded in Molise, which elects only two senators.

6 news.bbc.co.uk/1/hi/world/europe/5117992.stm (consulted 22 January 2007).

7 The male pronoun will be used here because thus far no female has occupied the post of president of the Italian Republic.

8 Gürsel had only just been dismissed from his post as Commander of Land Forces because of a memorandum he had written to the Ministry of Defence expressing support for the prime minister; he did not participate in the 1960 coup, but was seen by the officers who did organize the coup as a potential unifying force. Sunay and Korutürk had been appointed to the Senate by the president (Gürsel appointed Sunay and Sunay appointed Korutürk) toward the end of their military careers; see en.wikipedia.org/wiki/List_of_Presidents_of_Turkey (consulted 30 January 2007).

9 Erdoğan was convicted of inciting religious hatred in 1998 for delivering a controversial poem while he was mayor of Istanbul, and was thus ineligible to serve as a member of parliament. Since prime ministers must also be members of parliament, though he was party leader, he was ineligible to serve as prime minister.

8 The resolution of regional conflict

1 Daniel Ziblatt (2006) contends that instead of military power, it may be infrastructural power that is the key to explaining the establishment of federations. That is, federalism is the state structure chosen when the capacity of subunits to govern, raise taxes, etc. is high because this capacity provides the newly created state with the resources and legitimacy that it requires.

2 Note that South Tyrol did not become a region of its own. Constitutional designers like De Gasperi were concerned about continued attempts at separatism if the region was granted its own government, and so it was lumped together with the Italian-speaking Trentino region and the region as a whole was called Trentino-Alto Adige. In the newly created region, the Germans, while guaranteed use of their language, would always be in the minority in the regional assembly (Clark 1984: 322).

3 As indicated above, many of the elites in Galicia have worked in the Spanish bureaucracy and thus have benefited from the centralized administration; moreover, while the Franco dictatorship discouraged official use of Galician, the techniques used in this region were far less repressive than those used in the Basque Country and Catalonia (see Heywood 1995: Chapter 1).

4 Mosul is approximately 120 kilometres south of the current Turkish border.

5 Kirisci and Winrow contend that there were three main groupings of Kurds around the time that the boundaries were set. One group identified themselves with the resistance movement. Another wanted an independent state or at least autonomy within an Ottoman or Turkish state. The third group consisted of powerful Kurdish tribal leaders who seemed mostly interested in creating their own kingdoms in the Kurdish populated areas they controlled. These groups were simply unable to cooperate and organize themselves into an effective movement (Kirisci and Winrow 1997: 79).

6 'Independence Tribunals' were created and these were used to try the leaders of

the rebellions, many of whom received the death penalty (Kirisci and Winrow 1997: 100).

7 BBC online, news.bbc.co.uk/1/hi/world/europe/3634024.stm (consulted 25 June 2007).

8 BBC online, news.bbc.co.uk/1/hi/world/europe/3789913.stm (consulted 25 June 2007).

9 BBC online news.bbc.co.uk/1/hi/world/europe/3242825.stm (consulted 25 June 2007).

9 The professionalization of the military

1 For instance, between 1861 and 1922, states of siege were declared ten times, sometimes as a result of serious conflict and rioting and sometimes only as a result of threats of general strikes. A state of siege means that those arrested are tried under military rather than civilian law (Clark 1984: 49).

2 That is, it was feared that soldiers would develop sympathies for problems facing peasants and workers and the former could be co-opted for the causes being promoted by groups organizing the latter.

3 Also see Martínez and Barker (1988).

4 The most serious threat to Franco's rule came from General Alfredo Kindelán who challenged Franco in meetings in 1941. Franco 'responded cordially' to these criticisms; however when Kindelán organized a meeting of generals and other senior officers at his home in the Catalan military region to discuss the restoration of the monarchy, he was relieved of his post and made the director of a military school, which Kindelán himself recognized meant that he was unable to organize any direct action against the Franco regime (Preston 1990: 99–100).

5 Note that the attack on the Janissaries is known in Turkish history as the 'Auspicious Incident'.

6 See Hale (1994: 29–550), Ahmad (1969) and Buxton (1909) for overviews of this period in Ottoman history.

7 Fourteen of the radicals were expelled from the ruling committee, the National Unity Committee, and sent into exile (Hale 1994: 136).

8 See www.worldvaluessurvey.org.

10 External influences and democratic consolidation

1 An association agreement is an agreement between the EU and a non-member-state that outlines the process by which trade association between the two parties will increase. It generally includes provisions for a closer trade association than would be the case with other trade agreements that the EU has at its disposal. It is often the case that an association agreement includes the possibility of full EC/EU membership, but this is not always the case (Piening 1997).

2 After Greece orchestrated a coup in Cyprus to displace the elected president of the Cypriot Republic, Turkey invaded the island to restore constitutional order, primarily to protect the sizeable Turkish population living on the island. The Greek military's performance during this invasion discredited the military regime in Greece because the result of the coup and subsequent invasion was the division of the island into Turkish-occupied and Greek-occupied zones, as well as the long-term occupation of Cyprus by the Turkish military. That is, the regime of the colonels was unable to defeat the Turkish army.

3 The Empty Chair Crisis occurred when French President Charles de Gaulle recalled the French delegation from the Council of Ministers and insisted that Gaullist party members in the EP boycott participation in a dispute with the

European Commission president over the attempt by the latter to create the EU's 'own funds' and generally change budgetary rules as well as the Common Agricultural Policy. Thus, France's chairs at the EU institutions remained vacant during this period (July 1965–January 1966) and the rest of the community refused to take any major decisions until the French delegation returned.

4 See the Council of Europe website at www.coe.int/ (consulted 25 June 2007, for details about history, membership, etc.).

5 DISK was a member of the World Federation of Trade unions and was actively supported by counterparts in Europe; TURK-IS is a member of the Confederation of Free Trade unions (Karaosmanoğlu 1991: 169).

6 meria.idc.ac.il/journal/2002/issue2/jv6n2a4.html (consulted 25 June 2007).

7 This is not to say that economic concerns were unimportant (see Muftuler-Bac 1997: 54, 56), but it is likely that they were somewhat secondary.

8 meria.idc.ac.il/journal/2002/issue2/jv6n2a4.html (consulted online 25 June 2007).

9 Given the influence of modernization approaches to political development at the time, it seems likely that EU leaders might have believed that if they took action to help Turkey's economy to modernize, political modernization would follow.

10 This is seen as a fairly minor reform because the death penalty had not been used since 1984 and the phrasing of the abolition still allowed for the possibility of executing those convicted of terrorism; in effect, this would mostly mean the execution of Kurdish terrorists, and particularly Kurdish separatist leader Abdullah Öcalan, who had been captured in February 1999.

11 It is not clear that a reduced number of generals on the NSC would, in fact, reduce their ability to affect policymaking.

12 Bureaucratic red tape had held up the implementation of the original legislation.

11 Conclusion

1 Given the large number of variables investigated here, the only realistic way to address this problem would have been to turn to a large-scale quantitative analysis. This book has, however, investigated several historical factors to discover similarities and differences across the cases, and much of this investigation and discussion of the histories of the cases would be unrealistic in a large-scale quantitative analysis.

Appendix: research design and case selection

1 It must be noted that many small-N researchers see this approach as being far more useful than large-N analyses and would reject the statement just made here. However, the statement made refers to the logically possible but practically impossible situation of having an infinite capacity not just for quantitative analyses but also for analysing long historical processes across all possible observations. I do assume the latter to be preferable but acknowledge the impossibility of such analyses due to human limitations.

2 I acknowledge the statements made by European leaders that question Turkey's European 'credentials', as well as the ongoing difficulties regarding Turkey's EU negotiations. It is important to note, however, that (a) it is actually only a handful of leaders making such statements, (b) the member states in question have had the opportunity to reject Turkey's bid for candidacy on multiple occa-

sions and instead supported Turkey's bid to join the EU, and (c) the problems surrounding Turkey's negotiations are not connected (at least not directly) to questions about its European 'credentials' but instead to the very thorny issue of Cyprus.

3 Note also that while this book makes reference to 'Southern Europe', it is not contending that this is necessarily a completely unique region. As discussed in this appendix and throughout the book, the countries generally included in the 'Southern Europe' category do share many traits in common, but not all countries that might be counted as geographically southern are generally included in the category (e.g. France). Some researchers do contend that Southern Europe is indeed a unique region and that countries like Turkey are not historically part of it, though (see, for instance, Malefakis 1995).

References

Absalom, R. (1995) *Italy since 1800: a nation in the balance?* London: Longman.

Adams, J.C. and Barile, P. (1966) *The Government of Republican Italy*, 2nd edn, Boston, MA: Houghton Mifflin.

Agranoff, R. (1993) 'Intergovernmental politics and policy: building federal arrangements in Spain', *Regional Politics and Policy: An International Journal* 3(2): 1–28.

—— (1996) 'Federal evolution in Spain', *International Political Science Review* 17(4): 385–401.

—— and Bañon, R. (eds) (1997) *Toward Federal Democracy in Spain*, special issue of the journal *Publius* 27: 4.

—— and Gallarin, J.A.R. (1997) 'Toward federal democracy in Spain: an examination of intergovernmental relations', *Publius* 27 (4): 1–38.

Agüero, F. (1995a) *Soldiers, Civilians, and Democracy*, Baltimore: Johns Hopkins University Press.

—— (1995b) 'Democratic consolidation and the military in Southern Europe and South America', in R.P. Gunther, N. Diamandouros, and H.-J. Puhle (eds) *The Politics of Democratic Consolidation: Southern Europe in comparative perspective*, Baltimore, MD: Johns Hopkins University Press.

Ahmad, F. (1969) *The Young Turks: the Committee of Union and Progress in Turkish politics, 1908–1914*, Oxford: Oxford University Press.

—— (1977) *The Turkish Experiment with Democracy, 1950–75*, London: Hurst for Royal Institute of International Affairs.

—— (1993) *The Making of Modern Turkey*, London: Routledge.

—— (1995) 'The development of class consciousness in republican Turkey, 1923–45', in D. Quataert and E.J. Zurcher (eds) *Workers and the Working Class in the Ottoman Empire and the Turkish Republic: 1839–1950*, London: Tauris.

Aksoy A, and Robins K. (1997) 'Peripheral vision: cultural industries and cultural identities in Turkey', *Environment and Planning* A 29 (11): 1937–1952.

Alcaide, J. (1976) 'Una revisión urgente de la serie de Renta Nacional española en el siglo XX', in Instituto de Estudios Fiscales, *Datos básicos para la historia financiera de España, 1850–1975*, 2 volumes, Madrid: Ministerio de Hacienda.

Allen, K. and Stevenson, A. (1974) *An Introduction to the Italian Economy*, London: Martin Robertson & Co.

Allum, P.A. (1973). *Italy: republic without government?*, London: Weidenfeld and Nicolson.

Almond, G. (1956) 'Comparative political systems', *Journal of Politics* 18(3): 391–409.

—— and Verba, S. (1963) *The Civic Culture: political attitudes and democracy in five nations*, Princeton, NJ: Princeton University Press.

Altuğ, S. and Filiztekin, A. (2006) 'Productivity and growth, 1923–2003', in S. Altuğ and A. Filiztekin (eds) *The Turkish Economy: The Real Economy, Corporate Governance and Reform*, London: Routledge.

Amodia, J. (1983) 'Union of the Democratic Centre', in D.S. Bell (ed.) *Democratic Politics in Spain*, London: Pinter.

Anderson, B. (1991) *Imagined Communities*, rev. edn, London: Verso Books.

Arango, E.R. (1996). *Spain: democracy regained*, 2nd edn, New York: The Perseus Books Group.

Aslan-Akman, C. (2005) 'Being an opposition MP in the 22nd Turkish parliament', *European Journal of Turkish Studies*, Thematic Issue No. 3, 'Being an MP in contemporary Turkey'. Online. available at: www.ejts.org/document500. html (accessed 29 January 2007).

Bachrach, P. and Baratz, M.S. (1970) *Power and Poverty: theory and practice*, New York: Oxford University Press.

Balcells, A. (1996) *Catalan Nationalism: past and present*, London: Macmillan.

Balfour, S. (2004). *The Politics of Contemporary Spain*, London: Taylor & Francis.

Bañon R and Tamayo M. (1997) 'The transformation of the central administration in Spanish intergovernmental relations', *Publius* 27 (4): 85–114.

Bañon Martinez, R. and Barker, T. (eds) (1988) *Armed Forces and Society in Spain Past and Present*, New York: Columbia University Press.

Barbagallo, F. (1994) *Storia dell'Italia Repubblicana*, Turin: Einaudi.

Barbé, E. (1999) *La Política Europea de España*, Barcelona: Ariel.

Barkey, H.J. and Fuller, G.E. (1998) *Turkey's Kurdish Question*, Lanham, MD: Rowman & Littlefield.

Barnes, S.H. (1966) 'Ideology and the organization of conflict: on the relationship between political thought and behavior', *Journal of Politics* 28 (3): 513–30.

Barton, S. (2003) *A History of Spain*, Houndsmills: Palgrave Macmillan.

Bassols, R. (1995) *España en Europa: historia de la adhesión 1957–1985*, Madrid: Política Exterior.

Battente, S. (2000) 'Nation and state building in Italy: recent historiographical interpretations (1989–1997), I: unification to fascism', *Journal of Modern Italian Studies* 5(3): 310–21.

—— (2001) 'Nation and state building in Italy: recent historiographical interpretations (1989–1997), II: from fascism to the republic', *Journal of Modern Italian Studies* 6(1): 94–105.

Beales, D. (1971) *The Risorgimento and the Unification of Italy*, London: George Allen & Unwin Ltd.

Beliaev, M. (2003) Institutional Factors in Consolidation of Post-Communist Democracies, *Globalization*. Online. available at: globalization.icaap.org/content/v3.2/03_beliaev.html#1 (accessed 18 August 2006).

Bell, D.S. (1983) 'The Spanish Communist Party in transition', in D.S. Bell (ed.) *Democratic Politics in Spain*, London: Pinter.

Berman S. (1997) 'Civil society and the collapse of the Weimar Republic', *World Politics* 49 (3): 401–29.

Bermeo, N. (1992) 'Democracy and the lessons of dictatorship', *Comparative Politics* 24 (3): 273–91.

Boix, C. and Stokes, S.C. (2003) 'Endogenous Democratization', *World Politics* 55(4): 517–549.

Bollen, K.A. (1979) 'Political democracy and the timing of development', *American Sociological Review* 44(4): 572–87.

Born, H., Caparini, M., Haltiner, K.W., and Kuhlmann, J. (eds) (2006) *Civil-Military Relations in Europe: learning from crisis and institutional change*, London: Routledge.

Bosworth, R.J.B. (2004). *Italy and the Wider World 1860–1960*, London: Routledge.

Botella, J. (1989) 'The Spanish "new" regions: territorial and political pluralism', *International Political Science Review* 10(3): 263–71.

Boxer, A. (2000) *The Rise of Italian Fascism*, London: HarperCollins Publishers.

Brady, H.E. and Collier, D. (2004) *Rethinking Social Inquiry: diverse tools, shared standards*, Lanham: Rowman & Littlefield.

Brassloff, A. (1989) 'Spain: the state of the autonomies', in M. Forsyth (ed.) *Federalism and Nationalism*, Leicester: Leicester University Press.

Briand, M.A. (1987) *The Generals' Coup in Turkey: an inside story of 12 September*, London: Brassey's Defence Publishers.

Browne, H. (1996) *Spain's Civil War*, Harlow: Pearson Education Ltd.

Bull, A.C. and Gilbert, M. (2001) *The Lega Nord and the Northern Question in Italian Politics*, London: Palgrave Macmillan.

Bull, M. and Newell, J. (2005) *Italian Politics: adjustment under duress*, Oxford: Blackwell.

Bunce, V. (2000) 'Comparative democratization: big and bounded generalizations', *Comparative Political Studies* 33(6–7): 703–34.

Burgess, M. (1993) 'The European tradition of federalism: Christian democracy and federalism', in M. Burgess and A.G. Gagnon (eds) *Comparative Federalism and Federation*, Toronto: University of Toronto Press.

—— (2000) *Federalism and European Union: the building of Europe, 1950–2000*, London: Routledge.

Busquets, J. (1984). *El Militar de Carrera en España*, 3rd edn, Barcelona: Ariel.

——, Aguilar, M.A., and Puche, I. (1981) *El golpe: anatomía y claves del asalto al Congreso*, Barcelona: Ariel.

Buxton, C.R. (1909) *Turkey in Revolution*, London: T. Fisher Unwin.

Çağlar, A.N. (1990) 'The Greywolves as metaphor', in A. Finkel and N. Sirman (eds) *Turkish State, Turkish Society*, London: Routledge.

Calvo Sotelo, J. (1974) 'Mis servicios al Estado', *Seis Años de Gestión: apuntes para la historia*, new edition, Madrid: Inst. De Estudios de Admón.

Cañaveral, R.C. *et al.* (1981) *Todos al Suelo*, Madrid: Putno Crítico.

Capano G. and Giuliani M. (2001) 'Governing without surviving? An Italian Paradox: law-making in Italy, 1987–2001', *Journal of Legislative Studies* 7(4): 13–36.

Cardona, G. (1983) *El Poder Militar en la España Contemporánea Hasta la Guerra Civil*, Madrid: Siglo Veintiuno.

Çarkoğlu, A. (2002) 'The rise of the new generation of pro-islamists in Turkey: the Justice and Development Party phenomenon in the November 2002 elections in Turkey', *South European Society and Politics* 7(3): 123–56.

Carr, R. (1980) *Modern Spain: 1875–1980*, Oxford: Oxford University Press.

—— (2000) *The Spanish Tragedy: civil war in perspective*. London: Weidenfeld.

—— (2001a) 'Liberalism and reaction, 1833–1931', in R. Carr (ed.) *Spain: A history*, Oxford: Oxford University Press.

—— (2001b) *Modern Spain, 1875–1980*, Oxford: Oxford University Press.

—— and Fusi, J.P. (1981) *Dictatorship to Democracy*, Winchester, MA: Allen and Unwin.

Castro, A. (1984) *España en Su Historia. Cristiano, moros y judíos*, 3rd edn, Barcelona: Crítica.

Ceballos, T. and José, G. (no date) *Historia Económica, Financiera y Política de España en el Siglo XX*, vol. 7, Madrid: Talleres tip. El Financiero

Cento Bull, A. (2002) 'Towards a federal state? Competing proposals for constitutional revision', in P. Belluci and M. Bull (eds) *Italian Politics: the return of Berlusconi*, Oxford: Berghahn.

Cervetti, G. (1999) *L'Oro di Mosca: La verità sui finanziamenti Sovietici al PCI raccontata dal diretto protagonista*, 2nd edn, Milan: Baldini & Castoldi.

CESS (Centre for European Security Studies) and IPC (Istanbul Policy Center) (2005) *Turkish Civil–Military Relations and the EU: Preparation for Continuing Convergence*. Final Expert Report. Wim van Eekelen, chairman. November 2005. Online available at: www.cess.org/publications/occasionals/pdfs/occasionals3.pdf (accessed 5 June 2007).

Cizre, U. (1997) 'The anatomy of the Turkish military's political autonomy', *Comparative Politics* 29(2): 151–66.

—— (2004) 'Problems of democratic governance of civil-military relations in Turkey and the European Union enlargement zone', *European Journal of Political Research* 43(1): 107–25.

Clark, M. (1984) *Modern Italy 1871–1982*, London: Longman.

Clark, R. (1987) 'The question of regional autonomy in Spain's democratic transition', in R.P. Clark and M.H. Haltzel (eds) *Spain in the 1980s*, Cambridge: Massachusetts: Ballinger Publishing.

Clegg, T. (1988) 'Spain', in E. Page and M. Goldsmith (eds) *Central and Local Government Relations*, London: Sage.

Closa, C. (1995) 'National interest and convergence of preferences: a changing role for Spain in the EU?', in S. Mazey and C. Rhodes (eds) *The State of the European Union*, Vol. III, Boulder: Lynne Rienner.

—— and Heywood, P. (2004) *Spain and the European Union*, London: Palgrave Macmillan.

Clough, S. (1964). *The Economic History of Modern Italy*, New York: Columbia University Press.

—— and Livi, C. (1956) 'Economic growth in Italy: an analysis of the uneven development of North and South', *Journal of Economic History* 16(3): 334–49.

Collier, D. and Levitsky, S. (1997) 'Democracy with adjectives: conceptual innovation in comparative research', *World Politics* 49(3): 430–51.

—— and Mahoney, J. (1996) 'Insights and pitfalls: Selection bias in qualitative research', *World Politics* 49(1): 56–91.

Colomer, J.M. (1991) 'Transitions by agreement: modeling the Spanish way', *American Political Science Review* 85(4): 1283–302.

—— (1995) *Game Theory and the Transition to Democracy*, Aldershot: Edward Elgar.

—— (1998) 'The Spanish "state of autonomies": non-institutional federalism', *West European Politics* 21(4): 40–52.

Commission of the European Communities (2006) *Turkey 2006 Progress Report*, Brussels: Commission of the European Communities.

COM (2006) 649 final. Online available at: ec.europa.eu/enlargement/pdf/ key_documents/2006/nov/tr_sec_1390_en.pdf(accessed 5 June 2007).

Conversi, D. (1990) 'Language or race?: the choice of core values in the development of Catalan and Basque nationalism', *Ethnic and Racial Studies* 13(1): 50–70.

—— (1993) 'Domino effect or internal developments? The influences of international events and political ideologies on Catalan and Basque nationalism', *West European Politics* 16(3): 245–70.

—— (1997) *The Basques, the Catalans and Spain: alternative routes to nationalist mobilization*, London: C Hurst and Co.

Cook, M.A. (ed.) (1976) *A History of the Ottoman Empire to 1730: chapters from the Cambridge History of Islam and the New Cambridge Modern History*, Cambridge: Cambridge University Press.

Cotta, M. (1990) 'The "centrality" of parliament in a protracted democratic consolidation: the Italian case', in U. Liebert and M. Cotta (eds) *Parliament and Democratic Consolidation in Southern Europe*, London: Pinter Publishers.

—— (1992) 'Elite unification and democratic consolidation in Italy: a historical overview', in J. Higley and R. Gunther (eds) *Elites and Democratic Consolidation in Latin America and Southern Europe*, Cambridge: Cambridge University Press.

Coufoudakis, V. (1977) 'The European Economic Community and the "freezing" of the Greek Association, 1967–1974', *Journal of Common Market Studies* 16 (2):114–31.

Couloumbis. Th. (1983) *The United States, Greece and Turkey: the troubled triangle*, New York: Praeger.

Cutright, P. (1963) 'National political development: measurement and analysis', *American Sociological Review* 28(2): 253–64.

Dahl, R.A. (1971) *Polyarchy: participation and opposition*, New Haven: Yale University Press.

Dalton, R.J. (2001) *Citizen Politics: public opinion and political parties in advanced industrial democracies*, 3rd edn, Washington, DC: CQ Press.

del Mar del Pozo, A.M. and Braster, J.F.A. (1999) 'The rebirth of the "Spanish race": the state, nationalism, and education in Spain, 1875–1931', *European History Quarterly* 29: 75–107.

Della Sala, V. (1997) 'Italy: a bridge too far?' *Parliamentary Affairs* 50(3): 369–409.

De Mauro, T. (1976) *Storia Linguistica dell'Italia Unita*, Laterza: Bari.

Demirel, T. (2005) 'Lessons of military regimes and democracy: the Turkish case in a comparative perspective', *Armed Forces & Society* 31(2): 245–71.

Diamond, L. (1992) 'Economic development and democracy reconsidered', in G. Marks and L. Diamond (eds) *Reexamining Democracy*, Newbury: Sage.

—— (1999) *Developing Democracy: toward consolidation*, Baltimore, MD: Johns Hopkins Press.

—— and Linz, J.J. (1989) 'Introduction: politics, democracy, and society in Latin America', in L. Diamond, J.J. Linz, and S.M. Lipset (eds) *Democracy in Developing Countries: Latin America*, Boulder: Lynne Rienner.

Diaz-Lopez, C. (1985) 'Centre-periphery structures in Spain: from historical conflict to transitional consociational accommodation?', in Y. Meny and V. Wright (eds) *Centre–Periphery Relations in Western Europe*, Winchester, MA.: Allen and Unwin.

Dion, D. (1998) 'Evidence and inference in the comparative case study', *Comparative Politics* 30(2): 127–45.

Di Palma, G. (1977) *Surviving Without Governing: the Italian parties in parliament*, Berkeley: University of California Press.

—— (1990) *To Craft Democracies: an essay on democratic transitions*, Berkeley: University of California Press.

Dodd, C.H. (1969) *Politics and Government in Turkey*, Manchester: Manchester University Press.

—— (1976) *Democracy and Development in Turkey*, Walkington: Eothen Press.

—— (1983) *The Crisis of Turkish Democracy*, Walkington: Eothen Press.

Domínguez Ortiz, A. (1976) *Sociedad y Estado en el Siglo XVIII Español*, Barcelona: Ariel.

Drake, R. (2004) 'The Soviet dimension of Italian communism', *Journal of Cold War Studies* 6(3): 115–19.

Duchacek, I. (1970) *Comparative Federalism: the territorial dimension of politics*, New York: Holt, Rinehart and Winston.

Duman, O. and Tsarouhas, D. (2006). ' "Civilianization" in Greece versus "demilitarization" in Turkey: a comparative study of civil Di Palma, G military relations and the impact of the European Union', *Armed Forces and Society* 32 (3): 405–23.

Earle, E.M. (1925). 'The new constitution of Turkey', *Political Research Quarterly* 40(1): 73–100.

Elazar D.J. (1993) 'International and comparative federalism', *PS: Political Science and Politics*, 26(2): 190–5.

Epstein, D.L., Bates, R., Goldstone, J., Kristensen, I., and O'Halloran, S. (2006) 'Democratic transitions', *American Journal of Political Science* 50 (3) 551–69.

Erdoğdu, E. (2002) 'Turkey and Europe: undivided but not united', *Middle East Review of International Affairs*, 6(2). Online. available at: meria.idc.ac.il/journal/2002/issue2/jv6n2a4.html (accessed 25 June 2007).

Ergil, D. (2000) 'The Kurdish question in Turkey', *Journal of Democracy*, 11(3): 122–35.

Esenwein, G. and Shubert, A. (1995) *Spain at War: the Spanish Civil War in context, 1931–1939*, London: Longman.

Ethier, D. (1997) *Economic Adjustment in New Democracies: lessons from Southern Europe*. London: Macmillan.

—— (2003) 'Is democracy promotion effective? Comparing conditionality and incentives', *Democratization*, 10(1): 99–120.

Evans, G. (ed.) (1999) *The End of Class Politics? Class voting in comparative context*, Oxford: Oxford University Press.

Farneti, P. (1985) *The Italian Party System (1945–1980)*, London: Pinter.

Feis, H. (1948) *The Spanish Story: Franco and the nations at war*, New York: Alfred A. Knopf.

Fernández, C. (1982) *Los Militares en la Transición Política*, Barcelona: Argos Vergara.

Fernández-Armesto, F. (2000) 'The improbably empire', in R. Carr (ed.) *Spain: a history*, Oxford: Oxford University Press.

Field, B.N. (2005) 'De-thawing democracy: the decline of political party collaboration in Spain (1977 to 2004)', *Comparative Political Studies* 38 (9) 1079–103.

Filippov, M., Ordeshook, P.C., and Shvetsova, O. (2004) *Designing Federalism: a theory of self-sustainable federal institutions*, Cambridge: Cambridge University Press.

Finer, S.E. (1988) *The Man on Horseback: the role of the military in politics*, 2nd edn, London: Pinter.

Finkel, A. and Hale, W. (1990) 'Politics and Procedure in the 1987 Turkish General Election', in A. Finke, and N. Sirman (eds) *Turkish State, Turkish Society*, London: Routledge.

—— and Nüket, S. (eds) (1990) *Turkish State, Turkish Society*, London: Routledge.

Finkelstein, M.S. (1999) *Separatism, the Allies, and the Mafia: the struggle for Sicilian independence, 1943–1948*, Cranbury: Lehigh University Press.

Flynn, M.K. (2001) 'Constructed identities and Iberia', *Ethnic and Racial Studies*, 24(5): 703–18.

Foot, J. (2003) *Modern Italy*, London: Palgrave Macmillan.

Forsyth, D.J. (2002) *The Crisis of Liberal Italy*, Cambridge: Cambridge University Press.

Forsyth, M. (ed.) (1989) *Federalism and Nationalism*, Leicester: Leicester University Press.

Franklin, M.N., Mackie, T.T., and Valen, H. (eds) (1992) *Electoral Change: responses to evolving social and attitudinal structures in western countries*, Cambridge: Cambridge University Press.

Friedrich, C. (1968) *Trends of Federalism in Theory and Practice*, New York: Prager Press.

Fuentes Quintana, E. (1995) 'El modelo de economía abierta y el modelo castizo de desarrollo económico en la España de los años 90', in E. Fuentes Quintana (ed.) *Problemas económicos españoles en la década de los 90* (Galaxia Gutenberg/Círculo de Lectores), Madrid: Galaxia Gutenberg

Gagnon, A.-G. (1993) 'The Political Uses of Federalism', in M. Burgess and A.-G. Gagnon (eds) *Federalism and Federation: competing traditions and future directions*, Toronto: University of Toronto Press.

—— (1996) 'Quebec: from its nonrecognition as a nation qua distinct society to its quest for a nation-state', *Regional and Federal Studies*, 6(1):21–29.

García de Añoveros, J. (1984). 'Autonomías, un proceso abierto', Madrid, *El País*, 29–30–31 May.

García Ferrando, M. López-Aranguren, E., and Beltrán, M. (1994) *La conciencia nacional y regional en la España de las Autonomías*, Madrid: Centro de Investigaciones Sociológicas.

Gasiorowski, M.J. (1995) 'Economic crisis and political regime change: an event history analysis', *American Political Science Review*, 89(4): 882–97.

—— and Power, T.J. (1998) 'The structural determinants of democratic consolidation, evidence from the Third World', *Comparative Political Studies*, 31(6): 740–71.

Geddes, B. (1999) 'What do we know about democratization after twenty years?', *Annual Review of Political Science* 2: 115–44.

—— (2003) *Paradigms and Sand Castles: theory building and research design in comparative politics*, Ann Arbor: University of Michigan Press.

Geertz, C. (1973) *The Interpretation of Cultures*, New York: Basic Books.

Gençkaya, Ö.F. (1998) 'Turkey', *World Encyclopedia of Parliaments and Legislatures*, 1, Washington, DC: Congressional Quarterly.

Gentile, E. (1996) *La Grand Italia. Ascesa e decline del mito della nazione nel ventesimo secolo*, Milan: Mondadori.

George, A.L. and Bennett, A. (2004) *Case Studies and Theory Development in the Social Sciences*, Cambridge, MA: MIT Press.

Gerschenkron, A. (1955) 'Notes on the rate of industrial growth in Italy', *Journal of Economic History* 15 (4): 360–75.

Gibb, H. and Bowen, H. (1950) *Islamic Society and the West*, vol. 1, part 1, London: Oxford University Press.

Gibbons, J. (1999) *Spanish Politics Today*, Manchester: Manchester University Press.

Gil, F. and Tulchin, J. (eds) (1988) *Spain's Entry Into NATO*, Boulder: Lynne Rienner Publishers.

Gilmour, D. (1985) *The Transformation of Spain: from Franco to the constitutional monarchy*, London: Quartet Books.

Giner, S. (1984) 'Ethnic nationalism, centre and periphery in Spain', in C. Abel and N. Torrents (eds) *Spain: conditional democracy*, London: Croom Helm.

Ginsborg, P. (1990) *A History of Contemporary Italy*, London: Penguin.

—— (1991) 'Risorgimento rivoluzionario. Mito e realità di una Guerra di popolo', *Storia e Dossier*, 47: 61–97.

—— (2005) *Silvio Berlusconi: television, power and patrimony*, London: Verso Books.

Giol, C., Garrido, D.L., and Subirats, L. (1990) 'By consociationalism to a majoritarian parliamentary system: the rise and decline of the Spanish Cortes', in U. Liebert and M. Cotta (eds) *Parliament and Democratic Consolidation in Southern Europe*, London: Pinter Publishers.

Gleditsch, K.S. and Ward, M.D. (2006) 'Diffusion and the international context of democratization', *International Organization* 60 (4): 911–33.

Gold, T. (2003) *The Lega Nord and Contemporary Politics in Italy*, London: Palgrave Macmillan.

Grabbe, H. (1999) 'A partnership for accession? the implications of EU conditionality for the Central and East European applicants', European University Institute Working Paper, San Domenico di Fiesole, RSC No. 99/12.

—— (2001a). *Profiting from EU Enlargement*. London: Centre for European Reform.

—— (2001b) 'How does Europeanisation affect CEE governance? Conditionality, diffusion and diversity', *Journal of European Public Policy* 8(4): 1013–31.

—— (2002) 'Enlargement puts EU credibility on the line, Turkey is the litmus test', *Wall Street Journal*, 11 October.

—— (2003) 'Europeanisation goes east: power and uncertainty in the EU accession process', in K. Featherstone and C. Radaelli (eds) *The Politics of Europeanisation*, Oxford: Oxford University Press.

—— and Hughes, K. (1998) *Enlarging the EU Eastwards*, London: Royal Institute of International Affairs.

Graham, H. and Labanyi, J. (1996) *Spanish Cultural Studies: an introduction: the struggle for modernity*, Oxford: Oxford University Press.

Gray, L. (1980) 'From Gramsci to Togliatti: the *Partito Nuovo* and the mass basis of Italian Communism', in S. Serfaty and L. Gray (eds) *The Italian Communist Party: yesterday, today, and tomorrow*, London: Aldwych Press.

Greenwood, D.J. (1977) 'Continuity in change: Spanish Basque ethnicity as a historical process', in M.J. Esman (ed.) *Ethnic Conflict in the Western World*, Ithaca: Cornell University Press.

Grugel, J. (1990) 'The Basques', in M. Watson (ed.) *Contemporary Minority Nationalisms*, London: Routledge.

Guibernau, M. (2001) 'Spain: Catalonia and the Basque Country', *Parliamentary Affairs* 53(1):.55–68.

Güneş-Ayata, A. (1990) 'Class and clientelism in the Republican People's Party', in A. Finkel and N. Sirman (eds) *Turkish State, Turkish Society*, London: Routledge.

—— (2002) 'The Republican People's Party', *Turkish Studies*, 3(1): 102–21.

Güney, A. (2002) 'The military, politics and post-Cold War dilemmas in Turkey', in K. Koonings and D. Kruijt (eds) *Political Armies: The Military and Nation Building in the Age of Democracy*, London: Zed Books.

—— and Karatekelioglu, P. (2005) 'Turkey's EU candidacy and. civil–military relations', *Armed Forces and Society* 31(3): 439–62.

Gunter, M.M. (1997) *The Kurds and the Future of Turkey*, London: Palgrave Macmillan.

Gunther, R. (1997) 'Managing democratic consolidation in Spain: from consensus to majority in institutions', in M. Heper, A. Kazancigil, and B.A. Rockman (eds) *Institutions and Democratic Statecraft*, Boulder: Westview Press.

——, Montero, J.R., and Botella, J. (2004) *Democracy in Modern Spain*, New Haven: Yale University Press.

——, Puble, H.-J., and Diamandouros, P.N. (1995) 'Introduction', in R. Gunther, P.N. Diamandouros, and H.-J. Puhle (eds) *The Politics of Democratic Consolidation: Southern Europe in comparative perspective*, Baltimore, MD: Johns Hopkins University Press.

——, Sani, G., and Shabad, G. (1992) *Spain After Franco: the making of a competitive party system*, Berkeley: University of California Press.

Güzel, M.S. (1995) 'Capital and labor during World War II', in D. Quataert and E.J. Zurcher (eds) *Workers and the Working Class in the Ottoman Empire and the Turkish Republic: 1839–1950*, London: Tauris.

Haggard, S. and Kaufman, R.R. (1995). *The Political Economy of Democratic Transitions*, Princeton: Princeton University Press.

Hale, W. (1980) 'The role of the electoral system in Turkish politics', *International Journal of Middle East Studies*, 11: 401–17.

—— (1981) *The Political and Economic Development of Modern Turkey*, London: Croom Helm.

—— (1990) 'The Turkish army in politics, 1960–73', in A. Finkel and N. Sirman (eds) *Turkish State, Turkish Society*, London: Routledge.

—— (1994) *Turkish Politics and the Military*, London: Routledge.

Hanley, D. and Loughlin, J. (eds) (2006) *Spanish Political Parties*, Cardiff: University of Wales Press.

Hansen, B. (1991) *The Political Economy of Poverty, Equity, and Growth: Egypt and Turkey*, Washington, DC: World Bank Oxford University Press.

Hardgrave Jr., R.L. (1994) 'India: the dilemmas of diversity', in L. Diamond and M.F. Plattner (eds) *Nationalism, Ethnic Conflict, and Democracy*, Baltimore, MD: Johns Hopkins University Press.

Harris, G.S. (1965a) 'The role of the military in Turkish politics, part I', *Middle East Journal* 19 (1): 54–66.

—— (1965b) 'The role of the military in Turkish politics, Part II', *Middle East Journal*, 19(2): 169–76.

—— (1985) *Turkey: coping with crisis*, Boulder: Westview.

—— (1988) 'The role of the military in Turkey in the 1980s: guardians or decision makers?', in M. Heper and A. Evin (eds) *State, Democracy and the Military: Turkey in the 1980s*, Berlin and New York: Walter de Gruyter.

Harrison, J. (1985) *The Spanish Economy in the Twentieth Century*, London: Croom Helm Ltd.

—— and Corkhill, D. (2004) *Spain: a modern European economy*, Aldershot: Ashgate.

Haughton, T. (2007) 'When does the EU make a difference? Conditionality and the accession process in Central and Eastern Europe', *Political Studies Review* 5(2): 233–46.

Hearder, H. (1983) *Italy in the Age of the Risorgimento 1790–1870*, London: Longman.

Heiberg, M. (1989) *The Making of the Basque Nation*, Cambridge: Cambridge University Press.

Held, D. (1996) *Models of Democracy*, 2nd edn, Oxford: Polity Press.

Hennessy, C.A.M. (1989) 'The renaissance of federal ideas in contemporary Spain', in M. Forsyth (ed.) *Federalism and Nationalism* Leicester: Leicester University Press.

Heper, M. and Başkan, F. (2001) 'Politics of coalition government in Turkey, 1961–1999', *International Journal of Turkish Studies*, 7(1–2): 68–89.

—— and Çinar, M. (1996) 'Dilemmas of parliamentarianism with a strong presidency: the post-1980 Turkish experience', *Political Science Quarterly* 111(3): 483–503.

Hershlag, Z.Y. (1959) *Turkey: an economy in transition*, The Hague, Uitgeverij van Keulen.

Heywood, P. (1995) *The Government and Politics of Spain*, Houndsmills: Macmillan Press.

—— (1998a) *Politics and Policy in Democratic Spain: no longer different?*, Southgate: Taylor & Francis Ltd.

—— (1998b) 'Power diffusion or concentration? In search of the Spanish policy process', *West European Politics* 21(4): 103–23.

—— (1999) 'Power diffusion or concentration? In search of the Spanish policy process', in P. Heywood (ed.) *Politics and Policy in Democratic Spain*, London: Frank Cass.

—— (2003) *Marxism and the Failure of Organised Socialism in Spain, 1879–1936*, Cambridge: Cambridge University Press.

Higley, J. and Burton, M. (2006) *Elite Foundations of Liberal Democracy*, Lanham, MD: Rowman & Littlefield Publishers.

Hine, D. (1990) 'The consolidation of democracy in post-war Italy', in G. Pridham (ed.) *Securing Democracy: political parties and democratic consolidation in Southern Europe*, London: Routledge.

—— (1993) *Governing Italy: the politics of bargained pluralism*, Oxford: Clarendon Press.

—— (1996) 'Federalism, regionalism and the unitary state: contemporary regional pressures in historical perspective', in C. Levy (ed.) *Italian Regionalism: history, identity and politics*, Oxford: Berg Publishers Ltd.

Hobsbawm, E.J. (1990) *Nations and Nationalism Since 1780: programme, myth, reality*, Cambridge: Cambridge University Press.

Holguin, S. (2002) *Creating Spaniards: culture and national identity in Republican Spain*, Madison: University of Wisconsin Press.

Hooper, J. (1987) *The Spaniards: portrait of a new Spain*, London: Penguin.

Hopkin, J. (2001) 'A "southern model" of electoral mobilisation? Clientelism and electoral politics in Spain', *West European Politics* 24 (1): 115–36.

—— (2005) 'From consensus to competition: the changing nature of democracy in the Spanish transition', in S. Balfour (ed.) *The Politics of Contemporary Spain*, London: Taylor & Francis.

Horowitz, D.L. (1985) *Ethnic Groups in Conflict*, Berkeley: University of California Press.

Howard, H. (1931) *The Partition of Turkey: a diplomatic analysis 1913–1923*, Norman: University of Oklahoma.

Hughes, H.S. (1965) *The United States and Italy*, New York: Norton.

Huntington, S.P. (1957) *The Soldier and the State*, New York: Vintage Books.

—— (1968) *Political Order in Changing Societies*, New Haven: Yale University Press.

—— (1991) *The Third Wave*, Norman: University of Oklahoma Press.

Hutchinson, J. and Smith, A.D. (2000) *Nationalism: critical concepts*, London: Taylor & Francis.

Hyslop, B.F. (1950) 'French Jacobin Nationalism and Spain', in E.M. Earle (ed.), *Nationalism and Internationalism*, New York: Columbia University Press.

İba, Ş. (2004) *100 Soruda Parlamento (The Parliament in 100 Questions: an introduction to the law of parliament)*, Ankara: Nobel.

ILO (1979) *Statistical Yearbook of Turkey*, Geneva: International Labour Office.

—— (1985) *Statistical Yearbook of Turkey*, Geneva: International Labour Office.

Inglehart, R. (1990) *Culture Shift in Advanced Industrial Society*, Princeton: Princeton University Press.

International Social Survey Project (1995) 'National identity I'. Online. available at: www.social-science-gesis.de/en/data_service/issp/data/1995_National_Identity. htm (accessed 23 August 2007).

Issawi, C. (1980) *The Economic History of Turkey 1800–1914*, Chicago: University of Chicago Press.

Itzkowitz, N. (1972) *Ottoman Empire and Islamic Tradition*, Chicago: University of Chicago Press.

Izady, M. (1992) *The Kurds: a concise history and fact book*, Washington: Taylor & Francis.

Jacobson, S. (2004) '"The head and heart of Spain": new perspectives on nationalism and nationhood', *Social History* 29 (3): 393–407.

Janowitz, M. (1964) *The Military in the Political Development of New Nations*, Chicago: University of Chicago Press.

—— (1977) *Military Institutions and Coercion in the Developing Nations*, Chicago: University of Chicago Press.

Kadt, E. de (2002) 'The military in politics: old wine in new bottles?' in K. Koonings and D. Kruijt (eds) *Political Armies: the military and nation building in the age of democracy*, London: Zed Books.

Kaplan, L.S. (1999) *The Long Entanglement: NATO's first fifty years*. Westport: Greenwood Press.

Karakisla, Y.S. (1995) 'The emergence of the Ottoman industrial working class, 1839–1923', in D. Quataert and E.J. Zurcher (eds) *Workers and the Working Class in the Ottoman Empire and the Turkish Republic: 1839–1950*, London: Tauris.

Karaosmanoğlu, A.L. (1991) 'The international context of democratic transition in Turkey', in G, Pridham (ed.) *Encouraging Democracy: the international context of regime transition in Southern Europe*, Leicester: Leicester University Press.

Karpat, K.H. (1959) *Turkey's Politics: the transition to multi-party system*, Princeton: Princeton University Press.

Keyder, Ç. (1987) *State and Class in Turkey: a study in capitalist development*, London: Verso.

King, G., Keohane, R., and Verba, S. (1994) *Designing Social Inquiry: scientific inference in qualitative research*, Princeton: Princeton University Press.

King, R. (1992) 'Italy: from sick man to rich man of Europe', *Geography* 335 (Part 2): 153–69.

Kirisci, K. and Winrow, G.M. (1997) *The Kurdish Question and Turkey*, Southgate: Taylor & Francis.

Koff, S.Z. and Koff, S. (1999) *Italy: from the 1st to the 2nd Republic*, London: Routledge.

Kogacioğlu, D. (2003) 'Dissolution of political parties by the constitutional court in Turkey: Judicial delimitation of the political domain', *International Sociology* 18 (1): 258–76.

—— (2004) 'Progress, unity, and democracy: dissolving political parties in Turkey', *Law & Society Review* 38(3): 433–62.

Kolaycıoğlu, E. (1988) 'The 1983 Parliament in Turkey: changes and continuities', in M. Heper and A. Evin (eds) *State, Military and Politics in Turkey*, Berlin and New York: de Gruyter Press.

—— (1990) 'Cyclical breakdown, redesign and nascent institutionalization: the Turkish Grand National Assembly', in U. Liebert and M. Cotta (eds) *Parliament and Democratic Consolidation in Southern Europe: Greece, Italy, Portugal, Spain and Turkey*, London, Pinter.

Koonings, K. and Kruijt, D. (2002) 'Military politics and the mission of nation building', in K. Koonings and D. Kruijt (eds) *Political Armies: the military and nation building in the age of democracy*, London: Zed Books.

Kreyenbroek, P.G. and Sperl, S. (1991) *The Kurds: a contemporary overview*, London: Taylor & Francis.

Lai, B. and Melkonian-Hoover, R. (2005) 'Democratic progress and regress: the effects of parties on the transitions of states to and away from democracy', *Political Research Quarterly* 58(4): 551–64.

Lanaro, S. (1988) *L' Italia nuova. Identità e sviluppo (1861–1988)*, Turin: Einaudi.

Landau, J. (1981) *Panturkism: a study of Turkish irredentism*, Connecticut: The Shoe String Press Inc.

Landau, M. (1973) 'Federalism, redundancy and system reliability', *Publius Journal of Federalism* 3(2): 173–95.

Lange, P. and Vannicelli, M. (eds) (1981) *The Communist Parties of Italy, France and Spain: postwar change and continuity*, London: George Allen and Unwin.

Laver, M. and Schofield, N. (1991) *Mulitparty Government*, Oxford: Oxford University Press.

Lawlor, T. *et al.* (1998) *Contemporary Spain: essays and texts on politics, economics, education and employment, and society*, London: Longman.

Leffler, M.P. (1985) 'Strategy, diplomacy, and the Cold War: the United States, Turkey, and NATO, 1945–1952', *Journal of American History*, 71(4): 807–25.

Leonardi, R. (1991) 'The international context of democratic transition in postwar Italy: a case of penetration', in G. Pridham (ed.) *Encouraging Democracy: The international context of regime transition in Southern Europe*, Leicester: Leicester University Press.

—— and Wertman, D.A. (1989) *Italian Christian Democracy: the politics of dominance*, Houndmills: Macmillan Press.

Lepschy, A.L., Lepschy, G., and Voghera, M. (1996) 'Linguistic variety in Italy', in Carl Levy (ed.) *Italian Regionalism: history, identity and politics*, Oxford: Berg Publishers.

Lerner, D. and Robinson, R.D. (1960) 'Swords and ploughshares: the Turkish army as a modernizing force', *World Politics* 13 (1): 19–44.

Levy, C. (ed.) (1996) *Italian Regionalism: history, identity and politics*, Oxford: Berg Publishers.

Lewis, B. (1968) *The Emergence of Modern Turkey*, 2nd edn, London: Oxford University Press.

Li, R.P.Y. and Thompson, W.R. (1975) 'The "Coup Contagion" Hypothesis', *Journal of Conflict Resolution*, 19(1): 63–88.

Lieberman, S. (1995) *Growth and Crisis in the Spanish Economy: 1940–93*, London: Routledge.

Liebert, U. (1990) 'Parliament as a central site in democratic consolidation: a preliminary exploration', in U. Liebert and M. Cotta (eds) *Parliament and Democratic Consolidation in Southern Europe: Greece, Italy, Portugal, Spain, and Turkey*, London: Pinter.

Lijphart, A. (1968) *The Politics of Accommodation: pluralism and democracy in the Netherlands*, Berkeley: University of California Press.

—— (1977) *Democracy in Plural Societies: a comparative exploration*, New Haven: Yale University Press.

—— (1985) *Power-Sharing in South Africa*, Berkeley: Institute of International Studies, University of California.

—— (1996) 'Constitutional choices for new democracies' in L. Diamond and M. Plattner (eds) *The Global Resurgence of Democracy*, Baltimore, MD: Johns Hopkins University Press.

—— (1999) *Patterns of Democracy: government forms & performance in thirty-six countries*, New Haven: Yale University Press.

—— and Waisman, C.H. (eds) (1996) *Institutional Design in New Democracies*, Boulder: Westview.

Linz, J. (1990) 'The perils of presidentialism', *Journal of Democracy* 1(1): 51–69.

—— (1999) 'Democracy, multinationalism and federalism', in W. Busch and A. Merkel (eds) *Demokratie in Ost und West*, Frankfurt am Main: Suhrkamp.

—— (2000) *Totalitarian and Authoritarian Regimes*, Boulder: Lynne Rienner Publishers Inc.

—— and Stepan, A. (1996) *Problems of Democratic Transition and Consolidation: Southern Europe, South America, and Post-Communist Europe*, Baltimore, MD: Johns Hopkins University Press.

Lipset, S.M. (1959) 'Some social requisites of democracy: economic development and political legitimacy', *American Political Science Review* 53(2) 69–105.

—— and Rokkan, S. (1967) 'Cleavage structures, party systems and voter alignments: an introduction', in S.M. Lipset, and S. Rokkan (eds) *Party Systems and Voter Alignments: cross-national perspectives*, New York: Free Press.

Londregan, J.B. and Poole, K.T. (1996) 'Does High Income Promote Democracy?', *World Politics*, 49(1): 1–30.

Lutz, V. (1962) *Italy: a study in economic development*, Oxford: Oxford University Press.

Lybyer, A.H. (1913) *The Government of the Ottoman Empire in the Time of Suleiman the Magnificent*, Cambridge, MA: Harvard University Press.

Lyttelton, A. (1973) *The Seizure of Power*, New York: Charles Scribner's Sons.

Mack Smith, D. (1959) *Italy: a modern history*, Ann Arbor: University of Michigan Press.

MacLennan, J.C. (2000) *Spain and the Process of European Integration, 1957–85*, Houndmills: Palgrave.

Magone, J.M. (2003) *The Politics of Southern Europe: integration into the European Union*, Westport: Praeger Publishers.

—— (2004) *Contemporary Spanish Politics Textbook*, London: Taylor & Francis.

Mainwaring, S. (1993) 'Presidentialism, multipartism, and democracy: the difficult combination', *Comparative Political Studies* 26(2): 198–228.

Majone, G. (1996) *Regulating Europe*, London: Taylor & Francis Ltd.

Malefakis, E. (1995) 'The political and socioeconomic contours of Southern European history,' in R. Gunther, P.N. Diamandouros, and H.-J. Puhle (eds) *The Politics of Democratic Consolidation: Southern Europe in comparative perspective*, Baltimore, MD: Johns Hopkins University Press.

Mansfield, E.D. and Pevehouse, J.C. (2006) 'Democratization and international organizations', *International Organization*, 60(1): 137–67.

Maravall, J.M. (1982) 'Introduccion' in *Parlamento y Democracia: problemas y perspectivas en los anos 80*, Madrid: F. Pablo Iglesias.

—— (1997) *Regimes, Politics, and Markets: democratization and economic change in Southern and Eastern Europe*, Oxford: Oxford University Press.

—— and Santamaria, J. (1986) 'Political change in Spain and prospects for democracy', in G.A. O'Donnell, P.C. Schmitter, and L. Whitehead (eds) *Transitions from Authoritarian Rule Prospects for Democracy: Southern Europe*, Baltimore, MD: Johns Hopkins Press.

March, J. and Olsen, J. (1989) *Rediscovering Institutions*, New York: Free Press.

Martín Rodríguez, M. (1999) 'Disparidades regionales: perspectiva histórica y Europea', in J.L. García Delgado (ed.) *España, Economía: ante el siglo xxi*, Madrid: Espasa Calpe.

Martínez, R.B. and Barker, T.M. (eds) (1988) *Armed Forces and Society in Spain Past and Present*, Boulder: Social Science Monographs.

Martinez-Herrera, E. (2002) 'From nation-building to building identification with political communities: consequences of political decentralisation in Spain, the Basque Country, Catalonia and Galicia, 1978–2001', *European Journal of Political Research* 41(4): 421–53.

Mattli, W. (1999) *The Logic of Regional Integration, Europe and Beyond*, New York: Cambridge University Press.

—— and Plümper, T. (2002) 'The demand-side politics of EU enlargement: democracy and the application for EU membership', *Journal of European Public Policy* 9(4): 555–74.

Ma Valles, J. and Cuchillo Foix, M. (1988) 'Decentralisation in Spain: a review', *European Journal of Political Research* 16: 395–407.

McKay, D. (1999) *Federalism and the European Union*, Oxford: Oxford University Press.

—— (2001) *Designing Europe: comparative lessons from the federal experience*, Oxford: Oxford University Press.

McLaren, L.M. and Baird, V.A. (2006) 'Of time and causality: a simple test of the requirement of social capital in making democracy work in Italy', *Political Studies* 54(4): 889–97.

Medhurst, K. (1977) *The Basques and the Catalans*, London: Minority Rights Group.

Mill, J.S. (1958 [1861]) *Considerations on Representative Government*, New York: Liberal Arts Press.

Mondini, M. (2006) 'Between subversion and coup d'etat: military power and politics after the Great War (1919–1922)', *Journal of Modern Italian Studies* (11) 4: 445–64.

Morales, J.L. and Celada, J. (1981) *La Alternative Military: el golpismo después de Franco*. Madrid: Ed. Revolución.

Morata, F. (1998) *La Unión Europea: procesos, políticas, actors*, Barcelona: Ariel.

Moreno, L. (1995) 'Multiple ethnoterritorial concurrence in Spain', *Nationalism and Ethnic Politics*, 1(1): 11–32.

—— (2001) *The Federalization of Spain*, London: Frank Cass.

Morlino, L. (1995) 'Consolidation and Party Government in Southern Europe', *International Political Science Review*, 16(2): 145–67.

—— (1998) *Democracy Between Consolidation and Crisis: parties, groups and citizens in Southern Europe*, Oxford: Oxford University Press.

Moss, H. (2000) 'Language and Italian national identity' in G. Bedani and B. Haddock (eds) *The Politics of Italian National Identity*, Cardiff: University of Wales Press.

Müftüler-Baç, M. (1997) *Turkey's Relations with a Changing Europe*, Manchester: Manchester University Press.

—— (1999) 'Turkish women's predicament', *Women's Studies International Forum* 22(3): 303–15.

—— (2005) 'Turkey's political reforms and the impact of the European Union', *South European Society and Politics* 10 (1): 17–31.

—— and McLaren, L. (2003) 'Enlargement preferences and policy-making in the European Union: impacts on Turkey', *Journal of European Integration* 25(1): 17–30.

Mujica, A. and Sanchez-Cuenca, I. (2006) 'Consensus and parliamentary opposition: the case of Spain', *Government and Opposition*, 41(1): 86–108.

Muller, E.N. and Seligson, M.A. (1994) 'Civic culture and democracy: the question of causal relationships', *American Political Science Review* 88 (3): 635–52.

Munck, G.L. (2001) 'The regime question: theory building in democracy studies', *World Politics* 54(1): 119–44.

Muro, D, and Quiroga, A. (2005) 'Spanish nationalism: ethnic or civic?', *Ethnicities*, 5(1): 9–29.

Naredo, J.M. (1974) *La Evolución de la Agricultura en España: desarrrollo capitalista y crisis de las formas de productión tradicionales*, 2nd edn, Barcelona: Laia.

Nash, E. (1983) 'The Spanish Socialist Party since Franco: from clandestinity to government: 1976–82', in D.S. Bell (ed.) *Democratic Politics in Spain*, London: Pinter.

Natali, D. (2005) *The Kurds and the State: evolving national identity in Iraq, Turkey, and Iran*, New York: Syracuse University Press.

Newton, M. (1983) 'The peoples and regions of Spain', in D.S. Bell (ed.) *Democratic Politics in Spain*, London: Pinter.

—— (1997) *Institutions of Modern Spain*, Cambridge: Cambridge University Press.

Nunez, X.M. (2001) 'The region as essence of the fatherland: regionalist variants of Spanish nationalism (1840–1936)', *European History Quarterly* 31(4): 483–518.

Nye, R.P. (1977) 'Civil–military confrontation in Turkey: the 1973 presidential election', *International Journal of Middle East Studies* 8(2): 209–28.

O'Donnell, G. (1973) *Modernization and Bureaucratic-Authoritarianism: studies in South American politics*, Berkeley, CA: Institute of International Studies.

—— (1994) 'Delegative democracy', *Journal of Democracy*, 5(1): 55–69.

——, Schmitter, P.C., and Whitehead, L. (1986) *Transitions from Authoritarian Rule: Prospects for Democracy*, Baltimore: Johns Hopkins University Press.

OECD (1987) *Economic Survey of Turkey*. Paris: OECD.

Oliveira, A.R. (1946) *Politics, Economics and Men of Modern Spain*, London: Victor Gollancz Ltd.

Olson, M. (1993) 'Dictatorship, democracy, and development', *American Political Science Review* 87 (3): 567–76.

Oneto, J. (1982) *La Verdad Sobre el Caso Tejero*, Barcelona: Planeta.

Ortega, A. (1994) *La Razón de Europa*, Madrid: El País/Aguilar.

Ortiz, D. (2000) *Paper Liberals: press and politics in restoration Spain*, Westport: Greenwood Press.

Özbudun, E. (1981) 'Turkey: the politics of clientelism' in S.N. Eisenstadt and R. Lemarchand (eds) *Political Clientelism, Patronage and Development*, Beverly Hills: Sage.

—— (1988) 'The status of the President of the Republic under the Turkish Constitution of 1982: presidentialism or parliamentarism?' in M. Heper and A. Evin (eds) *State, Democracy and the Military: Turkey in the 1980s*, Berlin: Walter de Gruyter.

—— (1998) 'Constitution making and democratic consolidation in Turkey', in M. Heper, A. Kazancigil, and B.A. Rockman (eds) *Institutions and Democratic Statecraft*, Boulder: Westview Press.

—— (2000) *Contemporary Turkish Politics: challenges to democratic consolidation*, Boulder: Lynne Rienner Publishers.

Pamuk, Ş. (1987) *The Ottoman Empire and European Capitalism, 1820–1913: trade, investment and production*, Cambridge: Cambridge University Press.

Panebianco, A. (1986) 'La dimensione internazionale dei processi politici', in G. Pasquino (ed.) *Manuale di Scienza della Politica*, Bologna: Il Mulino.

Parker, S. and Natale, P. (2006) *Contemporary Italian Politics*, London: Taylor & Francis.

Partridge, H. (1998) *Italian Politics Today*, Manchester: Manchester University Press.

Pasquino, G. (1980) 'From Togliatti to the *Compromesso Storico*: a party with a governmental vocation', in S. Serfaty and L. Gray (eds) *The Italian Communist Party: yesterday, today, and tomorrow*, London: Aldwych Press.

—— (1986) 'The demise of the first fascist regime and Italy's transition to democracy: 1943–1948', in G.A. O'Donnell, P.C. Schmitter, and L. Whitehead (eds) *Transitions from Authoritarian Rule Prospects for Democracy: Southern Europe*, Baltimore: Johns Hopkins University Press.

—— (1995) 'Executive–legislative relations in Southern Europe' in R. Gunther, P.N. Diamandouros, and H-J. Puhle (eds) *The Politics of Democratic Consolidation: Southern Europe in comparative perspective*, Baltimore, MD: Johns Hopkins University Press.

Payne, S. (1967) *Franco's Spain*, London: Routledge.

—— (1987) *The Franco Regime, 1936–75*, Madison: University of Wisconsin Press.

—— (1991) 'Nationalism, regionalism and micronationalism in Spain', *Journal of Contemporary History* 26(3–4): 479–91.

—— (1993) *Spain's First Democracy: The Second Republic, 1931–36*. Madison, Wisconsin: University of Wisconsin Press.

—— (2006) *The Collapse of the Spanish Republic, 1933–1936: origins of the Civil War*. New Haven: Yale University Press.

Payno, J.A. (1984). 'España: características de la economía y motivos para la adhesión', in J.A. Payno and J.L. Sampedro (eds), *La segunda ampliación de la CEE: Grecia, Portugal y España ante la Comunidad*, Madrid: Servicio de Estudios Económicos, Banco Exterior de España.

Perez-Agote, A. (2006) *The Social Roots of Basque Nationalism*, Reno: University of Nevada Press.

Perez Diaz, V. (1984) 'Politicas economicas y pautas sociales en la Espana de la transicion: la doble cara del neocorporativismo', *Espana: un presente para el futuro*, Barcelona: Planeta.

—— (1993) *The Return of Civil Society: the emergence of democratic Spain*, Cambridge, MA: Harvard University Press.

Pevehouse, J.C. (2002a) 'With a little help from my friends? Regional organizations and the consolidation of democracy', *American Journal of Political Science* 46(3): 611–26.

—— (2002b) 'Democracy from the outside-in? International organizations and democratization', *International Organization* 56(3): 515–49.

—— (2005) *Democracy from Above: regional organizations and democratization*, Cambridge: Cambridge University Press.

Piening, C. (1997) *Global Europe: the European Union in world affairs*, Boulder: Lynne Rienner Publishers.

Pierson, Paul (2000) 'The limits of design: explaining institutional origins and change', *Governance*, 13(4): 475–501.

Pierson, Peter (1999) *The History of Spain*, Westport: Greenwood Press.

Pi-Sunyer, O. (1985) 'Catalan nationalism: some theoretical and historical considerations', in E. Tiryakian and R. Rogowski (eds) *New Nationalisms of the Developed West*, Boston: Allen and Unwin.

Plattner, M.F. (1998) 'Liberalism and democracy: can't have one without the other', *Foreign Affairs*. Online. available at: www.foreignaffairs.org/19980301faresponse1382/marc-f-plattner/liberalism-and-democracy-can-t-have-one-without-the-other.html%20Marc%20Plattner (accessed 23 August 2007).

Porras Nadales, A. (1983) 'Ordenamiento de la defensa, poder militar y régime constitucional en España', *Revista de Estudios Políticos*, 35: 183–234.

Powaski, R.E. (1994) *The Entangling Alliance: The United States and European security, 1950–1993*, Westport: Greenwood Press.

Powell, C. (1996) *Juan Carlos of Spain*, London: Macmillan.

—— (2001) 'International aspects of democratization: the case of Spain', in L. Whitehead (ed.) *The International Dimensions of Democratization: Europe and the Americas*, Oxford: Oxford University Press.

Powell, G.B. (1982) *Contemporary Democracies: participation, stability, and violence*, Cambridge, MA: Harvard University Press.

Preston, P. (1978) *The Coming of the Spanish Civil War: reform, reaction and revolution in the Second Republic*, 2nd edn, London: Routledge.

—— (1986) *The Triumph of Democracy in Spain*, London: Routledge.

—— (1990) *The Politics of Revenge: fascism and the military in twentieth-century Spain*, London: Routledge.

—— (1996) *A Concise History of the Spanish Civil War*, London: Fontana.

—— (2006) *The Spanish Civil War: reaction, revolution and revenge*, New York: HarperCollins.

—— and Smyth, D. (1984) *Spain, the EEC and NATO*, London: Routledge.

Pridham, G. (ed.) (1990) *Securing Democracy: political parties and democratic consolidation in Southern Europe*, London: Routledge.

—— (1991) 'International influences and democratic transition: problems of theory and practice in linkage politics', in G. Pridham (ed.) *Encouraging Democracy: the international context of regime transition in Southern Europe*, Leicester: Leicester University Press.

—— (2000) 'Confining conditions and breaking with the past: historical legacies and political learning in transitions to democracy', *Democratization* 7(2): 36–64.

Przeworski, A. and Limongi, F. (1993) 'Political regimes and economic growth', *Journal of Economic Perspectives* 7(3): 51–69.

——, Alvarez, M., Cheibub, J.A., and Limongi, F. (1996) 'What makes democracies endure?', *Journal of Democracy* 7(1): 39–55.

—— (1997) 'Modernization: theories and facts', *World Politics*, 49(2): 155–83.

—— and Teune, H. (1970) *The Logic of Comparative Social Inquiry*, New York: Wiley-Interscience.

Putnam, R.D. (2001) *Bowling Alone: the collapse and revival of American community*, London: Simon & Schuster.

—— (with Leonardi, R. and Nanetti, R.Y.) (1993) *Making Democracy Work: civic traditions in modern Italy*, Princeton: Princeton University Press.

Rabushka, A. and Shepsle, K.A. (1972) *Politics in Plural Societies: a theory of democratic instability*, Columbus: Merrill.

Radcliff, P.B. (2000) 'The emerging challenge of mass politics', in J.A. Junco and A. Shubert (eds) *Spanish History Since 1808*, London: Hodder Arnold.

Ragin, C. (1987) *The Comparative Method: moving beyond qualitative and quantitative research strategies*, Berkeley: University of California Press.

Ragionieri, E. (1976) 'La storia politica e sociale', in *La storia d'Italia, IV Dall'Unità ad oggi*, vol. 3, Turin: Einaudi.

Rees, T. and Grugel, J. (1997) *Franco's Spain*, London: Hodder Education.

Reilly, B. (2001) *Democracy in Divided Societies: electoral engineering for conflict management*, Cambridge: Cambridge University Press.

Remmer, K. (1990) 'Debt or democracy? The political impact of the debt crisis in Latin America', in D. Felix (ed.) *Debt or Transfiguration? Prospects for Latin America's economic revival*, Armonk: M.E. Sharp.

Renan, E. (1947) 'Qu'est-ce qu'une nation?', in *Oeuvres completes*, Paris: Calmann-Lévy.

Requejo, F. (2005) *Multinational Federalism and Value Pluralism: the Spanish case*. London: Taylor & Francis.

Riall, L. (1994) *The Italian Risorgimento: state, society and national unification*, London: Routledge.

—— (1998) *Sicily and the Unification of Italy: liberal policy and local power, 1850–1866*, Oxford: Clarendon Press.

Riker, W. (1964) *Federalism: origins, operation, significance*, New York: Little, Brown.

Riley, D. (2005) 'Civic associations and authoritarian regimes in interwar Europe: Italy and Spain in comparative perspective', *American Sociological Review* 70(2): 288–310.

Río del Luelmo, J. and Williams, A. (1999) 'Regionalism in Iberia', in P. Wagstaff (ed.) *Regionalism in the European Union*, England: Intellect.

Riva, V. (1999) *Oro da Mosca: I Finanziamenti Sovietici al PCI dalla Rivoluzione d'Ottobre al Crollo dell'URSS*, Milan: Arnoldo Mondadori Editore.

Robinson, R.D. (1963) *The First Turkish Republic: a case study in national development*, Cambridge, MA: Harvard University Press.

Rochat, G. (1967) *L'esercito Italiano da Vittorio Veneto a Mussolini (1919–1925)*, Bari: Laterza.

——— (2005) *Le Guerre Italiane 1935–1943: Dall'impero d'Etiopia alla disfatta*, Torino, Einaudi.

Romero Maura, J. (1976) 'After Franco, Franquismo? The armed forces, the Crown and democracy', in *Government and Opposition*, 11(1): 35–64.

Romero Salvado, F.J. (2005) *The Spanish Civil War*, Palgrave Macmillan.

Ross, C. (2004) *Spain 1812–2004*, London: Hodder Arnold.

Rothstein, B. (2004) 'Social capital and the quality of government: the causal mechanism', in J. Kornai and S. Rose-Ackerman (eds) *Trust in Post-Socialist Transition*, vol. 2, London: Palgrave Macmillan.

Rueschemeyer, D., Stephens, E.H., and Stephens, J.D. (1992) *Capitalist Development and Democracy*, Chicago: University of Chicago Press.

Ruscoe, J. (1982) *The Italian Communist Party, 1976–81: on the threshold of government*, Houndmills: Macmillan Press.

Rusconi, G.E. (1993) *Nazione Etnia Cittadinanza in Italia e in Europe*, Brescia: La Scuola.

Rustow, D.A. (1959) 'The army and the founding of the Turkish Republic', *World Politics*, 11(4): 513–552.

——— (1970) 'Transitions to democracy: toward a dynamic model', *Comparative Politics*, 2(3): 337–63.

Sakallioglu, U.C. (1997) 'The anatomy of the Turkish military's autonomy', *Comparative Politics*, 29(2): 151–66.

Sapelli, G. (1995) *Southern Europe Since 1945: tradition and modernity in Portugal, Spain, Italy, Greece and Turkey*, London: Longman.

Sartori, G. (1976) *Political Parties: a framework for analysis*, Cambridge: Cambridge University Press.

Sassoon, D. (1997) *Contemporary Italy: economy, society and politics since 1945*, 2nd edn, London: Longman.

Savolainen, J. (1994) 'The rationality of drawing big conclusions based on small samples: in defense of Mill's methods', *Social Forces*, 72(4): 1217–24.

Schattschneider, E.E. (1960) *The Semisovereign People: a realist's view of democracy in America*, New York: Holt, Rinehart and Winston.

Schedler, A. (1998) 'What is democratic consolidation?', *Journal of Democracy* 9(2): 91–107.

Schimmelfennig, F. and Sedelmeier, U. (eds) (2005) *The Europeanisation of Central and Eastern Europe*, Ithaca: Cornell University Press.

———, Engert, S., and Knobel, H. (2003) 'Costs, commitment and compliance: the impact of EU democratic conditionality on Latvia, Slovakia and Turkey', *Journal of Common Market Studies* 41(3): 495–518.

Schmitter, P.C. (2001) 'The influence of the international context upon the choice of national institutions and policies in neo-democracies', in L. Whitehead (ed.) *The International Dimensions of Democratization: Europe and the Americas*, Oxford: Oxford University Press.

——— and Karl, T.L. (1996) 'What democracy is ... and is not', in L. Diamond and M. Plattner (eds) *The Global Resurgence of Democracy*, 2nd edn, Baltimore, MD: Johns Hopkins University Press.

Schubert, A. and Esenwein, G. (1995) *Spain at War: the Spanish Civil War in context 1931–1939*, London: Longman Publishing Group.

Schwartz, P. (1976) 'Politics first: the economy after Franco', *Government and Opposition* 11(1): 84–105.

Segal, G. (1991) 'International relations and democratic transitions', in G. Pridham (ed.) *Encouraging Democracy: the international context of regime transition in Southern Europe*, Leicester: Leicester University Press.

Servicio de Estudios del Banco de Bilbao (1983) *Informe economico, 1982*. Bilbao: Banco de Bilbao

Shabad, G. and Gunther, R. (1982) 'Language, nationalism and political conflict in Spain', *Comparative Politics* 14(4): 443–77.

Shambayati, H. (1994) 'The rentier state, interest-groups, and the paradox of autonomy: state and business in Turkey and Iran', *Comparative Politics* 26(3): 307–31.

Shaw, S.J. and Shaw, E.K. (1977) *History of the Ottoman Empire and Modern Turkey. Volume II: reform, revolution, and republic: the rise of modern Turkey, 1808–1975*, Cambridge: Cambridge University Press.

Simeon, R. and Conway, D.-P. (2001) 'Federalism and the management of conflict in multinational societies', in A.G. Gagnon and J. Tully (eds) *Multinational Democracies*, Cambridge: Cambridge University Press.

Smith, A. and Heywood, P. (2000) *Regional Government in France & Spain*, London: The Constitution Unit.

Solbes Mira, P. (1990) 'La economia española ante la CEE: el proceso de negociación', in J.L. Garcia Delgado (ed.) *Economía española de la transición y la democracia*, Madrid: Centro de Investigaciones Sociologicas.

Sole-Vilanova, J. (1989) 'Spain: developments in regional and local government', in R.J. Bennett (ed.) *Territory and Administration in Europe*, London: Pinter.

Soto J.L.P. (1997) 'Spain: a fledgling parliament 1977–1997', *Parliamentary Affairs* 50(3):410–22.

Soysal, Y.N. (1994) *Limits of Citizenship: Migrants and Post-national Membership in Europe*, Chicago: University of Chicago Press.

Spotts, F. and Weiser, T. (1986) *Italy: a difficult democracy*, Cambridge: Cambridge University Press.

Steinmo, S, Thelen, K. and Longstreth, F. (eds) (1992) *Structuring Politics: historical institutionalism in comparative perspective*, Cambridge: Cambridge University Press.

Stepan, A. (1986) 'Paths toward redemocratization: theoretical and comparative considerations', in G.A. O'Donnell, P.C. Schmitter, and L. Whitehead (eds) *Transitions from Authoritarian Rule: comparative perspectives*, Baltimore, MD: Johns Hopkins Press.

—— and Skach, C. (1993) 'Constitutional frameworks and democratic consolidation: parliamentarism versus presidentialism', *World Politics* 46(1): 1–22.

Stokes, S.C. (2007) 'Political clientelism', forthcoming in *Handbook of Comparative Politics Oxford University Press*. Online. available at: www.columbia.edu/~mv2191/stokes.pdf (accessed 13 August 2007).

Story, J. and Pollack, B. (1991) 'Spain's transition: domestic and external linkages', in G. Pridham (ed.) *Encouraging Democracy: the international context of regime transition in Southern Europe*, Leicester: Leicester University Press.

Subirats, J. (1987) 'Monopolio Politico e Conflitto Sociale', *Micromega*, 2: 87–96.

Sunar, I. and Sayari, S. (1986) 'Democracy in Turkey: problems and prospects', in G.A. O'Donnell, P.C. Schmitter, and L. Whitehead (eds) *Transitions from Authoritarian Rule: comparative perspectives*, Baltimore, MD: Johns Hopkins Press.

T.C. Çalişma ve Sosyal Güvenlik Bakanlığy (1983) *Çalişm Hayaty Istatistikleri*. Çalişma ve Sosyal Güvenlik Bakanlığy Yayın, No. 45.

Tanör, B. (1990) 'The place of parliament in Turkey', in A. Finkel and N. Sirman (eds) *Turkish State, Turkish Society*, London, Routledge.

Teza, J.F. (1979) nos*Estructura de Clases y Conflictos de Poder en la Espana Postfrancuista*. Madrid: Edicusa.

—— (1981) 'Identificacion de clase y conciencia obrera entre los trabajadores industriales', *Sistema* 43–4: 87–124.

Thelen, K. (1999) 'Historical institutionalism in comparative politics', *Annual Review of Political Science* 2: 369–404.

Tobia, B. (1991) 'Una patria per gli italiani', *Spazi, Itinerary, Mnumenti Nell'Italia Unita (1870–1900)*, Rome: Bari.

Tovias, A. (1984) 'The international context of democratic transition', in G. Pridham (ed.) *The New Mediterranean Democracies: regime transition in Spain, Greece and Portugal*, London: Frank Cass.

—— (1991) 'US policy towards democratic consolidation in Southern Europe', in G. Pridham (ed.) *Encouraging Democracy: the international context of regime transition in Southern Europe*, Leicester: Leicester University Press.

—— (1995) 'Spain in the European Community', in R. Gillespie, F. Rodrigo and J. Story (eds) *Democratic Spain: reshaping external relations in a changing world*, London: Routledge.

Traina, R. (1968) *American Diplomacy and the Spanish Civil War*, Bloomington: Indiana University Press.

Tsoukalis, L. (1981) *The European Community and its Mediterranean Enlargement*, London: George Allen & Unwin.

Tuna, O. (1964) 'Trade unions in Turkey', *International Labour Review*, 90(5): 413–31.

Turan, İ. (1985) 'Changing horses in mid-stream: party changers in the Turkish Grand National Assembly', *Legislative Studies Quarterly* 10: 21–34.

—— (1994) 'The Turkish legislature: from symbolic to substantive representation', in G.W. Copeland and S.C. Patterson (eds) *Parliaments in the Modern World: changing institutions*, Ann Arbor: University of Michigan Press.

—— (2000) 'The effectiveness of parliaments and the Turkish Grand National Assembly', in İ. Turan (ed.) *The Effectiveness of the TBMM*, Istanbul: TESEV.

—— (2003) 'Volatility in politics, stability in Parliament: an impossible dream? The Turkish Grand National Assembly during the last two decades', *Journal of Legislative Studies* 9(2): 151–76.

Umbach, M. (2000) *Federalism and Enlightenment in Germany, 1740–1806*, London: Hambleton Press.

Urbano, P. (1982) *Con la Venia: Yo Indagué el 23-F*, Barcelona: Argos Vergara.

US Department of State (1972) 'Memorandum of conversation (Secretary Byrnes, Prime Minister De Gasperi, Ambassador Tarchiani, and Ambassador Dunn) by the Appointed Ambassador to Italy (Dunn)', in *Foreign Relations of the United States, 1947*, Vol III, Washington, DC: Government Printing Office.

—— (1974) 'The position of the United States with respect to Italy (NSC ½), 10 February 1948', in *Foreign Relations of the United States, 1948*, Vol III, Washington, DC: Government Printing Office.

US Library Congress (1995) 'Turkey' report at lcweb2.loc.gov/cgi-bin/query/r?frd/cstdy:@field(DOCID+tr0082) (viewed 10 January 2007).

Uslaner, E.M. (2002) *The Moral Foundations of Trust*, Cambridge: Cambridge University Press.

Vachudová, M.A. (2005) *Europe Undivided: democracy, leverage, and integration after communism*. Oxford: Oxford University Press.

Valenzuela, S. (1992) 'Democratic consolidation in post-authoritarian settings: notion, process and facilitating conditions', in S. Mainwaring, G. O'Donnell and S. Valenzuela (eds) *Issues in Democratic Consolidation: the new South American democracies in comparative perspective*, Notre Dame: University of Notre Dame Press.

Velarde Fuertes, J. (1973) *Política económica de la Dictadura*, 2nd edn, Madrid: Guadiana de Publicaciones, D.L.

—— (1995) 'Evolución del comercio exterior Español: del nacionalismo económico a la Unión Europea', in E. Fuentes Quintana (ed.) *Problemas económicos españoles en la década de los 90*, Madrid: Galaxia Gutenberg.

Verney, S. and Couloumbis, T. (1991) 'State-international system interaction and the Greek transition to democracy in the mid-1970s' in G, Pridham (ed.) *Encouraging Democracy: the international context of regime transition in Southern Europe*, Leicester: Leicester University Press.

Vincent, M. (2007) *Spain, 1833–2002: people and state*, Oxford: Oxford University Press.

Weiker, W.F. (1963). *The Turkish Revolution, 1960–61*, Washington: Brookings Institution.

Wiessner, S. (1993) 'Federalism: an architecture for freedom, *European Law Review*, 1(2): 129–42.

Welch, C.E. (1976) 'Civilian control of the military: myth and reality', in C.E. Welch (ed.) *Civilian Control of the Military*, Albany: State University of New York Press.

Wexler, I. (1983) *The Marshall Plan Revisited: the European recovery program in economic perspective*, Westport: Greenwood Press.

Whealey, R. (1977) 'How Franco financed his war – reconsidered', *Journal of Contemporary History*, 12(1): 133–52.

Wheare, K.C. (1964) *Federal Government*, New York: Oxford University Press.

Whitehead, L. (1986) 'International Aspects of Democratization', in G.A. O'Donnell, P.C. Schmitter, and L. Whitehead (eds) *Transitions from Authoritarian Rule: comparative perspectives*, Baltimore, MD: Johns Hopkins Press.

—— (1989) 'The consolidation of fragile democracies: a discussion with illustrations', in R.A. Pastor (ed.) *Democracy in the Americas: stopping the pendulum*, New York and London: Holmes and Meier.

—— (1991) 'Democracy by convergence and Southern Europe: a comparative perspective' in G. Pridham and Geoffrey (ed.) *Encouraging Democracy: the international context of regime transition in Southern Europe*, Leicester: Leicester University Press.

—— (2001) 'Democracy by convergence: Southern Europe' in L. Whitehead (ed.) *The international dimensions of democratization: Europe and the Americas*, Oxford: Oxford University Press.

World Politics (1996) 'The role of theory in comparative politics: a symposium', 48(1) 1–49.

Yavuz, E. (1995) 'The state of the industrial workforce, 1923–40', in D. Quataert and E.J. Zurcher (eds) *Workers and the Working Class in the Ottoman Empire and the Turkish Republic: 1839–1950*, London: Tauris.

Yilmaz, H. (2002) 'External–internal linkages in democratization: developing an open model of democratic change', *Democratization*, 9(2): 67–84.

Zamagni, V. (2000) 'Evolution of the economy', in P. McCarthy (ed.) *Italy Since 1945*, Oxford: Oxford University Press.

Ziblatt, D. (2006) *Structuring the State: the formation of Italy and Germany and the puzzle of federalism*, Princeton: Princeton University Press.

Zürcher, E.J. (1984) *The Unionist Factor: the role of the Committee of Union and Progress in the Turkish national movement, 1905–1926*, Leiden: Brill.

—— (2004) *Turkey: A Modern History*, London: I.B. Tauris.

Index

For Product Safety Concerns and Information please contact our EU
representative GPSR@taylorandfrancis.com
Taylor & Francis Verlag GmbH, Kaufingerstraße 24, 80331 München, Germany

www.ingramcontent.com/pod-product-compliance
Lightning Source LLC
Chambersburg PA
CBHW070901080426
R18103400001B/R181034PG41932CBX00001B/1